The Hispanic World
in Crisis and Change

A History of Spain

General Editor: John Lynch

The Hispanic World
in Crisis and Change

1598–1700

John Lynch

BLACKWELL
Oxford UK & Cambridge USA

Copyright © John Lynch 1969, 1981, 1992

The right of John Lynch to be identified as author of this work has been asserted in accordance with the Copyright, Designs and Patents Act 1988.

First published 1992
First published in USA 1992
First published in paperback 1994

Blackwell Publishers
108 Cowley Road
Oxford OX4 1JF
UK

238 Main Street
Cambridge, Massachusetts 02142
USA

A CIP catalogue record for this book is available from the British Library.

Library of Congress Cataloging-in-Publication Data

Lynch, John, 1927–
The Hispanic world in crisis and change, 1598–1700 / John Lynch.
p. cm.—(A History of Spain)
Rev. ed. of: Spain under the Hapsburgs, v. 2. 2nd ed. 1981.
Includes bibliographical references (p.   ) and index.
ISBN 0–631–17697–7—0–631–19397–9 (pbk.)
1. Spain—History—Philip III 1598–1621. 2. Spain—History—
Philip IV, 1621–1665. 3. Spain—History—Charles II, 1665–1700.
I. Lynch, John, 1927–. Spain under the Hapsburgs. II. Title.
III. Series.
DP182.L96 1994
946'.05—dc20   91–27601
CIP

Typeset in 11 on 13 pt Garamond
by Graphicraft Typesetters Ltd., Hong Kong
Printed in Great Britain by T. J. Press, Padstow, Cornwall

This book is printed on acid-free paper.

Contents

Plates

Maps

To
W. K. L.

Preface

The present book is a new edition of *Spain under the Habsburgs*, Volume II, substantially revised and incorporated into the series *History of Spain*. Many sections have been re-written in the light of works published in the last two decades, in some cases to add new material, in others to refine an argument or revise an interpretation. The seventeenth century, even more perhaps than the sixteenth, has gained from the resurgence of historical studies in Spain and from the contributions of historians outside the peninsula. The attributes of Habsburg government in its middle phase are now more clearly observed, its kings and their subjects better understood. The reign of Philip III has been brought onto centre stage, while the rule of Philip IV and Olivares has been subject to extensive research and reappraisal. And beyond kings and favourites, the longer-term trends of government, its increasing deconstruction in favour of regional power bases and interest groups have become new themes of Habsburg history. The rural world in which most Spaniards lived has been recreated by recent research, and tithe records have become the key to laying open the reality of Spain's condition. There is virtually no region of the peninsula that has not had its population counted, its production computed, its society analysed, and its chronology of progress and recession restated, while cities, towns and ports have been scoured for signs of industry and trade. The last decades of the century, once a territory without maps, has now been explored and charted. Charles II, it seems, presided over promise as well as poverty, and as the survival of Spanish power and resources has been extended in time, so the chronology of recovery has been advanced, leaving the mid-century depression to occupy a shorter space and a lesser role. The history of the Indies trade in the second half of the seventeenth century has been transformed out of all recognition, while the calculation of American treasure receipts has been totally revolutionized. And behind the Atlantic sector the American home of mineowners, *hacendados*, Indians and slaves repays closer study as we search for the ultimate explanation of the shifts in the Hispanic world.

Students of the seventeenth century now encounter a more interesting Spain, still complex and contradictory, but subject no less than other countries to the logic of conditions and events. I have tried to do justice to the new history in the following pages, and to acknowledge its authors in a revised bibliography. But I have not sought to alter the essential framework and character of the book nor, apart from finer tuning, have I changed the hypotheses and speculations which were inherent in it and which belong to the unfinished debate on the rise and fall of Habsburg Spain.

J. L.

1

The Hispanic World in 1600

Spanish society and economy were built on the twin foundations of land and silver, Castilian agriculture and American mining. The conspicuous luxury of court and aristocracy, the palaces and the mansions, the Baroque splendour of the church, the complex apparatus of bureaucratic government, the fleets and the armies that spanned Europe and the wider world, the entire fabric of this aristocratic society and the power of its empire were supported ultimately on the backs of Castilian peasants and American Indians. The nobles, as well as the crown, drew their wealth from both sources, for in addition to the vast estates and the numerous vassals working for them in Castile, they also primed their fortunes with lucrative viceroyalties and other earnings in the Indies.

These two pillars of Spanish society were interdependent. In the heyday of empire Castilian agriculture provisioned the Indies fleets and supplied the colonists with grain, oil and wine. And the mineral wealth of America, directly or indirectly, took some of the pressure off the peasants of Castile and lightened their tax burden. In the years around 1600, however, the imperial relationship was profoundly transformed. The changing economies of Mexico and Peru now required not agricultural products but manufactured goods, which Spain was not equipped to supply. Diminishing trade returns, together with recession in silver mining and retention of capital in American hands for local investment, all combined to reduce the yield of empire, and ultimately to shift the burden of responsibility towards the peasants of Castile, as the crown demanded greater sacrifices from its taxpayers, and landlords from their vassals.

Spain was a rural society and land was the source of peninsular wealth. The numerous and growing towns, not being centres of industrial production, were essentially parasitic growths on an agrarian economy. Most people who actually worked lived in the countryside, and their horizons were bounded by the next harvest. But abundant harvests would stimulate other sectors of the national life, and in their wake taxes would be paid, lords and clerics would receive their rents and urban rentiers their interest, artisans would have employment and merchants something to sell. Conversely, if the crops failed or agriculture became depressed, then the whole nation suffered, from the king downwards. So everyone watched the weather and the work-force with acute personal interest, an interest turning to alarm as they noticed the first signs of rural distress. Towards 1575–80 Castile began to experience a reversal of the demographic trend, and by 1600 depopulation was notorious. The primary cause was rural migration, which peasants attributed to 'lack of land'. Some of them went to the Indies; others, following the trail of the *hidalgos*, sought their El Dorado in neighbouring towns or in Madrid. 'Lack of land' was a complex phenomenon, but one feature was clear enough – the peasants were losing their commons. The great territorial magnates, the nobles and the church, increasingly encroached on common land as they rounded off their estates, sometimes to increase their grain production in a period of rising prices, sometimes simply for the sake of social prestige.

For one reason or another, many peasants were forced out of agriculture. As the village of Taracena in the province of Guadalajara reported in the late 1570s,

> numbers here have diminished, because many *hidalgos* and *caballeros* have gone to live in the nearby city, although they have their estates in the countryside. The farmers who remain in the village have very little substance; poverty has forced many of them to leave for Guadalajara and Madrid, for the village is so destitute that there is no livelihood in it. The majority of its people are now landless labourers, and some of these are leaving for Guadalajara.[1]

Urban growth, rural depopulation, this was the sombre picture of Castile in the years around 1600.

[1] Quoted by Noël Salomon, *La campagne de Nouvelle Castille à la fin du XVIᵉ siècle d'après les Relaciones topográficas* (Paris, 1964), p. 48.

At a primitive level these agricultural communities were self-sufficient. In New Castile the dominant products were cereals and wine; for a period these crops managed to win the battle for land against the claims of livestock, and they accounted for 70–80 per cent of agricultural production.[2] Local artisan manufactures, some of them practised by unemployed peasants, supplied the simple needs of farms and villages – coarse textiles, leather, pottery and building materials, soap and candles. There was little surplus capital for more sophisticated consumer goods. Most of the peasants did not own the land they worked: they were tenants or seasonal labourers. And they themselves were 'owned' by great lords, lay and clerical, who possessed *señorío*, conferring rights of service, taxation and jurisdiction over their vassals. The Castilian peasant was closely martialled by seigneurial controls, and these spread their net more widely in the late sixteenth and early seventeenth centuries. Infatuation with noble status, abdication of responsible government, and royal penury, these were the pressures which swept aside the barriers against seigneurial advance erected by Philip II and gradually covered the Castilian country-side with a network of feudalism. Ministers and favourites began a mad scramble for vassals. The Duke of Lerma, favourite of Philip III, used his political influence unashamedly to amass *señoríos*. Already before 1600 he owned many townships and villages; at the peak of his power he acquired many more, and in 1611–12 alone he bought a further twelve. Philip IV's financial needs were still more pressing, and he alienated jurisdiction on an even greater scale. In 1625 the crown concluded an *asiento* with a group of bankers, who advanced 1,210,000 ducats to the treasury against the security of 20,000 vassals; these were regarded as property, the sale of which would guarantee the advance. To alienate jurisdiction on this scale the crown needed the formal agreement of the cortes; the size of the transaction disturbed the assembly and it was reluctant to give its sanction. Eventually, to secure agreement, the royal spokesmen had to pull out all the stops of patriotic and religious appeal,

> considering the great and urgent needs of His Majesty caused by the unavoidable expense involved in the capture of Breda, the recovery of Brazil, the provision of the great armed forces main-

[2] Ibid., p. 96.

tained by land and sea, and the forces in the Low Countries which are defending the Holy Catholic Faith and the king's patrimony against the assaults of the rebels.[3]

The efforts of the early Habsburgs to curtail and reclaim private jurisdiction were nullified, and the years around 1600 saw a 'feudal reaction', as tens of thousands of Castilian peasants passed from royal to aristocratic control, with harsher taxes, exactions and justice.[4]

Having lost their land and their freedom to the great magnates, the peasants also lost their income, for they were now more vulnerable to service exactions and financial pressure. The Castilian labourer became a beast of burden bearing on his shoulders the whole top-heavy structure of an aristocratic society, church and state, nobles and rentiers, merchants and bankers. The cortes of Castile, by no means a commoner's institution, described in 1573 how one of the basic taxes, the *alcabala* (sales tax), operated in the case of grain:

> The prelates, grandees, lords of vassals and nobles procure all the grain which the peasants produce but do not pay a thing in *alcabala*; the prelates because they are exempt; the grandees and lords of vassals because normally they do not pay this tax but charge it on their wretched vassals; and other nobles because most of them employ similar methods in their villages and estates to divert the tax from themselves. The whole burden therefore falls on the peasants who are unable to escape payment on any grain they sell.[5]

As the cortes of 1593 pointed out, the peculiar tax structure of Castile made the peasants 'the people who sustain this kingdom'.[6] It was their labour which supported Spanish government and society, financed the armies and fleets, and subsidized the allies. In 1600 the distinguished lawyer and *arbitrista* Martín González

[3] *Actas de las Cortes de Castilla*, 1563–1632 (51 vols, Madrid, 1861–1929), xliii, p. 125.
[4] See F. Braudel, *La Méditerranée et le monde méditerranéen à l'époque de Philippe II* (Paris, 1949), p. 635, who refers to a 'seigneurial reaction', dating it from an earlier period.
[5] *Actas de las Cortes de Castilla*, vi, p. 369.
[6] Ibid, xii, p. 505.

.de Cellorigo argued that the whole social and economic structure of Spain rested on the peasants, 'for the peasant who works in the field has to support himself, his lord, the clergy, the money-lender, and all the others who batten on him.'[7]

What were the various charges which crushed the rural masses? First there was the visible token of their vassalage, payments in money, in kind and in services to their lords. These varied from region to region, and in Castile they were not so oppressive as in Aragon and Valencia, but they were still heavy enough. Even more extortionate was the tithe owed to the church and charged on grain, livestock and other agricultural products. In New Castile the tithe took ten or twenty times more of a peasant's income than did seigneurial payments, and it was impossible to evade or reform, for the church had acknowledged rights to the fruits of the earth, enforced with all the rigour of canon law and spiritual sanctions. The tithe, it is true, financed the pastoral, social and educational work of the church, as well as its more extravagant consumption. But for the peasant it was a nightmare.

In addition to the regular visits of bailiffs and tithe commissioners, the peasant also endured the attentions of the royal tax-collectors, charging *alcabalas, servicios* and, from the late sixteenth century, the *millones,* a new tax on basic foodstuffs. Many *arbitristas* considered this the last straw. According to Sancho de Moncada, professor at the University of Toledo, the *millones* took 'the drop of wine from the mouth of the needy farmer, the morsel of meat and oil from the poor widow'.[8] But having paid his taxes, the peasant still had to find the rent he owed his landlord. In New Castile this was even more exacting than the tithe, taking between one-third and one-half of the value of crops produced.[9] Between rent and tithe the peasant was trapped, and the only escape was migration. González de Cellorigo, writing in 1600, regarded rent as the greatest cause of rural distress and the prostration of the Castilian peasants, 'for having paid the tithes owed to God, they pay an even greater amount to the owner of

[7] *Memorial de la política necesaria y útil restauración de la República de España* (1600), quoted by Salomon *La campagne de Nouvelle Castille,* p. 214. The *arbitristas* were literally 'projectors' of schemes of financial and economic reform, but they may be regarded as the political economists of the time.

[8] *Fin y extinción del servicio de millones,* in *Restauración política de España* (Madrid, 1619), fols. 41–41v.

[9] Salomon, *La campagne de Nouvelle Castille,* p. 243.

land; and then follow innumerable seigneurial obligations, impositions, payment of debts and dues; and finally the various state taxes to which they are subjected.'[10] Altogether more than half of a peasant's product was consumed in payments which enriched non-peasant classes. On the remainder he had to keep his family, defray his overheads, pay his labourers, and renew his equipment.[11] Is it surprising that he was forced to cut down on production or abandon the land, seeking release from a standard of living which had become intolerable?

The structure of rural society was rigid, a harsh reflection of prevailing values.[12] At the bottom were the *jornaleros*, the landless labourers, who formed more than half the rural population of New Castile and lived more like beasts than human beings, in mud or wooden huts, with no furniture and few belongings, the whole family sleeping on the earth floor. The *jornaleros* were seasonal labourers, moving from place to place in search of work and bread, and in the intervals turning their hands to some rough craft or begging for charity. Above them were the *labradores*, peasant farmers who had actual possession of land by ownership or more commonly on lease. In New Castile they formed 25–30 per cent of the rural population, and most of them were wretchedly poor, their joyless lives containing few hopes. A farmer was rich if he had 1,000 ducats a year, and perhaps some of them had, but they were a small minority, no more than 5 per cent of rural inhabitants. These were the only dynamic group among the peasants and they fought to preserve their modest fortunes in the midst of rural crisis, looking down on the *jornaleros* below and resenting the *hidalgos* above. But they were not agents of change, for they themselves aspired to *hidalgo* status and in some cases secured it. So the one vigorous element in the countryside worked not to dissolve the social structure but to reinforce it. As for the *hidalgos* themselves, some were proud and destitute, others were reduced to working for a living, and all of them worked hard at maintaining their tax immunity, if only formally. But the *hidalgos* came well behind the *caballeros* and *títulos* in land, income, and prestige; these were the greatest proprietors, the real landed aristocracy.

[10] Quoted ibid., p. 245.
[11] Ibid., p. 250.
[12] Ibid., pp. 257–302.

The defects of the agrarian structure were becoming more pronounced towards the end of the sixteenth century. Land, jurisdiction and tax immunity gave the aristocracy a monopoly of power in the countryside, while the peasant, more vulnerable than ever before, joined a growing exodus to the towns. This was the first cause of rural depopulation. But these over-crowded towns became death-traps of another kind.

In the years around 1600 Spain was struck by devastating disease, the first wave of a repeated assault which decimated the Spanish people and from which no generation of the seventeenth century escaped. The first great bubonic plague entered through Santander in 1596 and spread westwards along the northern coastal provinces, leaving heavy mortality in its wake. About 1598 it penetrated central Spain and began to feed on the two Castiles. In 1599 it reached Andalucía, and in Seville alone claimed 8,000 victims. It is difficult to calculate the total casualties of this prolonged scourge, but they amounted perhaps to 500,000.[13] There was a direct connection between rural depression and the high mortality of these plague-ridden years. Masses of distressed peasantry, already suffering from acute malnutrition, were easy victims of epidemic disease.[14] Once contagion had taken root agriculture further deteriorated, for the labour force was weakened and diminished. As for the densely packed towns, they were particular foci of infection, which shortage of food supplies then prolonged. Coastal districts were open to relief, for emergency supplies could be rushed in by sea. But the heartland of Castile, at the mercy of a slow and inefficient transport system, was isolated from the outer world. Its enclosed rural communities depended on their own agricultural resources, and to them the coincidence of famine and plague brought disaster – and panic. As towns were placed under quarantine, movement of the meagre food supplies available became even more difficult. And it was the

[13] Antonio Domínguez Ortiz, La sociedad española en el siglo XVII (Madrid, 1963), pp. 68–70. The prolific writings of this distinguished historian, full of research and understanding as they are, have made him one of the greatest authorities on the Spanish seventeenth century; this book is particularly indebted to his works.

[14] J. Nadal and E. Giralt, La population catalane de 1553 à 1717 (Paris, 1960), discusses the relation between famine and pestilence; see also Vicente Pérez Moreda, Las crisis de mortalidad en la España interior. Siglos XVI–XIX (Madrid, 1980), p. 453, who places life expectancy in seventeenth-century Spain between twenty-four and twenty-six years.

urban poor, living in unsanitary slums and shanty towns, who
suffered most; while the wealthy could escape to their country
houses and isolate themselves behind armed guards, the poor had
no refuge and if they fled from the towns they were driven off
from country villages at gunpoint.

The great plague of 1596–1602, a precursor of other lethal
epidemics, inaugurated a century of demographic recession. A
decade later, inspired with a kind of death wish, Spanish society
purged itself of impurity and expelled the moriscos, the last
remnants of Islam in the peninsula. These two amputations deprived Castile of some 600,000 to 700,000 people, about one-
tenth of its population, within the short period of 1596–1614.
Spain bore the scars for many decades to come. According to
González de Cellorigo, 'the loss of the strength, valour and
greatness of Spain' was due to the 'lack of people which has
become apparent in recent years'. This lack was particularly noticeable in the Castilian plain watered by the River Duero, a
region which included Valladolid, Burgos and Medina del Campo; but the provinces of Toledo and Seville were not far behind.
And there was no respite. The years 1630–2 were particularly
harsh, with a crushing combination of crop failure, famine and
plague. In 1632 the cortes lamented:

> Many people have died, and many have abandoned their houses
> and farms, with great loss to agriculture. Livestock is scarce,
> savings are consumed, and many villages are so destitute that they
> ought to be relieved of their burdens rather than be asked for more
> to contribute to the needs of other kingdoms.[15]

But plague and depopulation had secondary consequences, for
they disrupted trade and business, and labour shortage inflated
wages to an unprecedented level.

Demoralized by death and destruction, the people of Castile
were further castigated in these years by a rampant rise in the cost
of living. After a century of relentless inflation prices suddenly
spiralled beyond all control. In Andalucía the price of grain rose
from 430 maravedis per fanega in 1595 to 1,041 in 1598, in Castile
from 408 in 1595 to 908 in 1599.[16] The price revolution culmin-

[15] *Actas de las Cortes de Castilla*, li, p. 97.
[16] Earl J. Hamilton, *American Treasure and the Price Revolution in Spain,
1501–1650* (Cambridge, Mass., 1934), pp. 215–16.

ated in 1601 when prices reached their peak. Thereafter, inflation did not cease, in spite of demographic recession and the onset of diminishing silver receipts from America; now it was caused by the progressive depreciation of base money, especially from the early 1620s. In Andalucía and the two Castiles the average price level showed a downward tendency in 1601–10, and trade, particularly to America, began to recede.[17] Prices then remained stable in 1611–20, with a slight trend upwards. This stability was upset by the enormous coinage of vellon (debased copper coinage) in 1621–5, as the government sought to create quick money for itself. On average the indices rose about 20 per cent in 1621–30; in 1626–7 Castile experienced one of the most violent price upheavals in its history, its average indices rising 20.21 points in two years.[18] This was caused not by economic activity nor by the American trade – imports of precious metals fell sharply in 1630 – but almost exclusively by monetary inflation. There was a further price rise in 1636–8, with an advance of 21.8 points in Old Castile. After a brief fall, prices surged upwards again in 1641–2, owing to the heavy increase in vellon during the wars and revolutions of the early 1640s, but they were brought down in 1642 by official deflation. This did not last long, and further depreciation of vellon caused another great upswing in Castile in 1646–50, while the rise was aggravated in Andalucía by the great plague of 1648. The average price level in Andalucía, the two Castiles and Valencia was approximately 38.7 per cent higher in 1650 than in 1625. 'Hence the net advance under the stimulus of vellon inflation in Castile and silver inflation in Valencia in the second quarter of the seventeenth century was not far behind the most violent upheaval of silver prices in any quarter century of the Price Revolution.'[19]

Grains, particularly wheat, were the most important item of consumption for the vast majority of the population and absorbed a high percentage of the income of the common people. Until about 1570 there was little divergence between grain prices and those of other commodities. Up to 1650 this still held good for Old Castile and Valencia. But in Andalucía and New Castile grain prices rose much more than those of general commodities in

[17] Ibid., pp. 217–21.
[18] Base 1571–80.
[19] Hamilton, *American Treasure and the Price Revolution in Spain*, p. 220.

the period 1575–1650. The rise of the New Castilian indices in the first half of the seventeenth century, in spite of demographic recession, was probably due to exports to other parts of Spain and to over-planting of vineyards on wheat land after the steep rise of wine prices in the previous century. And the lag of grain prices in Old Castile behind those of other regions is probably accounted for by depopulation and price control.[20]

The wage rise of the sixteenth century continued into the seventeenth.[21] The demographic reversal caused by the great plague of 1596–1602 led to an abrupt increase of wages; a labourer in Castile who was paid 3,470 maravedis in 1599 received 9,000 in 1603. Under the stimulus of vellon inflation, money wages continued to rise from 1626, and the wage index for 1650 exceeded that of 1600 by 47.77 per cent. But a labourer had to buy food and clothing and house his family, and his real earnings were eroded by inflation. In the course of the sixteenth century the purchasing power of labourers suffered by almost 30 per cent. It also suffered in the first half of the seventeenth century. Prices responded much more rapidly than wages to the great depreciation of vellon money in 1622–7, and this disparity caused real wages to drop more than 20 per cent. From then onwards wages never caught up with the steep rise in the cost of living. The index for real wages in 1650 was about 10 per cent less than in 1645 and considerably under that for 1627. For the labouring masses of Castile, therefore, the inflation induced by vellon debasement was a calamity; it defrauded them of their wages and depressed their already low living standards to the margin of subsistence.

Historians have been tempted to argue that Spain forged its own economic ruin by tolerating the sharp increase of wages in the early seventeenth century, especially in the period 1611–20 when real earnings briefly attained a summit. In these years, it is suggested, wages did not lag sufficiently behind prices to allow the accumulation of capital for investment in production.[22] The argument is not convincing. It is unrealistic to suppose that Spain needed a policy of compulsory saving at the expense of depressed

[20] Ibid., pp. 241–2.
[21] Ibid., pp. 273–82.
[22] See Earl J. Hamilton, 'American Treasure and the Rise of Capitalism, 1500–1700', *Economica*, ix (1929), pp. 338–57.

labouring groups. Surplus capital already lay in other hands, innocent of useful employment. And there is no evidence to suggest that better industrial profits would have been invested productively. Spanish entrepreneurial and manufacturing groups, few in numbers and low in spirits, thwarted by state policy, war, social values and economic adversity, were already in difficulties by the end of the sixteenth century. And there could be no improvement until the agrarian structure had been remodelled, for the depressed rural sector did not provide a market for consumer goods. The towns themselves, swarming with unemployed or underemployed migrants from the countryside, were simply an extension of rural depression, so they in turn provided little outlet for agricultural expansion.

Towards the end of Philip III's reign the sense of crisis rose to a new pitch. Amidst a chorus of lamentations from officials and economists, from towns and countryside, the crown commissioned the Council of Castile to report on measures needed to revive the ailing economy. In its celebrated *consulta* of 1 February 1619 the Council examined the causes of depopulation and depression, and concluded, among other things, that the 'excessive burdens and contributions' imposed on the people had led to the 'greatest depopulation', for in order not to die of hunger people were forced to emigrate to other regions or overseas.[23] In a gloss on this report, the *arbitrista* Pedro Fernández Navarrete argued that the income from agriculture, the country's basic economic activity, was not sufficient to cover various costs such as taxes, rent to the landowner and interest payments to money-lenders; in his view, output was falling because the costs of production were too high.[24] A somewhat different opinion was expressed by Sancho de Moncada. Writing in 1619, he dated rapid deterioration as beginning during 'the last four or five years'; this would coincide with the expulsion of the moriscos and the first stage of recession in the American trade. But Moncada did not regard poor harvests as the root cause of depression; following the crop shortages of 1606–7, he argued, production had improved.

[23] Angel González Palencia, *La Junta de Reformación, 1618–1625 (Archivo Histórico Español*, v, Valladolid, 1932), doc. 4.
[24] *Conservación de Monarquías* (1626) *(Biblioteca de autores españoles*, 25, Madrid, 1947), pp. 445–7.

Many parts of Castile and elsewhere are depopulated by the very abundance of crops, and we see grain and grapes remaining to be harvested. The reason is the lack of demand, which arises from the dearth of people and money for buying essentials; for those who remain have no means of earning money to spend on food.[25]

He saw the depression as the inevitable consequence of a diminishing population, excessive import of foreign goods and a social mentality which inhibited industrial production. Yet a further viewpoint was given by the Count of Gondomar, Spanish ambassador to England, who referred to the 'depopulation, poverty and deprivation in contemporary Spain; foreigners proclaim that to travel through our country is more painful than to traverse any other waste land of Europe, for there are no beds, lodgings or meals, on account of the great and oppressive taxes the natives pay'.[26]

Government revenue was heavily compromised by Philip III. He did not create new taxes, but he anticipated revenue by several years and he inaugurated one of the great evils of the century, monetary inflation. From 1618 in particular, to finance Spain's entry into the Thirty Years War, his government debased the currency on a large scale, a practice continued with even less responsibility by Philip IV. Unwilling to reduce expenditure, which was regarded as essential for national defence, or to increase taxation, which would be unpopular, the govenment persisted in reckless borrowing until it reached the point of inevitable bankruptcy in 1627. This year was a further stage in the crisis. Castile now staggered under the impact of vellon inflation, diminution of American trade and a year of poor harvests. In 1628 the Dutch captured the Mexican silver fleet, and hostilities with France pushed up defence expenditure still higher. Adverse weather conditions in the following years caused further crop failures. Emergency grain supplies were desperately sought in the Mediterranean, North Africa and the Baltic; and the few existing stocks were bought up by the powerful and wealthy, while the mass of the people lived next to starvation.[27]

---

[25] *Restauración política de España y deseos públicos* (1619), quoted by Domínguez Ortiz, *La sociedad española en el siglo XVII*, pp. 26–7.
[26] Gondomar to Philip III, 1619 *Documentos inéditos para la historia de España* (new series, 4 vols, Madrid, 1936–45), ii, pp. 131–46.
[27] Dominguez Ortiz, *La sociedad española en el siglo XVII*, pp. 33–4.

The syndrome of rural poverty, depopulation, financial chaos and recession of American trade produced Spain's first great crisis in the modern period.[28] The crisis can be dated between 1598 and 1620, and it was a crisis of change, denoting a reversal of the economic trends of the sixteenth century. The worst was still to come. From 1640 political disintegration and military collapse compounded the economic disorder and reduced Spain to absolute depression. And by this time there was less hope of relief from America.

In the sixteenth century the economy of the Hispanic world was an integrated economy. Spain expended men, money and prolonged effort in the colonization of America and the development of its resources. The annual shiploads of American treasure, therefore, were the returns on an investment – the greatest investment by any country in the sixteenth century – and not the rewards of a parasite. The injection of expanding amounts of silver into the peninsula compensated to some degree for the failings of the domestic economy. These receipts stimulated some sectors such as shipbuilding and, at first, agriculture; they bridged the gap in the balance of payments; they alleviated the tax burden; and they joined the contributions of the Castilian peasantry to maintain the nation's armies and fleets, and to support its war effort in northern Europe. In the years around 1600 the continuing yield of colonial wealth redeemed the poor performance of domestic agriculture and still more of industry by providing capital to buy abroad. But this closely-knit economy was bound to contract when its most fruitful branch began to wither. Between 1606–10 and 1646–50 gross tonnage in the American trade dropped by 60 per cent, from 273,560 tons to 121,308. This long period of recession can be dated from 1609, and it would take some time to reverse.[29] No doubt the crisis of the transatlantic trade was aggravated by the attack of foreign enemies and the penetration of foreign interlopers. But its basic cause was the transformation of the colonial economies and the shift of economic power within the Hispanic world.

The American colonies were no longer exclusively orientated

[28] See P. Vilar, 'Le temps du "Quichotte"', *Europe*, xxxiv (1956), pp. 3–16, for an interpretation.

[29] See the references to H. and P. Chaunu, *Séville et l' Atlantique* (1504–1650) (8 vols, Paris, 1955–9), in Chapter VII below.

towards mining production. The trends of silver output, of course, differed between Mexico and Peru. From 1545 to the mid-1560s Peru disgorged a vast amount of treasure, especially from Potosí. There followed a recession in the late 1560s and early 1570s until the adoption of the *patio*, or amalgamation, process unlocked the lower grade ores and released an immense and rising output. While this was not sustained throughout the seventeenth century, Peru remained a mining economy, more 'colonial' and less developed than Mexico. But Peru, too, had other sources of wealth and these now absorbed more of the colony's capital, leaving a reduced surplus for Spain. Mexico's mining output was more erratic in the sixteenth century until the introduction of mercury amalgamation in 1553. Thereafter silver production rose steadily, though at its peak, in the 1580s and 1590s, it probably amounted to no more than a third or quarter of that of Peru. From the beginning of the seventeenth century Mexican silver mining suffered from shortage of capital and labour, technical deficiencies and rising costs, but survived in one region or another and it never went out of production.[30] The vicissitudes of silver returns from America, therefore, reflected more than simple mining recession. It was also evidence of the development of the colonial economies, the decrease of their primitive dependence on mining, their exploitation of other sources of wealth and their retention of capital for local use in administration, defence contracts, public works and private investment. In Mexico the demographic factor alone was sufficient to stimulate a new investment pattern. The simultaneous growth of the white population and decimation of the Indians caused the colonists to overcome shortage of labour and therefore of food supplies by renewed investment in agriculture, to concentrate more on land and less on mining.

Spain was powerless to prevent these developments. Indeed she had necessarily assisted them. In the process of colonization Spaniards introduced from the peninsula and the Canary Islands the domestic animals, cereals, vegetables and fruits which flourished in the temperate and highland regions of the New World; they also transferred tropical and sub-tropical plants, such as the orange, sugar cane, and later coffee and rice, which took root in

[30] John J. TePaske and Herbert S. Klein, 'The Seventeenth-Century Crisis in New Spain: Myth or Reality?', *Past and Present*, 90 (1981) pp. 116–35.

the humid and warmer lowlands. Furthermore, a number of plants cultivated by the Amerindians – cacao, cotton and maize – were taken over by the colonists and produced in quantities to become, with sugar, hides and woods, important articles of trade. Towards colonial industry and commerce Spanish policy was at best liberal and at worst too inconsistent to be a serious obstacle. Some American products such as wine – the vine too was transplanted from Spain – expanded into direct competition with Spanish exports, but by the time this was identified as a danger, towards the 1590s, the development could not be reversed. The textile industry was specifically authorized. Mexico produced raw and manufactured silk, and being well endowed with wool had a sizeable cloth industry. Peru also had a textile industry; this became a target of restrictive policy, but too many Peruvian interests were involved to permit its curtailment. While colonial textiles were inferior in quality and could not command the luxury market, they could certainly satisfy the mass market and remove it from Spanish control. Many of the new products were sold outside the colony which produced them; inter-colonial trade developed a buoyancy of its own, independent of the Spanish liaison, and carried by a merchant marine constructed in American shipyards.

Economic shift was accompanied by social change. By 1600 the first generation of American-born Spaniards had taken root and occupied dominant positions as landowners, manufacturers, merchants and capitalists. Spanish American whites now called themselves *criollos* and were conscious of a difference between themselves and *peninsulares*; they displayed some aversion to Spanish immigrants and began to demand access to office.[31] They were subjects of the crown, of course, and not basically hostile to Spain, but nor were they closely attached and they would brook no interference with their private interests. The recession of imperial trade and navigation provided favourable conditions for the growth of an independent society, and in the course of the seventeenth century American elites came into being, elites of land and large-scale commerce, the guardians of creole interests, whom imperial administrators could not ignore.

The crisis in the transatlantic trade in the years after 1600,

[31] D. A. Brading, *The First America. The Spanish Monarchy, Creole Patriots, and the Liberal State 1492–1867* (Cambridge, 1991), pp. 224–5, 294–9.

therefore was rooted in economic forces over which Spain had no control. The development of the empire, the new variety of its economic activities, and its growing self-absorption, were all signs that America was detaching itself from peninsular requirements and was no longer content to be a mere provider of precious metals for the metropolis. By the 1640s certain sectors of the American economy – shipbuilding, agriculture and investment in overseas trade – were far more buoyant than their counterparts in Spain. The economic independence of America, and its superior capital resources, denoted a fundamental shift of balance within the Hispanic world. Economically at least the dominant partner was now America, and America did not share the peninsular and European interests of Spain, nor did it now contribute in any significant degree to Spain's defence needs and foreign policy. If this interpretation is correct, Spain lost her colonial wealth not so much to foreign rivals and interlopers – the familiar heroes or scapegoats according to point of view – as to her own American subjects who now appropriated their own resources for themselves.

The reorientation of the Hispanic world in the years around 1600 has gone largely unnoticed in European historiography.[32] Observers have been so impressed by the waning of Spanish power in Europe that they have tended to see this exclusively in terms of the depression and depopulation within the peninsula, the suicidal foreign policy of Spain's rulers between 1621 and 1658, and the relative improvement in the power of other states. In these terms, however, how can we explain the enduring facts of the case – that an enfeebled metropolis retained its American empire unimpaired for another two centuries, and that the unity of the Hispanic world survived all assaults until 1810? The reason, of course, is that this was still a great complex of wealth and power, though the centre of gravity had moved across the Atlantic. America in effect preserved its own territory, and in addition defended imperial communications. America was now the guardian of empire. This is the story of the seventeenth century – not the waning of the Hispanic world, but the recession of Spain within that world.

---

[32] Except of course by Chaunu; see below, pp. 287–98.

2

The Government of
Philip III

King and Favourite

Philip II died on 13 September 1598, leaving to his last surviving son, then aged twenty, the government of the largest, the most powerful and the most complex empire in the world. He delivered his charge with some misgivings: 'God, who has given me so many kingdoms, has denied me a son capable of ruling them.' And, referring to the aristocratic friends hovering about the heir to the throne, he confided to his secretary a few days before his death, 'I fear they are going to rule him.'[1]

Ill-endowed in mind and character for his vast responsibilities, regarded by his officials and his subjects with a mixture of indulgence and exasperation, and condemned by later opinion as totally unfit to rule, Philip III put personal monarchy to the severest test it had yet endured.[2] Physically he seemed to have shed the ill health of his childhood. Short in stature and inclined to stoutness, he was agreeable enough in appearance, with the red hair typical of his dynasty but without the degenerate physiognomy of the later Habsburgs. His education and upbringing had followed

---

[1] Modesto Lafuente, *Historia general de España* (30 vols, Madrid, 1850–67), xi, pp. 77–8.

[2] The reign of Philip III has recently been brought out of obscurity by the research of Patrick Williams, reference to which is made in subsequent footnotes. Among older works, Ciriaco Pérez Bustamente, *Felipe III. Semblanza de una monarca y perfiles de una privanza* (Madrid, 1950), is a useful source of information though not of analysis. The distinguished works of the nineteenth-century statesman and historian, Antonio Cánovas del Castillo, *Historia de la decadencia española* (Madrid, 1854, 2nd edn 1911) and *Bosquejo histórico de la Casa de Austria* (Madrid, 1869, 2nd edn 1911), are still valuable for their scholarship and judgement.

conventional lines for an heir to the throne, and he had lived a
courtly life in the company of clerical tutors, spiritual advisers
and aristocratic friends Weak and timid by nature, he was further
inhibited by the greatness of his father and the superior knowledge of his advisers. His father had arranged his betrothal,
predictably, to a Habsburg cousin, Margaret of Austria, a
fourteen-year-old, whom he married in Valencia on 18 April 1599;
she bore him eight children, five of whom survived infancy, and
she died in childbirth in 1611. Benign and pious, he impressed
contemporaries for his moral virtues at least. If his court was
frivolous and extravagant, it was probably an inevitable reaction
to the austerity of Philip II's household. The king himself had no
strong interests, except perhaps eating and hunting. He travelled
extensively and seemed to prefer country houses, above all the
Escorial, to Madrid. But his mind was empty, his will supine. His
political ideas were based on a belief in the divine mission of
Spanish kingship, and he identified the interests of religion with
those of Spain, interpreting the vicissitudes of Spanish policy in
terms of divine pleasure or displeasure. Otherwise he seemed to
view his office primarily as a source of patronage for the Spanish
aristocracy. His irresponsible generosity drove his treasury officials to despair, though it was never directed, as far as is known,
to cases of real destitution. Even more damaging to the interests
of good government, however, was his incurable apathy. Philip
III was the laziest king in Spanish history.

The new monarch could not hope to emulate his father. Philip
II, as well as being a great king, had been a great civil servant. But
his system of government, in which the king was at once his own
counsellor, policy-maker and executive, placed an intolerable burden on the incumbent. Philip III at least recognized his own
limitations. He took one look at the situation and promptly
withdrew. Before doing so he made, for a Spanish monarch, an
unprecedented decision: he delegated power to a chief minister.
Even in this rare moment of resolution, however, he could not
escape his own mediocrity. His choice fell upon Francisco
Gómez de Sandoval y Rojas, Marquis of Denia and soon promoted Duke of Lerma, his closest friend and confidant, and a
man hardly more fit to exercise power than he himself was.

Lerma and his family were from Old Castile – he was born in
Tordesillas – and he consolidated his lineage by marrying the

daughter of the Duke of Medinaceli. Indeed, his social status and his friendship with the king were his only qualifications for office. Intelligence and judgement he possessed to only a moderate degree. At the age of forty-five he was deficient in political experience; he had occupied, without distinction, only one major office, that of Viceroy of Valencia, and he had been given this by Philip II not on his merits but in order to remove him from proximity to the impressionable prince. Ranke believed that Lerma possessed qualities verging on statesmanship.[3] And it is true that he consistently advocated a policy of peace and sought to disengage Spain from imperial commitments in northern and central Europe. But these qualities would have been more convincing had Lerma shown any disposition to use peace as a means of reassessing Spanish priorities, of relieving the taxpayer, and of pursuing a policy of retrenchment and reform. As it was he seemed to have little interest in the details of government, and his normal response to a crisis was either to declare his intention of entering the religious life or, more convincingly, to take to his bed and indulge his chronic hypochondria. In this respect at least he was far from being a precursor of Olivares, the great favourite of Philip IV.

Lerma wanted power not in order to make policy but in order to acquire prestige and, above all, wealth. In pursuit of wealth he was active and uninhibited. Beginning his public career in financial difficulties he gradually amassed a vast personal fortune and used his political power shamelessly to sustain and extend it.[4] If Philip III was the laziest ruler Spain has had, Lerma was incomparably the greediest. And his care for his own interests was closely followed by that for his family and friends. He dismissed García de Loaysa, Archbishop of Toledo, and Pedro de Portocarrero, Inquisitor General, and gave both posts to his uncle Bernardo de Sandoval. He distributed titles and offices to select

[3] Leopold von Ranke, L'Espagne sous Charles-Quint, Philippe II et Philippe III (Paris, 1845), pp. 219–23.

[4] 'The circumstances of the Marquis of Denia are extremely reduced', Mateo Vázquez to Philip II, 12 January 1585, Correspondencia privada de Felipe II con su secretario Mateo Vázquez, 1567–1591, C. Riba García, ed., (Madrid, 1959), i, p. 351; according to the Venetian ambassador, Lerma was bankrupt in 1598, Simon Contarini, Relazione of 1605, in Luis Cabrera de Córdoba, Relaciones de las cosas sucedidas en la corte de España desde 1599 hasta 1614 (Madrid, 1857), p. 579. On Lerma see also Cánovas, Decadencia, p. 60.

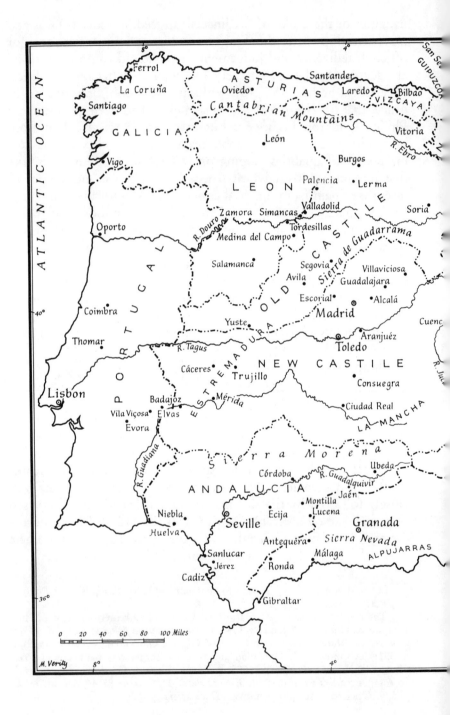

ATLANTIC OCEAN

Ferrol
La Coruña
Santiago
GALICIA
Vigo
Oporto
Coimbra
Thomar
Lisbon
PORTUGAL

ASTURIAS
Oviedo
Santander
Laredo
Bilbao
VIZCAYA
Cantabrian Mountains
Vitoria
GUIPUZCOA
San Se.
R. Ebro

León
Burgos
LEON
Palencia
Lerma
Valladolid
Zamora
Simancas
Tordesillas
Medina del Campo
Salamanca
Soria
OLD CASTILE
Sierra de Guadarrama
Segovia
Villaviciosa
Avila
Guadalajara
Escorial
Alcalá
Yuste
Madrid
Aranjuéz
Cuenc
Toledo
ESTREMADURA
Cáceres
Trujillo
NEW CASTILE
Consuegra
R. Jua
Badajoz
Mérida
Vila Viçosa
Elvas
Evora
Ciudad Real
LA MANCHA
R. Guadiana
Sierra Morena
Ubeda
Córdoba
R. Guadalquivir
Jaén
ANDALUCIA
Montilla
Niebla
Ecija
Lucena
Seville
Granada
Huelva
Antequéra
Sierra Nevada
Sanlucar
Málaga
ALPUJARRAS
Jérez
Ronda
Cadiz
Gibraltar

R. Douro
R. Tagus

0 20 40 60 80 100 Miles

M. Verity

BÉARN

Pyrenees

Marseilles
Toulon

plona

RIBAGORZA

ROSELLÓN

Urgel

Monzón

CATALONIA

Gerona

Zaragoza

Lérida

Cervera

Manresa

pila

RAGON

Barcelona

Tarragona

Tortosa

40°

BALEARIC IS.

MINORCA

MALLORCA

VALENCIA

Valencia

Gandia

IBIZA

Játiva

Alicante

rcia

Cartagena

MEDITERRANEAN SEA

SPAIN IN THE
SEVENTEENTH
CENTURY

36°

favourites until he had an entire faction beholden to him. Lerma's venality can hardly be questioned. Whether he had a corrupting influence on Spanish public life is more difficult to determine. The distribution of favours to political clients is one thing; perverting an entire administration is another. It is hardly likely that the hard core of the bureaucracy was affected by Lerma's influence. The Spanish civil service was not so sensitive to change. The king, on the other hand, was more impressionable. Lerma wanted titles, land and wealth, and he wanted them in Old Castile, not in Valencia, where the family held the Marquisate of Denia. With this in mind he moved the capital. While Philip III hated Madrid, it was Lerma's influence which was behind the inconvenient transfer of court and government to Valladolid in 1601–6. This was a move designed to increase his personal power, influence and property, and was followed by extensive travels throughout Old Castile at a time when problems of state were mounting and decisions were needed, a blatant exercise in irresponsibility much criticized at the time.[5]

The novelty of a weak king and a powerful favourite so impressed contemporary Spaniards that they regarded the year 1598 as the end of an age. Political theorists, too, reacted quickly to the change. In Spain the age of the great political philosophers, like the age of the great kings, had passed. The successors of Vitoria, Soto and Suárez were mediocrities, writers who compiled precepts of moral philosophy for the instruction and edification of the ruler and his ministers.[6] They took for granted that the perfect form of government was personal monarchy; they did not question that sovereignty should be absolute; and it never occurred to them to consider the role of representative institutions. They were looking, indeed, not for the origins and nature of power but for the ideal Christian prince. Their search was appropriate but in vain; Spanish kingship was never so weak as when it was exposed to most exhortation. As though despairing of the monarchs, some political theorists turned to the monarchs' favourites and began to preach on the education, qualities and tactics of the *perfecto privado*. This type of literature reached the

[5] Patrick Williams, 'Lerma, Old Castile and the Travels of Philip III of Spain', *History*, 73, 239 (1988), pp. 379–97.
[6] J. A. Maravall, *Teoría española del Estado en el siglo XVII* (Madrid, 1944).

depths of bathos in the conclusions drawn by Padre Joseph Laynez: 'If the favourite is as good as he ought to be then he is the noblest and richest gem in the crown of the king.' And as kings rule by divine right so do favourites: 'God chooses the favourite as he does the king.'[7] However preposterous Spanish political theory became in its didactic period, it reflected the view that Spanish kings needed encouragement and their favourites recognition. This in itself was a radical change from the theory and practice of kingship in the reign of Philip II. Later historians, too, have seen the year 1598 as a turning point in the history of Spain, the time when personal rule by the monarch gave way to the rule of favourites.[8]

Yet these developments masked a basic continuity in Spanish history, a continuity of institutions, personnel and policy. This was appreciated by an older tradition of Spanish historiography: 'the truth is that, with less power and less fortune, neither Philip III nor Philip IV professed any other principles of government than Philip II established and practised'; and it has even been claimed that it was not in the *valimiento*, the office of favourite, but in the councils 'in which resided in effect all the political power at that time'.[9] No doubt this is an exaggeration. The formulation of policy is not the same as the exercise of sovereignty. Nor was it the councils in general which formulated basic policy but one council in particular, the Council of State.[10] Nevertheless, in underlining the continuity provided by the administrative machine, these views have a certain validity.

Councils and Councillors

Spain continued to be governed by the conciliar apparatus developed by the earlier Habsburgs. In this system power was distributed among a number of agencies which specialized in different aspects of government. But is was not distributed even-

[7] Ibid., pp. 303–17.
[8] Pérez Bustamente, *Felipe III*, p. 7.
[9] Antonio Cánovas del Castillo, *Estudios del reinado de Felipe IV* (2 vols, Madrid, 1888), i, p. 258.
[10] Charles Howard Carter, *The Secret Diplomacy of the Habsburgs, 1598–1625* (New York, 1964), pp. 71–2.

ly. At the top was the Council of State which considered major policy and had exclusive jurisdiction over foreign policy. This council had no president, as the king was regarded as its convenor. And all the other councils were subordinate, either formally or in practice, to its jurisdiction. It was the parent body of the Council of War, which had begun its career as little more than a specialized sub-committee of the senior council. In the last decades of Philip II's reign, in response to Spain's growing military commitments, the Council of War had acquired its own secretariat and a distinct identity, but it was still basically a subordinate of the Council of State both in function and membership; all the councillors of state were *ex-officio* members of the Council of War, though they did not all necessarily attend it, and its role was simply to administer the military consequences of policy decided in the Council of State.

There was a group of superior or supreme councils, so called because they were theoretically independent of any other. In order of rank these were the Council of Castile, the Council of the Indies, the Council of Aragon, the Council of the Inquisition, the Council of Italy, the Council of Flanders and the Council of Portugal. Constitutionally 'supreme', in fact they were, to a greater or lesser degree, essentially administrative agencies, applying policy not making it; matters of importance, particularly those affecting defence and security, had to be referred to the Council of State. The Council of Aragon considered the affairs of the three realms of the Crown of Aragon, that is Aragon proper, Catalonia and Valencia. It acted as a liaison between the king in Madrid and his viceroys in Zaragoza, Barcelona and Valencia, Like the other councils in this group it had its own president and secretariat, and a membership which was a mixture of minor nobility and *letrados*; but it also possessed a unique 'constitutional' feature in that all its councillors, with the exception of the treasurer-general, had to be natives of the Crown of Aragon.[11] The Council of Castile had administrative and judicial jurisdiction in the territories of the crown of Castile alone, and was the nearest Spain approached to a council for home affairs. But even within this specialized field major policy decisions – the expulsion

[11] See John Lynch, *Spain 1516–1598: From Nation State to World Empire* (Oxford, 1991), pp. 3–4, 11–12, 70, 272–3, 472–3.

of the moriscos, for example – had to be referred to the Council of State. The councils specializing in regional affairs outside Castile and Aragon – the Council of Italy, the Council of Flanders and the Council of Portugal – had an even more humble role. They handled the day-to-day trivia of administration, much of it concerned with applications for pensions and preferment, and any business of importance within their areas went to the Council of State. The Council of the Indies, on the other hand, occupied a more distinguished position in the administrative hierarchy, corresponding to the importance of the oveseas empire which it administered. It had competence in every sphere of colonial government, legislative, financial, judicial, military, ecclesiastical and commercial.[12] And so specialized was its function that it was necessarily the major influence in the formation of colonial policy. Nevertheless, in matters concerning imperial defence and security it might have to defer to the Council of State; and its control over Indies revenue and expenditure was severely limited by the general fiscal jurisdiction of the Council of Finance.[13] The latter administered the crown's revenue and expenditure; and although in the field of taxation its jurisdiction was confined to Castile, in effect it had international responsibilities, for it was Castile which financed the general policy of the monarchy. But as this policy was formulated in the Council of State, the Council of Finance was little more than a service department for its superior.

Conciliar government, which was essentially government by committees, was weak in two respects: it provided neither an efficient executive nor sufficient centralization. It was subject, of course, to relentless pressure. Over the vast expanse of the Hispanic world, from the Low Countries to the Philippines, hundreds of officials spent much of their working lives writing reports to the central government, posing problems, requesting advice, demanding action. As wave after wave of paper reached Madrid it was processed according to a procedure which was now fairly standardized. Each conciliar secretary selected and prepared his particular material for the attention of the king; the latter, working with the secretary, decided what the appropriate council

---

[12] Ernesto Schäfer, *El Consejo real y supremo y de las Indias* (2 vols, Seville, 1935–47), provides an authoritative and detailed study of the Council of the Indies, a task which has not been performed for any other council.

[13] Ibid., i, pp. 102–10.

should see and requested its opinion; the council discussed the matter and presented its conclusions in a *consulta*, which was a document drawn up by the secretary summarizing the various arguments and recording the vote of each councillor; this then went to the king for his decision, a decision which would be returned to the secretary and/or council for action. Before they were subverted by declining standards of appointments in the course of the seventeenth century, the councils themselves and their secretaries worked with reasonable efficiency and despatch. And the *consulta* was a useful instrument for the formulation of policy. The weakness of the system lay in the excessive reliance it placed upon the executive, the king. Too much depended on his personal action. Under Philip II, who worked prodigiously, the machinery was already beginning to creak; under his successors it almost ground to a halt. Delay occurred at two key points: having received the incoming material the king took too long to send it to council for an opinion; and having received the opinion he took too long to act upon it. The efficiency of the subordinate councils in particular was blunted by the evasive tactics of the king in sending their *consultas* to the Council of State for a further *consulta* and even then delaying his decision. The precious decision, once obtained, had to reach a distant agency, or a number of agencies, for actual enforcement. This was the final flaw in the system.

Conciliar government, radiating from the centre though it did, was not really a centralized system of administration. Reflecting to some degree the constitutional structure of the Monarchy, with its semi-autonomous regional components, it could hardly aspire to centralization. But regional barriers were not the only ones. Madrid was not linked with its outlying provinces by a bureaucracy. Few of the councils – the Inquisition and the Council of the Indies were exceptions – employed their own officials in the localities; liaison between the centre and the periphery hardly penetrated beyond viceregal level. Thus the councils could only govern indirectly. The Council of Finance, for example, which had most need of its own local officials, had to rely for the collection of taxes on tax-farmers who were not responsible to the central government.[14] The regional councils had virtually no

---

[14] Antonio Domínguez Ortiz, *Política y hacienda de Felipe IV* (Madrid, 1960), pp. 171–80.

full-time administrative officials in the areas under their jurisdiction. Even Castile, within its own boundaries, lacked bureaucratic centralization.

Philip III inherited these structural defects in Spanish administration and aggravated them by his own habits of work. But his very indolence allowed the councils to assume greater direction of their affairs and to this extent promoted institutional development. This was particularly noticeable in the Council of State. Under Philip II, who did his own work, its powers were limited and its meetings irregular. In 1598, shortly after his accession, Philip III revived the Council of State, pressed it into more frequent meetings, and filled it with leading members of the nobility.[15] In April 1600 the Council was reorganized and from now it began to meet regularly – about once a week – and to assume a more active and comprehensive role in the formulation of policy. This can be seen in the greater number of *consultas* coming from the Council of State, indicating that Philip III was sending it more material and relying more on its advice than his father had ever done. This advice he normally accepted. The only drawback was the intolerable length of time he took to do so.

In the first three years of his reign Philip III grossly neglected his responsibilities. He was unbelievably slow in sending incoming material to the councils, and he sometimes took as long as six months and frequently two or three months to reply to a *consulta*. From about 1602 he seemed to bestir himself, but his performance was still erratic. His addiction to public ceremonial and his excessive travelling habits further isolated him from officials, who were left to administer affairs of state as best they could, waiting with increasing frustration for the king's perfunctory agreement to their *consultas*. Liaison with the councils he left in the hands of Lerma, who pushed material around from one to another and kept an eye on their activities. But it is difficult to determine the extent to which Lerma influenced conciliar decisions. He rarely attended the Council of State – twenty-two out of 739 sessions in 1600–18 – and he seems to have been content to let the administration get on with its own job. Councillors, of course, had other means of knowing the favourite's opinions than listening to them at the council table; and he was known to be a dangerous man to

[15] Patrick Williams, 'El reinado de Felipe III', in *Historia General de España y América* (Edn Rialp, Madrid, 1986), viii, p. 422.

cross. But in many respects Lerma was the image and likeness of the king; he was remote, itinerant, and just as ready to accept conciliar advice as his master. There were two subjects, however, in which he took a close interest – finance, especially expenditure, and patronage. On these matters at least he made it clear who was in command.

The remoteness of the executive threw greater responsibility on the councils and forced them to review their own procedure. In the process the Councils of State, War, and Finance became more professional bodies; the Council of War entered a new phase of its history, acquiring long-serving and experienced personnel, and a firm dedication to its task. If Philip III's way of life encouraged courtiers, his political preferences promoted good government, staffed by efficient administrators, and preoccupied with the problems of the day.[16] In 1598 the councils had employed twenty-two secretaries; by the mid-1620s they had forty-seven. At the same time they reacted to the growing burden of work by producing from within themselves a number of *juntas*, or sub-committees, whose function was to consider urgent and special problems of the moment. They were usually composed of a few members of the parent body reinforced by specialists from other councils or from outside the councils. The Council of the Indies, whose problems encompassed many areas of government, sought relief in the junta system. In 1600 it produced a *Junta de guerra de Indias*, specializing in the military and naval affairs of the empire, and composed of four councillors of the Indies and four members of the Council of War. In the same year it also formally constituted a special finance committee, the *Junta de hacienda*, to which were added two members of the Council of Finance; this was an *ad hoc* body which had first appeared in 1595 and operated until 1605.[17] Finally, appointments and patronage in the Indies were put in the hands of a small standing committee, the *Consejo de cámara de las Indias*; constituted in 1600, this committee soon acquired a reputation for the venality associated with the Duke of Lerma and it was abolished in 1609, an indication perhaps of conciliar resistance to blatant corruption. The junta

---

Patrick Williams, 'Philip III and the Restoration of Spanish Government, 1598–1603', *The English Historical Review*, 88 (1973), pp. 759, 769.
[17] Schäfer, *El Consejo real y supremo de las Indias*, i, pp. 170–4, 203–6.

system was particularly useful to the Council of State and enabled it to cope with the increasing business coming its way. It set up a number of sub-committees to specialize in the various areas of foreign policy, such as the *Junta de Italia*, the *Junta de Inglaterra* and the *Junta de Alemania*. In this way the Council could have a number of urgent matters considered simultaneously without tying down the whole Council to one problem. The proliferation of juntas in the reign of Philip III has usually been regarded as a disorderly process and a symptom of decline in standards of government. In fact it was a realistic development, sponsored by the administration itself, in response to the growing burden of work.[18] And it had perfectly respectable precedents in the reign of Philip II.

Continuity between the old regime and the new can also be seen in the personnel of Philip III's administration. The new king did not take over the conciliar team of his father in its entirety. Some officials were demoted and new ones were brought in. Among the latter Lerma himself was the outstanding example, and he is often supposed to have had a pernicious influence on the new administration by filling it with his own creatures. The Venetian ambassador reported:

> In Spain the Council is everything, but it is not free, or only nominally so, for no one dares to give his opinion freely, especially if it is against the will of the Duke of Lerma. For having done so García de Loaysa, Archbishop of Toledo, fell in disgrace, and Rodrigo Vázquez, president of the Council of Castile, was deprived of his office and expelled from court. The same happened to Pedro Portocarrero, Inquisitor General, and to don Pedro de Guzmán, royal chamberlain, who spoke ill of the duke to the king.[19]

The Venetian ambassadors were not infallible guides to the Spanish political system. It can be queried whether there was anything sinister in these dismissals and whether they were due exclusively to the favourite's malice. García de Loaysa and Vázquez de Arce had both been members of the junta appointed by Philip II for

[18] See Carter, *Secret Diplomacy*, pp. 73–4, for a vigorous reappraisal of the junta system.
[19] Contarini, in Cabrera de Córdoba, *Relaciones*, p. 579.

the education of the heir to the throne, and it may be that the latter had seen enough of them not to require their services further. A new regime, moreover, might be expected to react against members of the old who take their power and influence too much for granted. This seems to have been the case with Cristóbal de Moura, former secretary of Philip II; while not dismissed by the new king, he was posted away from Madrid, returning subsequently to the Council of State a strangely muted figure.[20] Baltasar de Zúñiga was also posted abroad, but this was because his great diplomatic talents were especially needed in the key embassies at Brussels, Paris and Vienna; and he too returned to conciliar office for a brief, though influential, term.[21] Lerma's patronage can certainly be seen in appointments to a number of offices, including some at secretarial level; but there is no evidence that he attempted the impossible task of subverting the entire administration.

The Council of State provides a good example of the new dispensation. Most of the men who were now brought in – the Duke of Alba, the Duke of Infantado, and the Constable of Castile – were obvious candidates for preferment by reason of their noble rank, their experience and their past service to the crown. The inclusion of the royal confessor, Fray Gaspar de Córdoba, was acceptable by the standards of the time and he too had experience of administration under Philip II. Even the Count of Miranda, regarded by many historians as an obvious creature of Lerma, had viceregal and conciliar experience in the previous reign and qualified for further office on his own merits.[22] The clearest line of continuity, however, was provided by two men who had been among the principal officials of Philip II, Juan de Idiáquez, Comendador de León, and the Count of Chinchón. The latter was a seasoned and forceful administrator, whom Philip II had employed on various councils and had marked with his approval. Idiáquez had been brought into the royal secretariat after the fall of Antonio Pérez and was one of those men around

[20] Matías de Novoa, Memorias (Colección de documentos inéditos para la historia de España, lx–lxi, lxix, lxxvii, lxxx, lxxxvi, Madrid, 1875–8), lx, p. 58; Williams, 'El reinado de Felipe III', p. 424.
[21] Carter, Secret Diplomacy, pp. 70, 208, 281.
[22] Schäfer, El Consejo real y supremo de las Indias i, p. 178; Cánovas, Decadencia, p. 61.

whom Philip II had built a new and hard-line administration
in the 1580s. As a member of the junta which had supervised
his education he was well known to the new king, who now
appointed him to the Council of State; there he became one of its
most influential members. A tough, faceless and realistic administrator, Idiáquez was a witness to the survival of professionalism
in govenment.[23] Fashioned round men like this, the new Council
of State was no irresponsible creation. The criterion of appointment seems to have been experience and talent, not favouritism.
By the end of the first decade of the reign, with the departure of
Chinchón and Miranda, its composition was modified; the Marquis of Spinola and the Marquis of Villafranca were brought in,
while Cristóbal de Moura returned in 1612. But its character
remained unchanged. It was a conservative body and a fairly
unanimous one, applying the received doctrines of Spanish policy
on which virtually the whole ruling class was agreed. It was not a
body which could be bullied or corrupted by the Duke of Lerma,
even if he had tried.

The members of the Council of State were drawn almost exclusively from the higher aristocracy, as they had been under Philip
II. Of the twenty-seven who served on the Council during the
reign of Philip III, sixteen were already titled nobles at the time
of appointment, though its leaders were not necessarily the highest nobles. In the other councils Philip III, like his father, employed a greater proportion of middle and lesser nobility and a
hard core of *letrados*, whose university qualifications were usually
enhanced by gentry status. Like his father, he rarely, if ever,
employed commoners. Granted the bias towards aristocracy,
Philip III's choice of servants seems to have been guided by a
concern for expertise and efficiency. The Count of Miranda, for
example, president of the Council of Castile and a specialist in
home affairs, had numerous *ad hoc* duties assigned to him in the
field of internal administration, all of which he performed with
great competence. Another experienced official inherited from the
previous regime, the secretary Esteban de Ibarra, was used as an
executive in military and defence matters and as a man who could
keep the Council of War on its toes and implement its decisions.
These and others like them, such as the secretaries Andrés de

[23] See Lynch, *Spain 1516–1598*, p. 432.

Prada, Antonio de Aróstegui and Juan de Ciriza, were professional bureaucrats who formed a reserve of talent on which the king
could draw to reinforce the various juntas and commissions
which were busy examining Spanish policy and problems. And
their presence in the administration enabled it to absorb amateurs
like the royal confessor and Lerma's *criados* without too much
damage to standards of government.

The *Valimiento*

After 1598 Spanish government began to move beyond the system of personal rule practised by Philip II and to break through
the restraints imposed on its development. Much of the impetus
towards change came from the administration itself. But Philip
III, out of his own inadequacy, was responsible for the greatest
change of all, the creation of an office closely resembling that of
chief minister. The fact that the office was unnamed, that the
minister of his choice was his closest friend the Duke of Lerma,
and that Lerma's appointment initiated a permanent line of *validos*, or favourites, whose chief qualification was their personal
friendship with the king, has tarnished its development in the
eyes of later historians and obscured those elements in it which
represented real institutional growth.[24] It is true that the appointment of *validos* was in part a device by which the later Habsburgs, lacking the talent and the will for personal rule, sought to
shield themselves from the problems of government. But it was
more than this. It was, in the first place, an adjustment to circumstances. The burden of governing Spain and its vast empire
had grown beyond the point where one man could carry it alone.
As a mere administrative problem, with paper mounting inexorably day by day, it was more than a one-man executive could be
expected to resolve. The time had come for the king to share his
burden and delegate power.

In the past the crown had shared administrative work, though
not policy making, with its secretaries. Less than a minister, the

[24] Francisco Tomás Valiente, *Los validos en la monarquía española del siglo
XVII* (Madrid, 1963), provides an illuminating institutional study of the *valido*,
to which the following pages are indebted; see also Carter, *Secret Diplomacy*,
pp. 66–71, for a notable revision of the subject.

secretary had become more than a clerk. He had access to all state papers, his advice was sought by the king, and he was the main link between king and council. The secretaries of the Council of State in particular were key figures in the administration, especially under Philip II, who had worked his secretaries hard and his Council little. Indeed the secretaries' permanent access to the king, contrasting with the irregular meetings of the Council, must have been galling to aristocratic councillors, who regarded themselves as the king's rightful advisers. For it was clear to them that the secretaries were no longer merely the Council's clerks: the *secretario de estado* had become the *secretario del rey*. Yet the development of the secretaryship did not alter the character of the secretary. He remained a professional bureaucrat without political ambition; he usually had a university qualification and some previous administrative experience; and socially he came from the lesser nobility, a matter of preference to Philip II and of resentment to the grandees.

The rise of the *valido* meant the decline of the secretary. Writing in the 1620s, Francisco Bermúdez de Pedraza, an authority on the office, lamented the passing of the golden days of the secretaryship in the sixteenth century and its depreciation at the hands of the *validos*:

Philip III did not have a private secretary, because the grandees of Spain in his administration made sure they discussed verbally with the king the *consultas* and files of the secretary. It is the exercise of the office which counts, not the title. And it was the grandees who were now exercising the real function of the office; the secretaries were left with the title but they were merely clerks, deprived of the most important part which is to discuss and resolve personally with the king the highest affairs of state.[25]

The grandees had won their point. The secretaries of state were now literally secretaries of the Council of State. They were no longer private counsellors of the king. They were no more than civil servants, important ones no doubt, but completely overshadowed by the *valido*. It was the *valido* who now supervised the councils, managed the written instruments of government, and advised the king. His office had greater political content than

[25] Quoted in Valiente, *Los validos*, p. 50.

the secretaryship had ever had; it was unique, undivided, and carried more power. The *valido*, moreover, was closer to the king, whose friendship was at once his badge of authority and his chief qualification for office. Finally, the *valido* had greater social assets than the secretary: he almost invariably came from the higher aristocracy.[26]

The rise of the *valido* reflected not only the inadequacy of the king and the growth of administration but also the ambitions of the aristocracy. In the role of Lerma and his successors one can observe perhaps a certain reaction of the higher nobility against the type of secretary who had stood between them and the king in the reign of Philip II. In this sense the emergence of the *valido* represented an aristocratic bid, if not to control, at least to monopolize the crown, and the outcome was a political victory of the grandees over the *hidalgos* and the lesser nobility. For although the grandees, like other elements in Spanish society, overtly criticized the *validos*, their criticism was directed at individual incumbents, not at the office, and it was motivated by resentment of a rival's success or in expectation of similar preferment. This was only to be expected, for the *valido* was simply the apex of a system which permeated the whole of Spanish society, as it did other European societies in the early modern period, the system of patronage and clientage.[27]

The Spanish crown was regarded not only as a law-giver but also as a benefactor. From all parts of Spain and its dependencies a constant stream of suitors pressed on Madrid in search of appointments, honours, privileges, pensions and grants of all kinds. They could hardly expect to reach the fount of patronage itself, the crown, so they would try to get someone highly placed to intercede for them, a councillor or an important official who had the king's ear, and naturally they would be expected to pay for this service in one way or another. Clients, then, sought to attach themselves to a powerful patron who disposed of influence and wealth, and the most influential of all was the king's favourite, and after him the favourite's favourite. For their part patrons,

---

[26] Ibid., pp. 51–3, 109–10.
[27] The penetrating study of patronage and faction in England by Sir John E. Neale, 'The Elizabethan Political Scene', *Proceedings of the British Academy*, xxxiv (1948), provides an interpretation which can usefully be applied to Spain.

anxious to build up a large following as a measure of their own power and status, were willing to oblige. This accounts for the manoeuvring for strategic positions around the king and for the constant agitation at court. Fray Antonio de Guevara, one of the many observers of the scene, recorded:

> I see the majority of courtiers swearing, blaspheming, muttering and snarling about the evils and evil-doers there are at court. But I am confident that their discontent does not stem from the vices they see practised there but from the simple fact that their rivals are prospering in the king's favour while they are not.[28]

The patronage system had political implications. There were, of course, no political parties: these could not develop in a situation where the crown controlled policy, where the obligation of councillors to the crown was a personal and not a corporate one, and where the ruling class was agreed about basic objectives. This did not mean that there were no political differences among statesmen. But the form these differences took was faction. The rivalry of factions was concentrated on what mattered most, namely influence over the king and thereby control of patronage and all that this meant. It meant not only wealth but power. If a politician disposed of patronage and influence he could attract a large following and so create a faction of men who expected their patron to sponsor their interests at court. It was inevitable, therefore, that just as Lerma and his successors sought the king's patronage, so they in turn should distribute patronage to their clients and thus acquire their own *validos*. It was at this point that the patronage system engendered corruption.

Lerma's technique was to accumulate major offices in the royal household until he monopolized access to the king; minor offices he acquired to give to his family and clients and to erect a further barrier against rivals. At the same time he collected offices controlling access to the royal palaces, and the governorship of those cities – Valladolid and Madrid, for example – where the king would be staying. In this way he came to isolate the king from the influence of rivals and prevented anyone of whom he disapproved from approaching the royal presence. He fortified his

---

[28] Quoted in Valiente, *Los validos*, p. 54.

family with titles and marriage alliances, headed by a dukedom for himself. He bought palaces, houses, landed property, and of course jurisdiction and revenues, the latter either donated by the crown or purchased as a secure investment. His annual income in 1620 was 200,000 ducats, and at the end of the reign his total wealth amounted to 3 million ducats.[29] Lerma blatantly favoured his relations, promoting his son-in-law, the Count of Lemos, to the presidency of the Indies, the viceroyalty of Naples, and the presidency of Italy, and his brother Juan, Marquis of Villamizar, to the viceroyalty of Valencia. Patronage of this kind could backfire; in favouring his eldest son, Cristóbal, Duke of Uceda, he created a rival and an alternative focus of interest. And some of his *criados* were badly chosen. Don Pedro Franqueza, for example, younger son of impoverished Catalan gentry, became a *valido* of Lerma and through him acquired a title, Count of Villalonga, and the offices of secretary and councillor of Finance; but success went to his head and after a brief if spectacular career he was purged from the administration for blatant venality. The most notorious example of the private *valido* was Rodrigo Calderón whose rapid rise from obscurity to fame and fortune at once fascinated and scandalized contemporaries.[30] Beginning as a retainer in Lerma's household he soon became his principal liaison officer, in much the same way as Lerma was the king's. His patron procured him numerous offices and grants, including the titles of Count of Oliva and Marquis of Siete Iglesias, and put him in the way of a large income. Calderón in turn had his creatures, rather lower down the ladder, and predictably a large number of enemies. His disreputable behaviour made him particularly vulnerable once his patron fell. Indeed his fate was worse than Lerma's. He was arrested on various charges ranging from murder to peculation, and after lengthy imprisonment he was tortured, convicted and executed at the hands of a rival faction in the following reign. The downfall of Lerma and Calderón attested to the ruthlessness of the patronage system and the vindictiveness of the 'outs' when they became the 'ins'. There was too much at stake to expect clemency.

The crown itself was a passive spectator of these events,

---

[29] Williams, 'El reinado de Felipe III', p. 430.
[30] Cánovas, *Decadencia*, pp. 61–2.

trapped in a system it had helped to create. Instead of distributing their favour among a number of ministers, who could be played off one against the other, the later Habsburgs allowed one man to monopolize patronage and power. They thereby lost their independence, for they were subject to the pressure of a single interest. They became victims of powerful *validos* and aristocratic factions. What had begun as delegation of power ended as abdication of control.

Yet their original objective was valid enough. They may not have been able to formulate the problem precisely, but they were searching in effect for a chief minister. The term is actually used in contemporary texts and state papers, and although its meaning is not precise its use is sufficient to identify the official and public status of the *valido* as head of the central administration. Some political commentators viewed the development with the deepest misgivings; that a king should share his sovereignty was thought to be incompatible with absolute monarchy. And, paradoxically, in order to control the *valimiento* they sought to institutionalize it. Diego Saavedra Fajardo, the distinguished diplomat, was affronted in all his instincts by the emergence of the *valido*, and his writings show a deep concern to reduce the position to acceptable limits. The *valimiento*, he argued, 'is not only a grant, it is an office; it is not a favour but a delegation of work'.[31] For Saavedra the *valimiento* was an office without a name; far better that it be regarded as a public institution than allowed to drift into crude personal power.

As an institution the *valimiento* was not static but evolved throughout the course of the seventeenth century. The first important stage of its growth was the long tenure of the Duke of Lerma, who occupied the position for twenty years. The decision of the young king to share his responsibilities with his friend and mentor must have been taken before his accession to the throne. At any rate within a few days of his father's death, and in spite of the disapproval of Moura and Idiáquez, he dissolved the small junta which Philip II had created to ease the transition, and he thus left the way open for Lerma to acquire a unique position. Simultaneously he seems to have given Lerma verbal authority to

[31] *Idea de un Príncipe político-cristiano* (1640) (*Biblioteca de autores españoles,* 25, Madrid, 1947), p. 126.

sign state papers in the king's name, in order to legitimize that position. The delegation of power can be inferred from a remarkable decree issued some years later, on 23 October 1612, in which the king, to stave off perhaps growing criticism of the favourite, declared his complete satisfaction with the service rendered by Lerma and confirmed the power given to him at the beginning of the reign. The decree ordered each council and its president 'to comply with whatever the duke instructs or orders . . . and also to furnish him with any information he requires'.[32] This was the formal instrument of delegation, with retrospective validity to the beginning of the reign. It stated in effect that orders signed by Lerma had the force of royal orders, and thus placed the entire conciliar system at the disposition of the *valido*. This was how Lerma himself interpreted his powers. He received incoming material from the secretary, distributed it to the councils, and made executive decisions on the councils' *consultas*. No doubt he discussed these matters with the king privately, and he was always careful to couch his instructions in the form of a written or verbal order from the king himself. But he was acting in fact as the executive. This was so in his relations with the Council of State, the chief policy-making body; and as he exercised his own discretion in deciding what matters should be remitted from the other councils to the Council of State he became the controlling link in the whole system, though not a particularly efficient one.[33] Towards the other councils, such as the Council of Aragon and the Council of the Indies, he also assumed the attitude of the executive, though preserving the form of merely transmitting 'the king's orders'.[34] The Council of Finance, it is true, was an object of more particular interest to the king, and he usually looked more closely at its *consultas*, though he also usually agreed with them. But Lerma himself sent frequent and peremptory orders, overtly in the king's name, to the president of the Council of Finance, ordering payments of various kinds, including military expenditure. Finally, Lerma was careful to keep control of pat-

[32] Valiente, *Los validos*, pp. 9, 161.
[33] Ibid., pp. 63–4.
[34] For examples of Lerma's relations with the Council of Aragon see J. Reglà, 'La expulsión de los moriscos y sus consecuencias', *Hispania*, xiii (1953), pp. 215–67; for the Council of the Indies see Schäfer, *El Consejo real y supremo de las Indias*, i, pp. 188–9.

ronage in his own hands. In July 1605 he instructed the secretary of the Council of State that matters concerning appointments and grants must be submitted directly to the king, and that the Council could only consider them if they were expressly remitted to it by the king. In practice all decisions on patronage matters were sent by Lerma, again acting in the name of the king, to the secretary for communication to the applicant.[35]

For twenty years, until 1618, Lerma was chief minister in all but name. In the course of this time he grew in wealth and in unpopularity; inevitably he became the target of criticism of Spain's economic condition and international policies. His unbridled greed, his unscrupulous use of patronage, and the scandalous behaviour of some of his clients, notably Calderón, outraged public opinion; his enemies began to sharpen their knives and his subordinates to edge away. In the course of twenty years the king too grew, if not in wisdom at least in maturity. The tutelage of his childhood mentor, to which he had clung with relief as a young king of twenty-one, was becoming increasingly ridiculous as he approached middle age. After about 1615, moreover, a sense of disillusionment possessed him, as he became aware of the shortcomings of Lerma and his clients, of growing dissatisfaction in the country, and above all of the real state of government finances. The appointment of Fernando Carillo as president of the Council of Finance in 1609 was already a sign that the king realized the need to reform the administration. Carillo had led the case against Villalonga and established his political priorities; he quickly became one of the most efficient and energetic of administrators. Meanwhile, as the king emancipated himself from Lerma, new voices were making themselves heard in council, especially those of Baltasar de Zúñiga, now returned from his embassies abroad, and of Fray Luis de Aliaga, the new confessor. On the international front Spain was facing new problems. The situation in Germany was deteriorating; Spain's commitment to the Habsburg cause and her position in the Low Countries had to be reappraised. Lerma stood for a policy of peace and non-intervention in the affairs of northern Europe, a policy which in itself had much to recommend it but which coming from Lerma lacked moral conviction. He had wasted the opportunity given by

[35] Valiente, *Los validos*, p. 68.

peace to effect retrenchment and reform. Instead he had advised
the young king badly and set an even worse example of private
extravagance and public waste.

Court and administration lived in expectation, trying to detect
the next candidate for royal favour; and clients awaited the decision of the supreme patron. Opposition to the ageing favourite
was mobilized by Aliaga, whose opinions on foreign policy coincided with those of Lerma but who otherwise abhorred the latter's influence on public affairs. An anti-Lerma faction began to
form, grouped around a new contender for the *valimiento*, none
other than Lerma's own son, Cristóbal de Sandoval y Rojas,
Duke of Uceda. And in the Council of State the views of Zúñiga,
the principal advocate of a hard-line policy in northern Europe,
began to win support. Faction and policy alike were moving
against Lerma. In a desperate attempt to strengthen his position
he procured a cardinalate from Rome, a typical move by a man
who viewed politics almost exclusively in terms of personal prestige. Even Philip III was unimpressed. From about April 1618 he
began to withdraw his confidence from Lerma, restricting his
access to state papers and warning him to prepare for retirement.
When during July and August the Council of State was unCharac-
teristically divided over a major policy issue, whether or not to
intervene in Germany, Lerma found himself in a distinct minority, powerless to keep Spain out of a war that was going to
ensnare her for forty years. On more than one occasion in the
past Lerma had indicated his wish to retire to his estates or to
religious life. Now, with rivals manoevring for position and more
imperialist voices dominating the Council of State, he may even
have come to consider these ideas, torn between the attractions of
retirement and reluctance to leave court. At the end of September
1618, when he asked the king's permission to retire, his request
was granted, and the decision communicated to him on 4
October.[36] Did Lerma retire, or was he dismissed? An element
of ambiguity surrounds the occasion. He retired to his estates
at Lerma, south of Burgos, then to Valladolid, where he died on
17 May 1625.

Philip III acted with unwonted resolution in accepting the
retirement of Lerma. According to an anonymous chronicler,

---

[36] Patrick Williams, 'Lerma, 1618: Dismissal or Retirement?', *European History Quarterly*, 19 (1989), pp. 307–32.

'even the lamb has to roar once; for it was important that His Majesty should overcome his meekness and show his favourites that he was determined enough to perceive and punish misdeeds and dismiss their authors'.[37] Lerma's clients, moreover, inevitably felt the cold wind blowing through the Escorial, and his particular favourites like Calderón were mercilessly pursued by their enemies in the new regime. Yet his fall was not the occasion of a general upheaval of government, and the hard core of the administration continued unchanged. As for government by *valido*, that was too valuable to the king to be entirely relinquished and he still clutched at the support which it offered him.

Uceda succeeded Lerma in the *valimiento*, and the transfer of power was instantaneous.[38] It was also incomplete. On 15 November 1618 Philip III issued a decree which had the effect of revoking that of 1612; from now onwards all policy statements, orders and matters of patronage emanating from the royal will were to be signed by the king and by no one else.[39] This ended, formally at least, the almost total delegation of power by king to *valido*, and it meant that the councils were not so dependent on Uceda as they had been on Lerma. It is a sign perhaps that Philip III had learnt some lessons and was determined this time not to abandon all his responsibilities. If this is so, he did not keep his resolution. Before long Uceda was handling a good deal of conciliar business on behalf of the king, and the administration seemed to regard him as chief minister. Nevertheless, his position was never as well defined as that of Lerma. He did not monopolize liaison between king and councils; and to some extent traditional avenues of communication reasserted themselves. Uceda himself had no political gifts and there was a certain hollowness about his regime. Was this featureless man a figure-head behind whom other advisers operated, Aliaga, the keeper of the king's conscience, and, in foreign affairs, Baltasar de Zúñiga? If the suspicion is correct it would signify a sharing of delegated power, in itself a healthier political development. But the evidence is too vague to yield firm answers. If the chroniclers are to be believed, Philip III died repenting that he had abandoned power into the

[37] Valiente, *Los validos*, p. 9.
[38] On the fall of Lerma and the succession of Uceda see Novoa, *Memorias*, lxi, pp. 145–59.
[39] Valiente, *Los validos*, pp. 10–11, 162.

hands of *validos*. And on the day of his death, at the express wish of the new king, Uceda was obliged to hand over state papers and the management of government to Baltasar de Zúñiga.

The Poverty of Government

The empire which Philip III inherited was based on Castile, but it was not governed by the laws of Castile or assessed by the taxes of Castile. Even Philip II, absolutist though he was, had not attempted to challenge the autonomy of his various kingdoms or to incorporate them into a centralized state. Although Philip III described himself as king of Spain, he was first and foremost king of Castile and his power was absolute only in Castile. Even within the kingdom of Castile the provinces of Vizcaya (Biscay), Guipúzcoa and Alava enjoyed a degree of fiscal and administrative autonomy. Outside Castile separatism was even more pronounced. The Crown of Aragon, which included the realms of Aragon, Catalonia and Valencia, had its identity enshrined in highly developed *fueros*, or constitutional rights. Each of these realms was governed independently, each had its own laws and tax system, and in each the king was represented by a viceroy. Castilian sovereignty was even more attenuated in Italy, where the kingdoms of Sicily and Naples and the duchy of Milan were governed for the king of Spain by viceroys or governors and administered by their own institutions. In the Low Countries Spanish sovereignty, where it was effective, was exercised by the archdukes, who were something less than independent rulers and something more than mere governors, and who ruled through local institutions with the assistance of local personnel.[40] This constitutional structure cannot be described as a federal one, for there was no federal agency at the centre, other than the crown itself. It was a personal union, which fully respected the independence of each of the parts. In practice Castilian power made itself felt to some degree. The permanent residence of the king in Castile, the preponderance of Castilians in public office, and the

[40] Charles Howard Carter, 'Belgian "autonomy" under the Archdukes, 1598–1621', *Journal of Modern History*, xxxvi (1964), pp. 249–59.

situation of the councils in Madrid made unity rather more effective in practice than it was in theory. But there was one area of
government where the constituent kingdoms were particularly
sensitive to attacks on their prerogatives – in matters of finance.
One of the greatest problems of the Castilian government was to
persuade them to contribute to common expenditure in proportion to their resources.

The Spanish Low Countries contributed only modest amounts
to the general expenses of the monarchy and these were swallowed up in local administration; defence expenditure was subsidized from Castile. From the time of the dissolution of the States
General in 1600 a subsidy (*subsidio ordinario*) of 3,600,000 florins
was collected annually; this was voted by the various provincial
estates, but it was understood that they could not refuse it without compromising the king's sovereignty; and in order to allow
them to discuss it without danger the administration usually
asked them for a higher amount than it was likely to get.[41] In
addition, and more reluctantly, they also voted an extraordinary
subsidy of varying amounts. The Italian dependencies contributed
much more to imperial expenditure than did the Low
Countries.[42] For Spanish policy imposed upon them an important
and costly role in Europe and the Mediterranean, a role which
they sustained to a great extent out of their own resources; these
resources were severely strained by tax demands which, at the end
of the sixteenth century, were being met to the tune of 5.5 million
ducats a year by Sicily, Naples and Milan combined.

Within the peninsula Portugal was completely autonomous in
fiscal maters and contributed nothing to the general expenses of
the monarchy. The Basque provinces, though part of Castile,
were also immune from Castile's demands.[43] They did not pay
the *alcabala*, the *millones* or the other standard taxes of Castile,
and they even complained that merchandise imported from Castile was already charged with these taxes. The only revenue which
the king received from the Basque provinces was the yield from
his feudal and seigneurial rights, and this was hardly enough to

[41] H. Pirenne, *Histoire de Belgique* (3rd edn, 7 vols, Brussels, 1909–32), iv,
p. 402.
[42] Domínguez Ortiz, *Política y hacienda de Felipe IV*, pp. 161–4.
[43] Ibid., pp. 159–60.

cover the cost of his administration in the area. In Vizcaya, for example, his patrimonial revenue – some 30,000 to 40,000 ducats a year – was normally expended on the grants and pensions of various kinds with which he was expected to regale his subjects in the province. The latter resisted all attempts of the central government to introduce ordinary taxation, no matter how temporary, for that would have compromised their *hidalguía* and consequently their permanent immunity from taxation. The attitude of the Basques, however, was not unreasonable, for theirs were small provinces, sparsely populated and economically undeveloped. Whenever Spain was at war with France they defended the frontier at their own cost, and to this extent contributed to imperial finances.

The Crown of Aragon was equally stubborn in its resistance to the tax demands of the central government, and actually contributed less than the Italian dependencies to general expenses. Royal income from Valencia was effectively confined to the revenue from crown property and seigneurial jurisdiction. This yielded the modest sum of about 100,000 libros a year, which was consumed in the maintenance of royal administration in the area. In the reign of Philip III the cortes of Valencia voted only one subsidy, in 1604, amounting to 400,000 ducats. From the cortes of Catalonia he received in 1599 a subsidy of 1,100,000 ducats. And from the cortes of Aragon he received nothing. In Aragon and Catalonia most of the taxes on merchandise were in the hands of the towns or of individual proprietors; the crown had the right to one-fifth (*quinto*) of these revenues annually, but in many cases had allowed it to fall into disuse. Philip III's local administration began to reclaim the *quinto* for the crown, and those towns which could not produce proof of legal immunity from the claim were gradually, and against much opposition, forced to pay. The campaign for the *quinto* was particularly intense in Catalonia, and when it reached Barcelona the latter flatly refused to contribute. The refusal was accompanied by the usual appeal to Catalan liberties, an appeal which would have been more convincing had the not inconsiderable revenues of Barcelona been administered with integrity by the municipal oligarchy. In any case nothing was further from the intention of Philip III's government than to initiate constitutional change.

Castile continued to be the treasury of the monarchy. And

general expenditure continued to outstrip Castile's resources. In the first decade of the reign defence expenditure, especially in the Low Countries, was still the major charge on revenue. In addition Philip III inherited the considerable debts incurred by his father. He made matters worse by his own extravagance. He spent far too much money on himself and almost as much on his favourites. Among the numerous gifts to the Duke of Lerma was one of 50,000 ducats made in the euphoria engendered by the arrival of the Indies fleet. On the occasion of the king's marriage in 1599 his lavish gifts to various favoured subjects passed all reason; the whole extravaganza cost 950,000 ducats, 300,000 of which were disposed of by Lerma. Philip III, in fact, behaved as though the public treasury was his private property. Traditionally this may have been a valid assumption, though the political economists of the time, the *arbitristas*, were beginning to challenge it.[44] Indeed Juan de Mariana, the Jesuit political philosopher, was quite clear on the subject: 'The king is not allowed to spend at liberty the money granted to him by his subjects as if it were income from his private possession.'[45] It was obvious, even to Philip III, that the grants of the cortes had a public character which placed them out of his reach; in any case they were usually appropriated to specific items of expenditure. But there were numerous other revenues on which he could lay his hands. In addition to his private patrimony, moreover, the king, as the highest official, possessed a kind of civil list – some 600,000 ducats a year – charged on public revenues. This, however, by no means covered all his expenses – royal household, secret service payments, gifts to clients, to mention only a few. The maintenance of the royal family alone cost Castile about 1,300,000 ducats a year under Philip III – over 10 per cent of the budget – compared to 1,000,000 a year under his two predecessors and his immediate successor.

The scale of expenditure called for greater revenue than the government possessed. Yet there was a real reluctance to impose new taxes. These were known to provoke resistance and criticism

[44] José Luis Sureda Carrión, *La Hacienda castellana y los economistas del siglo XVII* (Madrid, 1949), pp. 77–9.
[45] *De mutatione monetae*, in John Laures, *The Political Economy of Juan de Mariana* (New York, 1928), p. 299.

of government policies. And as its own conduct was particularly vulnerable to criticism, the government of Philip III and Lerma preferred not to stir up hostile interests or alienate public opinion; its policy was to let sleeping dogs lie. There were, in fact, two alternatives to heavier taxation. One was to reduce defence expenditure, an expedient which appealed to Philip III not out of conviction but on the assumption that peace was easier than reform. As other nations too had an interest in ending the long and costly conflict inherited from the previous century, the Spanish government was able to continue the process of peace-making begun by the Franco-Spanish treaty of 1598. Peace was made with England in 1604, and in April 1607 a cease-fire was arranged with the Dutch, followed by the Truce of Antwerp in 1609. Disengagement in northern Europe, of course, did not mean disarmament elsewhere, and Spain continued to have heavy defence commitments in Italy, the Mediterranean and the Atlantic. But recourse had already been had to a second expedient, one which branded the government as bankrupt of ideas as well as of money – debasement of the coinage.

In 1599 Philip III departed from a long Spanish tradition of sound money and issued in Castile a vellon coinage of pure copper in order to save the silver with which it had previously been alloyed. The 100 per cent profit accruing to the government from this operation encouraged it to decree even heavier issues of copper vellon in 1602 and 1603, in spite of the bitter protests of the cortes. In 1608, in return for a subsidy, Philip III promised the cortes not to coin further vellon for twenty years, but the enormous budget deficit in 1617 caused him to seek release from his promise, and the cortes agreed to a further issue sufficient to yield a profit of one million ducats. This was followed in 1621 by yet another issue, designed to yield a profit of 800,000 ducats. Altogether Philip III issued copper vellon to the amount of 27 million ducats.[46] The consequences were predictable, at least to many outside the government. Monetary instability drove gold and silver out of circulation. Vellon receded from parity with the precious metals; the average annual premium on the exchange of vellon for silver rose from 1 per cent in 1603 to 3 per cent in

---

[46] Earl J. Hamilton, *American Treasure and the Price Revolution in Spain, 1501–1650* (Cambridge, Mass, 1934), pp. 73–9, 88–93, 102–3.

1619. As taxes were paid in vellon and defence expenditure abroad had to be made in silver, the crown itself was one of the biggest losers. Currency debasement, moreover, prolonged into the seventeenth century the great price inflation generated by American silver in the sixteenth century, but with an important difference; whereas the price revolution of the sixteenth century had been a steady and continuous process, the new inflation moved by fits and starts and was periodically interrupted by sudden deflation, thus causing great harm to business activities and to all those who lived on annuities, pensions and fixed incomes. And inflation hit the greatest consumer of all, the government itself. Many of these disadvantages were identified by contemporaries, by the cortes and the *arbitristas*. Mariana wrote a treatise on the subject which he published in Germany in 1609. He denounced Philip III's monetary policy as hidden taxation and warned that it would drive out gold and silver and lead to inflation. But on this subject the government was hypersensitive. Mariana was arrested by the Inquisition and charged with lèse-majesté for criticising the monetary policy of the king before a foreign audience; and although he was released after a year his treatise was put on the Spanish Index.[47]

What were the main sources of revenue from Castile? First, there was the ordinary income from the *alcabala* and the customs. The latter covered a wide range of charges on internal and foreign trade and constituted a basic item of revenue, though one highly vulnerable to fraud. The *alcabala* was a 10 per cent tax on sales, which the larger towns had previously compounded for an agreed yearly payment. By 1612 it was raising 2,754,766 ducats a year, more than twice the amount yielded in the 1570s.[48] This was still well below its potential yield, for many places and people, including all ecclesiastics, had acquired exemption from the tax or paid at a reduced rate. In many parts of Castile, moreover, the *alcabala* had fallen into the hands of private proprietors, either through grants to powerful nobles in the Middle Ages or by purchase in the course of the sixteenth century; and the improvident govern-

[47] Laures, *The Political Economy of Juan de Mariana*, p. 282; see also G. Lewy, *Constitutionalism and Statecraft during the Golden Age of Spain: A Study of the Political Philosophy of Juan de Mariana, S. J.* (Geneva, 1960), pp. 30–2.
[48] Domínguez Ortiz, *Política y hacienda de Felipe IV*, pp. 194–203.

ment of Philip III continued the process of alienation in exchange
for a quick though short-term income. These traditional revenues
of the crown were supplemented by grants of the cortes.[49] The
servicio ordinario y extraordinario was granted by the cortes
every three years and since 1591 had been fixed at 405,000 ducats
a year. The most important grant, however, was the *millones*, a
tax on basic foodstuffs, which was supposed to yield 2 million
ducats a year but in fact grew to 3 million in the early years of the
reign, reverting to 2 million by the end of the reign. In an age of
inflation the value of these fixed grants effectively declined,
though the *millones* occasionally responded to rising prices. In
addition to this ordinary and extraordinary income, the crown
had revenues from ecclesiastical sources, and these extended
beyond Castile into all the king's dominions.[50] The most important was the *cruzada*, the revenue from the sale of bulls of
indulgence, whose average annual yield in Spain alone was
800,000 ducats paid in silver by the banker who administered the
revenue; the *subsidio* – some 420,000 ducats a year – was a
proportion of church revenues paid to the crown for the upkeep
of the naval establishment in the Mediterranean; and the *excusado*
was an income of 250,000 ducats a year derived from ecclesiastical
property. Finally, the crown possessed its celebrated revenue
from the Indies.[51] The decade 1610–20, however, saw the beginning of a noticeable decline in silver remittances from America,
reflecting a crisis in the Indies trade which hit both public and
private returns.[52] For the five-year period 1611–15 the crown
received 7,212,921 pesos, compared with 10,974,318 pesos in the
peak period 1596–1600. In the years 1616–20 there was an even
sharper drop, to 4,347,788 pesos, a level from which the American revenue never substantially rose during the rest of the seventeenth century.

In 1598 the crown's estimated revenue amounted to 9,731,405
ducats.[53] Of this, 4,634,293 ducats – drawn principally from
major taxes such as the *alcabala*, customs and the *subsidio* – were
either already assigned in advance to permanent items of expendi-

[49] Ibid., pp. 232–8.
[50] Ibid., pp. 241–9.
[51] Hamilton, *American Treasure*, pp. 34–8.
[52] See below, pp. 241, 269–70.
[53] Domínguez Ortiz, *Política y hacienda de Felipe IV*, pp. 3–18.

ture, principally *juros* (state bonds) and certain defence commitments, or had been recently alienated to tax proprietors. The rest
of the revenue, just over 5 million ducats – derived from the
millones and *servicio* granted by the cortes, the *cruzada* and the
income from the Indies – was theoretically free of charges but in
fact much of it was committed in advance to bankers in payment
of previous *asientos*, or defence contracts. Most of the defence
expenditure was incurred in the Low Countries, which in the first
twelve years of the reign consumed over 40 million ducats.[54] As
commitments increased the time came when the whole of the
'free' revenue for several years in advance was assigned to bankers
and there was nothing left to cover further *asientos*. This point
was reached in 1607; the government had now anticipated revenue up to 1611 and the total debt stood at 22,748,971 ducats.[55]
For this situation there was a classical remedy, known at the time
as the *medio general*: contracted revenues were released from
their commitments and the bankers were indemnified with
juros.[56] Operations of this kind, though frequently called bankruptcies, were in effect forced conversions of debts; Philip II had
recourse to them on three occasions, roughly every twenty years.
In using the device once, Philip III could claim not to have
exceeded his quota, but once was enough to worsen the crown's
credit, and the government was forced to re-think its defence
policy. Suspension of payments in 1607, therefore, was followed
by suspension of war in the Low Countries in 1609. Yet although
Spain was no longer involved in a major war, her financial trou-
bles were not at an end. A number of localized conflicts in Italy,
defence spending in Germany, the Mediterranean and the overseas empire, and the expenses of court and government actually
raised expenditure beyond previous wartime levels. In 1615 the
year's expenditure was expected to exceed 9 million ducats.[57]

On the eve of the Thirty Years War, therefore, Spanish finances
were badly overstrained. Much of the appropriated revenue in
1617 failed to meet its commitments. The remaining 'free' revenue

[54] 'Relación del dinero remitido a Flandes', 13 September 1598–20 June 1609, *Colección de documentos inéditos para la historia de España*, xxxvi, p. 509.
[55] *Actas de las Cortes de Castilla*, xxiii, pp. 543–59.
[56] See Lynch, *Spain 1516–1598*, pp. 209–10.
[57] J. H. Elliott, *The Revolt of the Catalans. A Study in the Decline of Spain (1598–1640)* (Cambridge, 1963), pp. 187–8.

amounted to 5,357,000 ducats, compared with an expenditure which had risen to some 12 million ducats. This comprised 5 million in defence costs (principally in the Low Countries, where Spain was now re-priming the military establishment, and in Milan), 3 million owed in unpaid *juros*, and the remainder for the royal household, officials' salaries, delayed debts and sundry other expenses.[58] The budget for 1618 looked even worse: 'free' revenue had now dropped to 1,601,000 ducats and was utterly inadequate for existing commitments. It was at this point that Spain intervened in Germany, on a modest scale at first but sufficient to aggravate expenditure. Long before its arrival the public income from the Indies for 1619 was assigned to bankers on account.

What could the government do? Advice there was in plenty. The Council of Castile took a long look at the economic situation before producing its notable *consulta* of 1619 on the state of the nation.[59] It drew attention to the damaging effects of excessive taxation on Castile, and underlined two particular causes of rising expenditure – the extravagant doling out of grants and pensions, and the exaggerated growth of the bureaucracy, much of which was becoming at once venal and superfluous. The results, it concluded, could be seen in the financial situation: the whole of the crown's income was committed in advance, except for the 'free' revenue, and this had been anticipated in *asientos*. But Philip III's mind was closed to argument of this kind. In the same year, in spite of the Council's advice to cut conspicuous expenditure, he decided to take a long-planned trip to Portugal to have his son recognized as heir apparent, an excursion which proved to be inordinately expensive. Yet he still shrank from taking the extreme step of imposing new taxes. He preferred more devious methods, such as issuing further quantities of vellon, sequestering a portion of private treasure on the Indies fleet in return for *juros*, and, of course, anticipating income. The last *asiento* contracted by Philip III shortly before his death in March 1621 was for 4.5 million ducats, most of it for defence expenditure in the Low

[58] 'Relación de la Real Hacienda', 1617, *Actas de las Cortes de Castilla*, xxx, pp. 15–32.
[59] Angel González Palencia, *La Junta de Reformación*, 1618–1625 (*Archivo Histórico Español*, 5, Valladolid, 1932), doc. no. 4.

Countries, the Atlantic and the Mediterranean. This consumed all his current 'free' revenue and that of the future up to 1624. The crushing weight of defence expenditure fell almost exclusively on Castile. Inevitably Castilians began to demand that the tax burden should be shared by other parts of the monarchy. The argument was developed by a number of *arbitristas*. In a paper presented to Philip III on his accession Baltasar Alamos de Barrientos pointed out that 'in other states all the parts contribute to the maintenance and greatness of the head, as is only fair.... But in ours, it is the head which does the work and provides the other members with their sustenance'.[60] Pedro Fernández Navarrete echoed these sentiments at the beginning of the following reign:

It is only fair that the burdens should be properly apportioned; that Castile should continue to provide for the royal household and for the defence of its own coasts and the route to the Indies; that Portugal should pay for its own military defences and for the East Indies fleets, as it did before incorporation with Castile; and that Aragon and Italy should defend their own coasts and provide the necessary military and naval forces for this. It is quite wrong that the head should be impoverished and weakened while the other members, wealthy and populous as they are, remain spectators of its burdens.[61]

In the eyes of Castilians, therefore, Aragon's constitutional barriers preserved a fiscal immunity which was at once outmoded and unjust. The *fueros* of the eastern kingdoms, of course, were not designed with the welfare of the underprivileged in mind; peasants and urban workers in those lands did not live in a tax-free paradise. But the taxes they paid went to the local governing bodies, dominated, as in the rest of Spain, by the aristocracy and the urban patriciate. They certainly did not go to the crown. There was, therefore, truth in the charge that the periphery paid much less revenue to the crown than did the centre.[62] In 1610, for example, income from Aragon, Catalonia

---

[60] Quoted in Elliott, *The Revolt of the Catalans*, p. 184.
[61] *Conservación de Monarquías* (1626) (*Biblioteca de autores españoles*, 25, Madrid, 1947), p. 496.
[62] For a quantitative comparison see Elliott, *The Revolt of the Catalans*, p. 185.

and Valencia together yielded no more than 600,000 ducats, whereas in Castile the *alcabala* and *millones* alone (taxes which the east did not pay) produced 5,100,000.[63] There is evidence, indeed, that Castile was actually subsidizing the administration and particularly the defence establishments of the eastern kingdoms.[64] It is not surprising that Philip III's treasury officials should have joined the *arbitristas* in demanding a fairer distribution of fiscal obligations among the component parts of the monarchy. Their demands were reinforced by the Council of Castile in its *consulta* of 1619, when it advocated, among other things, that the various partners should make greater revenue contributions in order to relieve Castile; for it was only just that 'they should provide, and should be requested to provide, some assistance, so that the whole burden should not fall on one weak and exhausted victim'.[65] To implement proposals like this, however, would mean attacking the laws and provoking the susceptibilities of the eastern kingdoms. And this was not the stuff that Philip III's government was made of.

[63] Sureda Carrión, *La hacienda castellana*, p. 114.
[64] Elliott, *The Revolt of the Catalans*, p. 190.
[65] González Palencia, *La Junta de Reformación*, p. 16

3

Recession and Reaction

Truce in the Low Countries

The government of Philip III was a conservative government. The national objectives developed in the course of the sixteenth century – defence of Spanish interests in northern Europe and, within the peninsula, maintenance of an equilibrium between the power of Castile and the rights of the regions – these it accepted in their essentials. But it was no longer possible to apply the classical precepts of Spanish policy undiluted. The environment was different. Economic circumstances were beginning to move against Spain; a basic sector of the economy, the Indies trade, after a century of almost constant growth, entered a period first of stagnation, then of depression. In a time of acute economic disorder political strategy developed its own neuroses. Financial stringency induced uncertainty and vacillation: in foreign policy aggression alternated with inertia, and at home Castile began to readjust its relations with the periphery.

The financial crisis in the last years of Philip II's reign was enough in itself to check Spanish action in northern Europe. Peace with France in 1598 was a recognition that Spain could not fight a war on three fronts simultaneously. In the Low Countries the transfer of sovereignty to the archdukes was a belated attempt to end the struggle with the northern provinces by peaceful means and to close one of the gaping holes of Spanish expenditure. The Archduke Albert was a realist and he used his sovereignty to reduce commitments still further. On his own initiative he sent an ambassador to London to open negotiations with the new king of England, James I, and he urged Madrid to take the dispute to the conference table; the policy bore fruit in the Treaty of London (1604) which ended the long Anglo-Spanish war. With the exception of Lerma, the government of Philip III was not enthusiastic over military withdrawal in northern Europe. But even Madrid had to bow to financial arguments. It was now clear that the economy was suffering severe dislocation. In the Atlantic sector, although the long period of growth had not yet finished its course, a series of fluctuations from 1597 brought the first signs of contraction in the Indies trade and the first indication that Spain could no longer rely on constant returns from America.[1]

It was the Low Countries, always the severest test of Spanish resources, which reacted most sharply to Spain's difficulties.[2] Since the 1590s, and the costly intervention in France, the Dutch Republic had made further political, economic and military advances. And the Spanish Road, the vital link between metropolis and its distant dominions, was now unmistakably dependent on French goodwill, the major power capable of cutting it. Events in 1600 were ominous. The war against the United Provinces was now being fought on yet another front – the Indian Ocean – and in the Low Countries itself a mutiny of unpaid troops worsened Spanish prospects. Yet Philip III's determination to continue the struggle was suddenly rewarded.[3] In 1602–3 a cyclical expansion in the Indies trade brought returns comparable to those of the peak years of 1584–7 and enabled the government to send larger remittances to the Low Countries. These provided the means for renewing military operations and led to the successful siege of Ostend, conducted by a brilliant new military commander, Ambrosio Spinola. The victory at Ostend in 1604 was the prelude to a large-scale offensive in which Spinola penetrated into Frisia with the object of driving a wedge into the United Provinces and cutting their communications with Germany. But the Yssel campaign came to an abrupt conclusion in 1606. The difficult terrain

---

[1] P. Chaunu, *Séville et l'Atlantique*, viii, 2, 1, pp. 767–8.

[2] P. Chaunu, 'Séville et la "Belgique" (1555–1648)', *Revue du Nord*, xlii, 2 (1960), pp. 259–92; Geoffrey Parker, *The Army of Flanders and the Spanish Road, 1567–1659* (Cambridge, 1972), pp. 68–70.

[3] Joseph Lefèvre, *Spinola et la Belgique, 1601–1627* (Brussels, 1947), pp. 29–31.

and the skilful tactics of the Dutch brought a halt to the Spanish offensive. But they were not the only obstacles. yet another large-scale mutiny of Spanish troops, in 1606, crippled the war effort from within; and mutiny was caused by lack of pay under the financial stringency imposed by the fall in returns from the Indies in the years 1604–5.[4]

The revolt of the *tercios* in 1606 shook Spain's belief in the possibility of reconquering the United Provinces; combined with the suspension of payments in 1607 and the losses suffered in the Indies trade in the same year, it persuaded the Spanish government that the time had come to negotiate. Again, however, it was the administration in Brussels which first faced up to realities. The Archduke Albert appreciated that the United Provinces would never agree to unconditional surrender. They were now a state, recognized as such by many European powers; they possessed an effective administration, a buoyant overseas trade, and natural protection against an invading army. The recent campaign, for all its initial success, simply showed the impossibility of reducing the Dutch by force. On his own initiative the archduke concluded a cease-fire with the Dutch in March 1607; containing as it did a recognition of Dutch sovereignty for the duration of the cease-fire, this was an enormous concession of principle.[5] Subsequent negotiations for a formal truce conceded even more. For it was clear that Spain would have to recognize Dutch sovereignty in such terms that there would be no saving clause in favour of Catholics. These were serious blows to Castilian pride, so much so that Madrid was loath to follow the pacificatory advice of the archduke, supported though it was by the military expert, Spinola. Philip III sought to evade the ultimate decision. The year 1608 was a record year in the transatlantic trade; and in August a sense of euphoria induced by massive returns from the Indies caused the Spanish government to toy with the idea of breaking off the peace negotiations and subsidizing a new offensive.[6] But the income of one exceptional year

---

[4] Chaunu, *Séville et l'Atlantique*, viii, 2, 2, pp. 1143–57, 1189–1252; for a different interpretation of the financial history of these years, and the policy implications, see Geoffrey Parker, *Spain and the Netherlands, 1559–1659: Ten Studies* (London, 1979), pp. 40–1.

[5] Lefèvre, *Spinola*, pp. 36–44.

[6] Chaunu, *Séville et l'Atlantique*, viii, 2, 2, pp. 1276–95. On the truce of 1609 see Parker, *The Army of Flanders and the Spanish Road*, p. 251.

could not solve Spain's financial problems. This was recognized even in Madrid, and the government was forced to accept the inevitable and to conclude a twelve years' truce with the United Provinces in 1609.

The decision of 1609 marked a stage in Spanish policy. In the Low Countries it gave Spain a breathing space. The Spanish army was reduced to a peace-time force of 15,000, and the annual provision was cut from 9 million to 4 million florins. Overseas, it is true, the Dutch onslaught on Iberian positions continued, though directed perhaps more at Portugal than at Spain. But by any standards Spain had suffered a political, military and ideological defeat; and the affront to its prestige was immense. A defeat for Spain was essentially a defeat for Castile, for it was Castile which provided the policy and the sustenance for Spain's role as a world power. Thwarted abroad, wounded in its self-esteem, Castile developed a new and a heightened sensitivity in its political relations; it began to seek compensation nearer home and to look more closely at its position within the peninsula.

The Expulsion of the Moriscos

The Truce of Antwerp was signed on 9 April 1609. On the same day Philip III took another decision – to expel the moriscos from Spain.[7] The two events were not a coincidence. Spanish statesmen of the time measured out their policy by calculation, not by accident, and Spanish policy was never more calculating than it was in 1609. The international situation was at last propitious for a measure which was regarded as one of national security. The detente achieved by peace with England in 1604 and with the United Provinces in 1609 enabled Spain to concentrate her land and sea forces in the Mediterranean in order to ensure the security of the operation against the moriscos.[8] But there was a further

[7] On the expulsion of the moriscos see particularly J. Reglà, 'La expulsión de los moriscos y sus consecuencias. Contribución a su estudio', Hispania, xiii (1953), pp. 215–68, 402–79; H. Lapeyre, Géographie de l'Espagne Morisque (Paris, 1959); Antonio Domínguez Ortiz and Bernard Vincent, Historia de los moriscos (Madrid, 1978); and Tulio Halperin Donghi, Un conflicto nacional: moriscos y cristianos viejos en Valencia (Valencia, 1980).

[8] F. Braudel, La Méditerranée et le monde méditerranéen à l'époque de Philippe II (Paris, 1949), pp. 592–3.

and more complex connection between the events of 1609. Behind them loomed the worsening economic situation, of which
the fluctuations in the Indies trade were at once a symptom and
a cause. On Spain's position in the Low Countries the impact
of economic restriction was direct. Its effect on the position of
the moriscos was more insidious. In a period of declining living
standards – the years 1604–5 saw a pronounced cyclical recession
in the Indies trade after a long period of expansion – the resentment of the masses towards a successful minority might be expected to become more acute. Not that the Spanish government
responded directly to public opinion; but its decision reflected
the general malaise. It also reflected the state of mind of Castile's
leaders. The time had passed when they could impose their will
in northern Europe; they had been forced to recognize the
sovereignty of people they regarded as rebel subjects and to
abandon the religious interests of their Catholic brethren. But in
Spain at least they were still masters and here they could find
moral compensation for their retreat abroad.[9] To expel the moriscos was to rid Spain of a group long identified as national enemies
and simultaneously to strike a blow for religious orthodoxy,
vindicating at once Castilian power and prestige. In a government
which wanted victories on the cheap the psychological factor was
not insignificant.

Ironically the war with Islam had lost much of its urgency and
by 1609 it was no longer a major preoccupation.[10] Of course the
depredations of the Barbary corsairs and their Ottoman allies
continued to pose a security problem in the western Mediterranean; Spanish shipping was still subject to constant attack, and
Spanish prisoners were still held for ransom money by the enemy
in North Africa. To this relentless pressure the Spanish naval
authorities reacted with vigour and some success, and in the
period 1601–16 they took the war into the enemy's own camp.
But no one seriously believed in waging a war of religion, and
there was no real danger of an invasion of Spain or of military
collusion between Algiers and the moriscos. The strategic argument, therefore, had lost much of its point. But it was still used.

[9] P. Chaunu, 'Minorités et conjoncture. L'expulsion des Morisques en 1609',
Revue Historique, ccxxv (1961), pp. 81–98.
[10] See Lynch, *Spain 1516–1598*, pp. 339–41.

Lerma himself used it. In 1596, as viceroy of Valencia, he had
reported his fears of an attack by sea combined with an insurrection of the moriscos. But the Council of Aragon thought he
exaggerated the danger and argued that, even were the Turkish
fleet to approach, the moriscos were in no position to act, 'for
they possess neither arms, nor supplies, nor fortified positions, nor
a base for the Turkish fleet.'[11]

The basic problem of the moriscos was a problem of integration. The moriscos remained a class apart, with their own lan-
guage and religion and a way of life directed by Islamic law. In
Aragon and Valencia, descendants of those who had submitted to
forced conversion, they were a genuine enclave of Islam within
Spain, resistant to christianization and hispanization, with their
own leaders and upper class, their rich and their poor, all equally
immune to integration. And as their spiritual home was outside
Spain so, it was suspected, was their political allegiance. In Castilian eyes it was an abnormal and monstrous situation, an admission of the failure of past policies. Yet public opinion, in so far as
it can be tested in the cortes and in the literature of the time, was
not pressing for a final solution, nor was there a mass campaign
for expulsion. There was no question of toleration: everyone
agreed that Islam was an inveterate enemy of the Catholic faith
and of Spain. But hostility towards the moriscos was normally
expressed against specific abuses – banditry, or competition for
jobs – rather than in a general condemnation or demand for
expulsion. The policy debate was limited to ruling groups in
church and state. There was a division of opinion over the religious issue: could not some moriscos be genuinely assimilated
into Christian belief and society? A number of ecclesiastics such
as Fray Luis de Aliaga, the royal confessor, and the bishops
of Tortosa and Orihuela, came to the defence of 'well-disposed'
moriscos and of genuine converts. But their advocacy was out-
weighed by more fanatical voices. Jaime Bleda, Dominican friar
and member of the Inquisition of Valencia, urged Rome to declare all moriscos apostates, and called on the king and the government to expel them *en bloc* and immediately. Juan de Ribera,

---

[11] Tulio Halperin Donghi, 'Recouvrements de civilisation: les Morisques au
Royaume de Valence au XVI siècle', *Annales. Economies. Sociétés. Civilisations*,
xi (1956), pp. 154–82; for the quotation see p. 178.

Archbishop of Valencia, whose excessive zeal for evangelization turned into hostility when this failed, demanded the expulsion of the moriscos as heretics and traitors, adding for good measure the argument that the king could profit from confiscating morisco property and from enslaving moriscos for work in the galleys and mines or from their sale abroad 'without any scruples of conscience'. Views of this kind were not well received in Rome, and they were not shared by all clerics, some of whom advocated a policy of patient assimilation, or by the church as an institution, which did not have an official opinion. In government circles, too, there was some division of opinion, reflected in the Council of State, between the majority who followed the advocacy of Idiáquez for total eviction and those who favoured the pleas of the Duke of Infantado for the exercise of discrimination. The most committed defenders of the moriscos, of course, were self-interested ones, the aristocracy of Aragon and Valencia, on whose estates they provided the labour force as tenants or vassals. But the nobles were not the only owners of morisco property: there was another group of proprietors, urban rentiers, clergy and religious houses, who were paid extremely low quit-rents – further devalued by contemporary inflation – and who had an incentive to get rid of their tenants in order to dispose of the land more profitably.[12] As for the mass of Christian peasants, they viewed their morisco rivals with envy and resentment and regarded them as satellites of the landowing aristocracy.

At the root of the morisco problem lay a matter of demography. On the eve of the expulsion the morisco population of Spain stood at 319,000 out of a total of under 8 million inhabitants.[13] But this 319,000 was not distributed evenly throughout the peninsula. More than 60 per cent of the moriscos were concentrated in the south-east quarter of the country. In Valencia, where the concentration was greatest, they amounted to 135,000, or about 33 per cent of the population, one morisco for every two Christians. In the eyes of the government, whose officials kept it extremely well informed on these matters, the problem was aggravated by the fact that the morisco population

---

[12] Ibid., p. 178.
[13] Domínguez Ortiz and Vincent, *Historia de los moriscos*, p. 83; for a lower estimate of morisco demography see Lapeyre, *Géographie*, pp. 203–4.

was growing more rapidly than the Christian. In Valencia, between 1565 and 1609, population growth among the moriscos was in the order of 69.7 per cent, compared with 44.7 per cent in the non-morisco sector.[14] In Aragon a similar situation prevailed, though on a smaller scale. There the moriscos numbered some 61,000, or about 20 per cent of the population, and again their growth rate was outstripping that of the Christians. In the area between Zaragoza and Alicante, therefore, there was a vast *morería* of some 200,000 aliens, facing a Christian population of 600,000 and growing faster than it. This was the real morisco problem, and it appeared insuperable. For the two communities lived in different worlds. The towns were Christians, the suburbs morisco; the rich lands of the plains were Christian, the hill scrub and the highlands were morisco. And the two worlds did not meet.

In Castile the situation was less tense. The ancient communities of *mudéjares*, a tiny minority, had never posed a problem. The dispersion of 84,000 moriscos from Granada throughout Castile after the suppression of their revolt in 1570 slightly modified the demographic picture. Together, *mudéjares* and Granadine moriscos numbered about 110,000 or 120,000, unpopular people no doubt, but hardly a threat to Castile's 6.5 million Christians. The two morisco communities were not even integrated among themselves; and they had little in common with their co-religionists in Aragon and Valencia. So it was not against this poor minority of small traders and artisans that the measure of 1609 was taken. Muslim Spain was south-eastern Spain. It was here that the real danger was seen to lie. The rapid population growth of the moriscos of Valencia and Aragon threatened soon to restore the balance of power between the two communities and eventually perhaps to tip it in favour of Islam. The expulsion of 1609, therefore, can be regarded as the second act of the Reconquest.

Yet there remains an element of uncertainty. In the final analysis it is difficult to identify the precise reasons why the moriscos

---

[14] Ibid., p. 30. 'In 1609', it has been aptly observed, 'roughly one Valencian in three still obeyed in secret the law of Islam'. James Casey, *The Kingdom of Valencia in the Seventeenth Century* (Cambridge, 1979), p. 2. The reason for the grater fecundity of moriscos is not precisely known. They seem to have married at an earlier age, but why? Was it due to Muslim customs, the precocity of young moriscos, or a communal determination to survive?

were expelled. It was not simply the result of 'demographic pressure', least of all after the epidemic and mortality of 1596–1602, when Castile began to experience a scarcity of labour. In Valencia and Aragon, it is true, the moriscos were numerous and popularly resented. But these conditions had long existed, without motivating a policy of expulsion. This was new, and it was the responsibility of a few people: Philip III, with whom sovereignty lay, and his immediate advisers, who placed this option before him. The king took a personal interest in the evangelization of the moriscos from the time of his visit to Valencia in 1599. Conversion of the moriscos by peaceful means remained official policy until 1608, in spite of the urgings of extremists. Then the duke of Lerma took the initiative: this was one matter on which he was an active policy maker and executive. Under his direction the Council of State debated the issue: from January 1608 the Council began to advocate expulsion, mainly on grounds of state security, and on 4 April 1609 it firmly recommended this measure to the king. Philip III accepted the advice: on 9 April it was decided to expel the moriscos from the whole of Spain, beginning with Valencia. It was here, as has been seen, that the problem of the moriscos was considered most acute, because of their numbers, their concentration in mountain fastnesses, their situation near a coastline easily accessible from North Africa. It was logical to expel them first, before they organized their defence or called in outside aid.[15] Preparations were begun in the utmost secrecy. The Mediterranean galleys were assembled; the Atlantic fleet was brought in; troops were mobilized. By September naval squadrons were stationed at three ports, Alfaques, Denia and Alicante; and three *tercios* withdrawn from Italy occupied strategic positions in the north and south of Valencia. On 22 September the Viceroy of Valencia, the Marquis of Carazena, ordered the publication of the decree of expulsion. This included a provision excepting children under four years – subsequently raised to fourteen years – if their parents agreed to their remaining; and Archbishop Ribera protested in vain that all morisco children should be reduced to slavery for the good of their souls. The decree also authorized six families out of every hundred in

---

[15] Pascual Boronat, *Los moriscos españoles y su expulsión* (2 vols, Valencia, 1901), ii, pp. 150–1.

each village to stay behind in order to maintain 'houses, sugar-mills, rice crops and irrigation works, and to initiate the new settlers'.[16] In fact very few took advantage of this permit and it was subsequently abolished.

The landed aristocracy of Valencia, task-masters and protectors of the moriscos, had already held various meetings and organized a protest to Madrid, arguing that expulsion would mean destruction of their estates and loss of their revenue.[17] Their protest was fruitless, though Lerma had in mind some form of compensation. The moriscos were allowed to take with them their moveable property, but their houses, seeds, crops, trees and other assets were to go as compensation to their lords, with the death penalty for any act of destruction or burning. But these orders were variously interpreted, and many moriscos quickly unloaded their products and property on to the market.[18] Otherwise they caused no trouble. They quietly left their villages, and under the direction of special commissioners they made their way in long columns to the ports of embarkation.

There, from 30 September, they were herded aboard the waiting vessels, most of them foreign merchantmen attracted by the good freightage opportunities; for, as a final affront, the moriscos were forced to pay their own passage. They left in successive convoys under naval escort to North Africa. In the first twenty days of October some 32,000 moriscos were transported across the Mediterranean. Incidents were few, but those which occurred had repercussions. There were some isolated cases of robbery and violence by ships' captains; and a few groups of moriscos were attacked and robbed by Arabs in North Africa. When news of these incidents reached Valencia it heightened the fears of those who had not yet embarked. Rebellion broke out on 20 October in the remote valley of Ayora in the south of the kingdom; about 6,000 insurgents defied the authorities and entrenched themselves in the wilderness of the Muela de Cortes. Five days later a more serious uprising of 15,000 moriscos occurred in an area near the coast of southern Valencia, and the rebels took up positions in

[16] Ibid., ii, pp. 190–3; Julio Caro Baroja, Los moriscos del reino de Granada (Madrid, 1957), pp. 232–3.
[17] Boronat, Los moriscos españoles, ii, pp. 183–4.
[18] Reglà, 'La expulsión de los moriscos', p. 231.

the valley of Laguar.[19] The government sent in the *tercios* and the local militia, and meanwhile continued the embarkations in order to stop the revolt spreading. By the end of November the rebels were overwhelmed; those who survived the slaughter were either sent to the galleys or summarily expelled. By now even the most recalcitrant were resigned to their fate, and few escaped the efficient machinery which operated the expulsion. In the first three months of the operation 116,022 moriscos were transported to North Africa. And when, by 1612, the stragglers and escapees had been rounded up, a total of 117,464 had been expelled from Valencia.

The operation was equally efficient in Aragon, where it was conducted in the course of 1610, once the security of Valencia was assured. Here too the aristocracy protested, and here too their protests were in vain.[20] By mid-September some 41,952 moriscos, including a few from Catalonia, had been expelled to North Africa via the port of Alfaques. The rest of the Aragonese moriscos, some 13,470, were sent over the Pyrenees into France, to be shepherded by exasperated French authorities to the port of Agde for shipment across the Mediterranean, and forced to pay transit dues as well as sea fares.[21] From Andalucía, where the moriscos were more difficult to identify because of their relative affluence, 36,000 were expelled by mid-1610. In the rest of Castile the operation was not a problem in point of numbers but was complicated by the existence of two groups of moriscos, the ancient *mudéjares* and the more recent emigrés from Granada. First, by decree of 28 December 1609, they were given the opportunity of emigrating voluntarily via France to Tunis. Many took advantage of this, and the remainder were expelled by decree of 10 June 1610, departing via the ports of southern Spain. By mid-1610 about 32,000 had left.

Although Spain had now expelled most of its moriscos, the operation was not absolutely complete. It took from 1611 to 1614

[19] Florencio Janer, *Condición social de los moriscos de España: causas de su expulsión y consecuencias que esta produjo en el orden económico político* (Madrid, 1857), pp. 321–6; Boronat, *Los moriscos españoles*, ii, pp. 225–7, 234–7, 557–60.

[20] Ibid., ii, pp. 296–8; Reglà, 'La expulsión de los moriscos, pp. 252–5.

[21] Lapeyre, *Géographie*, pp. 100–5; Reglà, 'La expulsión de los moriscos', pp. 258–62.

to round up the stragglers, who were particularly elusive in
Castile. Those who regarded themselves as true Spaniards made
desperate efforts to avoid expulsion, either by litigation or by
sheltering under ecclesiastical authority. Some of these were
successful; others managed to remain illegally, and yet others
returned clandestinely.[22] Gradually the mopping-up operations
were completed, and by 1614 from the whole of the country
some 275,000 moriscos had been expelled.[23] Most of them had
gone to North Africa, to Morocco, Oran, Algiers and Tunis,
where they got a mixed reception but eventually contributed their
industry and skills to their new homelands. A few made their way
to Salonica and Constantinople.[24] Perhaps about 10,000 managed
to remain in Spain.

Spain had finally settled her account with Islam. But how was
she herself affected by this vast diaspora? Most of the *arbitristas*
considered the event to be of slight consequence for the economy
of the country as a whole; the government itself professed indifference to the economic implications of the measure; and when
the Council of Castile reported on the state of the nation in 1619
it did not even refer to the expulsion. This complacency was
probably justified in the case of Castile, where the demographic
and economic consequences of the expulsion could only have
been slight, though even here there was a population drop in
certain zones, the wages of artisans and agricultural labourers
rose, and transport costs moved upwards.[25] While the diligence
and efficiency of the moriscos are not in doubt, it is a myth that
they were the only productive classes in Spain; most of the trades
and occupations in which they specialized, including irrigation,
were also practised by Spaniards. And even in Valencia they had
not been the only efficient farmers. The expulsion, of course,
represented a loss of capital as well as of labour, for in spite of
regulations to the contrary the moriscos sold as much of their
property as they could and took the cash with them; but it is
impossible to quantify this flight of capital. If we are to judge by
wage and price levels in those sectors of the economy where the
moriscos had been most productive, the expulsion had little mate-

[22] Ibid., pp. 407–15.
[23] Lapeyre, *Géographie*, pp. 204–5.
[24] Caro Baroja, *Los moriscos*, pp. 249–57.
[25] Domínguez Ortiz and Vincent, *Historia de los moriscos*, pp. 204–10.

rial consequence, even in Valencia, and economic activity continued undisturbed.[26]

When all this has been said, however, the fact remains that the expulsion of the moriscos was a major event in Spanish history which cannot be explained away by reference to wage and price levels in certain districts. The loss of 4 per cent of the population of Spain may seem small, but it represented a higher percentage of the working population, for the moriscos did not include hidalgos, soldiers, priests, vagrants or beggars, and most observers agreed that the quality of morisco work was superior. In some places the deportation of the moriscos left a sizeable gap in the labour and tax-paying force, and here depopulation was a reality for many decades to come. Certain occupations suffered particular labour shortage and consequent rise of wages, such as silk production, market gardening and transport. The most critical loss of population, of course, occurred in eastern Spain. Aragon lost a sixth of its population, most of it from the irrigated zones of Borja, Tarazona, and Vega del Jalón; these were recolonized by Old Christians who lacked the agricultural techniques of the moriscos and allowed production to fall. Valencia lost a third of its population. No doubt resettlement brought some demographic recovery to Valencia, through immigration from Castile and Aragon, though most of the new settlers came from immediate neighbourhoods. The fact remained that in Valencia the expulsion added itself to general economic poverty and under-development to cause a long depopulation. Forty years later, in 1646, Valencia remained depopulated.[27] Not only had the old morisco villages disappeared, but most Christian ones were depleted too; not only were the highland regions still empty but even the fertile *huertas* around Játiva and Gandia were under-

[26] Earl J. Hamilton, 'The Decline of Spain', *Economic History Review*, viii (1937–8), pp. 168–79, who indicates that wages in morisco-type occupations and prices of commodities, such as sugar and rice, which moriscos had produced underwent little significant change in the years after the expulsion. Hamilton's article, which is somewhat exaggerated in its interpretation and unreliable in its morisco population figures, was a reaction against previous historiography; a more balanced note has been struck in the works of Reglà, Lapeyre, Domínguez Ortiz and Vincent, and Casey.

[27] Boronat, *Los moriscos españoles*, ii, pp. 324–54; Reglà 'La expulsión de los moriscos', pp. 419–22; Lapeyre, *Géographie*, pp. 71–3; Domínguez Ortiz and Vincent, *Historia de los moriscos*, pp. 211–23; Casey, *Kingdom of Valencia*, pp. 6, 34, 58–61.

populated compared with their situation in 1609. With the exceptions of the province of Castellón and the *huerta* of Valencia,
every region of the kingdom of Valencia suffered a loss of vital
manpower. Many of these areas were too poor to attract new
settlers; and much morisco land was too heavily charged with
ground rents and other dues to make it a good investment.

Valencia remained a subsistence economy, though the basic
subsistence crop was now wheat, not the inferior grains favoured
by the moriscos. In some regions sugar cane production suffered
severe depression, later compounded by competition from Portuguese and Spanish American sugar. The rice crop also diminished,
although silk and wine production, presumably the work of Old
Christians, increased and approached commercialization. If wage
and price levels remained unchanged anywhere it was only in the
capital of Valencia, and this was not typical, for with fewer
moriscos the capital was less affected by the expulsion. Elsewhere
there is evidence that agricultural wages rose steeply and further
encouraged the trend towards rentier status on the part of the big
landowners. Poor farmers and peasants had the illusion of greater
prosperity from the removal of competition and the new wage
levels, but many of them inherited from the moriscos debts and
credit for agricultural supplies and cattle, which often amounted
to sizeable sums. Such debts were not cancelled but immediately
claimed by the crown as its own and subsequently handed over to
the nobles, whom it regarded as the real victims of the expulsion.

Almost all the seigneurial lords in Valencia, and to a lesser
extent in Aragon, had mortgaged their morisco property up to
the hilt; the mortgagees were usually private investors and ecclesiastical communities who were thereby assured of a regular
income charged on seigneurial revenue. Now the seigneurial
proprietors were driven to demand from new tenants extremely
heavy rents or else to default on their payments to creditors. The
government attempted to compensate the landlords by assigning
them ownership of morisco property and reducing the interest
rate on mortgages, but neither of these expedients was adequate.
So the landowners fell back on charging the few incoming tenants
excessive rents, which only deterred other settlers; and they still
failed to meet their mortgage payments. Another group of creditors hit by the expulsion were those who had invested directly in
agriculture by providing credit to morisco farmers. For many

creditors the revenue from morisco agriculture was their only income. As most of them were ecclesiastical communities and middle-income groups in the towns it is clear that the effects of the expulsion extended far beyond the countryside.[28] It was a further blow at the middle sectors in Spanish society and a further disincentive to investment in an already under-capitalized agriculture.

While the seigneurial lords of Valencia, with their thousands of morisco vassals, were severely affected by the expulsion, this was not the first blow to their prosperity. Self-destruction was their worst enemy. Long before 1609 the family fortunes of many noble houses had been damaged by the simple fact that they lived beyond their means, indulged in excessive luxury consumption, and administered their estates inefficiently. A family like the Borjas, dukes of Gandia, were so heavily mortgaged that they could not possibly keep up interest payments and they were literally bankrupt by 1604. The expulsion of the moriscos came as the final blow, and paradoxically it enabled many nobles to escape from their financial difficulties and start afresh. With the help of the crown, the interest rates on their mortgages were lowered from 10 to 5 per cent (decree of 22 September 1622), while they were authorized to impose the same obligations and charges on the new settlers as had been due from the moriscos. Some landowners were able to increase their holdings from morisco spoils; others, the feudal *senyors*, were more interested in strengthening their claims to agrarian production than in modernizing agrarian property. In one way or another, the expulsion of the moriscos was turned to some advantage by the Valencian aristocracy.[29] Yet in spite of the compensations in land and finance which they received, they did not recover the great prosperity they had enjoyed in the sixteenth century. Their new

[28] On the mortgage implications of the expulsion see Reglà, 'La expulsión de los moriscos', pp. 417–43, and the same author's, 'La expulsión de los moriscos y sus consecuencias en la economía valenciana', *Hispania*, xxiii (1963), pp. 200–18.

[29] The royal treasury drew a considerable revenue from the administration and sale of morisco property; in Alzira, Valencia, most of such property went to the nobility and creditors, thus increasing social polarization in the kingdom. See Encarnación Gil Saura, 'La expulsión de los moriscos. Análisis de las cuentas de la bailía de Alzira: administración y adjudicación de bienes', *Hispania*, 46, 162 (1986), pp. 99–114.

receipts, in spite of higher dues from their vassals after 1609, did not compare in real terms with the old; their debts encumbered them for the rest of the century; and if they survived at the top of society, they did so with the help of the crown and as loyal servants of the crown.[30] Valencia remained a conservative oligarchic society, in which under the king's government a relatively small aristocracy concentrated in their hands economic and social power.

As an administrative exercise the expulsion of the moriscos could hardly be faulted. Few government machines in Europe could have collected the statistical information on which it was based, or have organized the assembly and transport of so many people.[31] This was one test which the Spanish bureaucracy passed with vigour and efficiency; to conduct an operation of this magnitude and complexity was a sign of strength not of stagnation. Even the much-maligned Lerma emerged with credit – as an administrator if not as a policy-maker. It was an example, moreover, of central policy and direction reaching effectively into the provinces, on this occasion at least belying the usual criticism of Spanish government. This aspect of the operation had implications beyond the problem of the moriscos.

The expulsion of the moriscos was a policy decided in Castile and executed by Castile. To this extent it further altered the balance of forces within the peninsula. From the beginning of Philip II's reign the power of Castile had over-shadowed the eastern kingdoms: to finance the policy of Spain was to control the policy of Spain. But the government of Philip II had been careful not to encroach on the rights and resources of the non-Castilian parts of the nation. Now, by expelling the moriscos from Aragon and Valencia, Madrid was attacking the immunity of these kingdoms and increasing the disequilibrium between the centre and the periphery. This meant in effect an attack on the non-Castilian aristocracy. In its origin the aristocracy of Aragon was a military aristocracy, with pronounced feudal and seigneurial characteristics, owing its initial existence to its control over a large morisco population.[32] During the second half of the six-

---

[30] On the Valencian aristocracy after the expulsion see Casey, *Kingdom of Valencia*, pp. 70, 125–6.

[31] Lapeyre, *Géographie*, pp. 212–3.

[32] On the Aragonese aristocracy see Domínguez Ortiz, *La sociedad española en el siglo XVII*, pp. 300–3.

teenth century the feudal power of the higher nobility had already been eroded by royal jurisdiction, which had also begun to curb the severity of private seigneurial authority.[33] The expulsion of the moriscos was a further blow at the power and wealth of the Aragonese aristocracy. The same was true of Valencia, where the higher nobility was severely hit by the fall in income from seigneurial property after 1609.[34] The *fueros* of the eastern kingdoms were essentially the possession of the upper classes of the towns and countryside; to strike at the landed aristocracy, therefore, was to strike at the constitutional immunity of these regions. In the process Castile broke whatever power Aragon and Valencia possessed within the Monarchy, for it was there that the economic consequences of the expulsion were most severe. It was for this reason that the government of Castile remained indifferent to the economic arguments against expulsion. From the point of view of Castile, smarting under its defeat in the Low Countries where it alone sustained Spain's position without help from Aragon and Valencia, the policy of 1609 was not unreasonable. But this policy added two more dead weights to the empire, and made of Aragon and Valencia, as Castile had already made of the Low Countries, a liability rather than an asset to Spain.

There remained in eastern Spain one region virtually unaffected by the policy of 1609. Catalonia possessed few moriscos and on this issue at least did not enter the calculations of the central government. Catalonia's problems went deeper than the possession of a dissident minority. Indeed they were such as to justify a reappraisal of its relations with Madrid: Castile had much more reason to intervene in Catalonia than in Aragon and Valencia. Whether it was prepared to do so remained to be seen.

Catalonia: the Problem of Intervention

The crippling blows dealt at Aragon and Valencia in 1609 left Catalonia pre-eminent among the eastern kingdoms. Her advantage was a relative one, of course, for the Catalan economy was by no means buoyant. In the period 1599–1615 Catalan trade in

[33] See Lynch, *Spain 1516–1598*, pp. 472–81.
[34] Domínguez Ortiz, *La sociedad española en el siglo XVII*, pp. 303–5.

the Mediterranean was receding, incapable of competing with that of France and Italy.[35] The French were actually making inroads into the Catalan domestic market. One of the reasons for this was the poor industrial performance of Catalonia; with textile production slumping, Catalonia was becoming an exporter of raw materials alone.[36] Urban society reflected these conditions. Municipal government was controlled by urban oligarchies composed largely of businessmen; and this aristocracy of the towns, with a resentment born of frustration, was only too ready to attribute its difficulties to outsiders, especially the central government. The rural sector was faring no better. Agriculture in the principality suffered from poor technique and, in certain areas, from lack of irrigation. There was, it is true, some agricultural prosperity in the first half of the seventeenth century, at least in eastern Catalonia.[37] But elsewhere production was hit by the farmers' policy of keeping output down in order to keep prices up, and by the policy of Barcelona merchants whose commercial relations with Sicily involved the import of Sicilian corn.[38] The pressure of a growing population on limited food supplies and the inability to earn a sufficiency by foreign trade led to a price rise and severe unemployment. These conditions bred banditry, as in many other Mediterranean regions. And banditry was, in part at least, an aristocratic phenomenon.

The higher aristocracy of Catalonia was almost indistinguishable from that of Castile. Few in numbers and including only one grandee, the Duke of Cardona, it co-operated with the crown and in general played its part in the public life of the monarchy.[39] But it was not typical of Catalonia. The typical Catalan noble was poor, ignorant, far removed from the life of the court with its offices and opportunities; in seventeenth-century Spain he was an anachronism. Whereas the poor *hidalgos* of northern Spain either resigned themselves to a plebeian standard of living or sallied forth in search of careers in Castile or the Indies, in trade, office

[35] Pierre Vilar, *La Catalogne dans l'Espagne Moderne* (3 vols, Paris, 1962), i, pp. 588–92.
[36] Ibid., i, pp. 593–9.
[37] Ibid., i, pp. 599–602.
[38] Elliott, *The Revolt of the Catalans*, pp. 56–9.
[39] On the Catalan aristocracy see Domínguez Ortiz, *La sociedad española en el siglo XVII*, pp. 305–9.

or military service, the Catalan nobles showed little inclination to leave their homeland; they were rarely to be found in the Indies, the army, the central bureaucracy, or the commercial houses of Seville and Cadiz. Their alienation from the life of the nation was not due entirely to the exclusivism of Castile. It was also due to the parochialism of Catalonia. To reject the burden was to forfeit the fruits of empire. In any case the mass of the Catalan aristocracy was virtually unemployable, being more addicted to guns than to books. This petty nobility and gentry, harsh with its inferiors, narrow in its political vision, ill-qualified for office even within Catalonia, either remained unemployed or released its energies in crime and extortion. Banditry, contraband, counterfeiting money, these were the principal occupations of many of the Catalan nobility. For these men the Catalan *fueros* were a vital defence mechanism against the interference of royal officials.

The king's power in Catalonia was constitutional and contractual; the exercise of sovereignty depended on his observing the *fueros*. Philip III visited Catalonia in 1599 and held a session of the cortes.[40] In return for various concessions – he confirmed aristocratic privileges, distributed many new honours and cancelled the arrears of taxes owed to the crown – he was given a subsidy of 1,100,000 ducats, more than twice the amount of the largest subsidy granted to his predecessor. Philip III and Lerma were content to leave things at that. For the moment they had little option; their preoccupations first in northern Europe then in Moorish Spain left them little room for manoeuvre in Catalonia until some years after 1609. A series of innocuous viceroys maintained a holding operation against considerable odds. The Catalan aristocracy may have been impecunious but it was not powerless. Its extensive seigneurial jurisdiction – 71 per cent of all jurisdiction in Catalonia was in private hands – was a major obstacle to royal sovereignty.[41] Its poverty was matched by that of the crown, which did not have the revenue in Catalonia, nor reserves from outside, to implement a policy. And when all else failed, the aristocracy could fall back on the so-called Catalan liberties,

[40] On the policy of Philip III's government in Catalonia see Elliott, *The Revolt of the Catalans*, pp. 49–51, 65–6, 104–47, and J. Reglà, *Els segles XVI i XVII: els virreis de Catalunya* (Barcelona, 1956), pp. 123–8.
[41] Elliott, *The Revolt of the Catalans*, p. 98.

which it virtually monopolized in its own sectional interests. In these years a campaign against the carrying of arms, which was thought to have the benefit of cheapness, did little to restrict banditry for it was frustrated by the aristocracy with the usual invoking of the *fueros*. As Viceroy Monteleón reported in August 1603, 'the majority of these people live in a state of mutual conflict, belonging to bands and factions, which give rise to infinite excesses.' But if the crown took action then it was probably breaking some Catalan law, for as the viceroy explained, 'justice here is shackled by the laws and constitutions.'[42] The Catalans were a difficult people to govern; they resented intervention and they criticised indifference. The crown could hardly win.

During the viceregency of the Marquis of Almazán (1611–15) the crisis in Catalonia reached a peak. Banditry was now feeding voraciously on the country. Bandits had their protectors, chiefly among the rural nobility, who took a commission for their services; they had their enemies, in rival bands; and neutrals were bribed or terrorized into silence. A mafia-type regime prevailed in parts of Catalonia, sustained by violence and extortion.[43] By 1615, such was the anarchy in the country, even local interests looked to the crown to rescue them. The Bishop of Vic reported in 1615 that

> the people of this principality are blaming the bishops for not getting together to consider these evils [banditry] and request a remedy for them; and they say that if the king sends troops to occupy the country they will all support him in order to establish justice as in Castile and remove the perverse laws and customs which impede it.[44]

An exaggeration, no doubt, but a reflection of prevailing desperation.

At last the government of Philip III decided to act. In the post-1609 phase of policy reappraisal the moment was right from Castile's point of view: having secured peace in the Low Coun-

---

[42] Quoted by Reglà, *Els virreis de Catalunya*, pp. 124–5.
[43] J. Carrera Pujal, *Historia política y económica de Cataluña (siglos XVI–XVIII)* (Barcelona, 1947), i, pp. 165–75.
[44] Quoted by Reglà, *Els virreis de Catalunya*, pp. 127–8.

tries and expelled the moriscos, it had liquidated for the moment its major policy problems and was ready to turn its attention to Catalonia. The government appointed a tough viceroy, the Duke of Alburquerque, a Castilian aristocrat uninhibited by constitutional ideas. Alburquerque was realist enough to appreciate that strong government could only be applied at the expense of the Catalan *fueros*; believing that what masqueraded as liberty was really licence, he announced in advance that he would 'put the entire principality in the galleys'.[45] When he took office in March 1616, in fact, he discovered that he had some allies, at least among those who valued law and order – businessmen, property owners in town and country, peasant proprietors. But he also had some enemies, and the bitterest of these was the *Diputació*, the standing commission of the cortes, supposedly the guardian of the *fueros* and the representative of the whole Catalan people; in fact it was a corrupt oligarchy serving the interests of the aristocratic sector alone. The *Diputació* was the centre of an anti-government movement on the part of discontented nobles. It was also a financial power to be reckoned with; it had an income over four times as large as that of the royal administration in Catalonia, and it was hardly a secret that its members were lining their own pockets from the tax revenue they were supposed to administer.[46]

The new viceroy set about detaining and executing delinquents on a large scale; and he reached out to frighten off their aristocratic allies by destroying the latters' castles and strongholds. Predictably there was an outcry that the constitutions were being violated; and a nervous central government, once Alburquerque was seen to have the situation under control, ordered him to observe the *fueros*. By the time he left office in 1619, however, he had restored some order out of chaos and his policy could hardly be reversed. It was continued by his successor, the Duke of Alcalá, who provoked even more opposition than Alburquerque. His personal qualities were less attractive than those of his predecessor, but it was basically to his policy that interested parties in Catalonia objected. To strengthen the royal administration Alcalá decided to intensify the fiscal policy of Alburquerque and to reclaim for the crown the royal 'fifth' from those towns which

[45] F. Soldevila, *Història de Catalunya* (3 vols, Barcelona, 1935), ii, p. 262.
[46] Elliott, *The Revolt of the Catalans*, pp. 92, 101, 120–21.

were not already paying it and could not prove exemption.[47] In
view of the revenue enjoyed by the *Diputació* the object was not
unreasonable. Amidst growing protest Alcalá stubbornly extended the list of towns to be assessed, and in 1620 he decided to
tackle Barcelona itself, including its arrears since 1599. But Barcelona refused to pay, and it was still refusing when the reign of
Philip III ended in March 1621. The stand taken by Barcelona
strengthened the Catalan resistance to further intervention from
Castile. In the process of restoring law and order to the principality the crown and its representatives had alienated two groups,
the rural aristocracy, who made an issue of the attack on firearms
and the destruction of castles, and the urban oligarchies, who
took their stand on resistance to the 'fifth'. Yet they themselves
had no policy for the salvation of Catalonia. Who could take
seriously the Catalans' plea for more royal government, given
their record of impeding it? These were men who could obstruct
government but were incapable of promoting it. The initiative
would have to come from the central government. Philip III's
administration recognized the problem, and in its general readjustment of the balance of power within the peninsula it made a
tentative approach to re-ordering Castile's relations with Catalonia. But it did not have the nerve to risk a political confrontation
with the principality, and the problem was left unresolved.

The attitude of Catalonia towards Castile and the central government seems to have been conditioned by an assumption –
subsequently underwritten by Catalan historians – that as the
Catalans did not receive the benefits of empire they could hardly
be expected to share its obligations.[48] In particular Castile's
monopoly of the Spanish Indies has been cited as an example of
her exclusiveness, which reaped its logical reward in the alienation
of Catalonia. Historically, however, the situation had not developed in this way. The Catalans asserted and practised their
liberties long before Spain assumed an imperial role in Europe
and America. Their opposition to Castilian laws and taxes was
not the result of their exclusion from the Indies trade but preceded it.[49] Indeed the Castilians might have justly inverted the

[47] See above, p. 44.
[48] See, for example, J. Vicens Vives, *Aproximación a la historia de España*
(Barcelona, 1952).
[49] On the position of the subjects of the Crown of Aragon in relation to the
Indies see below, pp. 230–2.

argument: the Catalans could not expect to be admitted to Castilian privileges if they rejected Castilian responsibilities. But these were, and remain, debating points. The Catalan liberties had a long history, so long in fact that they were now out of joint with the time and the place; the world in which they had been forged had little relevance to the problems of seventeenth-century Spain.

Castile and Portugal

The year 1609 was a critical one for Castile, and it inaugurated a new stage in the political equilibrium within the peninsula. Peace in the Low Countries gave Castile the opportunity and the incentive to eliminate the last vestige of Islam in Spain. This involved breaking the constitutional barriers surrounding Aragon and Valencia and reducing them to Castile's will. And this in turn left Catalonia exposed in a Spain which was becoming increasingly unfavourable to the possession of special status and fiscal immunity. But 1609 was also significant for Castile's relations with Portugal. The policy of peace with the United Provinces was decided by Castile and for Castile. Portugal, whose overseas interests were particularly sensitive to international change, had no say in the conduct of her international affairs. Consequently she had no say in Spanish policy towards the United Provinces, though the latter were the greatest threat to her empire.

The population of Portugal, hit by emigration overseas and by the virulent epidemics of 1580 and 1598–9, underwent no real growth in this period, moving from about 1,100,000 in 1580 to 1,200,000 in 1640.[50] The effects of emigration were seen in periodic crises of food supplies, for there were not enough peasants to feed the growing urban centres with a sufficient margin for safety. The non-productive sectors of society – clerics, university graduates, the military and bureaucrats – were increasing in numbers. The nobility, in search of pensions and preferment, joined the service of the king at court, in the administration or in the empire. Commerce was largely in the hands of the New

[50] On Portuguese society and institutions under Habsburg rule see Damião Peres, ed., *História de Portugal* (8 vols, Barcelos, 1929–35), v, vi; on colonial organization see Frédéric Mauro, 'Portugal and Brazil: political and economic structures of empire, 1580–1750', Leslie Bethell, ed., *The Cambridge History of Latin America* (Cambridge, 1984), i, pp. 443–60.

Christians, nominally converts or the descendants of converts from the Jewish religion. Regarded by the Portuguese, probably justifiably, as crypto-Jews, they were persecuted by crown and Inquisition alike. They had two main avenues of escape – the purchase of immunity or emigration to Amsterdam. Those who remained performed an essential entrepreneurial function and constituted in effect a middle sector of society, though with second-class status.

Although Portugal was annexed to the crown of Castile in 1580, she retained her separate identity. Philip II observed the conditions of autonomy to which he had agreed at the cortes of Thomar. Portuguese offices were reserved to Portuguese. The Portuguese empire was administered by Portugal alone and its trade monopolized by Portuguese subjects; it remained, indeed, more firmly closed to Spaniards than the Spanish empire did to Portuguese. And Portugal retained its own institutions. Sovereignty, of course, resided in the king, and he was the head of the government structure. He was represented in Lisbon by a viceroy or by a board of three governors. But their jurisdiction was limited and matters of importance had to be remitted to Madrid; there they were considered by the Council of Portugal, which produced *consultas* for the king's decision. In Lisbon there was a Council of State to advise the royal representatives on major items of government, but it was a purely government council without precise administrative competence. Already, before 1580, it had employed two secretaries of state, one for home affairs and one for the colonies, whose functions were to transmit the king's decisions to the appropriate agencies. Philip II retained these officials. He also retained the *Mesa da Consciencia e Ordens* (Board of Conscience and Military Orders), which was at once a tribunal and council of religious affairs and the military orders, with jurisdiction in the metropolis and the colonies. And he preserved the *Desembargo do Paço*, the supreme tribunal of the kingdom which supervised the administration of justice. He did make, however, one significant institutional change: in 1591 he replaced the *Vedores da Fazenda* by a *Conselho da Fazenda*, which now became the supreme financial tribunal. Composed of a president, four councillors and four secretaries, this council conducted day-to-day financial administration on its own initiative, though it remitted important matters to the king. As Portugal's most important financial and economic interests lay in her overseas colonies, the *Conselho da Fazenda* constituted in fact a tribunal for colonial affairs. All normal and routine decisions regarding the Portuguese empire were made in Lisbon by the *Conselho da Fazenda*, which worked in close contact with, and often included in its membership, the viceroy of Portugal; major policy decisions they would remit, with their recommendations, to the king or the Council of Portugal in Spain. Co-ordination in policy matters between these two bodies was achieved by routine correspondence between the Council of Portugal on behalf of the king and the *Conselho da Fazenda* in Lisbon.

Philip II's conservative approach to Portugal and her institutions was not continued by his successor. In 1601 the Duke of Lerma created a *Junta da Fazenda*, composed of three Spaniards, with power to intervene in the *Conselho da Fazenda*. This was correctly interpreted in Portugal as an attempt to centralize financial administration in the interests of Spain and of Lerma's policy; the *Junta* was viewed with extreme mistrust, and it was abolished in 1605.[51] A further attempt to modify the structure of government was made with the creation of the *Conselho da India* (25 July 1604). The new council had a president and four councillors, and was given jurisdiction over colonial affairs, though the financial and economic business of the empire remained in the hands of the *Conselho da Fazenda*. This, too, was viewed with reservation in Portuguese government circles; the new agency clashed with the jurisdiction of the *Mesa da Conciencia e Ordens*, and it did not survive beyond 1614.[52] But there were other avenues into the Portuguese administration. Philip III began to appoint Spaniards to the Council of Portugal in Madrid and to the *Conselho da Fazenda* in Lisbon. In 1615 he attempted to appoint a Spaniard, the Count of Salinas, as his representative in Portugal, but he bowed to the inevitable protest and appointed the Archbishop of Lisbon instead. In 1617, however, he did in fact appoint the Count of Salinas, bestowing on him the Portuguese title of Marquis of Alenquer.

[51] Fortunato de Almeida, *História de Portugal* (6 vols, Coimbra, 1922–31), v, pp. 19–22.
[52] See F. P. Mendes da Luz, *O Conselho da India* (Lisbon, 1952), pp. 81–93, 97–195.

Behind this attempt to infiltrate the Portuguese administration lay another object. The crown's economic difficulties were causing it to look more closely at Portugal as a possible source of revenue. By the terms of the union Portugal enjoyed fiscal autonomy. But this was not impenetrable. Lerma proposed to raise a revenue by selling privileges to New Christians. They were first granted permission to leave Portugal in return for 170,000 cruzados. They were then offered the right to remain, together with a general pardon and admission to all offices in Portugal, but for a larger fee – ten times larger. Portuguese opinion was outraged: in a single deal the Spanish crown would simultaneously raise a revenue and soften up the administration. The three archbishops were sent to Spain to object. They offered the crown an alternative, 800,000 cruzados from the Portuguese towns; but there was one draw-back to this – the designated taxpayers refused to pay. So Madrid reopened negotiations with the New Christians. In the new bargain the right to office was dropped and they were offered only toleration for the full sum of 1,700,000 cruzados, which was in fact converted into an exaction. There was worse to come: in 1610 all the concessions granted to the New Christians were withdrawn and the Inquisition resumed its operations. One of the few escape routes left to the New Christians was to marry into distressed Christian families, which gave them some guarantee, producing what the Inquisition called 'half-Jews' or 'quarter-Jews'.

The attempt to tap the resources of Portugal was not, for the moment, carried further. As in the case of Catalonia, the government of Philip III did not really have the courage of its own convictions. But if in the union of the crowns Portugal did not lose its administrative and fiscal independence, it did lose its control over foreign policy. And while it acquired a powerful sovereign, it also acquired a powerful enemy. Whether the Dutch would have stayed their hand against an independent Portugal indefinitely, of course, is a matter of speculation. Philip II's policy in the 1590s, when he put an embargo on Dutch shipping in the Tagus and prohibited further trade between the Portuguese and the Dutch, was possibly provocative, but it was hardly more effective than the ban on Spanish trade with the Dutch, and it may be queried whether it was the policy of embargo which drove the Dutch to go direct to the Far East for goods which they had previously procured in Lisbon and thus initiated the Dutch attack on the Portuguese Asian empire. It can hardly be doubted that the Dutch would have made their way to the Far East even without provocation by Philip II. And if Spain brought enemies she also brought bullion to Portugal; for its trade with Asia Portugal needed a constant supply of silver, which the Spanish Indies alone could provide.[53] There was, therefore, an economic case for closer integration between the two countries. At the same time Dutch pressure in the Far East helped to precipitate a shift in Portuguese colonial interests. Although Portugal's Asian empire gradually succumbed to enemy penetration in the early seventeenth century, a second empire began to take shape in America. Brazil became the focus of increasing attention and by the 1620s had developed into a prosperous plantation colony; it possessed an expanding sugar industry, attracted growing emigration, and yielded more money to the metropolis than it cost in administration and defence.[54] Simultaneously Portuguese merchants made use of their advantageous position under the union of the crown to ease their way into the American trade of Seville and to infiltrate into Castile's colonial possessions.[55] Although the Portuguese received no special privileges to enter Spanish America and were legally regarded as foreigners there, even in the period 1580–1640, in fact their status was much superior to that of other foreigners – unlike the English and the Dutch they were allies of Spain – and they were allowed to travel and settle in the Spanish empire with relative immunity. In the years after 1580 they were particularly active and were to be found in all parts of Spanish America, as seamen and settlers, merchants and artisans; and by the second generation they had made their way into offices in church and state. Their preference was for the Río de la Plata and Peru; and Potosí was one of their principal targets. Brazil afforded a convenient base for their operations. Portuguese exports to Brazil far exceeded the colony's needs; many of them

[53] Chaunu, Séville et l'Atlantique, viii, 1, p. 261.
[54] See C. R. Boxer, Salvador de Sá and the Struggle for Brazil and Angola (London, 1952), pp. 1–39.
[55] On the Portuguese in Spanish America see Alice P. Canabrava, O comércio português no Rio da Prata, 1580–1640 (São Paulo, 1944); Boxer, Salvador de Sá, p. 31; Lewis Hanke, 'The Portuguese in Spanish America, with special reference to the Villa Imperial de Potosí', Revista de Historia de América, 51 (1961), pp. 1–48; Chaunu, Séville et l'Atlantique, iv, p. 570.

were designed as re-exports to the Río de la Plata and, beyond the pampas and Tucumán, to Upper Peru, where they competed with legitimate Spanish trade routed via Panama and Peru; and Portuguese traffic in slaves and merchandise siphoned off quantities of silver from Potosí.

As the Portuguese shifted the focus of their imperial interests from the Far East to America, so the Dutch followed them remorselessly. The Dutch had already penetrated Spanish imperial defences at certain points.[56] From the 1580s they were active in the Caribbean; and at the beginning of the seventeenth century they began the occupation and exploitation of the salt-pans of Punta de Araya on the coast of Tierra Firme, which became a base of an extensive contraband trade until the Spaniards hit back in 1605.[57] Conditions of war or peace made little difference to the Dutch. And although the Portuguese had no say in the Spanish decision to conclude a truce with the Dutch in 1609, it may be doubted whether any other decision would have altered the balance of power overseas. The chief obstacle to the truce negotiations was Dutch insistence on a right to trade in the East and West Indies, and Spain's refusal, following her usual practice, to admit in an international treaty any statement reflecting on her colonial monopoly. But one of the reasons which forced Spain to come to terms was the success achieved by the Dutch East India Company from 1602, which had effectively breached one sector of the Iberian monopoly. Spain, unable to defend both Asia and America simultaneously, was concerned to assert its determination to preserve the latter, in which Portugal too had a stake. The fourth clause of the treaty, therefore, was worded in such a way that it could be interpreted as allowing the Dutch a relatively free hand in the East Indies but not in America.[58] This merely recognized the existing situation, for treaties could not alter facts. It also reflected the policy of the 'peace party' of the burgher oligarchs in the United Provinces, who preferred to trade in the East Indies than to fight their way into America. Consequently, during the period of the truce (1609–21), the Dutch continued

---

[56] Frédéric Mauro, *Le Portugal et l'Atlantique au XVII siècle* (1570–1670). *Étude économique* (Paris, 1960), p. 463.

[57] Engel Sluiter, 'Dutch Maritime Power and the Colonial Status Quo, 1585–1641', *Pacific Historical Review*, xi (1942), pp. 29–41.

[58] C. R. Boxer, *The Dutch in Brazil, 1624–54* (Oxford, 1957), p. 2.

their progress in Asia, consolidating the dominant position in the Indian Ocean and the Far East which they had begun to acquire in the period 1600–9.

America, however, was another matter. The treaty of 1609 implied that, whatever happened in the Far East, America was to be regarded more strictly as an Iberian preserve. This too reflected the balance of power overseas. Spain sustained her position in the New World by virtue of occupation, military defence and naval power. The Dutch might make minor inroads into the Spanish monopoly; but they could not overthrow it. There was, it is true, a 'war party' in the United Provinces which advocated an attack on South America comparable to that in South-east Asia. This party argued that the truce of 1609 should be limited to Europe, with war continuing 'beyond the line'. Through the ambiguous wording of the fourth clause of the treaty the truce was in fact virtually limited to Europe. But there was also a limit to what the Dutch could accomplish in Spanish America. The latter remained immune from penetration on a large scale. In any case, as the Dutch could trade with relative freedom to the Iberian peninsula in the years of peace, it was easier to conduct a re-export trade to Spanish America from Seville than to breach the monopoly by direct assault. Portugal, however, was more vulnerable than Spain. So Dutch activity in America tended to focus on Brazil. During the years of truce Dutch trade with Brazil made a notable spurt.[59] The Spanish crown issued constant and explicit prohibitions of foreign trade with the colony, but its policy was subverted from within Portugal itself. The Dutch traded with Brazil through the connivance of Portuguese officials and of Portuguese merchants – New Christians in most cases – in Vianna and Oporto; it was they who provided the necessary facilities of cover agents and a flag of convenience.[60] Dutch merchants estimated that by the 1620s they had secured between one-half and two-thirds of the carrying trade between Brazil and Europe. By the end of the truce fifteen ships were being built yearly in the United Provinces for the Brazil trade alone, while some 50,000 bales of sugar, apart from Brazil-wood, cotton and hides, were being imported in Dutch vessels by way of Portugal.

[59] Mauro, *Le Portugal et l'Atlantique*, p. 261.
[60] Boxer, *Dutch in Brazil*, p. 20.

Most of this Brazilian produce was shipped via Oporto and Vianna, where duties on imports and re-exports were substantially lower than at the monopoly port of Lisbon. There was also an outward flow of traffic, for Brazil was a market for Dutch linens and textiles. A sector of opinion in the United Provinces wanted more than a contraband trade with Brazil: it sought the colony's annexation. This was viewed with alarm by the 'peace party', which believed that a profitable trade would only be damaged by war with the Iberian powers. According to one Dutch writer, the king of Spain regarded Portuguese Asia 'as his concubine, who can shift for herself if need be, but he does not count the cost of maintaining America, which he regards as his lawful wife, of whom he is exceedingly jealous and firmly resolved to maintain inviolate'.[61] And Dutch critics of an expedition to Brazil in the 1620s were convinced that the Spanish government would react more vigorously towards an attack on America than it had done in the Far East.

Portuguese opinion, too, disillusioned with the union of the crowns, subsequently tended to attribute Portuguese losses in the Far East to Spanish neglect. The charge was less than just to Spain. By the terms of the union the empires of the two powers remained independent, their burdens and their fruits in separate possession. This was what Portugal wanted. It was easy for the Dutch to identify the weaker member of the partnership and to focus their attack accordingly. In any case, Portugal's Asian empire, being essentially a trading complex with the minimum of political dominion, was not an easy object to defend by conventional methods of imperial defence, such as could be applied in America. There was little to prevent other trading powers moving in, if they had sufficient maritime resources. Spain could hardly be held responsible for failing to defend two empires at once. This was recognized at the time. There was no sign of resentment against Spain among the Portuguese officials administering and defending their Asian empire, and it seems to have been taken for granted that there was a division of labour over the defence of their respective possessions. The test of relations between Spain and Portugal would come if the Dutch attacked Brazil; then it would be seen if Spain had the will and the ability to come to the

---

[61] Quoted ibid., p. 16.

assistance of a Portuguese dominion situated within the heart of the Iberian monopoly. Meanwhile, however, Spaniards were taking note that while they possessed no legal status, much less privilege, in the Portuguese empire, the Portuguese were swarming over the empire of Spain. Again this raised the question, in Castilian minds at least, should not those who received benefits assume obligations? The government of Philip III was aware of the question but left it unanswered.

4

Olivares, Castile and Imperial Spain

Philip IV and the Rule of Olivares

Philip III died prematurely (31 March 1621), leaving the government of Spain and its empire to his son, a youth of sixteen, who had yet to be introduced to affairs of state and was already dominated by his childhood mentor, Gaspar de Guzmán, Count of Olivares. The accession of Philip IV, therefore, took placed before his political education was complete. His precipitate induction into kingship was enough in itself to cause him to reach desperately for the guiding hand of a powerful minister; and the habit of relying on the judgment of Olivares acquired in the early years of the reign proved difficult to outgrow. When, by about 1630, he had gained some maturity and experience and was in a position to question the decisions taken in his name, it was too late to assert his independence, had he so wished; for, under pressure of foreign wars and domestic crises, Spanish policy had become committed to certain objectives which were difficult to reverse and which the king could only leave to the government machine and the man who ruled it.

Modern historiography has attempted to rescue Philip IV from the obloquy heaped on the later Habsburgs.[1] Contemporaries

---

[1] There are few general studies of the reign. One of the first modern historians to attempt a reappraisal was A. Cánovas del Castillo, *Estudios del reinado de Felipe IV* (Madrid, 1888, 2nd edn, 2 vols, Madrid, 1927), a valuable work still. Martin Hume, *The Court of Philip IV. Spain in Decadence* (London, 1907), is based on original documentation and has considerable utility, in spite of its defects of analysis. These works are superseded by R. A. Stradling, *Philip IV and the Government of Spain 1621–1665* (Cambridge, 1988), a work of research and revision.

certainly recognized him as an improvement on his father, if not
in appearance – he had the pendulous lower lip and exaggerated
jaw characteristic of the Habsburgs – at least in intellectual and
political virtues. After the inertia and corruption of the previous
reign the new king was hailed as a leader and a reformer. Popular
enthusiasm was reflected even by the satirist Quevedo: 'His actions promise another Charles V; his words and decrees recall his
grandfather; his religion reflects his father.'[2] He himself claimed
that, having served no apprenticeship in kingship, he was forced
to learn it as he went along, by secretly attending council meetings, by reading history, and by examining 'all the reports which
come from the councils, juntas and individual ministers on every
matter concerning my kingdoms'.[3] And it is true that he did
a considerable amount of paper work, annotating the conciliar
material with his comments and decrees, sometimes extensive and
in his own hand. At this level he was a conscientious, even a professional, monarch, politically aware, far from indolent, and
no less informed than his ministers.[4] If he was more concerned
with the powerful than the poor, and saw Spain as a problem of
government rather than of people, these too were the limitations
of his contemporaries. In the event his efforts to intervene were
sporadic and inconclusive, little more than signs of periodic
remorse, a substitute for policy-making rather than a means
towards it. Philip IV was too much of a courtier to reproduce the
working habits of Philip II. But at least his court was cultivated.
His patronage of literature, the theatre and the fine arts gave a
distinct impetus to Spain's baroque culture, a model in its time
and a legacy for the future. The court of Philip IV exemplified the
splendour of Spanish kingship, its wealth and power, and the arts
became a showcase of the monarchy's values and ambitions.[5] But
the study and the studio were not the whole of his world. He was
even more interested in outdoor sports and martial display, in
equestrian contests and bull-fighting. Yet his passion for horses
took second place to his passion for women, exaggerated no

---

[2] Quoted J. Juderías, *Don Francisco de Quevedo y Villegas. La época, el hombre, las doctrinas* (Madrid, 1923), p. 110.
[3] Quoted in Cánovas, *Estudios*, i, p. 231.
[4] Stradling, *Philip IV*, pp. 276–84.
[5] On court culture and propaganda see J. H. Elliot, *Spain and Its World 1500–1700* (New Haven, Conn. and London, 1989), pp. 156–60, 164–78.

doubt by detractors then and since, but sufficient to impair his family life with his first wife, Isabel of Bourbon, if not with his second, Mariana of Austria; and while he had great difficulty in providing an heir to the throne, he casually fathered five or six bastards.

It has been argued that Philip IV delegated power to Olivares not out of feebleness of mind and will but because he believed that Olivares was the best man for the job.[6] Philip IV was not a puppet king. While he gave his confidence to Olivares, there were disagreements and outright clashes over policy. The king had ideas about government and was aware of his own interests. As he grew in experience he demanded a military role for himself, changes in foreign policy, revision of appointments. But his will was not normally strong enough to prevail, and he took refuge from public duty in private pleasure. He sought in the able and determined Olivares the counterpoise for his own irresolution and lack of judgment. It is true that his decision to delegate power corresponded to the conditions of seventeenth-century government, and was a necessary admission that the king of Spain could no longer administer the affairs of his vast empire unaided. His freedom of choice, moreover, was limited, for the higher aristocracy of Castile would not tolerate supreme power going to anyone outside their own ranks. Olivares was the only member of the ruling class whom Philip IV knew well enough to trust. These were the grounds on which he subsequently justified his abject reliance on a favourite minister, contrasting the man of his choice with the many 'pernicious ministers' who surrounded him, 'those people who to my way of thinking are more concerned with their own interests than with the service of God and the king'.[7] Self-justification of this kind, however, could not disguise the fact that Philip IV did more than delegate power: he abdicated control. This is implied in the barbed advice given by the same Quevedo who had once welcomed the young king. To give political power to a *valido*, argued Quevedo, was to alienate sovereignty: 'Whoever relieves the king of the work and the fatigue of his office is a thief, for he takes away the honour, pride

[6] Domínguez Ortiz, *Política y hacienda de Felipe IV* (Madrid, 1960), p. 9.
[7] Phillip IV to Sor María de Agreda, 30 January 1647, in Appendix VIII, Valiente, *Los validos*, pp. 181–4.

and fruits of that office'; and again, 'the minister who lets the king sleep does not serve him, he buries him.' Quevedo addressed himself directly to Philip IV: 'Most powerful, mighty and excellent Lord: kings are workers, and you are worth no more than you labour; to be idle is to forfeit your wages.'[8] Philip IV's neglect of public duty became an obsession with Quevedo and he returned to the theme in one of his most mordant verses:

> Filipo, que el mundo aclama
> Rey del infiel tan temido,
> Despierta, que por dormido
> Nadie te teme, ni te ama.[9]

The man who relieved Philip IV of these burdens was Gaspar de Guzmán, son of Enrique de Guzmán, ambassador and viceroy under Philip II.[10] The family was ambitious, and its pretension probably outstripped its resources. These, however, were substantial enough. The Guzmán were a junior branch of a famous noble dynasty headed by the Duke of Medina Sidonia; they came from Andalucía where they had estates in the region of Seville, nominally yielding the incumbent an income of some 60,000 ducats a year. But they aspired to higher things, and for years Gaspar de Guzmán, as his father before him, sought to convert his peerage of Castile into a grandeeship of Spain. After a socially, if not academically, productive career at the University of Salamanca – as contemporaries remarked, he became Rector before he even graduated – he succeeded to his father's title and estates in 1607 and thenceforth devoted his energy and patrimony to penetrating the source of power, the court of Philip III. In 1615, following eight years as a *señorito* in Seville, he received the first

---

[8] *Política de Dios y Gobierno de Cristo*, in *Obras* (*Biblioteca de autores españoles, 23*, Madrid, 1946), pp. 23, 69, 72.

[9] 'Philip, whom the world acclaims, king who keeps the infidel in fear, wake up! For while you sleep no one fears you and no one loves you!' Quoted in Hume, *The Court of Philip IV*, p. 355 n. i.

[10] Olivares is studied in the distinguished 'psychological' biography by Gregorio Marañón, *El conde-duque de Olivares (la pasión de mandar)* (Madrid, 1936, 4th edn, 1959), a valuable source of personal detail but lacking in political content. This, and much more, is supplied by J. H. Elliott, *The Count-Duke of Olivares. The Statesman in an Age of Decline* (New Haven, Conn. and London, 1986).

PLATE 1 *Philip IV, 1631*, by Velázquez (reproduced by kind permission of the Trustees, National Gallery, London)

return on his investment: he was appointed to the household of Prince Philip, the heir to the throne, who first apparently regarded his dominating senior with some aversion but soon came to rely on him in every detail of his life. Olivares secured complete control of the young prince's household, packing it with his own creatures. And as he monopolized the heir to the throne, so he indoctrinated him against Lerma and then against the remains of the Lerma faction. These were scattered in 1621 when Philip succeeded his father and Olivares succeeded Uceda. With his pupil on the throne Olivares received all the offices and honours he desired; he was able to purchase possession of additional lands and lordships in Andalucía; and in 1625 he was made Duke of Sanlucar la Mayor, and came to be known universally as the Count Duke. But what he desired above all was political power.

On the political front Olivares moved at first with caution, overtly deferring to the greater experience of his uncle, Baltasar de Zúñiga, and careful not to offend the susceptibilities of the new king, who seems to have had a brief period of aversion to rule by *valido*. But, as the king's closest friend, his tactical position was assured. Gradually and discreetly he began to intervene in matters of government, gaining confidence as he went along. By August 1622 he was a member of a junta consisting of all the presidents of councils whose function was to advise the king on major items of policy. There was now talk of diagreement between Olivares and Zúñiga, who was regarded by courtiers and officials as merely the uncle of the new favourite.[11] Zúñiga's death (7 October 1622) clarified the situation. The king now handed power officially and exclusively to Olivares, making it clear that he alone enjoyed his absolute confidence. Olivares believed that this was no less than his due, the reward for his talent and dedication.

Now in his early thirties, Olivares was dark and heavy in appearance, with hard eyes and an imperious bearing. His shortcomings were there for all to see – ruthless ambition, obstinacy, impatience with fools and opponents, and dangerous illusions induced by the power he wielded. But his qualities, too, were on a large scale. He possessed great political vision and he was capable of great magnanimity. In the king's service he worked

[11] Marañón, *El conde-duque de Olivares*, pp. 43–52.

himself to a standstill. He lived in the royal palace and attended to his master's slightest whim as well as to every aspect of government. He worked non-stop from early morning to late at night, interviewing, attending councils and juntas, reading dispatches, writing memoranda and seeing the king.[12] He brought to his office not only dedication but also a marked instinct for absolute rule and the ability to go with it. If there was a field of government which he did not understand, such as finance, he mastered it quickly. If there was an urgent problem which officials could not resolve he stayed up all night to resolve it. In a sense his vigour and impatience were his undoing, for he tried to take short-cuts to objectives which required a more elaborate approach. His vision of a greater Spain was too ambitious for the period of recession in which he lived, and he himself had no talent for political manoeuvre and compromise.

Unlike many seventeenth-century *validos* and ministers, Olivares was more interested in government than in patronage. Philip IV gave him almost exclusive power in matters of patronage, and he used it, to reward friends and punish enemies. But he did not like it and he tried to relinquish it, believing that it was a matter for the king, while he concentrated on policy and government. He was quite explicit about this, and one of his reasons was that control of patronage was the mark of a *valido*, while he preferred to be a minister. In a paper which he wrote for the king (4 September 1626) he argued that if the king assumed control of patronage 'there would be no need for the name and office of *privado*, for this is its essential feature. . . . At the same time Your Majesty's ministers would be relieved of the lengthy negotiations which patronage involves and would be able to concentrate on your royal service.'[13] But Olivares found that the distribution of *mercedes*, the award of offices, pensions and knighthoods in the military orders, were essential to the process of government and that he himself could not establish an administration of his own without a network of clients recruited and retained by *mercedes*.[14] The core of the Olivares administration consisted of his immediate clients bound to him by ties of kinship, friendship, depend-

[12] Ibid., pp. 167–72.
[13] Olivares to Philip IV, 4 September 1626, in Valiente, *Los validos*, Appendix V, pp. 171–4.
[14] Elliott, *The Count-Duke of Olivares*, pp. 113–14, 135–7, 169–70.

ence and Andalusian connections. Court, councils, embassies and viceroyalties swarmed with members of his own family, the Zúñiga, Guzmán and Haro. His power base spread out from the court itself into the key sections of the administration, held together by the pyramidal structure of clientalism, operating downwards from the *valido*, through the *valido*'s favourites, to the mass of clients at the bottom.

Olivares seems to have sought a working partnership and a division of labour between himself and the king. But this, he recognized, depended on the king doing much more work than he had hitherto done: 'the problems of government are such that Your Majesty cannot evade assuming your share of the burden, under pain of grave and mortal sin.' He sought to educate Philip in the art of government, to enlarge his knowledge, sharpen his judgement, improve his taste, making him a fitting ruler of a great monarchy, a Ferdinand, Charles V and Philip II in one.[15] If Philip needed Olivares, Olivares needed the king, partly to sustain him against his enemies, partly to legitimize his policy and projects. For this reason he never sought to reduce the king to a cipher; nor did he crave a *valimiento*, which, like many of his contemporaries, he seems to have regarded with distaste. He preferred power to prestige, politics to patronage. He saw himself in effect as a prime minister, an office which Spanish government needed but did not possess. In default of a single great office of state, therefore, Olivares had to acquire a number of offices in order to buttress his position and give it legal form. He was not entirely devoid of acquisitive motives, but he was not as greedy as Lerma and he was primarily interested in the institutional content of his offices.

One title to which he was particularly attached was that of *Canciller Mayor y Registrador de las Indias*, granted by the king on 27 July 1623.[16] This was an office which had long since lapsed and was now revived in order to give Olivares a base in an important institution, the Council of the Indies, and to enable him to share its jurisdiction over Spain's overseas empire.[17] At the other end of the scale he formalized his influence over the local

---

[15] Ibid., pp. 171–2.
[16] Valiente, *Los validos*, Appendix IV, pp. 162–70.
[17] See Schäfer, *El Consejo real y supremo de las Indias*, i, pp. 217–27.

government of Castile through the offices of *procurador* in the
cortes and *regidor* in the towns represented there; these offices
enabled him to intervene not only in the cortes but also in the
internal affairs of the constituent towns. His most important
office, of course, was that of Councillor of State, which gave him
legal entry to the highest policy matters. He became a member of
the Council in 1622 and soon came to dominate it. The extent of
his dominance is seen in the fact that he did not normally attend,
though when he did his interventions were extensive and decisive.
They were equally decisive when he operated, as a king would
do, from outside the Council. He controlled its assembly, its
agenda and, by making known his opinions in advance, its decisions. If, in spite of all this, its *consultas* still did not meet with his
approval, he sent them back for revision without even showing
them to the king. What the king finally received, therefore, if he
received it at all, was a *consulta* censored by Olivares, and what
he gave in return was a decision advised by Olivares. While he
neutralized the Council of State, Olivares replaced the presidents
of the other councils by 'governors' with more limited powers.
He was particularly interested in the Council of Finance, which
had to find the resources for his policy, and those brusk and
admonitory decrees descending so frequently on the Council,
though signed by Philip IV, bear all the marks of Olivares-
inspired documents.

If patronage enabled the system to work, it was the bureaucracy which provided institutional continuity and enabled government of this period to proceed with practised efficiency.
Olivares built up his own secretarial team, headed by his loyal
servant and closest assistant Antonio Carnero. He was also served
by the secretaries in the official administration. As the power of
the councils diminished that of the secretaries increased. The
secretaryship of state was divided into three secretaryships, one
for Italy, one for the North and one for Spain. This was assigned
to Jerónimo de Villanueva, who became the essential link between
king and favourite and the most powerful man in Spain after
Olivares.[18]

The junta system, which had taken firm root in the previous
reign, proliferated even more under Philip IV.[19] It is usually

[18] Elliott, *The Count-Duke of Olivares*, pp. 421–2.
[19] See above, pp. 28–9.

regarded as a device by which Olivares side-stepped the councils and placed administration in the hands of his creatures. Whether he needed to do this is debatable. In any case he did not invent the system nor was it necessarily a sinister development. It probably represented no more than the perennial habit of administrators who have to work through committees to create sub-committees for specialized tasks. Most of the new juntas had administrative, not political, implications. The *junta de armadas* specialized in naval affairs, the *junta de presidios* in frontier garrisons. Inevitably most of the juntas were concerned with raising or administering money. Some, such as the *junta de media anata*, the *junta del papel sellado*, the *junta de donativos*, were created for the administration of extraordinary revenues which the Council of Finance's machinery did not cover. Others were designated *juntas de medios* and ordered to find the 'means' to resolve the ever-present financial problems. These were usually composed of councillors of Castile and Finance, with a few ecclesiastics and Olivares; their object was to circumvent the ponderous and frequently unimaginative councils and to find answers to urgent questions of the day. They were smaller in composition than the councils and drawn from a fairly restricted number of public figures.[20] The *junta de estado* was in a different category, and it is not easy to discern the difference of jurisdiction between it and the Council of State. Both dealt with the same matters, mainly foreign policy, and some members of the Council also belonged to the junta. The junta, like the Council, depended for its agenda on items submitted to it by the king or Olivares, and like the Council, it directed its *consultas* to the king for action in fact by Olivares. Perhaps it was intended that the junta should provide a second opinion on *consultas* which Olivares considered had not been sufficiently aired in Council. Or perhaps it was an attempt to endow the *valido* with a type of council of his own, meeting in his private apartment, more flexible than the Council of State, and directly subordinate to his will.[21]

Possessed of the main instruments of power and secure in the backing of the king, Olivares set the direction and controlled the momentum of Spanish policy for the next twenty years.

[20] Domínguez Ortiz, *Política y hacienda de Felipe IV*, pp. 185–6. There was even a curious *junta de conciencia*, created in 1643, to consider the justification of new taxes, particularly as they affected the church.
[21] Valiente, *Los validos*, pp. 81–3.

In domestic affairs he was essentially a reformer. But domestic affairs were of secondary interest to him, a means to an end. His prime concern was the preservation of Spain as a world power, and this he conceived as a problem not of internal resources but of foreign and military policy.

Spain and the Thirty Years War

Olivares viewed the international role of Spain with the eyes of a traditionalist. He did not question the inherited ideas of Spanish foreign policy nor did he create new ones. He simply sought to apply received doctrine with greater vigour and more powerful resources. In a paper dated 28 November 1621, for the advice of the new king, 'the greatest monarch in the world in kingdoms and possessions', he reminded him of his essential duty:

> Almost all the kings and princes of Europe are jealous of your greatness. You are the main support and defence of the Catholic religion; for this reason you have renewed the war with the Dutch and with the other enemies of the Church who are their allies; and your principal obligation is to defend yourself and to attack them.[22]

Although this policy is frequently described as Spanish 'imperialism', in fact it was empty of aggressive content and of expansionist aims.[23] Spain had neither the desire nor the means to acquire new dominions in southern, central or northern Europe, and encroachment on French sovereignty and territory was now unthinkable. Why then, Spaniards were never tired of asking, did their policy provoke such suspicion and hostility throughout Europe?

The answer lay in two facts. First, Spain was an 'imperial' power in Europe in the sense that she possessed dominions outside her metropolis, in Italy and in the Low Countries. Secondly,

---

[22] 'Documento de gobierno del Conde-Duque de Olivares al Rey, en 1621', in Marañón, *El conde-duque de Olivares*, pp. 438–40.

[23] For a sensible discussion of Spanish foreign policy on the eve of the Thirty Years War see Carter, *Secret Diplomacy*, pp. 23–49; and Peter Brightwell, 'The Spanish Origins of the Thirty-Years' War', *European Studies Review*, 12 (1982), pp. 117–41.

to preserve communications between herself and these possessions she had to cut across spheres of interest and influence jealously guarded by other powers. The situation was aggravated by the conviction abroad that Spain was motivated by an aggressive Catholicism as well as imperialism. The conviction was largely misplaced: while Spanish statesmen might piously invoke religious arguments, they were under no illusions about the possibility of extending Catholicism by force. Here too, as with political dominion, they spoke only of defending existing positions. There was some justification for their attitude. Seventeenth-century Spain had inherited certain possessions in Europe which would have been difficult to relinquish even had she so wished. Most of these possessions were not ready for national independence, and it was arguable that no power had a better title to them than Spain. The one flaw in the argument was the United Provinces, which Spain regarded as rebel provinces but which by any realistic standards were a sovereign state. But even here Spain could invoke arguments of legitimate defence. For the Dutch were ready to subvert the Spanish position in the southern Netherlands and they waged outright war on the overseas possessions of the Iberian partners. At stake in the Low Countries, therefore, was imperial defence. And from the basic premise of defence in the Low Countries the rest of Spanish foreign policy flowed with a remorseless logic. To prevent the isolation of the Low Countries Spain was led to intervention in Germany, a break with England, conflict in northern Italy and eventually war with France. In the early seventeenth century Spain lost secure control of the overland military corridor so vital to the Army of Flanders. The recovery of France after 1595 and her resumption of an anti-Spanish foreign policy was to result by 1631 in French domination of the bridgeheads into Italy and Germany, and Spain's loss of her traditional military highways. Spain could not accept this with equanimity.

Spain's responses to the outbreak of the Thirty Years War in 1618 was carefully defined. To the emperor she sent financial subsidies and a token force of Spanish troops; these were present at the battle of the White Mountain in November 1620 when the imperial army defeated the Protestant forces, put the Elector Palatine to flight and crushed the Bohemian revolt. Meanwhile Spain had directed her principal military effort to targets closer to her immediate interests. In 1619 a Spanish army from Lombardy marched to defend Alsace and the Spanish Road for the Habsburgs. In July 1620 Spanish troops under the duke of Feria, governor of Milan, occupied the Alpine valley of the Valtelline, an essential pass linking the Spanish and Austrian Habsburgs, and an equally important passage for Spanish troops on their way from Milan to the Low Countries.[24] In September the powerful Spanish army of the Low Countries, under its distinguished commander, Ambrosio Spinola, struck quickly into western Germany, crossed the Rhine and occupied the Lower Palatinate. The object of this operation was not primarily to deprive the Elector Palatine of his patrimony while he was absent fighting the forlorn battles of the Bohemians. It was to safeguard the communication of the Low Countries with allied positions in Germany and with Spanish positions in northern Italy by securing control of the passage of the Rhine.

Spain's presence in the Lower Palatinate was resented by the German princes, including the Catholic electors and the Duke of Bavaria, who had himself acquired the Upper Palatinate and wanted the rest. But it was regarded by Spain as a place of great strategic importance, not least because the Dutch truce was due to expire in April 1621, and she was determined to stay until she had achieved the security of the Low Countries. In the early stages of the German war the Spanish Council of State had many reservations over giving continued assistance to the emperor. The money was badly needed in the Low Countries, and there seemed little point in promoting the ambitions of the emperor's ally, Maximilian of Bavaria. But in the ultimate analysis it was appreciated that Spain had too few allies in Europe to allow the destruction of the Austrian Habsburgs, and that she had a particular interest as well as a dynastic obligation in sustaining the imperial cause. From 1618 to 1640, therefore, in a period of appalling financial difficulties, Spain assigned substantial funds to the war in Germany.[25]

---

[24] On the Valtelline and Spanish lines of communication see Parker, *The Army of Flanders and the Spanish Road*, pp. 69–77.

[25] There is no full-scale study of Spain and the Thirty Years War, but Spanish relations with the Austrian Habsburgs and Germany are well discussed in Bohdan Chudoba, *Spain and the Empire* 1519–1643 (Chicago, 1952), pp. 229–61; Spanish policy in the 1620s is studied by R. Ródenas Vilar, *La política*

The basic reason for Spain's commitment in Germany was to be found in the Low Countries. If the imperial cause, and Catholicism, receded in Germany, the Spanish Netherlands would be correspondingly more isolated and vulnerable. Spain wanted the political frontier of the Habsburgs and the religious frontier of Catholicism maintained beyond the Low Countries. Here the moment of decision was approaching, one of the first big decisions Olivares had to make. The advice from Brussels was virtually unanimous: the Truce of Antwerp should be renewed, for with existing resources there was no possibility of winning a war. This was the policy of the Archduke Albert and after his death in July 1621 it was continued by his widow Isabella and her military expert, Spinola. They were overruled by Olivares and his advisers in Madrid, and their decision is usually regarded as a mistake. The renewal of the Dutch war, it is true, was a crippling blow to the Spanish economy. But the decision to renew it was not Spain's alone. The United Provinces too had a war party, led by Prince Maurice and including Calvinist extremists and Amsterdam merchants. The latter looked for profits in maritime war against the Iberian colonies. They had not wasted their time during the years of truce. The Dutch offensive against Portuguese positions in the tropics continued unabated, and if they were less successful against the Spanish empire this was due not to Dutch inhibitions but to Spanish defences. Now, with the prospect of official war, there would be even greater scope for action in the East and West Indies.[26] The renewal of the war in the Netherlands in 1621 was not a foregone conclusion. Spanish statesmen debated all the options of extending, renewing, or ending the truce, and even of converting it to permanent peace. They received no encouraging signals from the Dutch, who obtained and hoped to continue obtaining economic and financial benefits from Spain and the Indies whether war prevailed or not, but particularly if war prevailed. The Dutch colonial offensive justifiably bore great weight

europea de España durante la guerra de Treinta años, 1624–30 (Madrid, 1967); and two articles by Peter Brightwell add substantially to the subject, 'Spain and Bohemia: The Decision to Intervene, 1619', *European Studies Review*, 12 (1982), pp. 117–41; and 'Spain, Bohemia and Europe, 1619–21,' ibid., pp. 371–99.
[26] On the Dutch colonial offensive see C. R. Boxer, *The Dutch Seaborne Empire* 1600–1800 (London, 1965), pp. 25–7. On the options available to Spain see Peter Brightwell, 'The Spanish System and the Twelve Years' Truce', *English Historical Review*, 89, 350 (1974), pp. 270–92.

in Spain's decision to renew the war. In 1588 Philip II had dispatched his Armada against England in order to strike at the source of the greatest attack on his overseas empire. Similarly, in 1621, Spain resumed the struggle with the Dutch in order, in part, to remove the most serious contemporary threat to the Iberian empires. The motives in each case are intelligible, the means adopted less so.

The Dutch war had always been one of mixed motives. Sovereignty, religion, trade, all three had played their part in Spanish war aims. After 1621, however, while never disavowing her rights of sovereignty and religion, Spain saw the war for what it had become, a struggle for economic survival and defence of the American trade. It was a war which had to be fought by embargoes, river blockades and privateering, rather than by land campaigns and seige warfare, with the object of destroying Dutch trade and defeating the enemy by economic means.[27] Olivares seems to have understood this, and under him Spain achieved some success in developing her naval power in the north and in stemming the flow of Dutch exports and shipping; but, thwarted by rival policies and interests, he was unable to take his strategic ideas to their logical conclusion. Thus Spain still poured money into the defence establishment in the Netherlands, money which might have been more profitably invested in maritime and imperial defence where, in the case of the Spanish empire at least, the Dutch had shown that they were not invincible. The Portuguese empire was the more vulnerable of the two. With the expiration of the truce of Antwerp plans for the establishment of the Dutch West India Company were immediately implemented, and in the course of 1623 an expeditionary force was mobilized for an attack on Brazil. Spanish intelligence kept Portugal fully informed of Dutch preparations and destination, but it was difficult to defend the vast Brazilian coastline – one of the deterrents to heavy investment in imperial defence – and in May 1624 the Dutch force captured Bahia and took a large booty in sugar and other products.[28] With a foothold in Brazil the Dutch were now a greater menace to Spanish America.

[27] J. I. Israel, *The Dutch Republic and the Hispanic World, 1606–1661* (Oxford, 1982), pp. 150–3.

[28] C. R. Boxer, *Salvador de Sá and the Struggle for Brazil and Angola*, pp. 41–52.

While America entered into Spain's calculations in Europe, America also contributed to Spain's war effort there. Spain entered the Thirty Years War and renewed the conflict with the Dutch under favourable conditions in at least one sector of her economy, the Atlantic sector. The years 1616–20 were a kind of Indian summer in the Indies trade, with treasure receipts shooting up from 43.1 million pesos in the previous five-year period to 49.8 million.[29] The crown's share was not so buoyant, but it benefited indirectly from the boost given to the private sector and directly from its sequestrations of private treasure. In the period 1621–5 the crown's receipts were maintained at the previous level, while private returns dropped by about 3.5 million, but in general the favourable trading cycle was sustained, with marked results for the Spanish war effort. In December 1621 the Tierra Firme fleet was shipwrecked with much loss of treasure, and in the following year the New Spain fleet also suffered losses. Income from America, therefore, was poor in the years 1622–3, and military operations in the Low Countries were unspectacular. But in October 1624 both fleets reached Spain safely with one of the largest bullion deliveries in the history of the Indies trade.[30] There was nothing wrong with the Spanish army in the Low Countries that money could not repair. Now, with money available, Spinola led it to a spectacular success in May 1625 when he captured Breda after a ten-month siege. Perhaps even more interesting evidence of Spanish revival was the construction and equipment of a naval squadron based on Ostend and Dunkirk to wage maritime war on Dutch trade and shipping, though in the event it had to be employed primarily in a defensive role in protecting Spanish convoys through the Atlantic and the English Channel.[31]

In the Americas the Spanish war effort was equally robust. Madrid reacted promptly to the capture of Bahia, if only because it was believed, as the Council of Portugal informed Philip IV,

[29] Hamilton, *American Treasure and the Price Revolution in Spain*, pp. 34–5; Chaunu, 'Séville et la "Belgique" (1555–1648)', pp. 277, 291; Michel Morineau, *Incroyables gazettes et fabuleux métaux. Les retours des trésors américains d'après Les gazettes hollandaises (XVIᵉ–XVIIIᵉ siècles)* (Cambridge, 1985), p. 250.

[30] A. Domínguez Ortiz, 'Los caudales de Indias y la política exterior de Felipe IV', *Anuario de Estudios Americanos*, xiii (1956), pp. 311–83, particularly pp. 338–9.

[31] Lefèvre, *Spinola et la Belgique, 1601–1627*, pp. 82–3.

PLATE 2 *Reconquest of Bahia*, by Juan Bautista Mayno (reproduced by kind permission of the Museo del Prado, Madrid)

that the ultimate objective of the Dutch was 'not so much to make themselves masters of the sugar of Brazil as of the silver of Peru'.[32] This coincidence of interests produced a remarkable example of Luso-Spanish co-operation. A joint expeditionary force consisting of fifty-two vessels, carrying 12,566 men and 1,185 guns, was assembled under the command of Don Fadrique de Toledo; it quickly struck at Bahia and after a month's siege forced the Dutch garrison to surrender on 1 May 1625. The Spanish contingent followed up this success by pursuing the enemy in the Caribbean, and there too the Dutch were repulsed, notably at Puerto Rico. The Dutch, of course, had not yet shot their bolt. During the years 1626–7 the squadron under Piet Heyn wrought considerable damage on Portuguese shipping in the South Atlantic. But for the moment Spanish naval defences were equal to the threat and the silver fleets continued to get through. And this in spite of the fact that Spain was now at war with two naval powers.

Since 1604, and more particularly since 1618, peace with England had been one of the key objectives of Spanish foreign policy. On it was thought to depend the security of the Low Countries and Spain's freedom to intervene in Germany. During the crucial early years of the Thirty Years War Spain had neutralized England by means of the Anglo-Spanish marriage negotiations, under cover of which Spinola had struck into Germany and taken the patrimony of the Elector Palatine, son-in-law of James I of England.[33] In 1624, when the marriage negotiations had collapsed in ruins and the English were convinced of Spanish bad faith, English neutrality was even more important to Spain because of the latter's expanding commitments in the Low Countries, Germany and northern Italy. Olivares shied away from the impending war; indeed it was not until an English fleet appeared at Cadiz in the autumn of 1625 that the Spanish government reconciled itself to war with England. Once war was joined, however, Olivares and his collaborators indulged in an orgy of planning and for several months they seriously discussed a project for an

---

[32] Quoted in Boxer, *Salvador de Sá*, p. 55; see ibid., pp. 56–66 for the recapture of Bahia, and the same author's *The Dutch in Brazil, 1624–1654*, p. 28.

[33] Garrett Mattingly, *Renaissance Diplomacy* (London, 1955), pp. 255–68; Carter, *Secret Diplomacy*, pp. 120–33.

invasion of England on a scale even greater than that contemplated by Philip II. But while the Spaniards discussed incongruities the English practised them. At Cadiz, with a force of ninety vessels and 9,000 men, they committed every conceivable mistake. The Spanish Indies fleet was allowed to take evasive action; the attack on the town was badly conducted and was repulsed by local levies; and the whole operation ended in calamity, with loss of 1,000 men and thirty vessels. This war was not entirely of Spain's seeking. Charles I began it in 1625 because negotiations with Spain had failed to secure the restoration of the Elector Palatine's patrimony. While Philip IV had promised to use his influence with the emperor to further the cause of the elector, he had understandably refused to accept the English demand that he should undertake the restoration of the entire Palatinate by force of arms if necessary.

With France, too, Spain sought peace but was disposed for war. And here, too, the problem was one of preserving communications with the Low Countries, particularly through the Valtelline pass, a route which France and Spain's enemies in northern Italy were equally anxious to compromise. In January 1625 the French occupied the Valtelline and made an alliance with Venice and Savoy against Genoa, Spain's traditional ally. At the same time French naval forces blockaded Genoa and threatened to cut the vital supply lines between Barcelona, Milan and the Low Countries. Without a formal declaration of war, France and Spain confronted each other. In Spain French property was sequestered, while France prohibited trade with Spain. The Spanish government intrigued with the Huguenots while the French helped the Swiss Protestants. More to the point, a squadron under the Marquis of Santa Cruz raised the blockade of Genoa, and troops led by the Duke of Feria forced the French to retire across the Alps. These successes, combined with political instability within France, gave Spain the edge and enabled her to emerge unscathed. By the Treaty of Monzón (March 1626) peace was restored to Italy and the status quo to the Valtelline. Spain could continue to use the pass for military purposes.

The years 1624–6 were triumphant years for Philip IV and Olivares. Overseas Spain's naval and imperial defences had withstood and repulsed Dutch probings. In Europe Spain's military prowess had again been vindicated, moving Velázquez to celebrate it in his famous *Las Lanzas* depicting the capture of Breda. In a message to the Council of Castile on the state of the nation Philip IV alluded to the harsh economic consequences for Castile of this massive war effort, but he could not restrain his jubilation at the renewal of Spanish military power:

> Our prestige has been immensely improved. We have had all Europe against us, but we have not been defeated, nor have our allies lost, whilst our enemies have sued me for peace. Last year, 1625, we had nearly 300,000 infantry and cavalry in our pay, and over 500,000 men of the militia under arms, whilst the fortresses of Spain are being put into a thorough state of defence. The fleet, which consisted of only seven vessels on my accession, rose at one time in 1625 to 108 ships of war at sea, without counting the vessels at Flanders, and the crews are the most skilful mariners this realm ever possessed. . . . This very year of 1626 we have had two royal armies in Flanders and one in the Palatinate, and yet all the power of France, England, Sweden, Venice, Savoy, Denmark, Holland, Brandenberg, Saxony, and Weimer could not save Breda from our victorious arms.[34]

Yet the following years were an anti-climax and the big push forward in the Low Countries did not materialize. The reason was shortage of money, particularly from the Indies, that bonus on which Spanish foreign policy was so dependent. While total treasure receipts in 1626–30 rose to 55 million pesos, the true figure was disguised by fraud, and the crown's share was mediocre.[35] And not all the receipts reached Spain. In 1628 Piet Heyn's Atlantic squadron captured the entire New Spain silver fleet in the Cuban harbour of Matanzas, and the Spaniards offered virtually no resistance. This was the biggest blow to Spain's pride and purse since the discovery of America, and for the Dutch a windfall from which they financed another invasion of Brazil two years later. Piet Heyn owed his triumph to a combination of good luck and good seamanship. But the incident was out of character with current Spanish naval performance on

[34] Quoted in Hume, *The Court of Philip IV*, pp. 156–7.
[35] Hamilton, *American Treasure and the Price Revolution in Spain*, pp. 34–5; Domínguez Ortiz, 'Los caudales de Indias y la política exterior de Felipe IV', pp. 340–1; Morineau, *Incroyables gazettes et fabuleux métaux*, p. 250.

the Indies run, and this accounts in some degree for the exasperation it caused in Spain. The commander of the fleet, Admiral Juan de Benavides, was brought to trial for gross dereliction of duty; and after five years' litigation he was publicly executed in Cadiz.[36] Philip IV subsequently remarked: 'Whenever I speak of the disaster the blood runs cold in my veins, not for the loss of treasure but because we lost our reputation in that infamous defeat, caused as it was by fear and cowardice'.[37] But the loss to his treasury was grievous enough – 1 million ducats, and three times that amount if the galleons and artillery are included; and for private individuals the losses totalled about 6 million ducats. It happened, moreover, at a very inopportune moment.

Thwarted by the need to fight the Dutch and the English simultaneously, on resources inadequate to the task, Spain turned to her allies in Germany. From as early as 1624 Olivares had been thinking in terms of a Habsburg league, whereby Spain would unite with the emperor and the Catholic princes for the destruction of their respective enemies in Germany and the Low Countries.[38] As Spain had not hesitated to assist the emperor in his moment of need, it was thought reasonable that the Germans should reciprocate by lending their assistance against the Dutch. The idea was revived in 1626 but it made little headway in Germany.[39] While the emperor and Maximilian of Bavaria were anxious for Spanish aid in Germany, especially since Danish intervention there in 1626, they were not prepared to dissipate their resources on the Spanish war in the Low Countries.

A concomitant of Olivares's proposed league was a plan for a Habsburg naval and merchant base in the Baltic. The Baltic was of interest to Spain, as it was to the rest of western Europe, as a source of grain, timber and naval stores, and because it was a virtual monopoly of the Dutch shippers. In the course of 1626–8

---

[36] A. Domínguez Ortiz, 'El suplicio del almirante Benavides', *Archivo Hispalense*, xxiv (1956), pp. 159–71.

[37] Quoted in Domínguez Ortiz, 'Los caudales de Indias y la política exterior de Felipe IV', p. 341.

[38] Michael Roberts, *Gustavus Adolphus. A History of Sweden, 1611–1632* (2 vols, London, 1953–8), ii, pp. 315–16.

[39] Philip IV to Archduchess Isabella, 9 September 1626, 4 July 1628, in Henri Lonchay, Joseph Cuvelier, and Joeph Lefèvre, eds, *Correspondance de la Cour d'Espagne sur les affaires des Pays-Bas au XVIIe siècle* (6 vols, Brussels, 1923–37), ii, pp. 899, 1242.

Olivares sought to activate the policy of a joint Spanish and Imperial trade war against the United Provinces first discussed in early 1625 and reminiscent of initiatives made by Philip II. The idea was to establish a Habsburg-Hanseatic trading company to be based on ports in East Friesland. While this would challenge Dutch control of the Baltic trade, a Habsburg-Hanseatic fleet would strike at Dutch shipping and attack the enemies of the Iberian overseas empires near their homeland.[40] A further idea was to encourage Poland to take the war into Sweden and to contribute to the allied naval power. The weakness of the plan, which in many respects was a tempting and viable project, lay in the fact that none of the component parts was equal to the task; Spain's maritime protégés lacked confidence, its continental allies refused to move, and its own Dunkirk squadron was already underfinanced and overcommitted in the English Channel and the North Sea. An indispensable preliminary to a commercial and maritime league was Habsburg possession of a Baltic port. For this Olivares depended on the emperor, and the emperor's refusal to pledge himself not to lay down his arms until such a port was obtained virtually killed the scheme; the death blows were added by Hanse and Bavarian hostility. Thus the 'Baltic operation' came to an end in 1628–9, with each of the allies waiting for the others to do a little more, the emperor and the Poles for Spain to commit more naval forces and funds to the Baltic, the Spaniards for the allies to supply greater military action and support, while interests in Cologne and Brussels even pressed Spain to drop the economic blackade of the United Provinces. As the Habsburgs dithered, their enemies continued to dominate the Baltic by sea, and it was as much as Spain could do to preserve vital trade routes and keep the peninsula open to vessels from the north. One of the consequences of Olivares's project was that it alarmed Gustavus Adolphus and reinforced his motives for taking Sweden into the Thirty Years War.[41]

---

[40] The history of this policy has been clarified by José Alcalá-Zamora y Queipo de Llano, *España, Flandes y el Mar del Norte* (1618–1639) (Barcelona, 1975), pp. 229–30, 236–42, 267–76; see also Rafael Ródenas Vilar, 'Un gran proyecto anti-holandés en tiempo de Felipe IV. La destrucción del comercio rebelde en Europa', *Hispania*, xxii (1962), pp. 542–58; Israel, *The Dutch Republic*, pp. 150, 224; Elliott, *The Count-Duke of Olivares*, pp. 218–20, 333–4.

[41] Roberts, *Gustavus Adolphus*, ii, pp. 317–18, 346–56.

The frustrations he encountered in northern Europe caused Olivares to seek more fruitful terrain for the Spanish war effort. His eyes fell on northern Italy, where in December 1627 the Duke of Mantua died leaving a succession problem. The most convincing claimant to the duchy was the French Duke of Nevers, but Olivares feared that the succession of a French client would endanger Spain's interests in northern Italy and threaten her strategic communications. In March 1628, therefore, he ordered the governor of Milan, Gonzalo Fernández de Córdoba, to occupy Montferrat, a key position in the Mantuan estates situated on Milan's western frontier.[42] But what Olivares had conceived as a quick and decisive operation degenerated into a costly and bloody war. A French army predictably crossed the Alps and soon Spain was fighting to save Milan. The great Spinola was sent to command the Spanish and imperial forces, but when he died (25 September 1630) victory was no nearer and the Spaniards were thankful to accept an armistice, a prelude to the peace of Cherasco (April 1631) which ended the sterile conflict. Spain gained nothing from the War of Mantua, and her responsibility for it was a departure from the doctrine of defence on which her foreign policy was professedly based. On both counts her prestige suffered. So did her resources: by this miscalculation Olivares sabotaged any hopes his administration may have entertained of financial recovery. The Italian front swallowed up all the crown's returns from the Indies and a good portion of private returns. Of the 3 million ducats of private revenue brought on the Tierra Firme fleet in 1629 the crown laid its hands on 1 million and added it to its own 800,000 for immediate dispatch to Italy. In 1630 the crown received about 1.8 million ducats from the two fleets, a healthy sum for the time, which together with a 'loan' of half a million from Seville merchants also disappeared in defence costs.[43] In 1631 about 5 million ducats of American treasure went to the bottom of the sea through shipwreck. The Italian war had been no less wasteful.

The War of Mantua was a distraction from, not a contribution towards, the central issue of Spanish policy, the war against the

[42] See Manuel Fernández Alvarez, *Don Gonzalo Fernández de Córdoba y la Guerra de Sucesión de Mantua y del Monferrato* (1627–1629) (Madrid, 1955).

[43] Domínguez Ortiz, 'Los caudales de Indias y la política exterior de Felipe IV', pp. 342–9.

Dutch. Coinciding as it did with the financial stringency caused by the loss of the New Spain fleet in 1628, it brought the campaign in the Low Countries virtually to a halt. This intractable problem was extensively debated in the Council of State in the course of 1628, as the Spanish government doggedly sought the way to success. Spinola – temporarily recalled to Madrid – outlined two possible policies, either a firm renewal of a lengthy truce with the Dutch, or the dispatch of sufficient funds to permit a determined offensive. He himself favoured a truce, on the ground that the past sixty years had shown the impossibility of reducing the Dutch by force. The reply of Olivares was astonishingly unrealistic even for him. He demanded an energetic renewal of hostilities, without the slightest indication of how they were to be paid for; the object should be not a truce but a definitive peace treaty which would make the United Provinces a vassal state of Spain, forcing them to recognize explicitly the sovereignty of the king of Spain and to undertake to break off all alliances with Spain's enemies; they must accept a Spanish delegate in all their councils, promulgate their laws in the name of Philip IV, and perform a yearly act of deference to him.[44] Yet Olivares's policy, with all its delusions, was in substance the policy which Spain continued to follow. Not surprisingly Spinola declined to implement it and refused to return to his post. In 1629 the Spaniards lost Bois-le-Duc in Brabant, and in the following year the Dutch, switching their attack back to Brazil, began the conquest of Pernambuco.

What options were left to Spain? American revenue provided few windfalls in these years. Throughout the 1630s treasure receipts dropped from the high level of 1616–30.[45] Peace was made with England in 1630 and with France in 1631. But Sweden's powerful descent upon Germany worsened the prospects of the Habsburgs, and Spain had no confidence in the peace with France. Hitherto France had confined herself to giving subsidies to the enemies of the Habsburgs, but in the early 1630s she seemed to be making more warlike preparations. From 1632 to 1635 Spanish policy was indecisive, fearful of sudden attack but

---

[44] Lefèvre, *Spinola et la Belgique*, pp. 92–100; on Spinola, see also A. Rodríguez Villa, *Ambrosio Spinola, primer marqués de los Balbases* (Madrid, 1905).
[45] Hamilton, *American Treasure and the Price Revolution in Spain*, pp. 34–5.

uncertain whether to strike first. The Councils of War and of State constantly returned to the problem, and they began to make plans for an *exército real*, an army led by the king himself with all the nobility and their retainers. It was never clarified whether the role of this army would be defensive or whether it would strike beyond the Pyrenees; and the whole idea made little sense except in so far as it was a pretext for getting money in lieu of service out of the Spanish nobility. Meanwhile the Rhine fortresses fell into the hands of the Protestants. Spain had to send reinforcements to Germany and the Low Countries, and the latter were now threatened in the rear by France. As one front after another deteriorated, Olivares turned once more to Germany.

Spain still possessed one card in Germany, the Lower Palatinate, which was now regarded as an essential part of her strategic communications. As Philip IV remarked in 1638, 'the Palatinate is the best guarantee of our continued possession of the Low Countries and Italy.'[46] And in spite of German pressure Spain was determined to keep it until her possessions in northern Europe were secure. It was the only compensation she had ever received from the Empire for her military and financial aid, and it was a useful bargaining counter in her periodic attempts to interest her German allies in the problems of the Low Countries. From 1630 to 1648 Spain had strong diplomatic representation in Germany, including the Count of Oñate, the architect of Habsburg collaboration in 1618, and Diego Saavedra y Fajardo, a theoretician of government as well as a distinguished diplomat.[47] Their object was to persuade the emperor and the Catholic princes that the survival of Habsburg rule in the Low Countries was as important to Germany as to Spain. Their arguments were reinforced by subsidies to the Catholic electors, who were expected to counter the influence of the Duke of Bavaria. The latter's opposition to German intervention in the Low Countries and his neutralism with regard to France made him a great security risk in Spanish eyes, and it was Saavedra's task to watch him, to contain his influence, and to get him positively committed to the Habsburg

[46] Philip IV to the Cardinal Infante, 5 November 1638, Lonchay, *Correspondance*, iii, p. 807.
[47] See Manuel Fraga Iribarne, *Don Diego de Saavedra y Fajardo y la diplomacia de su época* (Madrid, 1956).

cause, especially in the Low Countries. It was recognized by Spanish planners that subsidies and diplomacy were not sufficient in themselves to procure active German co-operation in the war against the Dutch or in any war against France. Spain would have to convince by her example, to contribute a powerful military contingent to a joint Habsburg force which would serve at once imperial interests in Germany and Spanish interests in the Low Countries. The need was all the more pressing because of two recent development: at the end of 1631 the armies of Gustavus Adolphus and his German allies occupied the Lower Palatinate, and a few months later Richelieu acquired some strategic positions in Lorraine. Communications between Italy and the Low Countries were threatened anew.

Attacked by Sweden and threatened by France, the Habsburg cause required renewed collaboration between Vienna and Madrid. In February 1632 they signed a treaty of mutual help, and Olivares stirred himself to implement it.[48] Overwhelming problems of war and finance had momentarily reduced Olivares to a state of acute melancholia, and he seemed to despair of the future of Spain.[49] But his planning on this occasion was sound enough. In the course of 1633–4 a powerful army was assembled under the command of the Cardinal Infante Ferdinand, younger brother of Philip IV, a man who wore his sword more frequently than his cardinal's hat.[50] Moving north across the Alps from Milan he was joined by imperial forces under general Gallas and inflicted a crushing defeat on the Swedes at Nördlingen in September 1634. This campaign, one of the most spectacular of the war, brought a halt to Swedish successes, cleared southern Germany for the Habsburgs, and gave renewed confidence to the emperor and his allies. But it brought imperial armies no closer to the Low Countries. Count Oñate finally got the emperor's signature to an offensive and defensive treaty against the Dutch in October 1634. His active participation in the war was more difficult to procure.

[48] On plans for Habsburg military collaboration see Chudoba, *Spain and the Empire*, p. 259; Elliott, *The Count-Duke of Olivares*, pp. 458–60, 474–5.
[49] Marañón, *El conde-duque de Olivares*, pp. 80–2.
[50] See A. Van der Essen, *Le Cardinal-Infant et la politique européenne de l'Espagne (1609–1634)*, i (Brussels, 1944), and 'Le rôle du Cardinal-Infant dans la politique espagnole du XVIIᵉ siècle', *Revista de la Universidad de Madrid*, iii (1954), pp. 357–83.

When France intervened in 1635 and thus opened a new front in the Low Countries, Spanish appeals for imperial and German assistance became more insistent.[51] But apart from a token and temporary imperial contingent Spain received no German aid in the Low Countries.

Far from inaugurating an anti-Dutch Habsburg league, the victory of Nördlingen only worsened Spanish prospects. For it increased France's aversion to Habsburg power and reinforced her determination to enter the war, which she did in May 1635. This not only opened up new fronts for Spain but placed in jeopardy all the lines of communications with northern and central Europe which she had so laboriously built up over the years. And while France entered the war relatively fresh, Spain had been fighting for over fifteen years. The search for untapped resources now seemed hopeless. The Spanish economy was in a state of depression, its last prop, the Indies trade, suffering progressive contraction.[52] Between 1629 and 1631 occurred a decisive fall in the volume of the transatlantic trade and from then onwards it remained in deep depression. This was reflected in the mediocre silver returns of the 1630s which never came near to covering the deficits from defence expenditure.[53] The government was only too aware of this, and so was the Castillian taxpayer.

The Cost of War

In financial matters Philip IV was served by the most professional of all his councils, the Council of Finance. Established in 1523, reorganized in 1593, and reformed in 1621, it now consisted of a president, six councillors, a fiscal and a secretary.[54] The president tended to be a professional administrator rather than a member of the higher nobility, and the councillors were a mixture of

---

[51] Cardinal Infante to Castañeda, 24 August 1637, Lonchay, *Correspondance*, vi, p. 399.

[52] Chaunu, *Séville et l'Atlantique*, viii, 2, 2, pp. 1643–83.

[53] Domínguez Ortiz, 'Los caudales de Indias y la política exterior de Felipe IV', pp. 350–2.

[54] See Domínguez Ortiz, *Política y hacienda de Felipe IV*, pp. 176–80; Elliott, *The Count-Duke of Olivares*, pp. 68–71, 75–7, 87–8; Carmen Sanz Ayán, 'La figura de los arrendadores de rentas en la segunda mitad del siglo XVII. La renta de las lanas y sus arrendadores', *Hispania*, 47, 165 (1987), pp. 203–24.

bureaucrats, minor nobility and bankers. Its basic function was to administer the royal revenue, either farming it out on lease or keeping it under government administration. From the product it paid the *juristas* (owners of state bonds), and provided guarantees to the bankers for their *asientos* (contracts for the actual defraying of expenditure at home and abroad). The Council of Finance employed very few of its own officials in the collection of revenue.[55] *Sisas* (excise) and subsidies granted by the cortes were collected by local authorities; the *alcabala* was a composition tax paid by the localities; customs duties and taxes on wool, tobacco and such were usually on lease, with the lessees employing their own personnel and paying the product direct to the owners of *juros* charged on the revenue in question. Although administrative costs were apparently slight, in fact the system was expensive to the treasury and oppressive to the taxpayer. The lessees, most of whom were businessmen from Vizcaya or Portugal and were often Jews, pressed hard on the taxpayers in order to make a profit, and they not infrequently siphoned off the funds and declared themselves bankrupt. Municipal administration of taxes was often fraudulent, to the profit of those with places or creatures in the municipalities, powerful people who did not themselves pay but used the money of those who did for their own financial advantage. Fraud and evasion became more common as the state's demands became more pressing and its administration less efficient, as it did towards the end of Philip IV's reign. Excesses of this kind made Spanish taxation, which was not in itself immoderate, a highly discriminatory instrument and one regarded by those who suffered from it as an intolerable abuse.[56] But this was not the only trouble.

In the course of Philip IV's reign many new taxes were introduced. According to a report made to the cortes in 1623, Castile contributed more than 9 million ducats annually, of which 5.5 million were assigned to the payment of *juros*; this did not include revenue from America which, as has been seen, was now falling steeply. At the beginning of the following reign the Council of Finance reported (1667) an income of 12.7 million ducats, of which 9.1 million were already alienated; but this statement

---

[55] Domínguez Ortiz, *Política y hacienda de Felipe IV*, pp. 176–80.
[56] For an attempt to estimate the level of taxation see ibid, pp. 180–5.

did not include revenues administered by other bodies, the profits from debasement of coinage, or income from benevolences and sale of office; counting these, annual income probably then reached an average of 20 million ducats. These figures reflect the new taxes created during the reign of Philip IV. Some of them were more harmful in their consequential effects than the amount they yielded justified; devices such as coinage debasement, sale of office and sale of common lands were extremely damaging to different sectors of public and private life. Even the Inquisition was called upon to sell offices, raise revenue and help the government, contributing in the years 1629–44 considerable sums.[57]

The greatest cause for complaint was that this taxation was only part of the burden which the taxpayer had to carry. For it covered only part of the expenditure of the public sector – the royal household, diplomacy, administration, and above all defence, which together with the public debt represented by the *juros* absorbed the greater part of taxation. There still remained many services – public works, social welfare, education, medical facilities – which today the state assumes but which in seventeenth-century Spain were a charge on private or local enterprise and financed from various sources such as tithes, municipal taxes, pious foundations. The tithes alone represented taxation comparable in volume to all the regular revenues of the Castilian treasury put togther, and it weighed exclusively on farmers and peasants, most of whom were already subject to payment of rents and seigneurial dues. Public taxation, therefore, while not in itself excessive, fell on a sector of the population already burdened with other payments. Little wonder that it produced depopulation of entire villages.

Financial reform was a favourite theme in the early years of the new regime. It was canvassed principally by Olivares and co-incided conveniently, some thought, with his desire to punish his opponents of the previous reign. The Duke of Osuna, former viceroy of Sicily and Naples, was put on trial for peculation; the aged Lerma and his son Uceda were also brought to account and forced to disgorge some of their takings. But Olivares's attack on corruption went beyond vindictiveness: his reforms represented a

[57] Rafael de Lera García, 'Venta de oficios en la Inquisición de Granada (1629–1644)', *Hispania*, 48, 170 (1988), pp. 909–62.

determined attempt to impose financial restraint on the administration and the public alike. He had to begin with the king, who
regarded the treasury as his privy purse and, to the exasperation
of his officials, gave from it lavishly to an endless line of impecunious nobles, orphans, widows, ex-officers and other suitors who
thronged the court, some deserving, many less so. Olivares
insisted on restraint in the granting of *mercedes*, and as long as
he held influence they were in fact severely rationed and many
previously granted were pruned; it was only in the last decades of
the reign that the weak and irresponsible monarch shed the restrictions imposed by his former minister and lavished grants on
begging suitors from a treasury which could not afford them.

The royal household was another problem. In the reigns of
Charles V and Philip II its maintenance had cost the taxpayers of
Castile about one million ducats a year, about 10 per cent of the
budget; under Philip III this had grown to 1,300,000 ducats, and
the cortes were agitating for its reduction. Under the prompting
of Olivares, Philip IV began to reduce his household expenses,
reducing the numbers of courtiers and officials, cutting their
salaries, stopping the extravagant perquisites to which they had
been entitled, and generally saving money. The 'reduced' household was still enormous, but a start had been made and an
example set. Two years after these measures, in 1626, the king
wrote:

> I have twice reformed my household, and although my servants
> may be more numerous than before, I have had no other money to
> pay them with than honours, and they have received no pecuniary
> pay. As for my personal expenses, the moderation of my dress and
> my rare feasts prove how modest it is, and I spend no money
> voluntarily on myself, for I try to give my vassals an example to
> avoid vain ostentation.[58]

There was a measure of self-delusion in these claims, but if the
financial records are to be believed Philip IV did manage to
restore the level of royal household expenditure to that of the
sixteenth century.[59]

[58] Quoted in Hume, *The Court of Philip IV*, p. 35; see also pp. 131–2,
137–40.
[59] Domínguez Ortiz, *Política y hacienda de Felipe IV*, p. 179.

Olivares also attempted to reform the administration, partly by reducing the conciliar and municipal bureaucracy, partly by imposing new standards of integrity. In 1621 he set up a *junta de la reformación de costumbres* to prevent peculation among officeholders. The junta was to register the property of all senior officials appointed since 1952 and to compare it with the total of their possessions before their term of office began. It was further decreed (16 January 1622) that in future all senior appointees before taking office should make a sworn inventory of their private property and repeat the process at each promotion. These measures were extremely unpopular and in view of the resistance they met it is unlikely that they were permanently enforced. Olivares also tried to impose restraint on private spending. In the 1620s he caused to be enacted a series of sumptuary laws so extensive in their application – they embraced an incongruous range of items from clothes to coaches and from bullion to brothels – as to be quite unenforceable.[60] And like all sumptuary laws they attacked only symptoms. Meanwhile, as the *junta de reformación* had obviously failed to produce results, Olivares decided that more radical measures and a new committee were needed. In August 1622 the government set up the *junta grande de reformación*, composed of high-level councillors and possessing its own secretariat. The *junta* reported in October; amidst miscellaneous proposals, two ideas stood out, the establishment of a national banking system and the abolition of the *millones* in favour of defence contributions from all parts of Spain.[61] If Olivares was receptive to new ideas Spanish opinion and institutions were less so, and the report of the *junta* made little progress. In any case, all Philip IV's protestations of good faith and all Olivares's reforms suffered from a basic weakness: they regarded financial reform not as a function of the internal needs of Spain but as a means to practise foreign policy, a policy which was far more costly than that of any other reign and brought very few returns.

In July 1621, soon after the revival of hostilities in the Low Countries, the Council of Finance informed the king that he was beginning his reign with an empty treasury; much of his revenue

---

[60] Hume, *The Court of Philip IV*, pp. 131–2, 137–40.
[61] Elliott, The Count-Duke of Olivares, pp. 115–27.

was anticipated up to 1625, and 'resources are so exhausted that we do not know where to turn.'[62] The bankers, too, were aware of the facts and they advanced not the 1.5 million ducats requested but a mere 600,000, secured on various extraordinary revenues. The Low Countries, however, were soon absorbing annually not 1.5 million ducats as in the last years of the truce but 3.5 million, while naval defence in the Atlantic, a prerequisite in any war with the Dutch, more than doubled its cost to 1 million ducats. In spite of a reduction in court expenditure, therefore, the first budget of the reign produced an expenditure of 8.2 million ducats, almost double that of the last budget of Philip III. As available revenue up to 1625 only reached 5.8 million ducats, there remained an enormous deficit. Philip IV and Olivares were not impressed by these difficulties: they regarded them as a legacy for which they were not responsible; and nothing could shake their conviction that political problems took precedence over pecuniary ones, which were never insuperable. In the early years of the reign, to 1626, they simply adopted expedients which had been well tried in the past. First, they anticipated revenue. When this proved insufficient they continued the coinage of vellon initiated by Philip III, but on an even more massive scale. On 24 June 1621 the king decreed the coining of 4 million ducats, arguing that 'my chief obligation is to preserve and defend the kingdom against my enemies, and this does not admit delay.'[63] The decision was taken without reference to the cortes and it broke one of the conditions attached to previous subsidies. As a financial device it was extremely clumsy: copper was expensive to import and to coin; profits were slow and inadequate; and the consequent monetary disorder damaged the economy. But what was the alternative? The government was still reluctant to create new taxes, and it was still thought, as in Lerma's time, that there must be some way of procuring great sums without anyone having to pay them. This was the classical period of the *arbitristas*, those contrivers of schemes, or *arbitrios*, who searched for a 'universal means' to improve the situation; many of them favoured the invention of a single tax, though there was much disagreement as to the commodity on which it should fall.

[62] Domínguez Ortiz, *Política y hacienda de Felipe IV*, pp. 12–13.
[63] Quoted ibid., p. 14.

Meanwhile the government was frantically searching for money to rush to the Flanders front, remittances for which it wished to increase to 300,000 ducats a month in 1623. When the Council of Finance complained that it could not lay its hands on the money for these and other defence costs, it was rebuked by Philip IV: 'There is no need to warn me about the state of my treasury, for I am not responsible for its present situation .... It behoves the Council of Finance not to spend all its time pointing out difficulties but to attempt to resolve them.'[64] But the Council of Finance was not alone in its reservations about current financial policy. The bankers too were becoming restless, weary of being fobbed off with *juros* instead of hard cash, and steadily pushing up their rates of interest. For the contracts which backed the successful war effort of 1624–6 they insisted on extremely rigorous conditions, and at the beginning of 1626 Olivares had to stay up a whole night arguing with them before they agreed to the contracts for that year. The Genoese bankers, hitherto the mainstay of royal finances, were now anxious to cut their losses and retire from the *asiento* business. But this year, for the first time, a consortium of Portuguese Jewish financiers offered Olivares a loan of 400,000 escudos for payment in the Low Countries. Their capital resources were small compared to those of the Genoese, but Olivares encouraged their initiative as a means of keeping down the interest rates and as an alternative for the future.[65]

The Genoese had foreseen a crash. It came at the end of January 1627 when the crown, unable to anticipate revenue further, declared its bankruptcy, suspended its servicing of debts, and compensated its creditors with *juros*. Philip IV and Olivares were more complacent about this operation than were the bankers, regarding it simply as a conversion of short-term into long-term debts, as in a sense it was; it had become a regular device, adopted roughly every twenty years, and it was sometimes the prelude to financial restraint and reform. But it was useless to look to Philip IV and Olivares for financial reform: they regarded the treasury as an instrument for defraying defence costs. The late 1620s were bad years for Castile, with renewed inflation depressing living standards still further for its long-suffering people.

[64] Quoted ibid., p. 21.
[65] Ibid., p. 31.

PLATE 3   *Defence of Cadiz against the English*, by Zurbarán (reproduced by kind permission of the Museo del Prado, Madrid)

Inflation was aggravated by bad harvests and by the scarcity of imported goods caused by a partial closing of the frontiers during wartime. But it had already been induced by the massive coinage of vellon from the very beginning of the reign. Between 1621 and 1626 the crown minted 19.7 million ducats of vellon, from which it made a profit of 13 million ducats. The premium on silver soared from 4 per cent in 1620 to 50 per cent in 1626.[66] The treasury itself was a victim of this monetary disorder. At one point in the war it had to guarantee the Fuggers 180,000 ducats in vellon to make a payment of 80,000 ducats in silver in Germany. 'How am I going to rescue my stricken kingdoms from the oppression of vellon?', cried Philip IV to the Council of Finance.[67] One answer was to stop further issues. By a decree of 8 May 1626 minting was suspended. And on 7 August 1628 the crown reduced the tariff of vellon by 50 per cent.[68] This savage deflationary measure – which the crown promised was its last word on vellon – reduced the premium on silver, though at the cost of great hardship to individual holders of vellon, who were not compensated and suffered losses totalling some 14 million ducats. But it brought relief to the treasury by the reduction in the premium it had to pay the bankers for silver. And, in conjunction with the suspension of payments of the previous year, it could have been the point of departure for a new financial policy. In 1627 the Indies fleets returned with substantial remittances of precious metals. And on all fronts – England, the Low Countries and Germany – the war was dormant.

It was at this point that Olivares chose to go on the offensive and launched the aggressive and, in the event, fruitless war of Mantua, the only war which ever troubled the conscience of Philip IV. The heavy costs of the Italian war coincided (1628) with the loss of the treasure-laden New Spain fleet in the bay of Matanzas. The Tierra Firme fleet brought only 800,000 ducats for the crown, which took a forced loan of 1 million ducats from the silver which had arrived for private investors. Olivares could only complete the *asientos* for 1629 by bringing in the Portuguese financiers and persuading them to accept 15 per cent interest in

[66] Hamilton, *American Treasure and the Price Revolution in Spain*, pp. 80–1, 96; Domínguez Ortiz, *Política y hacienda de Felipe IV*, pp. 256, 276 n. 16.
[67] Quoted ibid., p. 38.
[68] Hamilton, *American Treasure and the Price Revolution in Spain*, p. 83.

place of the current 24–30 per cent. This was accompanied by minor palliatives such as selling *hidalguías*, seigneurial jurisdiction and municipal offices, in an attempt to meet the defence costs of 1629–30. The years 1627–34, therefore, saw no financial reform, only greater financial irresponsibility as the crown searched frantically for new sources of income.[69]

The years 1629–31 were a time of deep depression for Spain.[70] Agrarian crisis, brought on by a classic combination of drought, famine and malnutrition, pushed up mortality rates and drove many inhabitants of central Castile to migrate southwards to seek a living in Andalucía.[71] As bread prices rose, corn imports were needed, which cost silver. The government veered between price fixing and a free market, without noticeably increasing supplies for the starving. The usual 'remedies' for the restoration of agriculture, livestock farming, industry, and poor relief were subjects of discussion and legislation, but all came to grief against the wall of inertia, indifference, penury and war. And the resources of empire were least evident when most needed. The capture of the silver fleet by Piet Heyn in 1628 deprived the Indies trade of almost a whole year's returns; the crown's subsequent sequestration of a million ducats belonging to the private sector in the galleons of 1629 did nothing to restore confidence, revive investment or draw the Hispanic world out of its recession. There was no economic miracle for Olivares.

As the war in northern Europe gathered momentum in 1632 Olivares turned his frightening gaze once more on the taxpayers of Spain, and they rested as usual on those of Castile.[72] The cortes, which had already been held to a particularly long session in 1623–9, were convoked again in February 1632. They were asked to vote a three-year subsidy of 9 million ducats and given ten days to decide. They were understandably reluctant, pointing to the parlous state of the country, the multitude of taxes, the

---

[69] Domínguez Ortiz, *Política y hacienda de Felipe IV*, pp. 40–9, 359–64, 388–9.

[70] Elliott, *The Count-Duke of Olivares*, pp. 410–14.

[71] Angel García Sanz, *Desarrollo y crisis del Antiguo Régimen en Castilla la Vieja. Economía y sociedad en tierras de Segovia, 1500–1814* (Madrid, 1977), pp. 82–3; Pérez Moreda, *Las crisis de mortalidad en la España interior*, pp. 111, 299–300, 459.

[72] He was also, of course, unsuccessfully attempting to tax Catalonia; see below, pp. 136–9.

pernicious effects of debasement, the forced sale of offices and *hidalguías* to towns that had to pay for them out of municipal funds for want of takers, to all of which they added their customary warnings about rural deprivation and depopulation, concluding that 'the people ought to be relieved of impositions rather than given new ones for the benefit of other kingdoms.'[73] Then the browbeating began. The king warned them that he had been advised by the Council of Finance to send home those members who did not obey. Olivares tried to impress them with a statement of expenditure totalling, with some exaggeration, more than 18 million escudos. And the usual trading in pensions and honours was not neglected. Eventually the cortes voted 2.5 million ducats over six years, 416,666 ducats a year, to be raised from new taxes on sugar, paper, chocolate, fish and tobacco; they also doubled the regular *millones* subsidy to 4 million ducats a year by raising the taxes on basic foodstuffs, thus further depressing the living standards of the poor.

The expedition of the Cardinal Infante Ferdinand to Germany and the Low Countries in 1634 was a major financial undertaking, and on this occasion ecclesiastical revenue came to the rescue. The costs of the campaign were met in part by the numerous ecclesiastical benefices held by Ferdinand, particularly the wealthy see of Toledo and the Portuguese abbacies of Thomar and Crato; by the sale of seigneurial jurisdiction and municipal offices; and by the sale of a portion of the future *millones* revenue to financiers. But the victory of Nördlingen, presaging as it did French intervention in the war, only produced another financial nightmare. During 1634 Olivares worked feverishly with the Council of Finance and the *junta de medios* (committee of ways and means) to find supplies for the following year. A decree of 23 September fixed the expenditure for 1635 at 7,256,000 escudos: 5,656,000 for the Low Countries, 600,000 for Germany, 500,000 for northern Italy, and the rest for Spain. This was one of the largest Habsburg defence budgets ever. Olivares and his advisers appreciated the impossibility of the bankers providing such a sum, and they decided to negotiate for 5 million escudos, trying other expedients for the balance. The king rejected the advice indignantly: 'I do not know how you have the nerve to make

---

[73] On the proceedings of this cortes see *Actas de las Cortes de Castilla*, xlix.

such a proposal, which is offensive to my Council of State and, what is worse, to me. . . . I order you to set to and complete the negotiation with the bankers by dint of work, interest and prerogative.'[74] He ordered all senior ministers to buy *juros*, and local officials were instructed to promote a similar sales campaign in their districts. Foreigners were forced to pay to the treasury half of a year's returns on the *juros* they held. And, disregarding his promise of 1628, the king ordered further debasement of the coinage in March 1636.[75] This inaugurated a new period of financial disorder. From 1635 Castile entered a period of total war and its economy was subject to unprecedented pressure by the demands of defence expenditure. The financial planners ceased to plan and simply reacted despairingly to one circumstance after another, improvising from day to day and returning ever more frequently to the defenceless taxpayers of Castile. The people looked in vain for relief to their king. And they could expect little protection from their own representatives.

The Cortes of Castile

One of the sternest critics of the crown's financial practices was the cortes of Castile. In 1617 the town of Zamora instructed its representatives to resist further demands for subsidies and to seek a reduction of its tax assessment which had been set at 29,000 ducats fifteen years previously. 'The misery and poverty of this region and the great tax burden it bears are causing a daily flight of capital and labour. The countryside is exhausted, its farming and stock consumed. Trade, cattle and crops are down to a third of their previous volume.'[76] Denunciations like these were part of the stock-in-trade of the seventeenth-century cortes. But while they spoke like lions they acted like lambs.

The crown negotiated with the higher nobility and the clergy outside of the cortes, and these estates had long since ceased to attend. So the cortes in fact comprised the representatives of eighteen cities and towns of Castile – Burgos, León, Seville,

---

[74] Quoted in Domínguez Ortiz, *Política y hacienda de Felipe IV*, p. 48.
[75] Hamilton, *American Treasure and the Price Revolution in Spain*, p. 84.
[76] Manuel Danvila y Collado, *El poder civil en España* (6 vols, Madrid, 1885–7), vi, pp. 67, 76–7.

Córdoba, Murcia, Jaén, Toledo, Zamora, Toro, Soria, Valladolid, Salamanca, Segovia, Madrid, Avila, Guadalajara, Cuenca and Granada. Throughout the sixteenth century representation in the cortes was confined to these towns, each of which sent two *procuradores*, or deputies. Unrepresented towns resented their exclusion, not because they wished to bring themselves to the attention of the crown, but because in the actual voting and administration of taxes those who were represented were able to favour themselves at the expense of those who were not. Among the concession won by the cortes in first granting the *millones* in 1590 was a percentage cut from the tax for the deputies and their town councils. Membership of the cortes was made even more attractive by generous expenses paid by the crown during sessions and the rewards given in return for votes. For all these reasons debates over subsidies expressed not the voice of popular interests but the concern of deputies for the share they could obtain for themselves and their families. In the reign of Philip IV, when most things were up for sale, seats in the cortes too could be bought. In 1625 Galicia bought representation; so too, at the end of the reign, did Palencia. In 1639 Jérez sought to buy its way in, for a sum of 85,000 ducats, in order to free itself from the dominance of Seville. The cynical arguments used by the Council of Finance against the application are an interesting commentary on the role of the cortes. To admit Jérez, observed the Council, would simply give the government more trouble and expense, with one more town to manage in procuring majority votes, and two more deputies to satisfy with grants and honours; to raise 85,000 ducats the town councillors of Jérez, who alone would benefit from representation, would have to impose taxes on the mass of the citizens, who would get no benefit at all; in any case Jérez was already in arrears in its normal taxes and highly unlikely to be capable of raising the offered sum.[77] In the event the king granted the application on condition that the money came from the pockets of the twenty-four town councillors and not from taxes on the citizens. At that point the application was withdrawn.

[77] Consulta del Consejo de Hacienda, 21 July 1639, in Domínguez Ortiz, *Política y hacienda de Felipe IV*, Appendix XII, p. 372. See also the same author's 'Concesiones de votos en Cortes a ciudades castellanas en el siglo XVII', *Anuario de Historia del Derecho Español*, xxx (1961), pp. 175–86.

The cortes of Castile existed not to make laws, which was an exclusive prerogative of the crown, but to vote taxes.[78] In taxation the crown's sovereignty was limited by the basic principle, established since the beginning of the fourteenth century, that new taxes could not be imposed without the consent of the cortes. During most of the sixteenth century ordinary sources of income – existing taxes, ecclesiastical revenue, and returns from the Indies – enabled the crown to pay its way without going frequently to the cortes for extraordinary supplies. But the rising defence expenditure of Philip III and Philip IV forced these monarchs to have frequent and lengthy recourse to the cortes in search of new taxes. Philip III convoked the cortes on six occasions, Philip IV on eight occasions, one of which was a session lasting six years (1623–9). The cortes depended for their assembly on royal summons. There was no general rule regulating the election of deputies, and practices varied from town to town, some proceeding by elections, others by rotation or lot. The Spanish monarch did not normally go in person to his cortes but was represented by a minister, who opened the session with a speech from the throne, the *Proposición*, outlining the reasons for summoning the cortes, particularly the state of the treasury and its new needs, and exhorting them to do their duty. Having studied this message, and if proceedings went smoothly, the deputies then agreed on a sum to be granted, indicating the taxes by which it was to be raised, and imposing as a condition of the grant that it be applied to the expenditure for which it was requested. During the reign of Philip III the cortes encroached further on the royal prerogative. Lerma conceded conditions which enabled them to specify the uses to which the *milliones* revenue was put – coastal and mari-

[78] On the cortes of Castile see Manuel Colmeiro, *Introducción a las Cortes de los antiguos reinos de León y de Castilla* (2 vols, Madrid, 1888); Danvila, *El poder civil en España*, vi; and Danvila's series of articles, primarily documentation, on the cortes of Castile in the reign of Philip IV in *Boletín de la Real Academia de la Historia*, xv (1889), pp. 385–433, 497–542; xvi (1890), pp. 69–164, 228–90; xvii (1890), pp. 273–321. These are useful for raw material. The modern history of the cortes has been virtually rewritten by a series of key articles: Charles Jago, 'Habsburg Absolutism and the Cortes of Castile', *The American Historical Review*, 86, 2 (1981), pp. 307–26; I. A. A. Thompson, 'Crown and Cortes in Castile, 1590–1665', *Parliaments, Estates and Representation*, 2 (1982), pp. 29–45, and 'The End of the Cortes of Castile', *Parliaments, Estates and Representation*, 4 (1984), pp. 125–33; see also Stradling, *Philip IV*, pp. 135–7.

time defences, the bureaucracy and the royal household – and for this purpose they established a *comisión de millones*, which was under cortes control and independent of the Council of Finance. So the cortes had some power of appropriation, though this did not give them financial control; supply still took precedence over redress. Nor did it make them a constitutional opposition; they were divided into too many rival factions, motivated by too many private interests, subject to too much government manipulation to be capable of forming political groupings.

These specific, if limited, powers, combined with the needs of the crown, gave the cortes a certain bargaining capacity which they sometimes used to effect. They were particularly critical of the monetary policy of the crown and made more than one attempt to stop debasement of the coinage. In 1608, for example, as a condition of the *millones* grant of 2.5 million ducats a year for seven years, they procured a promise from the king not to coin additional vellon under any circumstances for the next twenty years.[79] But in 1617 in view of the enormous budget deficit, they released him from his promise and subsequently agreed to a vellon issue yielding 1 million ducats profit.[80] After this Philip III continued his inflationary measures without much reference to the cortes, and Philip IV issued vellon without reference to them at all, though he occasionally consulted them on some of its consequences. In April 1628 the deputies voted to have five hundred masses celebrated for the 'enlightenment of their intelligence' in studying the reform of vellon.[81] The cortes were in a stronger position when some particular financial proposal required the positive co-operation of the public. In 1622, searching frantically for additional sources of income, the government set up the *junta grande* which advanced the idea of establishing a system of banks, capitalized by forced loans from the public graded according to income; these banks would borrow at 3 per cent and lend at 5 per cent. The *junta* further proposed the replacement of the *millones* by a new form of contributions to national defence.[82] The first proposal met with the utter opposi-

---

[79] *Actas*, xxiv, pp. 637–9.
[80] *Actas*, xxx, pp. 109–19; xxxi, pp. 191–3, 196–201.
[81] Hamilton, *American Treasure and the Price Revolution in Spain*, p. 83 n. 3.
[82] Elliott, *The Count-Duke of Olivares*, pp. 124–7

tion of the cortes and the cities they represented, on the grounds that the contributions would be obligatory and unequal in incidence; as for the *millones*, many urban oligarchies now had a vested interest in this tax and argued that the cortes was the proper place to discuss it. So the matter had to be dropped.

The government of Philip IV was contemptuous of the cortes and unwilling to accept its recent encroachments on the royal prerogative, especially the procedures in the administration of the *millones*, which held up government and enabled the cortes to take the political initiative. There was money at stake, for the *millones* now represented 30 per cent of current annual revenue and was an important reassurance to the crown's bankers. For the same reasons, as well as to stem the rising demands for supplies, the towns of Castile reacted to government pressure and attempted to put some teeth into the cortes by modifying their procedure. Traditionally, in attaching conditions to grants, the cortes had presented petitions to the crown for redress of grievances. These were notoriously ignored. In 1623, therefore, many towns gave their deputies only the power of a *voto consultivo*, or provisional vote, reserving to themselves the *voto decisivo*, that is ratification of the grant offered; and the deputies were instructed that ratification would be withheld until the crown agreed to the conditions or gave good reasons why it should not.

The new procedure was soon put to the test. In 1623, under government prodding, a commission of the cortes produced proposals for a number of new taxes; these included a 12 per cent tax on public offices, a 'fifth' on all grants from the crown yielding the recipient an income, including *encomiendas* in the Indies, a 5 per cent tax on luxury textiles and on *juros* and *censos*. These proposals were a rare and promising development in tax policy, for they were aimed at the haves rather than the have-nots and would have spared the labouring masses in town and country. It was precisely for this reason that the cortes chose to dig in their heels. The deputies for Seville, Juan Ramírez de Guzmán and Francisco Ruidiaz de Pineda, opposed most of the new proposals on the grounds that they would impose further burdens on an already overtaxed city, whose returns from the Indies were under constant threat of sequestration. And they declared their incapacity to vote on the proposals as their municipality had reserved to itself the *voto decisivo*.[83] The opposition of Seville, however, was not as firm as it looked for its municipality was divided into two factions, the partisans of Olivares, who were backed by the Asistente, the crown's official in the area, and an independent faction including most of the twenty-four propriet-ary office-holders in the municipality; the latter were inspired by the local aristocracy led by the wealthy family of Ortiz de Mal-garejo, personal opponents of Olivares. One of the objects of Philip IV's visit to Seville in March 1624 was to break this opposition. While the king was being regaled in a series of fiestas, Olivares presided over a session of the *cabildo* and handled it with such effect that it not only ratified agreement to the propos-als before the cortes but also granted the king a benevolence of 30,000 ducats.

Meanwhile, however, other towns had decided to withhold ratification, and the cortes continued discussing the issue through-out 1624.[84] They maintained their opposition to virtually all the new taxes, particularly to those on offices, grants, *juros* and *censos*, for these affected the vital interests of the minor nobility, whom the cortes in effect represented. The result was that these particular taxes, advantageous in their social as well as their finan-cial implications as they would fall on the privileged and the unproductive, were eventually dropped, and the cortes confined themselves to approving a continuation of the *millones*, at the rate of 2 million ducats a year for six years, the money to be raised by taxes on basic consumer goods. Among the conditions attached to this grant was one that the crown should impose no extraordinary taxation outside the cortes; although the king agreed his ministers soon found ways of evading it. As for the attempt of the towns to retain in their own hands ratification of votes on subsidies, this hardly survived the cortes of 1623–9. The crown disliked the device: it insisted on deputies having full voting powers, and it met with little resistance. The incident, in fact, simply underlined two characteristics of the cortes of Castile, their class interest and their limited function.

When Philip IV convoked the cortes of 1632 he insisted that

[83] *Actas*, xl, *passim*; This was not a novel procedure but a reversion to sixteenth–century practice; see A. W. Lovett. *Philip II and Mateo Vázquez de Leca: The Government of Spain (1572–1592)* (Geneva, 1977), p. 104.
[84] *Actas*, xlii, *passim*.

cities grant their procurators full powers, thus enabling them to conclude agreements on their own directly with the crown; this they were now obliged to do, and for the rest of the decade and into the next they granted new subsidies additional to the traditional *millones*. Moreover, now isolated from the immediate control of their cities, they allowed the crown to take over the administration of the *millones*. The cortes returned to the fray in the late 1640s and challenged the crown both on the size of the *millones* and on the right to administer it. But through a series of ordinances issued during the 1650s the king wrested the *millones* from municipal control, and in 1658 he finally succeeded in annexing the commission of *millones* to the Council of Finance.[85]

How can the subservience of the cortes be explained? The basic reason was their lack of legislative power, which deprived them of a bargaining device and prevented them from insisting on redress of grievances before grant of supplies. They were, moreover, subject to government pressure of various kinds, ranging from holding the cortes to inconveniently lengthy sessions to outright corruption. The deputies were not paid a salary by their constituencies but received emoluments of one kind and another from the government. Their expenses were defrayed from a percentage of the subsidies they voted; in addition they spent much of their time in Madrid negotiating for offices, pensions and honours for themselves and their relatives, most of which were forthcoming if they co-operated with the crown. Methods of blatant bribery and corruption were first introduced by Lerma; Olivares and his successor, Luis de Haro, employed a mixture of cajolery and intimidation. As though this were not enough they were forced to admit to full membership of their sessions senior ministers of the crown, such as the president of the Council of Finance and the favourites Lerma and Olivares.[86]

Yet these factors do not in themselves completely account for the co-operation of the cortes of Castile with the crown. Their subservience was more apparent than real and it masked a measure of self-interest. They were generous, no doubt, but their generosity tended to be at the expense of sectors of society other

---

[85] Jago, 'Habsburg Absolutism and the Cortes of Castile', pp. 323–5.
[86] Cánovas, *Estudios*, i, pp. 125–33; Marañón, *El conde-duque de Olivares*, p. 333.

than the ones they represented. The cities and towns of Castile were dominated by aristocratic oligarchies; more particularly their government and economy were in the hands of the middle and lower nobility, who secured in the localities power to which they could not aspire at the centre. They were strategically placed to defend their property and their interests, for many taxes, and all those granted by the cortes, were administered by the municipalities. And, through the deputies whom they sent to the cortes, they were in a position to influence the actual incidence of taxation. In the sixteenth century the oligarchies of the larger towns had insisted on compounding the *alcabala*, one of the major taxes of Castile, for an agreed yearly payment. The reasoning behind this move was that in an age of inflation, with expanding trade and profits, it was advantageous to stabilise a sales-tax at a fixed level, particularly as this was one of the few taxes from which the nobility were not exempt. Subsequently, to compensate the crown for its losses on the *alcabala*, the cortes authorized a series of subsidies known as the *servicios ordinarios y extraordinarios*, payment of which was confined to commoners.[87] Thus the nobility arbitrarily passed on the tax burden to others. As there were relatively few commoners in northern Spain, a region notoriously populous in *hidalgos*, the north was effectively over-assessed compared to the centre and the south, with consequent economic hardship. The difficulties experienced by some regions in meeting their quota caused this tax, too, to be stabilized, and from 1591 its yield was fixed at 405,000 ducats a year. Consequently, like the *alcabala*, its yield to the crown failed to keep up with inflation. So it in turn was supplemented by a further series of subsidies known as the *servicios de millones*, which were first voted by the cortes towards the end of Philip II's reign. These were designed to raise 2 million ducats a year, by means of taxes on the *cuatro especies*, that is on wine, meat, oil and vinegar. These subsidies were generously renewed throughout the reigns of Philip III and Philip IV, and under pressure of the crown they showed a tendency to rise and to be extended to further commodities. In 1626 the cortes raised the *millones* subsidy from

---

[87] On the grants of the cortes see Domínguez Ortiz, *Política y hacienda de Felipe IV*, pp. 232–80, and the same author's 'La desigualdad contributiva en Castilla durante el siglo XVII', *Anuario de Historia del Derecho Español*, xxi–xxii (1951–2), pp. 1222–68.

2 million to 4 million ducats a year, by means of new taxes on paper, salt and ship anchorage. In 1632 they granted an extra subsidy of 2.5 million ducats every six years. And temporary subsidies were voted from time to time for specific items of expenditure and charged on various consumer goods.

From the *millones* the nobility were not exempt: in the grant of 1611 it was explicitly stated that there were to be no exemptions. Did this imply a change of fiscal policy on the part of the cortes? The change was more apparent than real. In the first place the affluent sectors whom they represented were less sensitive to taxes on basic foodstuffs than were the masses of labouring poor; in conjunction with the *alcabala* and local excise duties the *millones* were an intolerable burden on agriculture and on the farmers and peasants who practised it. Secondly, in a period when the financial officers of the crown were looking with disfavour on fiscal privilege, it obviously made sense for the nobility to choose the lesser of two evils, a purchase tax rather than a property tax. This is precisely what the cortes did when, as has been seen, they sabotaged the crown's proposals for taxes on public offices, pensions, *juros* and *censos* – all of which were vital property interests to the middle and lower nobility – and preferred instead to renew the *millones*. Thirdly, through their control of local government, the nobility were able so to administer the *millones* that they themselves paid as little as possible and even in some cases made a profit out of them, as did those officials who actually handled the tax and those nobles who sold untaxed goods from their own estates in their own houses in a respectable form of contraband.

Finally, the character of the *millones* was changing, to the benefit not of the mass of taxpayers but of the urban oligarchies and their clients in the cortes. From 1625, with the connivance of cortes and cities, the taxes linked to the *millones* had been steadily encumbered by state debts (*juros*). Among the greatest beneficiaries of this system were the urban elites, whose members included some of the largest bondholders in Castile. The practice of guaranteeing *juros* by the *millones* also had the effect of perpetuating the tax. Consent for renewal was now routinely given, not by the cortes but by the cities alone. Thus a kind of truce was observed: the *millones* survived, the urban elites were satisfied, and the towns preserved their local power. Once the cortes had defined and the crown had accepted the type of taxation they preferred, there was little reason for their further convocation. After the session of 1663–5 the cortes of Castile disappeared from the political stage, shorn of any useful purpose.[88] They possessed neither the motive nor the ability to enact tax reform and their consent to the renewal of existing subsidies had become redundant. From 1668 the *millones* were renewed by the *junta de asistentes a cortes*, the administrative commission of the cortes, which maintained the legal fiction of representation by sending circular letters to the towns indicating the need to renew the grant for a further six years.

Castile had been taxed too long and too heavily for anyone to mourn the demise of its cortes. Yet in one sense at least the cortes spoke for Castile. In the late sixteenth and early seventeenth centuries they often tried to insist that the money voted be spent exclusively on Castile, particularly on naval armament and defence of the Indies trade, and they had tried to appropriate supplies to this effect.[89] Their priorities were sound enough, and they were based on the conviction that Castile was bleeding itself in order to send supplies to other provinces which did not contribute fairly to their own defence, much less to the common cause of the monarchy. As taxation of Castile reached saturation point and brought diminishing returns, this conviction began to be shared by royal officials and advisers, and the non-Castilian provinces came under closer scrutiny. The call to action was given by Olivares.

[88] Thompson, 'The End of the Cortes of Castile', pp. 130–3.
[89] José Martínez Cardos, 'Las Indias y las Cortes de Castilla durante los siglos XVI y XVII' *Revista de Indias*, xvi (1956), pp. 207–65, 357–412.

5

The Great Crisis: 1640 and After

The Union of Arms

The defence of Spanish interests in Europe and overseas was more than Castile could bear alone. The Thirty Years War laid an extra burden on a land already depopulated and impoverished by previous calls on its resources. Increasing demands on Castile coincided with rapid diminution of Castile's remaining assets. The transatlantic trade now entered a period of severe crisis; it experienced a major contraction in the years 1629–31, which anticipated the great collapse of 1639–41.[1] The crown was thus starved of its revenue and the economy of its life-blood. It was not Castilian prejudice, therefore, but fiscal and military emergency which caused the central government to look more closely at the non-Castilian provinces and to seek to tap their resources.

Economists and ministers alike were calling for a more equitable distribution of taxation within the empire and demanding that the various provinces should pay at least for their own defence. In the reforming environment of the early 1620s the demands became more pressing. Fernández Navarrete spoke for many *arbitristas* when he argued that Castile was paying more than its fair share of defence costs: 'as far as possible there should be a just and proportionate adjustment of taxation in the Provinces, so that the whole weight does not fall on the centre.'[2] In April 1622 the Council of Finance was even more explicit:

---

[1] Chaunu, *Séville et l'Atlantique*, viii, 2, 2, pp. 1797–1848.
[2] *Conservación de monarquías*, p. 496.

The greatest benefit from these frontier garrisons accrues to the provinces themselves, and so they should reasonably be expected to maintain them, and Castile should not have to bear the entire burden, especially when the royal revenues are in such an impossible state, and the Castilians so exhausted and oppressed with tributes.[3]

Similar arguments had long been used by the cortes of Castile. A royal decree of 28 October 1622 to the towns represented in the cortes discussed the possibility of replacing the *millones* by a subsidy guaranteed to maintain 30,000 troops and of extending this to other provinces:

The greatest reform would be an arrangement whereby the other provinces, Aragon, Portugal, Navarre, Vizcaya and Guipúzcoa, made an equivalent contribution towards troops, for although they benefit equally from the defence and conservation of the monarchy they have hitherto escaped the costs. They have no justification for their exemption. Natural justice insists that all those who enjoy common benefits should make appropriate contributions. Moreover, they do not possess *fueros* or laws granting exemption; and, even if they did, they would not be justified in invoking them.[4]

These were likely to remain pious aspirations unless the central government was prepared to force the issue. The Italian states, it is true, contributed towards imperial defence in Italy, and they probably bore the greatest burden after Castile. The Low Countries contributed less, granted their resources, but they were in the front line of almost permanent warfare. Navarre, Aragon and Valencia gave only small and occasional amounts. Portugal and Catalonia utterly refused to contribute to general defence costs, as though what happened beyond their frontiers was no concern of theirs.[5] But the constitutional structure of the Spanish empire, and the diversity of laws within it, prevented the central government from taxing the periphery by executive means, and raised the issue of royal prerogative *versus* regional privilege. This was the problem which Olivares inherited in 1621 and to which he

---

[3] Quoted in Elliott, *The Revolt of the Catalans*, p. 192.
[4] Quoted in González Palencia, *La Junta de Reformación*, p. 406; Elliott, *The Count-Duke of Olivares*, pp. 123–4, 194.
[5] See Domínguez Ortiz, *Política y hacienda de Felipe IV*, pp. 157–9.

brought his feverish and dynamic talents. He took up ideas of fiscal uniformity which had been in the air for some time and incorporated them into a theory of empire. He then spent the rest of his political life attempting to apply the theory.

It was the object of Olivares to rationalize the imperial machinery in order to make it an efficient instrument of defence; this could be done by drawing into a common pool all the monarchy's resources of manpower and revenue for deployment where and when they were needed. To do this the empire had to be unified, and the obstacles were the different constitutions of the component parts. A precondition of uniform recruitment and taxation was a uniform law, and this inevitably meant Castilian law. But responsibilities would bring rewards. In return for their constitutional sacrifices, the provinces would receive the fruits of empire – offices and opportunities – as well as its burdens. To this extent Olivares was a champion not of Castile but of Spain, of a new and unified Spain where rights and duties were equally shared.[6]

These ideas were developed by Olivares in a secret instruction dated 25 December 1624, which he presented to Philip IV early in 1625.[7] At the heart of his argument was the idea of unification:

> The most important thing in Your Majesty's Monarchy is for you to become King of Spain: by this I mean, Sir, that your Majesty should not be content with being King of Portugal, of Aragon, of Valencia and Count of Barcelona, but should secretly plan and work to reduce these kingdoms of which Spain is composed to the style and laws of Castile, with no difference whatsoever. And if your Majesty achieves this, you will be the most powerful prince in the world.

But how was this object to be achieved? One method, according to Olivares, was to follow a policy of attraction, offering non-Castilians favours, offices, titles and brides in Castile; this was the best method, but the slowest. Alternatively the king could

[6] Elliott, *The Revolt of the Catalans*, pp. 198–208.
[7] Printed in J. H. Elliott and José F. de la Peña, *Memoriales y cartas del Conde Duque de Olivares* (2 vols, Madrid, 1978–80), i, pp. 49–100; see also Elliott, *The Revolt of the Catalans*, pp. 199–203, and *The Count-Duke of Olivares*, pp. 179–80, 196–8.

negotiate with the various provinces, but he should do this from a position of strength while his armed forces were not occupied on foreign fronts. There remained a 'third way'. The king could go in person to the province in question and provoke a rebellion there; this would give him a pretext for using an army to restore law and order, and thereby provide an opportunity to reorganize the province in conformity with Castile on the basis of conquest. This method, though not so justified as the others, would be more effective.

Olivares seems to have included the 'third way' in order to give the king a complete picture of the various options open to him, not because he favoured its adoption. There is no evidence that he ever sought to implement the proposal, while there is ample evidence that he preferred the ways of attraction and negotiation. For he recognized the aspirations of the non-Castilians and their resentment at exclusion from honours, offices and privileges, and he always argued that they should have equality of opportunity with Castile. These are not the sentiments of a crude Castilian nationalist: they imply a concept of empire transcending particularism, either of Castile or of the other parts. In the years following this memorandum, it is true, Olivares did little to widen the distribution of offices, apart from appointing an Aragonese, Miguel Santos de San Pedro, to the presidency of the Council of Castile. But the reason for his diffidence may have been the difficulty of synchronizing this reform with evidence of co-operation from the periphery. Such a plan would certainly provoke opposition in Castile and would have to be accompanied by a clear demonstration that the periphery was assuming its obligations. And this, as will be seen, was something which Olivares could not guarantee. Yet he remained remarkably free of the prejudices shared by most Castilian aristocrats, who regarded their regional neighbours with some contempt and treated them as second-class citizens. Olivares had no time for this attitude, and in the Council of State in 1632 he rebuked those who made discriminatory remarks against Catalans: 'In saying "Spaniards" it must be understood that there is no difference between one nation and another of those included within the limits of Spain, and the same is to be understood of the Portuguese as of the Catalans.'[8]

---

[8] Quoted in Elliott, *The Revolt of the Catalans*, p. 204.

As assimilation was a lengthy process and force not seriously contemplated, the memorandum of 1624 remained a long-term plan, to be achieved by evolutionary rather than revolutionary means. For the immediate defence of the empire and relief of Castile he had a second plan, more pragmatic in its approach, the co-called Union of Arms, which he explained to the Council of State in a two-hour speech in November 1625.[9] This was designed to secure an army of reservists, 140,000 strong, recruited and paid in appropriate proportions by the various provinces, for deployment wherever and whenever an emergency occurred. From each according to its resources, to each according to its needs. The idea was sound enough in principle and promising in prospects, for military and financial co-operation could be a step towards political unification. But it still came up against the autonomous rights of the regions. A decree from Madrid was not likely to overcome constitutional objection to raising money and troops in Aragon, Valencia and Catalonia for use outside these provinces. These may have been archaic privileges, inappropriate in a seventeenth-century state, but they could not be circumvented. There was no short cut to unification, only a long and tortuous road, with many pitfalls and obstacles. And at the end of it what had Olivares to offer the provinces? An interminable war and a devastated Castile, objects not of attraction but revulsion.

The eastern regions prepared for battle, mobilizing their legal reserves and polishing their constitutional weapons. Their first line of defence was their cortes. In January 1626 Philip IV opened the cortes of Aragon at Barbastro; despite the efforts of Olivares – a mixture of bullying and bribery – they proved decidedly refractory, and they had offered nothing to the Union of Arms when in March the king moved on to Monzón, where he had summoned the cortes of Valencia. The Valencians, too, were stubborn; they pleaded great poverty as a result of the expulsion of the moriscos and, like the Aragonese, they refused to supply troops for service outside the province. Olivares thereupon lowered his demands, making the military service voluntary but still insisting on the money to pay the men. After long and acrimonious debates the cortes of Valencia were finally persuaded to vote a subsidy of 1,080,000 ducats on these terms; this the king accepted as sufficient to maintain 1,000 infantrymen for fifteen

[9] Elliott, *The Count-Duke of Olivares*, pp. 245–9.

years, at the rate of 72,000 ducats a year. Eventually the Aragonese accepted similar terms, offering either 2,000 paid volunteers
for fifteen years or 144,000 ducats a year to maintain this number
of men.[10]

The Catalans were more difficult. They had already had one
brush with Philip IV over their refusal to accept a viceroy nominated by Madrid before the king had visited them and taken the
traditional oath to observe their laws; to resolve this conflict the
central government had had to back down on two important
items it had fought for in the previous reign, the carrying of arms
and the Barcelona 'fifths'.[11] When, on 28 March 1626, the king
opened in Barcelona the first cortes for twenty-seven years the
Catalans were no more ready to co-operate.[12] The Catalan cortes,
unlike those of Castile, had legislative powers, and they regarded
law-making as their first function; their second function was to
secure redress of grievances. Only after securing satisfaction on
these two matters would they pass to the third stage of their
proceedings, the granting of supplies; these depended on unanimity throughout the three estates of the cortes and were
accompanied by receipt of *mercedes*, or royal favours. The cortes
possessed a formidable instrument of resistance – the act of dissent, which any member could make in matters of grace and
justice and which, if accepted, then stopped all proceedings.The
crown could only overcome this tactic if it were prepared to buy
agreement with huge concessions.

Olivares merely wanted a quick vote of subsidy, but he re-
strained himself and accepted the order of proceedings with good
grace. By 18 April, however, the royal patience was wearing thin,
and the cortes were presented with an urgent message from Philip
IV:

My children, one and a thousand times I say and repeat that I have
no wish to remove your fueros and immunities, but only to give

[10] Danvila, *El poder civil en España*, iii, pp. 59–76, for extracts of debates at
Monzón and Barbastro. The sums voted, small in themselves, were further
eroded by resistance to actual collection.
[11] Elliott, *The Revolt of the Catalans*, pp. 148–81; Eulogio Zudaire Huarte,
El Conde-Duque y Cataluña (Madrid, 1964), pp. 1–33; see above,
pp. 69–75.
[12] Elliott, *The Revolt of the Catalans*, pp. 215–47, and *The Count-Duke of
Olivares*, pp. 262–6; Zudaire Huarte, *El Conde Duque y Cataluña*, pp. 35–59.

you many new ones. To serve with paid men, as is proposed to you, is not to infringe your constitutions nor to do anything contrary to custom, but to revive the glory of your nation, and the name that for so long has been forgotten, but was once feared throughout Europe. And by this means I wish your countrymen to obtain the leading places in my kingdoms – places to which their valour and heroism will surely take them.[13]

The cortes were not impressed by this call to greatness, but looked instead at its cost, 16,000 men. This, they argued, was beyond the capacity of Catalonia and a violation of its laws. So they returned to their practice of dissent; one town after another laid claim to fiscal and administrative concessions, and Barcelona led the way. No monarch could possibly submit to such demands if he wished to remain sovereign and solvent. The most that Olivares was prepared to concede was to cancel the request for paid infantrymen and to take instead a subsidy of 250,000 ducats a year for fifteen years. 'The money is to be spent solely in this province, for the defence its frontiers and the upkeep of galleys, not galleons. It is to be entirely collected by natives of the province, and is not to pass through the hands of royal officials.'[14] But the cortes found the new version no more acceptable than the old.

Olivares's estimate suffered to some degree from defective statistics. He assumed – as many Catalans did – that the population of the principality amounted to about 1 million. In fact it was probably no more than 400,000.[15] The population paid some 160,000 *lliures* a year in local taxes to the *Diputació*, the standing committee of the cortes. In addition Olivares was asking for 260,000 *lliures* a year for the central government. He was probably asking too much. Did the Catalans protest too much? The principality, if not as wealthy as Olivares imagined, was certainly wealthier than Aragon and Valencia, and these provinces decided, reluctantly, to co-operate with the crown. Could not the funds of the *Diputació* serve to defray a portion of the Catalan contribution? Unfortunately, in spite of the *Diputació's* regular income

[13] Quoted by Elliott, *The Revolt of the Catalans*, pp. 230–1.
[14] Quoted ibid., p. 237.
[15] J. Nadal and E. Giralt, *La population catalane de 1553 à 1717* (Paris, 1960), pp. 40–1, 341–4; Vilar, *La Catalogne dans l'Espagne moderne*, i pp. 617–20, 630.

over the last twenty years, its funds had been exhausted by a combination of peculation and maladministration. Catalan institutions were better equipped to resist than to govern. Olivares tried to ease the task of the local administration by offering to cancel the arrears of 'fifth's of all towns which voted the required subsidy and to make no further claims on them until the next cortes. But weeks of argument, negotiation and bribery were of no avail. On 3 May, in conditions of near riot, the cortes refused to vote the subsidy.[16] The next day the king left Barcelona in disgust.

On his return to Castile Olivares published the Union of Arms as though it were an accomplished fact and Castile were now going to be relieved of its burdens. But this was propaganda and no one was deceived. Castile and its dependencies continued to bear the brunt of defence expenditure. Peru was assigned a quota of 350,000 ducats, Mexico 250,000, to be applied to naval defence on the transatlantic route. So the colonies, already heavily taxed, made their contribution to the Union of Arms and in a form which became in fact a new permanent tax.[17] But Catalonia continued to resist, becoming, in its very isolation, a political as well as a fiscal problem, and one which Olivares had committed himself to solving. To the accompaniment of mounting resentment in Catalonia and of growing anti-Catalan sentiment among the Castilian ruling class, Olivares began to turn the screw more tightly on the principality, at a time, 1629–32, when commercial depression and plague were further reducing its fiscal capacity.[18] His methods were various. First he subverted the independence of the Council of Aragon, which he regarded as too closely tied to regional interests. In February 1628 the king replaced the office of vice-chancellor, hitherto a preserve of natives of the estern province, by that of president, after the fashion of the other councils; and to the new office was appointed the Marquis of Montesclaros, a close friend of Olivares. The Duke of Medina de las Torres, Olivares's son-in-law, became treasurer-general. But the key man in Olivares's system was Jerónimo de Villanueva, an Aragonese from a long-established bureaucratic dynasty. Nomi-

[16] Carrera Pujal, *Historia política y económica de Cataluña*, i, p. 196.
[17] Domínguez Ortiz, 'Los caudales de Indias y la política exterior de Felipe IV', pp. 317–19.
[18] Elliott, *The Revolt of the Catalans*, pp. 248–72.

nally Villanueva was simply *protonotario* of the Council of Aragon, an official in the chancery section of the Council. In fact he was to Olivares what Olivares was to the king, a *valido*. From 1626 he began to dominate the Council of Aragon and to control its business with the eastern provinces. He became, in addition, secretary of the Council of State, a member of the Council of War, and a member of all the important juntas. A powerful, intolerant and ruthless man, with a hint of religious heterodoxy about him, Villanueva was eager to relieve Olivares of the day-to-day burden of eastern affairs, much as Olivares relieved the king of the burden of empire.

Catalonia, meanwhile, with Barcelona in the lead, stubbornly refused to co-operate. Olivares therefore decided to appeal once more to the Catalan cortes. It is difficult to see what he hoped to achieve. In matters of *fueros* there were probably only two courses of action, either to leave well alone or to act with speed and force. Lengthy discussion was likely to produce neither peace nor profit. Yet in this his second appeal to Catalonia Olivares was prepared to give the cortes even more time to make up its mind. The king's place in Barcelona was taken by his brother, the Cardinal Infante Ferdinand, who acted simultaneously as president of the cortes and viceroy of Catalonia, while the count of Oñate was appointed his political adviser. The results were not encouraging. The business of the cortes was brought to a halt while the city of Barcelona wrangled interminably over its rights, privileges and demands, and resisted any concession to the crown. There is some evidence that members of the corrupt *Diputació* were working to sabotage relations between the cortes and the crown in order to prevent investigation of the *Diputació* itself. But subversion, if it took place, was hardly necessary. By now the crown did not even know how to withdraw from the conflict without loss of prestige. In August 1632 its exasperated officials in Barcelona were instructed to display the utmost 'tolerance and gentleness, and be prepared to consider any measure that would conclude the Cortes to the general satisfaction, even if it brings little benefit to the royal treasury'.[19] For the crown there was little satisfaction and even less benefit. At the end of October the

---

[19] Quoted ibid., p. 282; see also Elliott, *The Count-Duke of Olivares*, pp. 442–6.

cortes were prorogued. Catalonia still remained outside the Union of Arms and still constituted the major obstacle to Olivares's plans for fiscal uniformity.

The Revolt of Catalonia

For the government of Philip IV Catalonia was first a fiscal problem. Since 1626 it had also been a political problem. In May 1635, with the outbreak of the Franco-Spanish war, it became part of Spain's international problems. France's entry into the Thirty Years War had been foreseen for some time, but, harassed as it was on many fronts, the Spanish government was ill-prepared for the emergency. Now it had to improvise the raising of troops and money from a depopulated and impoverished community. Its methods were arbitrary taxation reinforced by appeals to patriotism.[20] *Juros* were heavily taxed, millions of ducats of vellon were coined, offices were sold on an unprecedented scale and the cortes of Castile were brow-beaten into voting new subsidies. Ministers were sent into the provinces to raise troops and loans. The higher nobility were ordered to raise companies at their own cost, *hidalgos* to hold themselves ready for military service. In Castile there was some response to these promptings, but it seemed like a drop in the ocean of Spain's commitments. Defence expenditure for 1636 exceeded 9 million escudos, most of it for the Low Countries. In 1637 defence and government costs rose to over 13 million escudos, while income was no more than 7.25 million; and *asientos* were becoming more difficult to obtain. The government now lived from hand to mouth, in the midst of financial chaos which lasted until the end of the reign.

The military returns from this expenditure were not impressive. In 1635 the Cardinal Infante took the offensive against France, striking hopefully from the Low Countries towards Paris; by August 1636 his army had reached Corbie. But his superiors in Madrid could not help him by opening a second front in southern France, and the Spanish war effort gradually lost its momentum. In October 1637 the Dutch recaptured Breda. In December 1638 Bernard of Weimar took Breisach, thus cutting the route from

[20] Domínguez Ortiz, *Política y hacienda de Felipe IV*, pp. 51–60.

Milan to the Low Countries. Attempts to supply and reinforce the northern army by sea were extremely hazardous and culminated in a major naval disaster; on 21 October 1639 Admiral Tromp destroyed the fleet of Antonio de Oquendo at the battle of the Downs. These reverses were due not so much to Spain's weakness as to her inability to concentrate her not inconsiderable military power on any one sector at any one time. She was now seriously overcommitted, with too many enemies and no major allies. Olivares appreciated the situation and in the late 1630s he seriously sought peace. 'God wants us to make peace', he remarked, 'for he is visibly depriving us of all the means of making war.'[21] By 1640 he had drastically reduced his terms in an effort to liquidate the war with France. But there was a limit to what he could concede. He could not countenance Dutch conquests in Brazil and expect to retain Portuguese allegiance.[22] And Richelieu refused to break his alliance with the Dutch and to press them into relinquishing their position in Brazil. So Olivares had to continue to plan for war. But where could he get additional supplies? American revenue in 1639 was not enough to cover the *asientos*; in 1640 nothing arrived from the Indies, and the whole budget was thrown out of gear. In these circumstances contributions from outside Castile were more urgently needed than ever. So attention was again focused on Catalonia.

By now, however, the Catalan problem had acquired a new dimension. From the standpoint of Madrid Catalonia was no longer simply a source to be exploited but a strategic problem to be solved, for Catalonia was France's immediate neighbour and Spain's outer defence against French invasion. Was Catalonia a security risk? The suspicion haunted some minds in Castile, but not that of Olivares. With typical ebullience he saw war on the Pyrenees front as a challenge which, if firmly grasped, might transform Catalonia from a liability into an asset. It became his policy in fact to force Catalonia into contributing to imperial defence by making the province a theatre of operations in the war with France.[23] This was not the sinister project so frequently attributed to Olivares. It was not his intention to put an army

---

[21] Report of Olivares to king, March 1640, in Cánovas, *Estudios*, i, p. 414.
[22] See below, pp. 151–3.
[23] Elliott, *The Revolt of the Catalans*, pp. 356–61, 375–90; Zudaire Huarte, *El Conde-Duque y Cataluña*, pp. 119–26.

into Catalonia in order deliberately to provoke a rebellion, the crushing of which would then be a pretext to abolish Catalan liberties; even Olivares at his most extreme did not plan the total destruction of the Catalan constitutions. He simply wanted to involve Catalonia in the problems, and therefore the finances, of the monarchy, and so to end its political and fiscal immunity.

Olivares worked on this principle from late 1635. But it was not easy to implement. Catalan resistance to taxation continued. Between 1626 and 1637, it is true, Barcelona provided 308,500 *lliures* in loans or gifts to the crown; but this was only half the value of arrears of 'fifths' owed by the city since 1599.[24] And it was not taxation. Recruitment of troops was equally difficult. The Catalans refused to supply a contingent for the hard-pressed Italian front. In the course of 1637 they also refused to supply troops for a diversionary blow into Languedoc to relieve the pressure on Italy and the Low Countries. In 1638, when French forces penetrated into Guipúzcoa and laid siege to Fuenterrabía, contingents from virtually the whole of Spain, including Aragon and Valencia, came to the rescue of the beleaguered town. Again Catalonia was absent. The Catalans, of course, invoked their constitutions, which prevented their recruitment for duties outside their own frontiers. But no power could possibly conduct a war on these principles, with one hand tied behind its back, never able to anticipate an attack or to take the offensive. Yet the Catalans were adamant. And now the resistance of Barcelona was reinforced by that of a resurgent *Diputació*, posing once again as the defender of the laws and liberties of the fatherland and taking advantage of the crown's financial difficulties to bargain more toughly.

If the laws of Catalonia frustrated legitimate defence interests there was an arguable case for changing the laws. This, at any rate, seems to have been the assumption of Olivares and his advisers. When they planned military operations for 1639 they deliberately chose Catalonia as the front on which to fight France, in order, among other things, to force Catalonia to contribute to the war effort, 'finding itself directly involved, as up to now it seems not to have been involved, with the common welfare of the Monarchy and of these kingdoms'.[25] In the event the

---

[24] Elliott, *The Revolt of the Catalans*, p. 333.
[25] Quoted ibid., p. 361.

campaign brought little credit to Madrid or Barcelona. Operations were seriously handicapped by constant bickering over the
raising and payment of troops in the principality, and by mutual
recriminations over Castilian charges that Catalan troops were
deserting on a large scale. Military ineptitude compounded the
confusion; and Salces, having been foolishly lost, was extra-
vagantly recovered, at heavy cost in Catalan lives. Nevertheless,
as a result of this campaign, Catalonia had been hounded into
raising troops, these had been harried to the front, and a royal
army about 9,000 strong now wintered in Catalonia in preparation for the spring campaign in 1640. Inevitably the army infring-
ed the constitutions, for these defined Catalan obligations of
billeting in such a way that they were insufficient for basic
maintenance. This in turn affected the behaviour of the troops,
whose excesses Viceroy Santa Coloma was too weak to prevent
and the Catalans too exasperated to stomach.

By the end of February 1640 the patience of Olivares was
exhausted. 'We always have to look and see if a constitution says
this or that', he wrote to Santa Coloma. 'We have to discover
what the customary usage is, even when it is a question of the
supreme law, of the actual preservation and defence of the
province .... The Catalans ought to see more of the world than
Catalonia.'[26] He ordered firmer measures for billeting and payment of troops in Catalonia, and for further recruitment there. A
member of the *Diputació* and two members of Barcelona city
council were gaoled. And preparations were made to involve
Catalonia irremediably in the campaign of 1640. Malice played no
part in the Count Duke's policy: far from trying to provoke the
Catalans into revolt, he was complacent enough to believe they
were basically loyal.

The Catalans, too, had had enough. Suddenly, in the first
weeks of May 1640, the pent-up resentments of the last four
decades and the more immediate anger at the presence of the
royal army exploded into rebellion. Peasants in the western areas
of Gerona and La Selva attacked the *tercios* which were billeted
on them. Violence was ruthless, organized, and inflamed by agitators. By the end of May peasant forces had infiltrated Barcelona.
In June they were joined by the *segadors*, casual labourers, who
soon had the city at their mercy. Royal judges were hunted like

[26] Olivares to Santa Coloma, 29 Februry 1640, ibid., pp. 400–1.

animals at bay, and the viceroy was killed on a beach of Barcelona as he sought to embark for safety.

The reaction of Madrid to these events was predictable. Ministers urged that the time had come to crush Catalonia once and for all. Olivares did not share this view. He still clung to his belief that reasonable accommodation was possible and that the Catalans would respond to a genuine offer of equal status and opportunity within the monarchy.[27] He therefore advocated leniency and the granting of a general pardon. The murder of the viceroy, however, shattered even Olivares; in a mood of hatred and despair he now lost his faith in the Catalans and appreciated that he had a major rebellion on his hands which no government could condone. But for the moment the government was impotent. Its armies and resources were already committed on several fronts and could not be focused on Catalonia.

If the rebellion was beyond the control of the government, it was soon out of the hands of the Catalan leaders. For alongside the political opposition which they represented there was a social revolution over which they had no control. From the beginning the rebels had attacked the property and the persons of wealthy citizens. Rural agitators infiltrated into the towns and collaborated with lawless elements among the urban poor. The leadership of Barcelona and its oligarchy was brushed aside as the forces of agrarian discontent swept into action. This was a rebellion of impoverished and landless peasants against wealthy farmers and noble landowners; of the underprivileged in the towns against the urban oligarchies; of repressed bandit elements against the forces of law and order.[28] The Catalan leaders had unleashed a tiger, and soon their country was rent by civil war as well as by revolution. Caught between the authority of the king and the radicalism of the mob, the leaders of the political revolution turned to France. The inconsistency of their position was now fully exposed. For all their opposition to the king they were incapable of ruling Catalonia independently, and so they sought the protection of the king's enemies. The *Diputació*, or people acting on its behalf, seem to have established contact with France as early as April 1640, before the revolution began.[29] The initiative

27 Ibid., pp. 433–42.
28 Ibid., pp. 431–2, 459–65; Zudaire Huarte, pp. 249–82.
29 José Sanabre, *La acción de Francia en Cataluña en la pugna por la hegemo-*

was taken by Pau Claris, canon of Urgell, member of the *Diputa-ció* and a leader of resistance to Madrid, and Franceso de Tamarit, another member of the *Diputació*, whose political activities had recently landed him in jail. And for his part Richelieu had his agents in Catalonia.

As the news from Catalonia became worse, Olivares too was caught in a dilemma. To offer reconciliation might be interpreted as weakness and set a bad example to other equally hard-pressed provinces. To crush Catalonia by military action, on the other hand, he really needed peace with France, as Richelieu knew to his advantage. Yet military action was now called for. Since the loss of Barcelona the government had used the port of Tortosa for the movement of troops to Italy and for supplying the remnants of its forces on the Catalan front. But in July Tortosa too revolted and deprived Spain of a vital link in its imperial communications. So preparations were made to send an army against Catalonia. Even now the intention of Olivares was not to destroy Catalonia's constitutions but only 'those laws which specifically obstruct good government and the administration of justice, and which stand in the way of uniformity with the other kingdoms of the Crown'.[30] As Castile laboriously mobilized, Catalonia too began to look to its defences. The *Diputació* could not rely on patriotism alone, for the Catalans were no more disposed to accept military service for defence against Castile than they had been for defence against France. So on 24 September the *Diputa-ció* submitted a formal request to Paris for French protection and military assistance. And in October it entered into an agreement with France whereby it allowed French ships to use Catalan ports and undertook to pay for the upkeep of 3,000 troops which France would send to Catalonia.[31]

As Olivares remarked, Spain had another Holland on its hands. He was now dispirited and pessimistic, believing that this was a war which no one could win, 'for one cannot talk of success in an action against one's own vassals, in which all gain must be loss'.[32]

nía de Europa (1640–1659) (Barcelona, 1956), pp. 91–4; Zudaire Huarte, *El Conde-Duque y Cataluña*, pp. 283–6, 299–300.

[30] Paper by Olivares, 11 August 1640, in Elliott, *The Revolt of the Catalans*, pp. 497–8.

[31] Sanabre, *La acción de Francia en Cataluña*, pp. 103–6.

[32] Quoted in Elliott, *The Revolt of the Catalans*, p. 504.

He had great difficulty in mobilizing an army in Castile and he had to rely on methods which had hardly changed since the Middle Ages. City militias were ordered to stand to, nobles to arm their vassals, *hidalgos* and *caballeros* of the military orders to follow the king to war.[33] The result was disappointing. Barely 1,000 nobility and gentry answered the call, and troops were equally difficult to find. When an army of 20,000 was finally assembled, it seemed the height of folly to entrust this precious commodity to the command of the Marquis of los Vélez, viceroy-elect of Catalonia, who had no military experience and few qualities of leadership. Tortosa was taken without much opposition at the end of November, but in the advance on Barcelona the army's behaviour, particularly the massacre of prisoners, reinforced the Catalans' determination to resist. On 23 January 1641 the principality placed itself under the government of the king of France in return for French military protection. The joint Catalan–French forces successfully defended Barcelona against the army of Castile, and the incompetent los Vélez promptly ordered a retreat. There would be no prompt return.

While Spain suffered temporary dismemberment by the revolt of Catalonia, the Catalans suffered much more. Now, with cruel irony, they had achieved a kind of parity with Castile: in the years following 1640 they too became the victims of war, and they too were forced to endure heavy defence expenditure, monetary inflation, economic stagnation, plague, famine, and finally loss of fertile territory.[34] They acquired the burden of power without any of the fruits. Their last state was worse than their first.

French policy in Catalonia was dominated by military considerations; they now had a base in Spain, to be used primarily for striking into Aragon and Valencia. They appointed a French viceroy and packed the administration with known friends of France. They insisted on the Catalans' billeting, supplying and paying the French troops, who looked increasingly like an army of occupation.[35] Catalonia became merely one of the various French theatres of war. In 1642, with the conquest of Rosellón and the capture of Monzón and Lérida, it was a successful theatre. But in

[33] Domínguez Ortiz, 'La movilización de la nobleza castellana en 1640', *Anuario de Historia del Derecho Español*, xxv (1955), pp. 799–823.

[34] Vilar, *La Catalogne dans l'Espagne Moderne*, i, p. 633.

[35] Sanabre, *La acción de Francia en Cataluña*, p. 148.

1643-4 Philip IV's armies began to strike back, recovering Monzón and Lérida where, in July 1644, the king took a solemn oath to observe the Catalan constitutions. Between 1646 and 1648 the French were held to a stalemate in Catalonia; when the Peace of Westphalia deprived them of their Dutch allies and the Fronde began to occupy their attentions at home, Catalonia ceased to figure prominently in French calculations.

France exploited Catalonia economically as well as militarily. French merchants poured grain and manufactured goods into the newly acquired market, and it soon became clear that commercially Catalonia had even less future with France than with Castile.[36] Unlike the Dutch, the Catalans had no colonial trade as a basis for independent growth; and as they constituted no threat to Castile's American monopoly their cause attracted little international interest.[37] The final blow to Catalan fortunes was delivered by the great plague of 1650-4 which caused severe mortality – claiming 36,000 victims in Barcelona alone – among a people already suffering from wartime malnutrition.[38]

The substitution of Louis XIII of France for Philip IV of Spain solved none of Catalonia's problems. All the complaints the Catalans had held against Castile they now held against France, but to a greater degree, and with less undertanding from the absolutist government in Paris. Internal divisions endemic in the principality came to the surface once more, and Catalonia was split between the partisan of France and those of Spain, between the few who profited from offices and opportunities with the French and the many who resented the depredations of the French armies and the predominance of French merchants. The growing alienation from France presented Philip IV with the opportunity to make a supreme bid to recover the principality. In mid-1651 the Spanish army under Don John of Austria, Philip IV's bastard son, advanced on Barcelona and began a lengthy siege of the city, while naval forces established a blockade. The French were unable to relieve Barcelona and it surrendered on 13 October 1652, accepting the sovereignty of Philip IV, with Don John as his viceroy, in return for a general amnesty and the king's promise to preserve

[36] E. Giralt, 'La colonia mercantil francesa de Barcelona', *Estudios de Historia Moderna*, vi (Barcelona, 1956), pp. 217–78.

[37] Sanabre, *La acción de Francia en Cataluña*, pp. 354–5.

[38] Nadal and Giralt, *La population catalane*, pp. 42–4.

the constitutions.[39] France still held Rosellón and continued to wage frontier warfare, but its object was now simply to win bargaining counters for the peace table. It had some success. By the Peace of the Pyrenees (7 November 1659) Spain – and Catalonia – lost both Rosellón and Conflent. But Spain had regained the allegiance of Catalonia and the Catalans could argue that they had preserved their laws and privileges. The Catalan ruling class had learnt some lessons. For the maintenance of their status and property and the supply of law and order they needed a superior sovereignty; their country did not possess the resources for independence and it did not wish to be a satellite of France; the best terms they could get were those from Spain.

In the course of discovering this they had led their people into bloodshed and deprivation and had inflicted a grievous wound on the rest of Spain. The role of the Catalan revolt in Spain's mid-century crisis is difficult to define with precision. England too had a civil war about the same time and came out of it a major military power. A basic factor in Spain's crisis was the depression in the Indies trade from 1629.[40] The collapse of maritime defences, the decay of Spanish shipping, the dwindling of trade with America and the decreasing returns therefrom, all caused a severe crisis in the Spanish Atlantic, a crisis seen to be temporary by later observers, but less obviously so to contemporaries. The crisis in colonial trade not only hit the crown's revenues directly but also reduced the influx of private capital into Castile and thus damaged all sectors of the economy. This was a novel experience and would have reduced Spain's power regardless of the revolt of Catalonia. But the depression in the Atlantic sector was one of the reasons why the crown had to look elsewhere – including Catalonia and Portugal – for additional revenue, and this was one of the causes of the alienation of these provinces. At this point the Catalan revolution played a crucial role. It prevented Spain from exploiting France's internal instability, and embroiled her in a disastrous and costly civil war at the very moment when she needed all her diminished reserves of money and manpower for campaigns abroad; these reserves now had to be diverted to

[39] Sanabre, *La acción de Francia en Cataluña*, pp. 533–44; Reglà, *Els virreis de Catalunya*, p. 142.

[40] Chaunu, *Séville et l'Atlantique*, viii, 2, 2, pp. 1793–1851.

Catalonia, thus precipitating Spain's collapse. At the same time the Catalan revolt provided an example and an opportunity to the Portuguese and encouraged them to make their own bid for independence. This in turn worsened the crisis in the Atlantic sector.

The Secession of Portugal

Catalonia was a small part of the Spanish imperium, a country orientated towards the Mediterranean and the past. For Spain there was a great security problem in its revolt but not much at stake economically. Portugal was an even greater security risk, for Portugal was more valuable, being an Atlantic power with an overseas empire.

Portugal, like Catalonia, presented a fiscal problem to Castile. It supplied no regular revenue to the central treasury, and its Iberian defences had to be subsidized by Castile, which was also expected to come to the periodic defence of Brazil. Olivares therefore planned to press Portugal too into his Union of Arms, and to the Portuguese, as to the Catalans, he wished to offer improved status and opportunities within the monarchy.[41] Continuing a policy begun by Lerma, though with hardly more success, he first tried to infiltrate the Portuguese administration; in 1634 Princess Margaret of Savoy was sent to govern the country, with a group of Castilian advisers who caused great resentment among the Portuguese bureaucracy. He then attempted to tax Portugal by introducing a regular contibution of 500,000 cruzados a year towards its own defence. In the period 1619–30 Lisbon had already made extraordinary contributions of one kind or another, some of them voluntary offerings, most of them forced loans, to the amount of 1 million cruzados.[42] New demands only increased the irritation of the Portuguese merchant class. They also led to tax riots in 1637 in Evora and other towns; but as these were essentially lower-class convulsions, from which the Portuguese leaders held aloof, they were put down without difficulty. Class divisions within Portugal gave the Spanish gov-

[41] Marañón, *El conde-duque de Olivares*, pp. 317–18, 441–2.
[42] Mauro, *Le Portugal et l'Atlantique*, pp. 468–9.

ernment a certain source of strength. While the lower sectors of society, and the lower clergy, traditionally resented Spanish rule, the aristocracy were reconciled to it by the greater opportunities available to them in a larger empire. By 1640, however, the Portuguese aristocracy too were alienated. The cause of their resistance was overtly the issue of military service. For in addition to money Olivares wanted troops from Portugal. Some 6,000 troops were impressed for service in Italy, but the revolt of Catalonia caused them to be diverted to the army recruited for the Catalan front. Olivares was even more anxious to mobilize the Portuguese nobility, with the Duke of Braganza at their head, in order that they should be employed in putting down revolution in Catalonia instead of fomenting revolution at home. But the Portuguese nobility, sensing that the time for action had arrived, refused to be lured out of the country; and in the autumn of 1640 some of them began to plan revolution.

Summons to military service was the occasion rather than the cause of Portuguese resistance. In a country which still remembered past independence there was bound to be latent resentment at the loss of sovereignty involved in the union of the crowns. But why did the Portuguese nobility, hitherto supporters of the union, withdraw allegiance in 1640? Olivares's attempt to press Portugal into the Union of Arms was too diffident to provoke a revolution. The revolt of Catalonia gave the Portuguese a model and an opportunity rather than a motive. The real cause of Portuguese alienation must be sought elsewhere, in an area of opportunity which the Portuguese particularly valued and in which they had a vital stake, the Iberian overseas empire. Olivares argued that as Castile helped Portugal in her attempts to recover Brazil then Portugal should help Castile to recover Catalonia. But what was Castile's record in Brazil? If the Portuguese ruling class ceased to find any advantage in union with Spain, was it because the transatlantic interests which bound Portugal to Spain in 1621 were no longer effective in 1640?

Portugal's loss of her Asian empire was not a valid test of Iberian collaboration. A trading empire in which Portugal had virtually no commodities to trade was not viable economically; and the Portuguese did not seriously regard Spain as responsible for its defence.[43] In any case loss of the spice trade was more than

[43] See above, pp. 75–83.

counterbalanced by the growth of a second Portuguese empire in Brazil. Brazilian sugar became one of the most spectacular growth industries of the early seventeenth century. By 1627–8 there were 200 sugar mills in Brazil, most of them in the north-east; and an average of 300 sugar ships left the colony every year carrying between 70,000 and 80,000 chests of sugar, worth some 4 million cruzados when landed in Portuguese ports.[44] Although this trade had been penetrated by the Dutch, it represented a major investment for Portugal and it yielded valuable returns. Its defence was therefore a vital test of the Iberian partnership. The most serious threat came from the Dutch West India Company, whose ships intercepted large numbers of Portuguese mechant vessels in the South Atlantic and appropriated their rich cargoes. Suggestions were frequently made that a convoy system on the lines of that operated by Spain's transatlantic shipping would provide the best defence against Dutch attacks; and in 1628 Philip IV instructed the Council of Portugal to investigate the possibility.[45] But the idea foundered on the established organization of the Brazil trade, which was not canalized through monopoly ports, and on the opposition of the sugar producers, merchants and shippers, who were either unable or unwilling to invest the capital needed for the provision of bigger and better armed escorts. Spain, therefore, could hardly be held responsible for the state of Portugal's maritime defences.

The Dutch not only attacked the sugar trade at sea, they also sought to appropriate it at its source. Their first conquest in Brazil drew swift retaliation; and Spain made a large contribution to the relief expedition which recaptured Bahia in 1625.[46] But in 1630 the Dutch West India Company, investing its windfall from the capture of the Mexican silver fleet in 1628, dispatched a second expedition which occupied Olinda and Recife. Within a few years the Dutch had laid the framework of a new colony in north-east Brazil based on the rich province of Pernambuco; there they remained for a quarter of a century and came to appropriate almost half of the sugar trade. Unless the Iberian powers could send a relief expedition and a fleet capable of contesting Dutch sea power in the South Atlantic, there was a

[44] Boxer, *Salvador de Sá*, pp. 178–81.
[45] Ibid., pp. 182–4.
[46] See above, pp. 99–101.

distinct possibility that the enemy would conquer the whole of the Brazilian littoral and begin to penetrate Spanish America.

Olivares appreciated that the union of the crowns was on trial. The restitution of Pernambuco became an indispensable Spanish condition for any peace with the Dutch, badly through Spain needed peace. By 1635 Olivares was even prepared to offer the Dutch Breda, 200,000 ducats, and the right to close the Scheldt, if they would return Pernambuco. But the Portuguese wanted more than diplomacy: they wanted military and naval assistance. This too the Spaniards were willing to provide, but they could not provide it quickly. It took over six years to organize a relief expedition, and it was September 1638 before a joint force sailed from Lisbon. Don Fadrique de Toledo, the victor of 1625, declined its command on the gound that it was under strength; the expedition's forty-one vessels and 5,000 troops did in fact compare unfavourably with the force dispatched in 1625, a further sign of deterioration in Spain's resources, but reinforcements from Buenos Aires and Rio de Janeiro brought its strength up to eighty-six sail and 10,000 troops and gave it a clear numerical superiority over the Dutch. In the event the expedition failed not because of the insufficiency of the force but because of the incapacity of its commander, the Portuguese Conde da Torre, who was unearthed only after a fruitless search for talent and proved to be totally unqualified for the task. He kept his armada immobile in Bahia for almost the whole of 1639, thus presenting the Dutch with a perfect opportunity to prepare for battle. He finally moved his fleet to Pernambuco; there, in January 1640, he was outfought by a Dutch fleet under half his strength, and after a few days fighting he weakly withdrew, leaving the greater part of his fleet to disperse to the West Indies.[47]

By 1639, therefore, the Iberian partnership had ceased to function effectively. Although the Portuguese themselves conspicuously neglected their imperial defences, Spain as the senior partner had to bear the odium of failure. If Spain failed Portugal it was not through infirmity of will but through poverty of resources. In the Portuguese view Spain was overcommitted elsewhere to the neglect of more vital interests. There had ceased to be any value in the union. Spain could bring to it in the 1630s

[47] Boxer, *Salvador de Sá*, pp. 116–20.

much less power than in the past. And the Portuguese resented their losses in Brazil from 1630 much more than they had resented their losses in Asia from 1600.[48] Their resentment was aggravated by the fact that they were also in the process of losing one of the greatest advantages accruing from Brazil, their foothold in Spanish America.

At the height of the Brazil trade between 200 and 300 vessels left Portugal annually to cross the South Atlantic; these included many vessels from northern Europe, without counting those which sailed directly from Amsterdam.[49] As Portugal was not a manufacturing country it was obvious that these vessels were exporting merchandise from outside Iberian sources, and on a scale which far exceeded the capacity of the Brazilian market. They were in fact exporting to Spanish America, circumventing the legal route via Panama and Peru, and competing on very favourable terms – these goods were untouched by Spanish taxes – with authorized Spanish exports. Brazil, therefore, became an entrepôt for a vast re-export trade which possibly took half of the Spanish South American market.[50]

The most important point of Portuguese penetration of Spanish America from about 1600 was the Río de la Plata. Merchants from Brazil, the *Peruleiros*, made their way across the pampas, through Tucumán and over the Andes into Upper Peru, where they sold their goods for the coveted silver of Potosí.[51] Across the same route there was a flourishing contraband trade in slaves from Angola, the supply of which the Portuguese virtually monopolized. In addition to trading illegally in Spanish America the Portuguese also settled there, with tacit if not formal permission. Some acquired land, like Salvador de Sá, who married a wealthy creole heiress in Tucumán and thus became the owner of estates strategically placed on the route to Potosí.[52] Others sought and

---

[48] Chaunu, 'Autour de 1640', *Annales*, ix (1954), pp. 44–54.
[49] Chaunu, *Séville et l'Atlantique*, vii, 2, 2, pp. 1328–9, 1833–4.
[50] Chaunu, 'Autour de 1640', p. 53; Canabrava, *O comércio português no Rio da Prata*, 1580–1640, pp. 20–8. Spaniards alleged that from fourteen to eighteen vessels a year entered Buenos Aires, carrying as much cloth as the *flota* took to Tierra Firme; officials were presumably being bribed into compliance.
[51] Boxer, *Salvador de Sá*, pp. 77–9; Canabrava, *O comércio Português no Rio da Prata*, pp. 96–131; Georges Scelle, *La traite négrière aux Indes de Castille* (2 vols, Paris, 1906), i, pp. 382–484.
[52] Boxer, *Salvador de Sá*, pp. 96–110.

obtained offices. In Peru the Portuguese were prominent in maritime occupations as pilots and owners of vessels; some settled in
towns and ports as resident traders, acquiring among other things
a virtual monopoly of the export of vicuña wool; others became
small landed proprietors.[53] They were also to be found in Mexico,
where most of them had improved their prospects as small independent farmers and traders or as wage employees; in the province of Tulancingo, for example, they constituted from 10 to 15
per cent of the adult male Europeans.[54] This Portuguese invasion
of the Spanish Indies was one of their most valuable assets under
the union of the crowns. In this sector, at least, Olivares's offer of
opportunities was temporarily vindicated; it was not the Castilians who penetrated the Portuguese empire, but the Portuguese
who penetrated the empire of Castile.

Inevitably there was a reaction. From about 1630 Spaniards
began to resist the Portuguese invasion of their empire. Merchants and colonists, Mexicans and Peruvians inundated the
imperial government with protests against the ubiquitous Portuguese, intruders who took the fruit from the mouths of Spaniards.
According to one memorial, 'the Portuguese are increasing in the
Spanish Indies, and go on every fleet, while they are careful to
keep the Castilians out of the East Indies'; another claimed that
Portuguese Jews controlled the trade of Lima 'from the vilest
African Negro to the most precious pearl'.[55] Many, though not
all, of the Portuguese who traded with and settled in Spanish
America were indeed New Christians, and therefore suspect as
judaizers as well as interlopers. From 1634 the Lima Inquisition
intensified proceedings against them and increased its confiscation
of their property.[56] The state too began to tighten the screw,
taxing the Portuguese and their property with growing severity.

The Portuguese now had an added resentment. At the very
moment when they looked to the Spanish empire to compensate

[53] María Encarnación Rodríguez Vicente, *El Tribunal del Consulado de Lima
en la primera mitad del siglo XVII* (Madrid, 1960), pp. 70–3, 173, 264–5, 268–9.
[54] Woodrow Borah, 'The Portuguese of Tulancingo and the Special *Donativo*
of 1642–1643', *Jahrbuch für Geschichte von Staat, Wirtschaft und Gesellschaft
Lateinamerikas*, iv (1967), pp. 386–98.
[55] Quoted in Boxer, *Salvador de Sá*, pp. 77–81.
[56] Rodríguez Vicente, *El Tribunal del Consulado de Lima*, p. 75; James
Boyajian, *Portuguese Bankers at the Court of Spain* (New Brunswick, N.J.,
1983), pp. 122–4.

for losses in their own, Spaniards reasserted their traditional exclusivism in the Indies. They were moved not merely by national
and religious emotions but also by a distinct awareness that the
Spanish Indies were themselves contracting economically, particularly from 1629, when the trend of prices and of trade went
into reverse and when a period of easy profits gave way to one of
acute difficulty. Between the 1580s and the 1620s, during its long
phase of expansion, the Spanish empire had easily absorbed Portuguese immigrants; but now that there was less cake to share
the guests were unwelcome.[57] Harassment of the Portuguese
mounted throughout the 1630s and when, early in 1641, news of
the revolt of Portugal reached Spanish America colonial officials
were already poised to punish the immigrants by fiscal discrimination, property confiscation, and in some cases expulsion.[58]

By 1640 the Portuguese had reasons, convincing to themselves
if not to Spaniards, to reject the union with Spain. They also had
the opportunity. Naval losses in the battle of the Downs (October 1639) and at Pernambuco (January 1640) had stripped Spain's
Atlantic defences and deprived her of a naval arm against Lisbon;
now the revolt of Catalonia pinned down the remnants of her
military forces. Richelieu had already promised the Portuguese
French assistance in the event of a revolt, and they hoped that
the Dutch would ease the pressure on their colonial territory if
they declared their independence of Spain. The Portuguese had
another asset in the person of Dom John, seventh Duke of Braganza, who, weak and vacillating though he was, could claim dynastic rights to the Portuguese throne and was a symbol of national
unity. He had been pressed for some time by a group of influential nobility to proclaim himself king, and when Olivares
attempted to lure the nobility out of the country both he and
his supporters were forced to commit themselves. They did so on
1 December 1640 when the Duke of Braganza was proclaimed
King John IV of Portugal in Lisbon.[59] Although there was some
attachment to Spain among elements of the nobility, higher clergy
and merchants, there was no real opposition to independence, and
it was received with positive enthusiasm by the mass of the

[57] Chaunu, Autour de 1640', p. 54.
[58] Borah, 'The Portuguese of Tulancingo', p. 394.
[59] On the Portuguese independence movement see Peres, ed., *História de
Portugal*, v–vi; Virginia Rau, *D. Catalina de Bragança* (Lisbon, 1941).

people. It also had the influential support of the Portuguese Jesuits, who played an important role in the movement and perhaps a decisive one in rallying Brazil to the cause in the early months of 1641.[60]

As long as the Catalan front absorbed Spain's energies within the peninsula she had no chance of recovering Portugal. For the moment therefore she had to remain on the defensive against the Portuguese until she were free to reduce them. Equally the Portuguese were not in a position to wage offensive war on Spain, even had John IV so wished. They had to give priority to the defence of Brazil, for it was the sugar trade which chiefly financed their independence and their armed forces. The major threat to their colonial life-line came from the Dutch, not from Spain. The Dutch concluded a ten-year truce with Portugal in June 1641, but far from helping her against the common enemy they exploited her difficulties. In August 1641 they occupied Luanda, the base of the Angola slave trade, thus threatening to starve Portuguese Brazil of its plantation labour.[61] Dependent now on their own initiative, the Portuguese began to fight back. In 1648 they reconquered Luanda; in 1654 they recovered Recife and expelled the Dutch from Brazil. Now they were free to focus on Spain. With the death of John IV (6 November 1656) and the regency of his widow, Doña Luisa de Guzmán, they adopted a more belligerent policy, if only to show France their value as allies and to dissuade her from making a separate peace with Spain.[62] While Spanish sea power was tied down in war with Cromwell's England, the Portuguese invaded Spain in 1657 and seriously threatened Badajoz; in January 1659 they themselves were invaded but inflicted a shattering defeat on the Spanish army at Elvas. France deserted Portugal at the Peace of the Pyrenees in 1659 and hardly compensated by allowing the dispatch of volunteers under Count Schom-

---

[60] Boxer, *Salvador de Sá*, pp. 142–7. Although in South America the Spanish crown had been an ally of the Jesuits in their conflict with the Paulista slave-hunters, in the Far East it had followed a policy more sympathetic to the missionary methods of the Dominicans than to those of the Jesuits; see Chaunu, 'Autour de 1640', p. 55.

[61] Boxer, *Salvador de Sá*, pp. 168–70, 248–92.

[62] On Portuguese diplomacy in this period see Eduardo Brazão, *A restauração. Relações diplomáticos de Portugal de 1640 a 1688* (Lisbon, 1939); on Luso-French relations see Edgar Prestage, *The Diplomatic Relations of Portugal with France, England and Holland from 1640 to 1688* (Watford, 1925), pp. 1–98.

berg. It was the English alliance of 1661 which rescued Portugal from her diplomatic isolation; she now secured the support of English sea power and the assistance of an English military contingent.

For Spain the war was a story of unrelieved disaster. After forty years of warfare the Spanish people had not the stomach for more; they could produce neither enthusiasm, nor an army, nor suitable officers. Philip IV had to rely on German and Italian *tercios*. Even with these Don John of Austria, the victor of Catalonia, was unable to make an impression on the Portuguese, and he was defeated by Schomberg at the battle of Ameixial in June 1663. Another army was laboriously assembled under the command of a veteran soldier, the Marquis of Caracena; this too was defeated, at Vila Viçosa on 17 June 1665, a few months before the death of Philip IV. By now the war had become his war alone; with his rigidly dynastic view of sovereignty he had stubbornly clung to the belief that the Portuguese were rebel subjects, to be reduced at all costs. The government which succeeded him had neither the will nor the resources to continue. On 13 February 1668 Philip's widow, the regent Mariana of Austria, recognized the independence of Portugal.

After Olivares

The revolts of Catalonia and Portugal reduced the Count Duke's policy to dust. Olivares was a victim of economic circumstances as well as of political illusions. Between 1638 and 1641 the vital transatlantic trade suffered an emphatic collapse; if there was an ultimate turning point in Spain's economic power this was it.[63] State revenue and credit inevitably suffered. In 1640 no treasure arrived from the Indies. In 1641 the Tierra Firme fleet brought the crown only half a million ducats, to be followed by an equally meagre consignment in the New Spain fleet.[64] In each instance the crown confiscated half the private returns and compensated the merchants with vellon. The policy was self-defeating. Sequestration of private silver, combined with the rising costs of convoy

[63] Chaunu, *Séville et l'Atlantique*, viii, 2, 2, pp. 1797–1848.
[64] Domínguez Ortiz, 'Los caudales de Indias y la política exterior de Felipe IV', pp. 358–60.

defence, encouraged yet greater recourse to fraud, aggravated the crisis in the Indies trade, and thus reduced the pickings available to the crown. From 1640 state finances were in chaos; the public had been taxed dry; and there were two new fronts to be supplied.[65] Vellon issues were recklessly increased but these so drove up the premium on silver that advances from the bankers became impossibly expensive. In September 1642, therefore, the government was forced to deflate by 25 per cent; this constituted in effect an unscrupulous form of taxation and was a further blow to private savings.[66]

These sacrifices might have been tolerable had they produced proportionate results. But the campaigns in Catalonia and Portugal revealed crass incompetence in the administration and inability to plan for predictable events. Although Olivares had always regarded war as an essential instrument of policy, he had done nothing to give Spain a military machine adequate to its needs. The professional troops were already deployed in Italy, Germany and the Low Countries. But there was virtually no organization for raising a national army in Castile. Recruits unfortunate enough to be pressed into service resembled nothing so much as a feudal host, untrained, inexperienced, and led by amateurs. As Spain came apart at the seams, Olivares worked feverishly to repair the damage, but his time was running out. In September 1642 Perpignan was lost to France. The royal army so frequently announced and so laboriously assembled, the army on which Olivares pinned all his hopes, now moved unsteadily from Aragon towards Lérida, the key to Catalonia. There it was firmly defeated and lost 5,000 men.[67] In retreat as in attack disorder was complete, and pitiful survivors reaching Zaragoza, to find neither food nor lodgings nor medicine, were visible victims of gross failure of leadership.

Failure made Olivares vulnerable. He had already alienated important political and social groups, notably the judiciary and nobility. The Council of Castile, a body composed of senior judges and lawyers, many of them of noble rank and independent means, was at the heart of this 'constitutional' conflict.[68] The

[65] Domínguez Ortiz, *Política y hacienda de Felipe IV*, pp. 62–4.
[66] Hamilton, *American Treasure and the Price Revolution in Spain*, p. 86.
[67] Sanabre, *La acción de Francia en Cataluña*, pp. 211–12.
[68] Janine Fayard, *Les membres du Conseil de Castille à l'époque modern (1621–1746)* (Geneva, 1979), pp. 10–30.

Council had the unenviable task of legalizing and applying many of the questionable fiscal measures the Count Duke adopted, such as the confiscation of private silver returns from America. As he took more and more short-cuts to solvency, so councillors and judiciary were antagonized. The judiciary belonged to a wider group, the powerful profession of *letrados*, or graduate lawyers, who were further outraged by the gradual diminution of royal justice. This was affected by a dual process. On the one hand, through administrative inertia and neglect, the crown allowed the jurisdiction of the municipal courts to expand at the expense of the royal *audiencias*. The profits of less litigation had to be shared among more officials, as the crown created and sold numerous minor clerical posts in the *chancillerías*, or high courts of justice.[69] At the same time, for short-term gain, the crown sold its own lands, taxes and jurisdiction, the so called *realengo*, assets which were often snapped up by ambitious nobles.

Olivares viewed the aristocracy with a mixture of hope and distrust, seeing them as sources of revenue and a focus of opposition. He demanded first their military collaboration, that they should join the royal army at the head of contingents raised and paid by themselves. In default of military service he would take money. As the Andalusian Marquis of Jódar was told by Philip IV in 1629: 'I charge you to provide me with as many soldiers as you can raise, and if the shortage of inhabitants does not permit this, you will let me have the money by which I can enlist and pay others.'[70] From 1630 levies were imposed on titled nobility and prelates, and the military orders were assessed for contributions. The privileged and normally exempt groups were thus taxed for the first time in a direct way, though disguised as a cash commutation of the armed service owed to the crown by the nobility. In 1632 six of the wealthiest grandees were required to equip 4,000 men each, and in 1634 eight were assessed for a unit of 1,500 each. Towards 1640, as events in Catalonia and Portugal called for desperate measures, Olivares became more dictatorial and he demanded the service of the entire nobility without exceptions. Even the king was alarmed and advised him that 'there is

[69] Richard L. Kagan, *Lawsuits and Litigants in Castile 1500–1700* (Chapel Hill, NC, 1981), pp. 220–30.
[70] Quoted by Stradling, *Philip IV*, pp. 158–9.

nothing of greater consequence than the condition of the major families of Castile.'[71] Noble families reacted in various ways. Some, like the Duke of Híjar and the Duke of Sessa, welcomed his difficulties in Catalonia and sought to exploit them. Others went further. In 1641 the Duke of Medina Sidonia, a cousin of Olivares and brother of the new queen of Portugal, headed a conspiratorial movement to oust Olivares and make Andalucía an independent kindom. The opposition of most of the nobility, however, took less eccentic forms. First they ostracized Olivares, staging in the last years of his rule a veritable *huelga de grandes* in which they abandoned court and king.[72] Then, in 1642, while Olivares was absent in Aragon, they focused their opposition more precisely and seem to have brought pressure on the king. The movement was organized by the Count of Castrillo, a member of the Haro family, who was inspired as much by personal as by political motives. For Olivares had alienated the Haros, who were closely related to him, by legitimizing a bastard son, Enrique Felípez de Guzmán, and giving him right of succession to his titles and estates.[73]

Olivares was not a defeatist. As his secretary Carnero remarked, 'even with the water over his head he keeps swimming.'[74] But even Olivares appreciated that this political career could not survive the disasters of 1640–2, and as the sources of opposition came together – cortes, municipalities, nobility and judiciary – he was realist enough to accept defeat.[75] Philip IV arranged his resignation honourably and without recrimination: on 17 January 1643 he gave him formal permission to retire on the grounds of ill health. The Count Duke left Madrid for his house at Loeches, fought a brief propaganda campaign in defence of his reputation, and was then exiled to his sister's house at Toro. There, deranged in mind and broken in body, he died on 22 July 1645. In spite of his extraordinary talents and achieve-

[71] Quoted ibid., p. 120.
[72] On the 'strike of the grandees' see Marañón, *El conde-duque de Olivares*, pp. 89–100; Elliott, *The Count-Duke of Olivares*, pp. 610, 646.
[73] Marañón, *El conde-duque de Olivares*, pp. 285–301; Elliott, *The Count-Duke of Olivares*, pp. 618–19, 631–2.
[74] Quoted by Elliott, *The Count-Duke of Olivares*, p. 280.
[75] On the fall of Olivares see Elliott, *The Count-Duke of Olivares*, pp. 640–51; Stradling, *Philip IV*, pp. 134–7.

ments, Olivares presided over failure and defeat. In Europe Spain's preeminence was passing to France. In Spain itself the attempt to reform constitutional and economic structures left the situation no better than before. Olivares was conscious of recession and sought to reverse it. He was a reformer at a bad time for reformers, when the king was weak, society resistant to change and the aristocracy avid for power. In these conditions Olivares's remedies for Spanish institutions, economy and society were ahead of their time.[76]

Superficially the new regime repudiated the rule of Olivares and all its manifestations. Yet it had the same problems and the same enemies. Did it have the same system of government? Olivares had waged a long campaign to subordinate the grandees and the conciliar bureaucracy to royal authority. Now his special juntas were dissolved, their business was returned to the councils, and the conciliar bureaucracy began to recover ground lost to *ad hoc* committees. Thus, within days of Olivares's fall, the aristocrats and bureaucrats were again asserting themselves at the centre of government.[77] Who could fill the space left by Olivares and resist the invasion of the elites? Philip IV did not appoint a new *valido* in the image and likeness of the old. Instead he made an attempt to rule personally. On the departure of the Count Duke Philip IV professed to be shocked by what he discovered of the state of his kingdoms; and he resolved that he must never again abdicate responsibility. In July 1643, on his way to the Aragon front, he met the celebrated mystic, Sor María de Agreda, with whom he corresponded for the next twenty-two years. Sor María was a highly politicized religious and from her convent she directed a flood of advice to the king on the affairs of the monarchy. She assured him that royal decisions were good, ministerial decisions usually bad; she inveighed against Olivares and denounced *validos*. Her nagging pen, naïve though it was, further stirred Philip's conscience, and he decided to work more and delegate less, 'seated in this chair, with papers before me and pen in hand, working on all the consultas sent to me and the despatches from abroad'.[78] He seemed determined not to appoint

[76] Elliott, *The Count-Duke of Olivares*, pp. 640–51, 677–82.
[77] Ibid., pp. 653–4.
[78] Philip IV to Sor María de Agreda, 30 January 1647, in Valiente, *Los validos*, p. 183.

another *valido*. In the decree which announced the retirement of Olivares he stated: 'The moment is opportune to inform the Council that such a good minister must be replaced only by me myself, since our present difficulties require all my personal attention for their remedy.'[79]

Philip's resolution soon came under strain. His judgement did not suddenly improve or the process of government become less complex. He needed advisers and ministers, whatever they were called. These he took from a group of noble councillors from whom emerged favourites, if not a unique favourite.[80] The nearest to approach such a position was Luis de Haro, nephew of Olivares, a discreet and modest man, then in his mid-forties, whose rise to power was less flamboyant than that of Olivares and less complete. Philip had been a friend of Haro since childhood and he admired his qualities. Soon he was not only taking his advice but accepting his decisions. By mid-1643 Haro was recognized by observers if not as the successor of Olivares, certainly as a *primus inter pares*. His peers, too, were favourites of a kind, such as the Duke of Medina Torres, who accumulated offices, established a *clientela* and offered alternative advice. But Haro seemed to have more staying power, was perceived as a threat to no one, king or nobility, and was never dismissed. Philip was too ashamed and Haro too discreet to acknowledge his special position, and they avoided the terms *valido* and minister. The king guiltily reassured the disapproving Sor María: 'I have always refused to give him the character of minister, in order to avoid previous mistakes.'[81] Nevertheless by 1647 Haro had acquired almost as many functions as Olivares. He was assisted by a *junta de estado*, which met in his own house as his uncle's had done. Although he was not a member of the Council of State he directed its affairs from outside; and he controlled state papers and their distribution between councils in much the same way as previous *validos*. In general he had the same power as Olivares, though perhaps there was a new

[79] 'Comunicación del Rey al Consejo de la Cámara', 24 January 1643, in Marañón, *El conde-duque de Olivares*, p. 464.

[80] Stradling, *Philip IV*, pp. 246–7, 267, distinguishes between *privados*, or close advisers, who continued to be employed by Philip IV, and a *valido*, or unique favourite, who did not exist after 1643. 'The age of the *valido* had come to an end with the passing of Olivares.'

[81] See note 78 above.

division of labour between king and *valido*, with the king attending to more business than he had previously done. Haro had no official titles and did not even use the personal ones he inherited from his uncle. But by the late 1650s Philip was referring to him in state papers as his *primer ministro*; in the Treaty of the Pyrenees he spoke of him as his *primer y principal ministro*.[82] Although the title was a general and occasional one, Haro was in fact first minister and remained such until his death in 1661. Philip IV did not replace him. In the last five years of his reign, either because he found no one to trust or because the call of duty now appealed more than the pleasures of the flesh, he retained personal direction of government, taking advice from many, giving power to none. As the crown freed itself from political control by a dominant *valido* and his faction, so it gradually rebuilt its relations with the rest of the nobility, reducing Olivares-type demands for money and military service, diverting their ambitions away from the centre of power, and leaving them to lord it in their local domains.[83]

If the new regime brought few governmental innovations, it did little to reorientate Spain's foreign policy. The replacement of Olivares could not work miracles. The war continued to devour men and money, and Castile still bore the brunt. Subsidies from the cortes, forced loans, sale of offices, manipulation of the currency, all the devices favoured by the old regime were also practised by the new. The only difference was that where Olivares ranted Haro reasoned. As long as the demands of war were paramount, however, reason had its limits; there was no opportunity to stop and reorganize public finances. By the beginning of 1644 the crown's income was pledged up to 1648. *Asientos* contracted for 1644 amounted to 5.3 million escudos – over 2 million for the Low Countries, the remainder for Germany, Italy and internal administration. But a further 3 million was needed for the armies on the Catalan and Portuguese fronts and for the royal household. It was therefore decided to sell in the form of *juros* the recent 1 per cent increase in the *alcabala* tax. Corregidores were instructed to seek the consent of the towns represented in the cortes but not to assemble the *cabildos* until they were sure of

[82] Valiente, *Las validos*, pp. 20, 185–6.
[83] Stradling, *Philip IV*, pp. 167–71.

getting a favourable vote; if the *cabildos* were not persuaded by the state of the treasury then they were to be told that the king ordered the measure by virtue of his rights under divine and human law.[84] Spanish constitutionalism was as defunct as ever.

The situation in 1645–6 was more or less the same and Haro continued to raise extraordinary revenue by executive measures. The estimate of projected expenditure in 1647 was 12.7 million ducats, while available revenue was 7 million short of this. All essential foodstuffs were already overtaxed; forced loans were bringing diminishing returns; and it was not known when the Indies fleets would arrive. Before 1646 was out the Spaniards at great cost forced France to raise the siege of Lérida, but in the Low Countries they lost Dunkirk, and in 1647 there was a revolution in Naples. Available revenue for the next four years was already assigned to bankers and there was nothing with which to make immediate *asientos*. So the crown had to declare the second bankruptcy of the reign, twenty years after the first. By suspending payments and freeing pledged income the crown at once procured some 10 million ducats. The *asentistas*, who were indemnified with *juros*, suffered great losses, particularly the Portuguese and the Genoese; but the four royal factors – Spinola, Imbrea, Centurión and Palavesia – were exempt in order not to deprive them of the means of making further *asientos*.

War and Peace

The political and financial disasters of the 1640s, not the fall of Olivares, forced Spain eventually to re-think her foreign policy and reduce her commitments abroad. There was no thought of retreat from basic objectives, and Philip IV was determined that his subjects should fight on until these were achieved. But there was a readjustment of priorities and a renewed search for peace. First the Spaniards accepted what they had long suspected, that the Habsburg alliance was obsolete. As the Thirty Years War dragged on the rift between Madrid and Vienna became wider. By the early 1640s they no longer had the same war aims. For Spain

---

[84] Domínguez Ortiz, *Política y hacienda de Felipe IV*, pp. 64–8.

the principal danger came from France and the United Provinces; for the emperor the main enemy was Sweden. Spain resented her precious subsidies being absorbed by the Swedish war and from 1640 she drastically reduced them. She also resented the emperor's failure to support her position in the Palatinate and his readiness to sacrifice her interests there to conciliate France and Sweden, as he did in 1648.

The Habsburg alliance had been expensive to Spain and had brought her few returns. She could now concentrate what resource she had on the French and Dutch fronts. Unfortunately, owing to the collapse of the Spanish-American trade from 1638, the Spanish forces in the Low Countries could no longer count on the treasure of the Indies.[85] In 1643 the army under Francisco de Melo, Portuguese governor of the Spanish Netherlands, went into action against the French without adequate cavalry, because horses were too expensive. On 19 May at Rocroi it was defeated and routed by the young French commander, the Duke of Enghien, and suffered 14,000 casualties in dead and wounded; although the mercenaries turned and fled, the Spanish veterans fought to the death. Rocroi has acquired a legendary reputation as the greatest defeat ever suffered by the incomparable Spanish infantry, and it is often taken to mark the end of Spain's military power. But one battle in a war which had already lasted twenty-five years and still had another fifteen to run could not have transcendental significance. There was still plenty of fight left in Spain. Her military effort in the Low Countries did not slacken and although she suffered further reverses, including the loss of Dunkirk, she managed to maintain her position in the southern Netherlands. There, in spite of the bankruptcies, mutinies and failures, Spain had a record of financial and military organization second to none in Europe. The massive revenue injections, the military supply routes, the machinery for army welfare and maintenance, all developed and sustained over seventy years were a great feat of military organization which constituted a kind of victory. Overseas the Dutch still found Spanish colonial defences impenetrable, and their expedition to Chile in 1642 was a conspicuous failure. But the Spanish government was reluctantly forced to conclude

[85] Chaunu, 'Seville et la "Belgique" (1555–1648)', p. 277.

that it could not fight the United Provinces and France simultaneously. In July 1644 Philip IV issued a decree informing his ministers that owing to lack of resources he wished peace to be concluded on all fronts as soon as possible. But Spain's enemies knew this and exploited her weakness. France in particular was a difficult enemy to deal with and likely to be even more difficult if, as now seemed possible, she made peace with the emperor and concentrated her attack on Spain. So Spain anticipated the Peace of Westphalia, which brought the Thirty Years War to a close, by making a separate peace with the Dutch in January 1648. It was a logical step to take. The greatest threat to her peninsular security came from France; and Mazarin's demands, including a proposal to send auxiliaries to the Portuguese rebels across Spanish territory, were plainly intolerable.[86] By January 1648 the Spanish government had reached agreement with the Dutch on the general terms of a peace treaty, and these formed the basis of the Treaty of Munster of 24 October 1648. Spain recognized the United Provinces as a sovereign, independent state; she procured neither the opening of the Scheldt nor official toleration for Roman Catholics, two of her more important peace aims; and she explicitly recognized the right of the Dutch to conquer all the Portuguese colonial territory to which they laid claim, although in Spanish eyes the Portuguese were still subjects of Philip IV.[87] Spain retained the southern Netherlands, and detached the Dutch from the French alliance. It seemed a meagre result from a war of eighty years.

The recognition of Dutch independence, though galling to Spain, was merely a recognition of long-standing facts. It was designed to isolate France at a time when that country was also weakened by domestic instability. In the event Spain was unable to exploit the anti-Mazarin Fronde, as she did not have the resources for a major effort. But at least she recovered Dunkirk and began the recovery of Catalonia. The war called for further sacrifices from Castile. The crown seized 1 million ducats of private returns from the Indies, anticipated revenue up to 1655,

---

[86] On peace with the Dutch see Parker, *The Army of Flanders and the Spanish Road*, p. 261. On Spanish policy at Westphalia see Fraga Iribarne, *Don Diego de Saavedra y Fajardo y la diplomacia de su época*, pp. 564–91.
[87] Boxer, *The Dutch Seaborne Empire*, p. 27.

and in November 1651 increased vellon to the level of the pre-1642 deflation.[88] The subsequent price rise was aggravated by poor grain crops; in Andalucía there were serious disturbances, and Seville was at the mercy of the mob for several days. In 1652 the government deflated again, but by now vellon was utterly discredited and monetary disorder could hardly be worse. Estimated expenditure for 1653 – 11.3 million ducats – was far in excess of the revenue from ordinary taxation, forced loans and sale of offices. So the government decreed yet another suspension of payments. At this point, if Spain had been able to finance a supreme war effort, she could probably have won a favourable peace, before France recovered from political instability and agricultural distress and before she was joined by England. As it was, Spain barely had the resources to maintain her positions on the various fronts. In the cortes of 1655 the speech from the throne stated that it had not been possible to reach a general peace; it enumerated the positions recovered in Italy, the Low Countries and Catalonia; and it pointed out that insurrections in Sicily and Naples had also been overcome. Defence costs from 1649 to 1654 had totalled 66.8 million escudos, and these had been met without imposing new taxes, 'whatever other means His Majesty has been forced to use with his prerogative'. In preference to new taxes the king requested 'a universal means which would yield the same yet would fall on those with personal fortunes and not on the poor beggar, the labourer, the artisan and other people who can only support themselves with their labour'. The cortes, of course, was the last institution from which to expect support for such a tax; it simply voted a renewal of previous subsidies, with an additional 2 million ducats in sale of offices, and financial reform was left for another day. Yet the demands of war drove the crown to impose one fiscal innovation which had social significance. In 1657 it imposed a *media anata* tax (a sum equal to half a year's income) on all grants, pensions and annuities bestowed by Philip IV and his predecessors, exempting only those serving in the armed forces, their dependants, and disabled ex-servicemen. This was the kind of tax which the gentry-dominated cortes had always

---

[88] Domínguez Ortiz, 'Los caudales de Indias y la política exterior de Felipe IV', pp. 366–8, and *Política y hacienda de Felipe IV*, pp. 68–75.

opposed; it was used frequently by Philip IV and his successor, though the nobility exerted their influence to procure exemption, and it yielded progressively lower returns.[89]

While Spain did not have the means for a major offensive, she was still capable of defending herself, and it is a comment on the alleged waning of her military power that she fought France to a stalemate. At this point, however, the military balance was tipped against Spain by the entry of England into the war. The Spanish government had reason to expect a more propitious outcome from its English policy, which was determined by pragmatism not ideology. In the 1640s Philip IV followed a policy of strict neutrality towards the English civil war, and he showed little sympathy for the Stuart cause. He quickly recognized the new republic and, appreciating its threat to the balance of power, was prepared to buy its alliance, or at least neutrality, at almost any price. But Cromwell's price was too high. He wanted an explicit statement of religious toleration towards Englishmen resident in Spain and the admission of English merchants to direct partici-pation in the Spanish colonial trade. These were gratuitous de-mands: the religious problem had been dealt with in previous treaties and Englishmen had an indirect trade with the Spanish Indies through re-exports from Seville. Indeed the demands were so provocative that they were presumably designed to be rejected. As if to emphasize the point, Cromwell raised them still higher, to include the cession of Calais and Dunkirk.

Cromwell seems to have decided on war with Spain as early as April 1654; from August he was planning a marauding expedition and in December, without declaration of war, this was dispatched with instructions 'to assault the Spaniard in the West Indies'. The operation was ill-planned and badly executed; its commanders failed to overcome Spanish defences at Hispaniola, the principal target, and had to be content with the capture of Jamaica.[90] Meanwhile another English squadron patrolled off Cadiz, waiting to intercept the silver fleets. Philip IV was incredulous. In June 1655 he dismissed warnings from the Duke of Medina that de-

---

[89] Domínguez Ortiz, *Política y hacienda de Felipe IV*, p. 74.

[90] On Cromwell's 'Western Design' see I. A. Wright, ed., *Spanish Narratives of the English Attack on Santo Domingo* (Camden Miscellany, xiv, London, 1926); J. M. Incháustegui, *La gran expedición inglesa contra las Antilles Mayores. Tomo I: El plan antillano de Cromwell, 1651–1655* (Mexico, 1953).

fence measures were needed: 'It is unbelievable that the English
would break public faith and the peace with exists between the
two nations; it is therefore unnecessary to take major defensive
measures.'[91] He was even ready to overlook – for the time being
at least – the conquest of Jamaica if that would facilitate peace
with England. But Cromwell did not want peace.

It was Spain's ultimate misforture, after a long and gruelling
war, to be suddenly confronted by a new military power whose
foreign policy was dominated by motives of gain and godliness
and who seized upon Spain as the most likely target for both.
Philip IV was forced into a war with England which he did not
seek. In September 1655 an embargo was placed on English
property in Spain and in December it was decided to apply the
proceeds from its sale to naval defence. The need was urgent, for
Spain's maritime communications were now vulnerable to English
naval power. In September 1656 a detachment of Blake's squadron intercepted the returning Tierra Firme fleet almost within
sight of Cadiz, captured the *capitana* and a merchantman, took
booty estimated at 2 million pesos and sank other valuable units.
The New Spain fleet was forewarned and took refuge in Santa
Cruz de Tenerife; there, on 30 April 1657, it too was sought out
by Blake and almost totally destroyed, with the loss of its cargo
and treasure.[92] For two years therefore no silver fleet reached
Spain, while her foreign trade was paralysed by the enemy blockade of the peninsula and control of the English channel. Spain
was now completely isolated, with two major enemies and not a
single ally. Yet in 1656 there was a distinct opportunity of peace
with France; Catalonia had now been recovered and the French
promised not to assist the Portuguese. Against the advice of his
ministers Philip IV refused to negotiate, insisting on conditions as
unreasonable as those which Cromwell demanded of Spain.[93]
Spain was severely punished for his folly. In June 1658 a combined French and English army overwhelmed the Spaniards at the

[91] Quoted in Domínguez Ortiz, 'España ante la Paz de los Pirineos', *Hispania*, xix (1959), p. 548. In fact the 1655 silver fleet got through safely.
[92] See C. H. Firth, *The Last Years of the Protectorate*, 1656–1658 (2 vols,
London, 1909), ii, pp. 260–1, who, however, exaggerates the significance of the
disaster; the transatlantic trade had suffered so many reverses in the last two
decades that one year's loss could hardly be decisive.
[93] F. J. Routledge, *England and the Treaty of the Pyrenees* (Liverpool, 1953),
p. 9.

battle of the Dunes and took Dunkirk. The Spanish Netherlands, their subsidy already cut from 3 to 1 million escudos a year, were now seriously exposed. And in the peninsula the Portuguese, by their victory at Elvas, added to Spain's retribution.

As the country reeled under these successive blows, Philip IV's ministers urged him to end the agony; Don John of Austria in the Netherlands, the councils in Madrid, Haro, the primate of Spain, all gave the same advice.[94] As for his subjects, from the aristocracy to the poorest peasant, they had long ceased to believe that the war bore any relation to their interests, and they had lost their military vocation. The final campaigns, even within the peninsula, were fought mainly by Italian conscripts, with Irish and German mercenaries. Want of money to pay for these various armies was reason enough for peace. Mazarin was seeking a solution, and the English government, reluctant further to assist France, was not averse to one. But even now Philip IV was loath to negotiate, and if France had not modified her demands he would have ordered his subjects to fight on. He was eventually moved, not by the sufferings of his people much less by financial distress, but by yet another illusion – that peace with France and England would enable him to isolate and reduce the Portuguese. He therefore agreed to an armistice in May 1659 and the Peace of the Pyrenees was signed on 7 November. The treaty provided for the marriage of Philip IV's daughter, María Teresa, to the king of France. Spain ceded to France territory in the Netherlands and, more significantly, Cerdagne and Roussillon in Catalonia. Further cessions, among them Artois, marked the end of Spanish control over the imperial route from Milan to the Netherlands.[95] In its territorial provisions, however, the treaty was not a disaster for Spain. Its principal defect was that it came years too late.

Experience taught Philip IV no lessons. It is true that after Olivares he made a determined effort to rule personally and to reassure his doubting subjects, not only by leading his armies in Aragon but also by intervening directly in government. His fortitude amidst public adversity and private grief earned him some sympathy when, in 1644, he lost his queen, Isabel, and two

[94] For the advice of the *junta de estado* see ibid., p. 17.
[95] Ibid., pp. 67–70, 81; see also Juan Reglà, 'El tratado de los Pirineos de 1659', *Hispania*, xiii (1953), pp. 101–66.

years later his only son and heir Baltasar Carlos. Otherwise his subjects were not convinced. The king *appeared* to be more conscientious, but basic policy objectives were unchanged, the war continued, and the monarchy was still dismembered. The political philosophy which informed his decisions remained unaffected by the events of 1640–59. He had no conception of a national monarchy transcending dynastic interests. Although he professed a love of his subjects and a desire to alleviate their miseries, he saw himself primarily as the representative of the Habsburg dynasty, charged with the preservation of its possessions. These he regarded essentially as an estate entailed in perpetuity, and he shrank from the responsibility of alienating or losing any part of his sacred inheritance. It never occurred to him to ask whether the continued possession of the Netherlands or Portugal was of any benefit to his Spanish subjects. His only criterion was his legal rights. This accounts for his almost total subordination of domestic to foreign policy and for his stubborn commitment to war in defence of Habsburg property. In 1648 he reluctantly abandoned the war with the Dutch in order to concentrate on that with France. Six years later, still at war with France, he acquired a second enemy, England. Now, in 1659, he ended Spain's forty-year war simply to fight another one, against Portugal. Again he miscalculated, for the Portuguese quickly escaped from their isolation and secured an alliance with England which enabled them successfully to defend their independence. The Portuguese war dealt the death blow to the crown's tottering finances. The campaign cost an estimated 5 million ducats a year. From 1660 to 1665, in a final orgy of taxation, the government wildly employed every unsound device known to Habsburg administration – taxes on *juros*, currency manipulation, increase of the *alcabala*, further taxes on foodstuffs, anticipation of revenue and, in 1662, yet another suspension of payments.[96] By 1664 the crown's total indebtedness amounted to 21.6 million ducats. Philip IV bequeathed to his successor an empty treasury, a discredited currency, and a multitude of new taxes already alienated to financiers. And Portugal remained independent.

Philip IV died on 17 September 1665. The last months of his life were marred by acute melancholia. His subjects too had little

[96] Domínguez Ortiz, *Política y hacienda de Felipe IV*, pp. 81–5.

cause for rejoicing. The political future looked unpromising, for Philip left, if not a succession problem, at least a problem successor, his son Charles, a child of his old age, who was destined to be the most degenerate of all the Spanish Habsburgs. Spaniards would look in vain for new leadership. Economic prospects were also bleak. Spain had been at war for almost half a century. The people had been taxed and conscripted beyond endurance, the population ravaged by epidemic disease, and the colonial life-line badly frayed. Excessive investment in war did not bring comparable returns. Some assets remained. The Spanish colonial empire was still intact, territorially at least. And Spain's military power, though badly eroded, was not extinct. In had taken the combined efforts of France and England to force her to the peace table in 1659 and neither could have done it alone. But basically Spain had nothing to show for her efforts in northern and central Europe. The Habsburg alliance was dead, imperial communications were meaningless; and if Spain retained the southern Netherlands it was less because of her military presence than because the other powers could not agree on an alternative sovereignty.

Nations can recover from the consequences of war and renew their life. But Spain's prostration was so prolonged that it points to a deeper malaise. War and taxation merely placed additional burdens on a society already carrying a dead-weight of privilege and on an economy already weakened by structural defects.

6

Society and Economy

Population and Pestilence

At the end of the seventeenth century there were fewer people in Spain than there had been at the beginning. By the 1590s the demographic upswing of the sixteenth century had spent itself. The population was then about 8.4 million. In 1717 it was 7.6 million.[1] The rest of Europe too suffered demographic recession, or stagnation, in the seventeenth century, but nowhere did reverses begin so early, last so long or attain such proportions as they did in Spain.[2] How can we explain this catastrophe? War, famine and pestilence were not exclusive to the seventeenth century; birth control, though not unknown, was hardly practised; and the birth-rate was normally high in Spain, in spite of the incidence of celibacy. A deficit of this magnitude, most of it in the first half of the century, could only be the result of an exceptional concurrence of adversities.

The secular demographic trend was not the same in every part of Spain. Most of the non-Castilian regions suffered stagnation rather than loss. In Valencia the expulsion of the moriscos

---

[1] A careful discussion of the sources and methods for the study of Spanish demographic history in this period, and considered estimates, are provided by Domínguez Ortiz, *La sociedad española en el siglo XVII*, pp. 53–157; see also Jordi Nadal, *La población española (siglos xvi a xx)* (3rd edn., Barcelona, 1973), pp. 16, 37–88; María F. Carbajo Isla, *La población de la Villa de Madrid. Desde finales del siglo XVI hasta mediados del siglo XIX* (Madrid, 1987).

[2] See Karl F. Helleiner, 'The Population of Europe from the Black Death to the Eve of the Vital Revolution', *The Cambridge Economic History of Europe*, iv (Cambridge, 1967), pp. 1–95.

reduced the population from approximately 450,000 to 300,000; by mid-century the vacuum had still not been filled when the province was struck by plague. At the end of the century Valencia probably had between 350,000 and 400,000 inhabitants.[3] Catalonia, like other parts of Spain, suffered from plague and famine; the principality was a battlefield from 1640, losing Rosellón in 1659; and French immigration, which had previously boosted its numbers, was much reduced in the second half of the century. In 1700, therefore, the population of Catalonia was between 400,000 and 450,000, no larger than it had been in 1600.[4] Aragon, where the moriscos were less numerous than in Valencia, recovered more quickly from their expulsion, but poor economic conditions caused a downward demographic trend after 1650. The relative immunity of Navarre and the Basque provinces from the great plagues was counterbalanced by their primitive economy which forced many younger sons to emigrate, and here too the population remained stationary, roughly 350,000 throughout the century. In the 1590s the population of the non-Castilian regions totalled some 1,785,000. A century later it was probably slightly less than this.

The greatest blows were reserved for Castile, and within Castile for its heartland. The periphery provinces – Galicia, Asturias, Andalucía and Murcia – escaped the worst incidence of depopulation. Some regions, for local reasons, differed from the general pattern of Castile; the province of Mondoñedo in Galicia experienced an increase of 15–20 per cent between 1587 and 1631, and stronger growth subsequently, with a pause in 1650–69.[5] The most vulnerable region was the arid and infertile central plateau, and it was this which bore the brunt of the deficit; Old Castile, New Castile and Extremadura all suffered grievous losses. Disaster was absolute. No doubt there was some shift of population towards less depressed regions and overseas; but most of the missing Castilians died of hunger or disease or in war, and adverse economic conditions retarded their replacement. Disaster was also sudden. It began in the 1590s, and sixty years later the worst was over. At the beginning of this period the population of

[3] Lapeyre, *Géographie*, pp. 30, 203–5; see above, pp. 59–64.
[4] Nadal and Giralt, *La population catalane de 1553 à 1717*, pp. 19–23, 337.
[5] Pegerto Saavedra, *Economía, política y sociedad en Galicia: La provincia de Mondoñedo, 1480–1830* (Madrid, 1985), pp. 66–70.

Castile was about 6,600,000. Between 1591 and 1614 severe epidemics and the expulsion of the moriscos reduced this number by 600,000–700,000, or about one-tenth. In 1630–2 plague and famine caused further heavy losses. From 1640 civil wars combined with the famine and epidemics of 1647–52 reduced the population of Castile to its lowest point, and it was now that Andalucía suffered its worst catastrophe. In 1665 the population of Castile was little more than 5 million, which was also the figure yielded by the censuses at the beginning of the eighteenth century. After the damaging years 1677–83, when disease and climatic adversity again struck Castile, the population tended to level off, with perhaps a slight tendency to rise.[6]

Spaniards were at the mercy of disease and the elements. The basic cause of demographic recession was an abnormally high mortality-rate, and the chief killer was epidemic disease.[7] Small-pox, typhus, dysentery and other malignant diseases all played their part in pushing up the death-rates. But the greatest enemy was plague, principally bubonic plague carried by flea-infested rats. The virulence of disease was enhanced by two conditions endemic in Spanish life. Periodic subsistence crises, the fate of a people who neglected arable farming, caused extreme malnutrition and lowered resistance to infection. And excessive urbanization, leading to overcrowding, working-class slums and neglect of hygiene, made Spanish towns breeding-grounds of disease.

The outbreak of 1596–1602, the first major epidemic of the period, devoured northern and central Spain and Andalucía. From December 1596 it attacked Santander, carried to the port by vessels from the Netherlands. In 1597 the infection travelled to San Sebastian and began to spread inexorably inland. In the course of the next three years it moved over Old and New Castile, striking Bilbao, Aranda de Duero, Burgos, Segovia, Madrid, Valladolid, Toledo, and dozens of smaller towns and villages, until it reached the centre and the south of Spain. The plague came in the wake of poor harvests and food shortages, to com-

---

[6] Domínguez Ortiz, *La sociedad española en el siglo XVII*, graph facing p. 112; for the 1590s see Annie Molinié-Bertrand, *Au Siècle d'Or. L'Espagne et ses Hommes. La Population du Royaume de Castille au XVIe Siècle* (Paris, 1985), p. 307.

[7] Pérez Moreda, *Las crisis de mortalidad en la España interior. Siglos XVI–XIX*, pp. 452–71.

munities already enfeebled by poverty and depression. In some towns the impact was catastrophic. Santander suffered 2,500 deaths in a population of 4,000. Valladolid lost about 6,500 of its people, or 18 per cent in four months, Madrid 3,500, or about 10 per cent, in eight months of 1599 alone. The social distribution of mortality was predictable. The rich and powerful could flee to other parts of Spain or isolate themselves in the security of their country estates; the great majority of the victims were the poor and the undernourished. Altogether about 500,000 people died in the northern plague.[8] Its successor, the great plague of 1647–52, struck chiefly eastern Spain and Andalucía. It first penetrated Valencia – perhaps from Algiers – and killed 30,000 people. From there it spread relentlessly to Andalucía and finally swept through Aragon and Catalonia. Andalucía was devastated. On the coast Málaga alone lost 40,000 people. Seville neglected quarantine measures and was contaminated in 1649; entire streets, whole districts were emptied of their inhabitants, and the city was brought to a standstill. Seville and its rural environs probably lost a quarter of their 600,000 people; the economy suffered a permanent shock.[9] Altogether Spain lost about 500,000 people in this monstrous epidemic. Twenty-five years later, between 1676 and 1685, the country was again visited by lethal disease, and again Valencia and Andalucía were the foci of infection. The poor harvests of 1682–3 caused famine conditions, weakening resistance and prolonging the crisis. This, the final great plague of the seventeenth century, claimed about 250,000 victims, and brought the total epidemic losses for the century to at least 1,250,000.

The spectre of death haunted Spain in the seventeenth century. Compared with disease other adversities were of minor significance, but they mounted in conjunction a further assault on human resources. The expulsion of the moriscos varied in its effects from region to region. The total deficit was in the order of 275,000.[10] Castile's share of this was relatively small; but Aragon lost 20 per cent of its population and Valencia 30 per cent.

---

[8] Bartolomé Bennassar, *Recherches sur les grandes épidémies dans le Nord de l'Espagne à la fin du XVIe siècle* (Paris, 1969), pp. 49–53.

[9] A. Domínguez Ortiz, *Orto y ocaso de Sevilla. Estudio sobre la prosperidad y decadencia de la ciudad en los siglos XVI y XVII* (Sevilla, 1946).

[10] This is the estimate of Lapeyre; Domínguez Ortiz would raise the figure to 300,000; see above, pp. 59–60, 64–5.

Repopulation of Valencia was slow, incomplete and chiefly at the expense of other parts of the province, for harsh seigneurial conditions were a deterrent to new colonists. Castilians would be more likely to emigrate to America than to Valencia. How many of them did so is open to speculation. Contemporaries had the impression that shoals of emigrants crossed the Atlantic every year, leaving in their wake an empty Castile. But the impression was misleading. Surviving evidence indicates that 150,000 emigration permits were issued during the entire colonial period; of these the seventeenth century would account for perhaps 40,000, or an average of 400 a year.[11] The figure is manifestly too low: the documentation itself is incomplete, and of its nature it fails to record the large number of illegal emigrants. A mixture of calculation and guess-work produces an estimate of 4,000 to 5,000 emigrants a year, an insignificant number in a population of 7 million.[12] But most of them probably came from Castile, and they were a further drain on the region's resources.

The demographic consequences of war cannot be precisely computed. As a warrior nation Spain obviously suffered heavy casualties: in the first half of the seventeenth century she was engaged in almost continuous warfare. But war was not total; the mass of the people were not in the firing-line, nor were they at first conscripted. Spain had forces fighting in the Low Countries, Germany, Italy, and on the French frontier. These were professional troops, with a hard core of volunteers and large numbers of foreign mercenaries. Her naval forces too consisted of professionals. The balance of naval warfare was moving against Spain, and her seamen, particularly in major defeats like the battle of the Downs (1639), suffered heavy casualties in the course of the century. All these, however, could be regarded as the normal hazards of the regular services. From 1635 the situation changed.

---

[11] For discussion of the evidence see Domínguez Ortiz, *La sociedad española en el sigo XVII*, pp. 86–91, and G. Céspedes del Castillo, 'Las Indias en el siglo XVII', in J. Vicens Vives, ed., *Historia social y económica de España y América* (5 vols, Barcelona, 1957–9), iii, p. 497; see also Lynch, *Spain 1516–1598*, pp. 213–14, and below, p. 230.

[12] The estimate is that of Domínguez Ortiz, *La sociedad española en el siglo XVII*, p. 90. Another estimate, suggesting 200,000 emigrants for the period 1601–50, approximates to this; see Magnus Mörner, 'La emigración española al Nuevo Mundo antes de 1810. Un informe del estado de la investigación', *Anuario de Estudios Americanos*, 32 (1975), pp. 43–131.

War with France forced the government to extend the range of its recruitment, to mobilize nobility, gentry and their retainers, to call up town militias, to take a quota of conscripts from each community. From 1640 the peninsula itself became a theatre of war, and Castile's conflict with Catalonia and Portugal assumed the character, if not of total war, at least of war to the death, with large-scale pillage and devastation, killing of prisoners and heavy conscription. For the Catalan front the government aimed at drafting 12,000 men a year in Castile by quotas from each district. The burden fell most heavily on the poorer classes, for the nobility and the rich paid for a substitute or bought an office which carried exemption from military service. The war with Portugal was fought at first by a series of skirmishes along the lengthy frontier and was largely a holding operation. Even so it exacted a heavy toll and civilian casualties were large; Galicia in particular was subject to constant conscription. After 1659 the attempt to reconquer Portugal was made with small armies composed largely of foreign troops.

The greatest military effort, therefore, was concentrated in the years 1635–59, and it was in this period that war-time mortality rates were highest. But death came by stealth rather than assault. For war bred disease and famine and then perpetuated them. It is probable that more people died from the secondary effects of war, from pestilence and malnutrition, than from the sword and the bullet. In Aragon the presence of the army and court in 1645–50 devastated the countryside, through consumption of crops, confiscation of animals and transport, and conscription of labourers, and was itself the cause of a subsistence crisis. The epidemic of 1651 then struck a population enfeebled by hunger, and Aragon's fate exemplified the classic combination of war, famine and plague, which reduced the region to a subsistence economy. In Zaragoza alone more than 6,000 people died in 1652–3.[13] In general the casualties of war are difficult to calculate, but a reasoned estimate places the average casualty rate (including Catalonia) at 20,000 a year, which gives a total of 288,000 for the crucial twenty-four years.[14] The presumption of heavy casualties

[13] Jesús Maiso González, *La peste aragonesa de 1648 a 1654* (Zaragoza, 1982), pp. 27–8, 109, 117, 124–5, 140.
[14] Domínguez Ortiz, *La sociedad española en el siglo XVII*, p. 95.

is reinforced by the abnormally high proportion of widows registered in the census of 1646; in Mérida, Extremadura, for example, widows constituted one-sixth of the population.

The syndrome of plague, famine and war brought demographic
catastrophe to Spain. The government was aware of the crisis, if
only through the reports of its tax-collectors and recruiting-
sergeants. But it did not have reliable statistics; it regarded war as
inevitable; and in matters of public health it was a creature of
its age. Standards of sanitation were abysmal, medical resources
primitive. The state was more interested in the consequences of
depopulation than in its causes. It occasionally tinkered with the
problem, to no visible effect.[15] Among the reform plans adum-
brated at the beginning of Philip IV's reign was the creation of a
junta de población, perhaps with the intention of creating industries and attracting foreigners; but as it had no funds it soon
ceased activity. And in an attempt to boost the birth rate the
government exempted from taxation fathers who begat eight or
more sons; these prolific Spaniards were derisively known as
hidalgos de bragueta.

Aristocracy

The polarization of Spanish society into two sectors, a privileged
minority monopolizing land and office, and a mass of peasants
and workers, continued with greater momentum in the seventeenth century. The basis of this social division was wealth. It is
true that function – originally military function – assigned the
nobility its social status and honour, and that this was juridically
recognized in the *fuero de hidalguía* which exempted the noble
from personal taxes and from the normal process of law. But in
the ultimate analysis it was money which bought nobility, and
money was the motor of social mobility. Class distinction was
recognized and reinforced by legislation. The various sumptuary
laws, while they were motivated by economic considerations, also
served to underline social differences. One such law prohibited the
wearing of silk by artisans, labourers, all who worked with their
hands, and their wives; another restricted the use of coaches and

---

[15] Ibid., pp. 98–9.

sedan chairs. Decrees of this kind simply helped to identify status symbols and to encourage social pretensions. But they were welcome to the poor nobility who resented the pretensions of tradesmen, professional people and other urban groups. For its part the crown preserved the nobility, even against itself. Nobles had to get royal permission to marry, to alienate their patrimony, to mortgage their estates, in short to do anything which might weaken their class. For the crown regarded the nobility, somewhat naïvely, as a reserve of talent at the service of the country.

The nobility were also favoured by the educational system. They now monopolized the Colegios Mayores, foundations originally created to finance the studies of clever students from poor families. From these they graduated to automatic preferment in church and state. A degree was a qualification for office, and in the course of the sixteenth century the universities had helped to produce a new and homogeneous social group, the *letrados*, a corps of legally trained prelates, councillors, magistrates and statesmen, together with a bureaucratic elite comprising *letrado* dynasties who occupied key posts in Spain and the empire. Preference was given to Castilians of pure blood, to those with family connections, to graduates of Salamanca, Valladolid and Alcalá, and to former lecturers. In the seventeenth century, however, economic depression reversed the academic boom of the sixteenth and worsened the job prospects of graduates. The result was greater exclusivism and still more emphasis on utility. The ideal of a university was not scholarship but office-holding. The Colegios Mayores began to admit the sons of more powerful sectors, not only the aristocracy but also the traditional *letrado* families, who wanted to study virtually nothing but law and wanted to study it cheaply. Universities came to be dominated by law studies, and university chairs became the preserve not of scholars but of passing *letrados* with their eyes on higher rewards. And while the Colegios Mayores continued to recruit their students from the ranks of privilege, their graduates gained easy preferment in the state. They constituted 58.5 per cent of the *oidores* in the *Chancillería* of Valladolid in the reign of Philip III, rising to 61.5 per cent in the reign of Philip IV and to 66.7 per cent in that of Charles II. On the Council of Castile they rose from 57.9 per cent to 68.5 per cent, reaching 72.5 per cent under

Charles II.[16] Thus the universities and their prime products, the *letrados*, were almost exclusively dedicated to the service of the state and had no alternative resources. When the economy went into depression in the seventeenth century, state and society alike were affected: the universities suffered from dwindling revenues, families from shortage of funds for education and graduates from lack of opportunities. At that point the universities had no reserves of independent strength to sustain themselves. Socially university students came from *hidalgo* families rather than from commoners. For the elder sons of the higher nobility there was a special institution, the Colegio Imperial in Madrid, founded by the Jesuits in the reign of Philip IV with the specific purpose of training an elite. The college justified itself with the claim that

> well-ordered states have usually derived their success from the good education of their youth, and although it would be very appropriate to extend such education to the common people it is much more important to give it to the sons of princes and nobles, because they are the principal part of the state and, for good or for evil, they lead the rest; moreover they subsequently control the government and administration of the kingdom.[17]

Higher education in Spain had becomes a powerful instrument for perpetuating the social and political dominance of the aristocracy.

In the course of its history the Spanish aristocracy bred its own hierarchy and its own distinctions. This was inevitable in a class which, by the beginning of the seventeenth century, had grown to 650,000 in Castile, or about one in ten of the population.[18] The original *nobleza de sangre* were joined in the sixteenth and seventeenth centuries by masses of *hidalgos*, who bought, earned or

---

[16] Richard L. Kagan, *Students and Society in Early Modern Spain* (Baltimore, 1974), p. 93, for these and other original details; see also Janine Fayard, *Les membres du Conseil de Castille à l'époque moderne (1621–1746)* (Geneva/Paris, 1979), p. 35.

[17] Quoted by Domínguez Ortiz, *La sociedad española en el siglo XVII*, p. 289; see also J. S. Diaz, *Historia del Colegio Imperial de Madrid* (Madrid, 1952).

[18] John C. Salyer, 'La política española en la época del mercantilismo', *Anales de Economía*, 31 (1952), pp. 319–21. See also Domínguez Ortiz, *La sociedad española en el siglo XVII*, pp. 189–91.

proved their noble status. In the face of this invasion the older and wealthier nobility sought to preserve social distinctions by insulating themselves in the ranks of the grandees and *títulos*. This re-grouping of the aristocracy became more pronounced in the course of the seventeenth century, and by the end of the period there was a wide gap between the grandees and *títulos*, who were the real nobility, and the mass of *caballeros* and *hidalgos*, who had little more than a coat-of-arms. The ultimate test was an economic one: some were wealthier than others. As Lope de Vega put it,

> No dudes que el dinero es todo en todo.
> Es príncipe, es hidalgo, es caballero,
> Es alta sangre, es descendiente godo.

At the bottom of the hierarchy swarmed the *hidalgos*, nobles by heredity or recent procurement, but debarred by their poverty or lack of office from further advancement. Their principal habitat was northern Castile and the highlands of Cantabria. Some scraped a living from petty estates, others performed work regarded as vile, and not a few were reduced to beggary. These were the classical targets of the satirists. Further south *hidalgos* who possessed any fortune at all preferred the more illustrious designation of *caballero*. The *caballeros* were nobles of middle rank; they lived in town houses, drew most of their income from their estates, and supplemented this by annuities from investments in *juros* and *censos*. They frequently held *regimientos* – seats in municipal councils – which gave them the opportunity of becoming procurators in the cortes and thus of diverting taxation from the property and interests of their class. But *caballeros*, especially the newly arrived, aspired to higher things. To enhance their status they sometimes bought, if they had not already inherited, seigneurial jurisdiction and thus became *señores de vasallos*, of whom there were 254 in Castile at the beginning of the seventeenth century. Above all they craved to be *caballeros de hábito* and *comendadores*, not because the military orders any longer fulfilled a function but because they conferred unimpeachable honour, proof of racial purity and test of nobility, while the *encomiendas* yielded a useful income.[19] In the seventeenth century,

---

[19] Ibid., pp. 200–1.

when pressure for *hábitos* increased, Olivares sold them in their hundreds and the government of Charles II further debased their currency.

Armed with a *señorío*, a *hábito* and perhaps an *encomienda*, the *caballero* strove to enter the ranks of the *títulos*. These were distinguished by their position and their wealth, and in popular estimation they were the real nobility. Again the criterion was wealth, especially in the seventeenth century. Those who had enough money to buy land, jurisdiction and vassals, to live a life of ease and ostentation, to advance substantial sums to the treasury, could expect to rise from the rank of simple *caballero* to that of count or marquis. The growth of the *título* class in turn enhanced the value of the *grandeza*, the most exclusive and class-conscious group of all. This constant struggle for preferment, for *caballeros* to become *títulos*, and *títulos* grandees, engendered a kind of social mobility and modified the composition of the nobility. The sixteenth century saw a moderate movement upwards: the original twenty grandees and thirty-five *títulos* had increased to ninety-nine at the end of Philip II's reign – eighteen dukes, thirty-eight marquises and forty-three counts. Philip III accelerated the process, creating a further twenty marquises and twenty-five counts. Philip IV, in a longer – forty-four years – and more penurious reign, created sixty-seven marquises and twenty-five counts. Charles II, in a reign of thirty-five years, sanctioned the creation of as many titles as in the previous two centuries – five viscounts, seventy-eight counts and 209 marquises.[20]

When, in 1520, Charles V legally defined the *grandeza*, it comprised twenty families, among them the dukes of Medinaceli, Alburquerque, Medina Sidonia, Alba, Frías and Béjar. The first gradees were a select and powerful group; they possessed specific juridical and diplomatic privileges; and to keep them out of politics the early Habsburgs employed them – and their fortunes – in war and diplomacy rather than in central administration. With the accession of the more pliant Philip III the grandees moved more noticeably towards the court, where they negotiated the best appointments in the Council of State and the viceroyalties. Philip IV added lavishly to their number. In 1627 there were about 168 titled nobles in Castile, an increase of almost fifty since

[20] Ibid., pp. 209–22.

1600. Of these twenty-five were dukes (all grandees), seventy marquises (nine grandees), and seventy-three counts (seven grandees); the total of forty-one grandees was twice what it had been in the early sixteenth century.[21] In 1640 the crown created ten new grandees, each of them undertaking to lead a military contingent to the Catalan front.[22] The older grandees regarded the newcomers with contempt and their patron with suspicion. Olivares returned the antipathy, turning his opponents into declared enemies. Haro treated the grandees more suavely. And under Charles II they reached the apogee of their power.[23] To satisfy their pride and exclusivism further refinements were introduced with the more elaborate distinction between grandees of the first, second and third class. All of them, however, were extremely wealthy men, owners of the greatest fortunes in the kingdom. That was precisely why they were grandees, and that was the basis of their revival in the seventeenth century.

While the grandees and *títulos* looked out from their lofty position, their humbler colleagues had to work hard at being noble. To acquire or confirm the status they had to prove their lineage, their purity of blood – meaning freedom from Jewish ancestry – and their exemption from taxation. Unless a man was of *notoria hidalguía* his claim to nobility would usually involve lengthy and expensive litigation, for it would be contested by his enemies or by remaining taxpayers. Yet the advantages were thought to justify the struggle, and in many cases they probably did. The law dealt more leniently with the noble than with the commoner, and he could not be tortured, sentenced to the galleys or imprisoned for debt. Nobility was also a card of entry to the bureaucracy. The best public offices were virtually monopolized by nobles, and nobles occupied about half of municipal offices. The Council of State was always dominated by the higher nobility. The other councils had a greater proportion of *hidalgos* and *caballeros* but no commoners. And other important offices, such as that of *corregidor* (district officer), were usually in the hands of *caballeros*. Finally nobility conferred exemption from personal taxation; indeed tax exemption was the crucial test of *hidalguía*.

---

[21] Elliott, *The Count-Duke of Olivares*, pp. 184–5.

[22] Domínguez Ortiz, *La sociedad española en el siglo XVII*, pp. 218–19.

[23] See below, pp. 354–9.

Minor nobles, on the margin of their class, watched the municipal tax registers with acute anxiety, for it was these which separated the *pecheros* (commoners or taxpayers) from *hidalgos*. Fiscal privilege was much eroded in the seventeenth century by the increase of indirect taxes – principally the *millones* – and other impositions which the crown developed in order to make the nobility contribute, sometimes heavily.[24] But they strenuously resisted personal taxes such as the *servicio ordinario y extraordinario*, for exemption identified their status and had great symbolic value. They also maintained their exemption from certain municipal taxes, including the *sisa* (excise duty); and some towns had special shops for nobles where they could buy food free of purchase tax. The financial advantages of fiscal privilege were not to be despised; but its prestige value was even greater, for it conferred *honor* and social status, and in pursuit of this many Castilians were prepared to sacrifice all.

Nobility was not synonymous with wealth. But the poor *hidalgo* of northern Castile, the object of so much ridicule then and since, was not typical of the whole of Spain. Elsewhere the nobility did more than make ends meet. The source of a noble's wealth, however, was just as important as its size. Could a noble work? The question was much debated in legal and genealogical literature, and the ideal answer was that he should not. In the event impoverished *hidalgos* had to work, and in northern Spain they were driven to occupations which were strictly speaking incompatible with nobility. Apart from these, a number of *títulos* and *caballeros* were involved in industry and commerce, and this was acceptable as long as they did not manage their own enterprises or run them in their own homes. In the trading ports, especially in Seville and Cadiz, where they had the example of uninhibited foreigners before their eyes, Spaniards saw virtually no incompatibility between nobility and commercial enterprise, as long as this was wholesale, successful and large-scale.

In practice, however, noble entrepreneurs were a rarity. The income of the nobility came primarily from land, secured by primogeniture and entail, and reinforced by *señoríos*. Whether

---

[24] A. Domínguez Ortiz, 'La desigualdad contributiva en Castilla durante el siglo XVII' *Anuario de Historia del Derecho Español*, xxi–xxii (1951–2), pp. 1222–68.

income from agriculture dropped in the seventeenth century is difficult to determine. The fact that a noble had a large estate, or even extended it, did not mean that he was economically motivated. Land was a social rather than an economic investment. Nobles were not normally improving farmers and it would need exceptionally favourable conditions to persuade them to invest in extension of farmland. Agricultural prices dropped in the period 1605–12, failed to rise faster than non-agricultural in 1612–25, and lagged far behind non-agricultural in 1625–65.[25] If nobles were incapable of improving their income from land, this could explain their renewed anxiety to supplement their resources by grants and offices. Those who failed to do so and continued to live exclusively on rural revenue tended to feel the pinch. Their more successful colleagues varied their sources of income.[26]

Income from land was frequently supplemented by seigneurial revenue. The Admiral of Castile was lord of ninety-seven towns and villages, the duke of Infantado was lord of 800 and owned the right to appoint 500 officials. The aristocracy had acquired *señoríos* either by virtue of immemorial possession, or by royal grant or by purchase.[27] The early Habsburgs sold *senoríos* chiefly from disentailed lands of the military orders, but Philip IV, who sold on a much bigger scale, alienated royal jurisdiction to do so.[28] Seigneurial jurisdiction over towns and villages gave a noble vassals, offices and frequently rents, the most important of which were the *alcabalas*. The noble's gain, therefore, was the crown's loss. It lost income from important taxes, cognizance of many law suits and revenue from litigation. *Alcabalas* were often sold simultaneously with *señoríos*, and by the mid-seventeenth century more than 3,000 townships and villages in Castile paid their

[25] Hamilton, *American Treasure and the Price Revolution in Spain*, pp. 260–1; Carmelo Viñas y Mey, *El problema de la tierra en la España de los siglos XVI–XVII* (Madrid, 1941), p. 30.

[26] Domínguez Ortiz, *La sociedad española en el siglo XVII*, pp. 223–8.

[27] Alfonso María Guilarte, *El régimen señorial en el siglo XVI* (Madrid, 1962), pp. 1–12, 173–201, 285–324; Salvador de Moxó, 'Los señoríos. En torno a una problemática para el estudio del régimen señorial', *Hispania*, xxiv (1964), pp. 185–236, 399–430; Henry Kamen, *Spain in the Later Seventeenth Century, 1665–1700* (London, 1980), pp. 228, 232, 236–7.

[28] Salvador de Moxó, *La incorporación de señoríos en la España del antiguo régimen* (Valladolid, 1959), pp. 13–18.

alcabala tax not to the crown but to their lords.[29] Paradoxically, as the Habsburgs alienated jurisdiction so they tried to reclaim it, either by decree or more commonly by litigation. In the 1630s and 1640s the fiscal of the Council of Finance, Juan Bautista Larrea, initiated a number of court actions against nobles whose right to possession of *alcabalas* was questionable. But the campaign was not uniformly successful, and the most that Philip IV's government accomplished was to oblige some of the wealthier holders to disgorge a lump sum to the treasury by way of composition. It was not until the eighteenth century that the incorporation of *señoríos* was seriously undertaken.

In the course of the seventeenth century general economic depression accentuated the tendency of the nobility to turn to courtly and urban functions; at the same time their educational opportunities improved through their success in usurping the funds of the Colegios Mayores and thus procuring a free university education. They cornered the embassies and the councils; they filled the *corregimientos*, seats in the cortes, desirable benefices in the church; they held most of the crown revenues which were out on lease, and they had heavy investments in *juros* and *censos*. Like the rest of society, of course, they were vulnerable to economic adversity and state policy. Monetary inflation hurt those who lived on fixed incomes. The aristocracy of Aragon and Valencia were hit by the loss of the morisco labour force from 1609. And from the 1620s they were all scrutinized more closely by finance ministers. Olivares was convinced that idleness made nobles trouble-makers. His idea was to create a service nobility, mobilizing lords and their retainers for war service at the lords' expense.[30] Alternatively, they could purchase exemption. In October 1632 the Duke of Béjar, the Duke of Medina Sidonia, and the Marquis of Priego were asked to supply 3,000 men each for the royal army, in effect to depopulate their estates. A year later they were asked to raise this to 4,000. Requests of this kind were issued so frequently that in 1638 the Duke of Béjar began to

---

[29] Salvador de Moxo, 'Los orígenes de la percepción de alcabalas por particulares', *Hispania*, xviii (1958), pp. 307–39; see also the same author's *La alcabala. Sobre sus orígenes, concepto y naturaleza* (Madrid, 1963).
[30] Elliott, *The Count-Duke of Olivares*, p. 509.

object.[31] Many of those who failed to comply were banished from court to their estates, with admonitions to save now and contribute later. This was one of the reasons for the alienation of the nobility, from Philip IV as well as from Olivares, and it required all the tact of Haro to win them back.

The nobles, however, were their own worst enemies. In spite of abundant incomes – from estate production, seigneurial dues, rents, *censos* and *juros* – many of the higher nobility lived close to bankruptcy. Their difficulties were due not, as they pleaded, to royal service and court etiquette, but primarily to personal ineptitude. So inefficiently did they run their estates that without the built-in check of entail they would have begun to sell out. As it was many of them tried to do so. The crown normally refused permission to alienate any part of an estate, but it looked more indulgently on requests to mortgage property, requests which now flooded into the Council of Castile. While they were amateurs in managing their affairs, the nobles were also prisoners of an expensive system. Great nobles had heavy overheads: they had to live in style and maintain a large household; they were expected to be generous alms-givers, supporters of foundations, chantries and hospitals, all of which ate into the income of any self-respecting noble. For one reason or another many nobles, including the highest, were heavily in debt, and any emergency – service to the crown, a daughter's dowry – found them in trouble. Even the Constable of Castile, Bernardino de Velasco, lord of vast territories, had to plead financial difficulties in 1635, claiming that on succeeding to his patrimony he had found it 'mortgaged up to 400,000 ducats, and most of this sum spent on service to the crown'. The estate of the Enríquez, Admirals of Castile, was constantly besieged by creditors, encumbered as it was with vast debts and heavy expenditure. By 1640 the Duke of Infantado was paying 30,000 ducats a year in mortgage repayments, and in 1661 the government took over the administration of the Infantado estates to pay creditors and allocate an income to the duke. The Duke of Osuna, a great lord of Andalucía with extensive revenue from land, feudal dues and *juros*, had difficulty in living on his income. In the middle of the century the house of Pastrana had

---

[31] Domínguez Ortiz, *La sociedad española en el siglo XVII*, pp. 228–32.

debts totally 400,000 ducats and the Council of Castile had to take over the administration of its revenues.[32]

As commerce and industry did not appeal to the higher aristocracy, they sought the sustenance of royal *mercedes*. These were not normally outright grants of money, but 'expenses' for services rendered, and offices, especially the lucrative viceroyalties in Italy and the Indies. Philip III was ridiculously generous with nobles and courtiers, and they looked back on his reign as a golden age. Olivares attempted to cut back on *mercedes*, but Philip IV was a difficult man to restrain and the aristocratic reaction which followed the count duke's fall unleashed a new flood of pensions and grants. In effect the taxpayers were forced to subsidize an expensive aristocracy. Given the depressed condition of Castile, the lavishing of *mercedes* on nobles while poorer people died of hunger was the most pernicious aspect of the bias towards aristocracy in Spanish society. Yet parasitism of this kind expressed an essential truth about seventeenth-century Spain. The aristocracy were rich in property but poor in revenues, while the crown needed the support of a ruling class. Mutual dependence brought the two together. The crown used the aristocracy to rule Spain, and from the crown the aristocracy received sanction for social hierarchy and seigneurial jurisdiction, while taxation was diverted from lands and properties towards newer forms of wealth, such as *juros* and *censos*.[33]

From various sources, then, the Spanish nobility derived enormous wealth, even though some of them, like the crown itself, had to live on credit. The fact that aristocratic income was used unproductively was bound to have a harmful effect on the Spanish economy. Some of this wealth, no doubt, was invested in pious and charitable works and, in the first half of Philip IV's reign, in service to the state. But most of it was spent in conspicuous consumption and social ostentation, to the neglect of saving and investment and to the detriment of the balance of payments. The aristocratic way of life stemmed from false ideals of honour and reputation which contaminated the whole of society and seriously compromised economic values.

---

[32] For these and many other examples, ibid., pp. 232–42.
[33] Charles Jago, 'The "Crisis of the Aristocracy" in Seventeenth-Century Castile', *Past and Present*, 84 (1979), pp. 60–90.

La Gente Común

A minister of Philip IV noted that Spaniards

> each in their station and estate desire above all else honour and
> esteem, and everyone tries to advance himself, as can be seen in the
> fact that sons rarely follow the occupation of their father; the son
> of a shoemaker hates that occupation, the son of a merchant
> wishes to be a gentleman, and so it is with the rest.

Spain had no law defining estates, and legally speaking there was
no third estate, simply a mass of people – some 6 million – of
varying fortune who were only defined by their exclusion from
the aristocratic and ecclesiastical estates. There was nothing to
stop a commoner who got rich and lived *noblemente* from wearing silk, using a coach, and in general aping the consumer pattern
of the nobility.

There were various avenues open to a man of ambition. In the
countryside an industrious and thrifty farmer might acquire an
entail, then make his presence felt in the local municipality, and
finally begin proceedings for ennoblement. In the towns a commoner could purchase an office and move on from there. Or he
could enter the church and rely on his qualifications for preferment. The way ahead was difficult and already crowded with
nobility. But those who persevered could succeed. '*No tener
oficio ni beneficio* came to be synonymous with personal incapacity.'[34] The social preferences were obvious: the most highly regarded careers were in the bureaucracy and the church. Trade and
industry attracted far fewer candidates.

Spanish society was not devoid of entrepreneurial instincts. It
had its manufacturers, shipowners and merchants, especially in
the periphery provinces. The transatlantic trade still sustained a
number of Spanish businessmen. No doubt their profits were
now reduced and increasingly shared by outsiders, but even in the
1640s the great merchants of Seville were capable of assembling
loans for the crown. In 1645 a consortium of Seville businessmen
provided an *asiento* of 340,000 escudos, one of a number of
transactions of this kind.[35] Spanish entrepreneurs, however, were

---

[34] Domínguez Ortiz, *La sociedad española en el siglo XVII*, p. 47.
[35] Domínguez Ortiz, *Política y hacienda de Felipe IV*, pp. 147–54.

few in number. They did not form a middle class, with the social and economic objectives of a middle class. Indeed they usually aspired to aristocratic status. In the course of the seventeenth century the textile manufacturers of Segovia lost ground economically and socially to the sheep breeders and wool producers, who in 1648 managed to obtain a declaration affirming their noble identity by passing a law in the municipal council, which they controlled, 'that no cloth manufacturer, merchant or dealer, notary or attorney, or their sons, can be *regidores* (town councillors)'.[36] Decades later, in 1682, the manufacturers found a spokesman in the corregidor of Segovia, who asked the court to set an example by wearing Segovia cloth and to assure its producers that textile manufacture was not a bar to nobility. The point was taken and on 13 December the crown issued a decree removing any legal obstacles to the participation of nobility in economic enterprises, as long as they did not work with their own hands. No doubt in all societies there is a tendency for groups to affirm their identity and defend their status against others, and if in Spain this took the form of acquiring nobility this could be interpreted as a reward for entrepreneurial success rather than abandonment of it. But the title itself was only the beginning: it usually involved the diversion of profits to a landed estate, a daughter's dowry, and mortgage-type securities, actions alien to the work ethic and depriving industry of vital investment. The mania for aristocratic status was also fed by racial prejudice. In the sixteenth century a number of prominent Spanish businessmen were undoubtedly of Jewish extraction. This fostered a bias against the whole entrepreneurial class and caused many of its members, including those with Jewish ancestry, to buy their way out, to procure land and ennoblement, and thus to make their social status impeccable.

Public policy reinforced private prejudice. In Aragon and Valencia urban middle groups were badly hit by the expulsion of the moriscos, for in effect they lost the income from their investment in morisco agriculture.[37] In Castile taxation fell principally

[36] Angel García Sanz. *Desarrollo y crisis del Antiguo Régimen en Castilla la Vieja. Economía y sociedad en tierras de Segovia, 1500–1814* (Madrid, 1977), pp. 219–20; Kamen, *Spain in the Later Seventeenth Century*, pp. 262–3.
[37] Juan Reglà, 'La expulsión de los moriscos y sus consecuencias en la economía valenciana', *Hispania*, xxiii (1963), pp. 200–18.

on the non-aristocratic sector and inhibited investment in trade and industry, while government support of monopoly practices stifled the spirit of competition. A distinguished *arbitrista*, González de Cellorigo, argued that disproportion in the incidence of taxation was dividing Spanish society into two groups: 'We lack people in the middle who are neither rich nor poor but follow their natural occupation. And the cause of this defect is our inequitable system of taxation.'[38] Cellorigo was no egalitarian. He wanted an equilibrium between the three social groups; for this reason he viewed with dismay the erosion of the middle sector, as some climbed out and others dropped below. Taxation, of course, reflected rather than created the social structure; from the 1630s, moreover, aristocratic immunity was diminished in various ways. Nevertheless the property and interests of nobles remained basically intact, while nothing was done to give tax relief to entrepreneurial activities. Fiscal policy therefore tended to perpetuate social polarization.

The result could be seen all over Spain. It could be seen in Madrid. The capital underwent rapid urban growth in the early seventeenth century, as immigrants from other parts of the country arrived in search of work and the opportunities offered by court, government and the urban market. Madrid grew from 90,000 inhabitants at the end of the sixteenth century to over 130,000 about 1630, becoming in the process the largest city in Spain and replacing Toledo as the leading urban centre. No doubt Madrid underwent a severe crisis in the years 1601–6, but it was less devastated by the plague than many other places, and the population remained stable, even stationary, from 1631 to 1694.[39] This was an essentially parasitic community, a focus of consumption rather than production, and not a stimulus to its hinderland. It comprised on the one hand nobles, courtiers and bureaucrats, an elite who lived on rents and offices, spent only a small part of its income on food and satisfied its consumer needs by buying foreign imports rather than national products. On the other hand, it contained a vast service sector, together with labourers, under-

---

[38] Quoted by Sureda Carrión, *La hacienda castellana y los economistas del siglo XVII*, p. 168.
[39] Carbajo Isla, *La población de la Villa de Madrid*, pp. 138–40, 302–35; for different estimates see David R. Ringrose, *Madrid and the Spanish Economy, 1560–1850* (Berkeley and Los Angeles, 1983), pp. 28–58, 106–7.

employed or unemployed, and hordes of adventurers, vagrants and beggars. This mass of urban poor, people of low incomes and poor productivity, lived on the edge of subsistence and were usually forced to spend all they had on food alone, forming in no sense a dynamic market. With its stark contrast between luxury and squalor, between the elegant palaces of the aristocracy and the adobe dwellings of the masses, Madrid was a microcosm of Spanish society. Burgos, on the other hand, a thriving business centre in the sixteenth century, suffered economic and demographic collapse. No doubt its trade with northern Europe was dislocated by war from the 1580s. But adverse trading conditions alone could not be responsible for the fall in the population of Burgos from 25,000 in the mid-sixteenth century to 8,000 at the end of the seventeenth.[40] The majority of the town's businessmen simply abandoned their class. While 119 merchants attended the *consulado* (merchant guild) assembly in 1535, in 1661 the number was reduced to eight and these were a majority of the guild's members.[41]

The role of entrepreneur, abandoned by Spaniards, was taken over by foreigners.[42] Since the sixteenth century the principal bankers of the crown had been foreigners. By the 1620s Italians, mainly Genoese, dominated the *asiento* business. The Fuggers were now past their peak, but they still possessed two assets, the lease of the *cruzada*, one of the most lucrative revenues in Spain, and the Almadén mercury mine. Whoever they were the foreign *asentistas* were a hated group, popularly regarded as leeches on the Spanish economy, accused of enriching themselves at the expense of the treasury and the taxpayer, charging excessive interest, appropriating the best revenues and using their right to export silver for the crown as a cloak for private transactions.

[40] Domínguez Ortiz, *La sociedad española en el siglo XVII*, pp. 143–5.

[41] The number of insurance policies issued in Burgos dropped drastically in the first decade of the seventeenth century; see R. S. Smith, *The Spanish Guild Merchant. A History of the Consulado* 1250–1700 (Durham, N.C., 1940), p. 71; see also Manuel Basas Fernández, *El Consulado de Burgos en el siglo XVI* (Madrid, 1963).

[42] A. Girard, 'Les étrangers dans la vie économique de l'Espagne au XVIe et XVIIe siècles', *Annales d'Histoire Economique et Sociale*, xxiv (1933), pp. 567–78; A. Domínguez Ortiz, 'Los extranjeros en la vida española durante el siglo XVII', *Estudios de Historia Social de España*, iv, 2 (1960), pp. 293–426; H. Sánchez de Sopranis, 'Las naciones extranjeras en Cádiz durante el siglo XVII', *Estudios de Historia Social de España*, iv, 2 (1960), pp. 643–877.

There was some truth in these allegations, but basically the foreign bankers simply supplied a demand, on a scale far beyond the capacity of Spanish financiers and with an eye to the customer's unreliability. Eventually, their resources much reduced by the suspension of payments in 1627 and the insatiable demands of Philip IV and Olivares, the Italians were joined by a number of Portuguese financiers.

The Portuguese *marranos* were convert Jews, some of them descendants of Spanish Jews expelled in 1492. They were prominent in the domestic and international trade of Portugal; they almost monopolized the slave trade; and they handled spices, sugar and other colonial commodities. In Portugal they were vulnerable. The Inquisition suspected their orthodoxy and the populace resented their wealth. So they welcomed the union of the crowns and began to seek new pastures in Spain. In return for a handsome subsidy to the crown they were given the right to emigrate in 1601, and many of them immediately entered Spain. There they extended their business operations, and were soon accused of every misdemeanour from cornering the Indies trade to organizing prostitution. The privilege of 1601 was revoked in 1610, but they simply evaded the law. From the beginning of Philip IV's reign they were lessees of royal revenues, notably the inland customs. Olivares, who seems to have been free of racial prejudice, brought them into the *asiento* business, and under his patronage they were allowed freedom of movement within the peninsula and to some extent protected from the attentions of the Inquisition.[43] In addition to the small group of *asentistas* – Duarte Fernández, Simón Suárez, Manuel de Paz and Juan Núñez Saravia – lesser Portuguese businessmen swarmed into Spain to deploy their enterprise and capital, and particularly to procure a foothold in the Indies trade. By 1640 there were probably 2,000 Portuguese merchants in Seville alone. Not all of these immigrants escaped intact. One of the principal *asentistas*, Juan Núñez Saravia, was accused of judaizing and exporting bullion to colleagues abroad, for which he suffered five years imprisonment, while others were subject to fines and confiscations.[44] Yet on the whole

[43] A. Domínguez Ortiz, 'Los conversos de orígen judío después de la expulsión', *Estudios de Historia Social de España*, iii (1955, pp. 226–431; Boyâjian, *Portuguese Bankers*, pp. 2–13, 44, 133–80.

[44] A. Domínguez Ortiz, 'El proceso inquisitorial de Juan Núñez Saravia, banquero de Felipe IV', *Hispania*, xv (1955), pp. 559–81.

the Portuguese in Castile had a good run for their money under Olivares, and even in the first years of the Portuguese rebellion the Spanish authorities shielded most of them from popular hatred. After the fall of Olivares, however, they were more vulnerable; some of them were further hit by the state bankruptcy of 1647; and the Castilian economy became too depressed to offer them easy profits.[45] The mid-seventeenth century, therefore, saw a further flight of merchants and capital from Spain, as the Portuguese went in search of new opportunities in northern Europe, leaving behind from their number only a few administrators of royal revenues.

Meanwhile other foreigners filled the ranks vacated by Spaniards and Portuguese. Spain's overseas trade, especially the Indies trade, drew increasing numbers of foreign merchants to her ports as importers, exporters, factors and agents.[46] This was simply another sign of the country's underdevelopment. Spain was a good export market for manufactured goods and a useful source of certain raw materials. As the foreigners had the goods, the capital and the shipping, they could retain in their own hands the whole import-export operation, reducing their Spanish counterparts to little more than commission agents. Many of the foreign merchants became permanent residents in Spain; they were to be found chiefly in Seville and Cadiz, where they could supervise the re-export of their goods to the Spanish Indies. In the course of the seventeenth century the Genoese and Flemings were joined in the ports of Andalucía by growing numbers of non-allied nationals, notably the French, English and Dutch. Spain had a liberal immigration policy and her reputation for religious intolerance was much exaggerated abroad; by the middle of the century the English had developed a working relation with the Inquisition and they were allowed in effect to reside in Spain without harassment; even during wartime, when their position was necessarily more difficult, many of them chose to remain. The actual number of foreigners in Spain at any one time is a matter of speculation. In 1640 Seville had about 12,000, one-tenth of its population; in 1665, after the ravages of the great plague, the city still had 7,000

[45] J. Caro Baroja, *Los judíos en la España moderna y contemporánea* (3 vols, Madrid, 1962), ii, pp. 68–131; Henry Kamen, *The Spanish Inquisition* (London, 1965), pp. 221–6.

[46] Sánchez de Sopranis, 'Las naciones extranjeras en Cádiz durante el siglo XVII', pp. 647–59.

foreigners. Altogether, in 1650, there were between 120,000 and 150,000 foreign residents in the whole country.[47] These in effect were Spain's entrepreneurial class.

The vast majority of Spaniards, peasants in the fields, labourers in the towns, had no hope of advancement, only the fear that they might fall even lower, into that underworld of Spanish society populated by vagabonds, beggars and bandits, the victims of widespread unemployment. Again, fiscal policy perpetuated social malaise, for it weighed most heavily on the underprivileged. The *alcabala* tax was particularly loaded against the poor; the ultimate consumer bought an article at a price inflated by an accumulation of taxes charged every time it changed hands. From the end of the sixteenth century a new tax appeared, the *millones*, and this fell chiefly on three basic foodstuffs – meat, wine and oil. For the poor this caused an intolerable rise in the cost of living, and one which they were less capable of evading than the nobility. Where towns or districts paid a composition tax, the municipalities, dominated by a wealthy oligarchy, fixed the tax rates to benefit themselves; then they frequently sold the products of their estates with the purchase tax added, passing only a portion to the treasury. The fiscal system accelerated the rural depopulation of Castile. And as some people fled from the tax-collector, the quota for that district fell entirely on those who remained, who in turn would be driven to emigrate. Not a few villages of Castile disappeared from the map in the course of the century, their inhabitants joining the urban proletariat, not because the towns were booming or could offer them work but because there was less likelihood of starving there than in the countryside. Many Spaniards lived more or less below subsistence level, and bitter experience taught them that from those who had least most was taken.

The Spanish poor tended to congregate in towns, where they usually formed at least 40 per cent of the population, an irreducible group of paupers, vagrants and unemployed. Beggars were part of the landscape, and alms-giving a serious obligation of the Church and the faithful. But reformist opinion preferred to institutionalize poverty, and poor relief was a duty recognized by

[47] Domínguez Ortiz, 'Los extranjeros en la vida española durante el siglo XVII', pp. 389–91.

most local authorities. By the end of the sixteenth century Castile
had a range of hospitals for the aged, beggars, foundlings and the
sick, variously founded and financed, but all expressions of
voluntary charity, and all, especially those for poor relief, the
subject of great debate concerning their size, performance, desira-
bility and inevitably finance.[48] They were not isolated from the
economic pressures of the age. In Toledo charitable societies and
institutions suffered from the city's loss of trade and population
in the early seventeenth century, and most of Castile's poor relief
provisions were affected by recession and cut-backs. The impetus
to reform was lost in the first half of the century, and it was not
until the 1660s that a movement to found *hospicios*, or beggars'
hospices, made any progress. In 1668 the Hermandad del
Hospicio was established in Madrid; it accepted only twenty-four
out of 800 qualified beggars, was hampered by shortage of funds,
and reluctant to improve its facilities for fear of encouraging yet a
greater influx of vagrants from the provinces. Money was eventually found from private sources and by 1674 the *hermandad*
was accepting 800 paupers.[49]

The efforts of the Church and of charitable organizations took
some of the danger out of social conditions, but did not remove it
entirely. Urban disorder, food and tax riots were permanent, if
sporadic, features of seventeenth-century Castile, and local oligarchies were frequent targets of angry artisans. Rural Spain, rooted
in unchanging routine, was also a place of crime and violence.
Banditry was endemic in highland Catalonia, Valencia, Murcia
and Andalucía, a product of rural deprivation, criminality and
lack of law enforcement.[50] Officials accepted minor incidents of
peasant violence, food and tax riots as part of the rural scene. But
there was an added dimension in the 1640s, when a conjunction
of political crisis, regional unrest, and failure abroad tested the
equilibrium of Spanish society and posed a new challenge to
authority. In these conditions poverty became less passive; in the
midst of war harvest failures, food shortages and rising prices
posed a greater risk, causing famine in central Castile and making

[48] Linda Martz, *Poverty and Welfare in Habsburg Spain. The Example of Toledo* (Cambridge, 1983), pp. 45–89, 199; Kamen, *Spain in the Later Seventeenth Century*, pp. 277–80.
[49] Martz, *Poverty and Welfare in Habsburg Spain*, pp. 90–1.
[50] Kamen, *Spain in the Later Seventeenth Century*, pp. 175–82, 207–12.

Madrid a potentially dangerous place in the crisis years of 1647–
8. In the event the government kept its nerve and managed to
avoid serious disturbance in Castile.[51]

Elsewhere, however, popular protest exploded into violence
and peasant unrest assumed a spreading form, spilling also into
the towns. Andalucía was hit by recession in the Indies trade
from 1640, diminution of treasure returns, harvest failure and
high food prices in 1646–7, a combustible mixture which only
needed exceptional fiscal pressure to ignite. There were tax riots
in a number of towns in eastern Andalucía in the early months of
1647. In March 1648 the evident collusion between grain merchants and the authorities in pushing up prices triggered off a
popular revolt in Granada in which the insurgents seized control
of the city and held it for some weeks before they were pacified.
In May 1652 insurgents from the poorer districts occupied the
streets of Córdoba demanding cheaper bread, until they were
eventually crushed by the city authorities supported by the local
aristocracy. These events culminated in an uprising in Seville in
May 1652, which brought thousands into the streets to erect
barricades and brandish arms, before they too were repressed.[52]
These were spontaneous protests, popular revolts, tax and bread
riots, not regional rebellions. They demanded replacement of
some officials, not Andalusian autonomy. Movements of this
kind became a feature of rural life in the second half of the
seventeenth century, reappearing in Galicia in 1673 and in Catalonia in 1688–9. The latter originated in harvest failure and grain
shortage, and was aggravated by tax and billeting demands during
war with France; under Catalan leaders it became an armed rural
revolt and an attack on the regional authorities, but it received no
support from the local oligarchy and was eventually crushed by
viceregal forces.[53]

The alliance between crown and aristocracy was too close and the
forces of law and order were too solid to leave any opening for
social revolution. In the event the mass of the Spanish poor
accepted their fate with mute resignation. Their only spokesmen
were a few *arbitristas*, though these did not always go to the root

---

[51] Stradling, *Philip IV*, pp. 203–6.
[52] Antonio Domínguez Ortiz, *Alteraciones andaluzas* (Madrid, 1973),
pp. 92–148.
[53] Kamen, *Spain in the Later Seventeenth Century*, pp. 213–18.

of the problem which lay in the maldistribution of agrarian property. Many of them criticized fiscal injustice or, as Jacinto de
Alcázar Arriaza put it, 'the inequality in the system of taxes,
which the poor pay and the rich enjoy'.[54] Fernández Navarrete
denounced tax exemption: 'It is not just that some should be
exempt at the expense of others and that the whole burden should
fall on the weak shoulders of peasants and labourers.'[55] Padre
López Bravo, writing at the beginning of Philip IV's reign,
attacked the distribution of property: 'It is highly pernicious that
poverty should have its origin in an unjust distribution of wealth,
causing the affluence of the few and the deprivation of the
many.... The result is that people abandon the countryside for
the towns; the poor become slaves of the rich; and the rich
intensify their pursuit of luxury and pleasure.'[56] In the 1620s the
Benedectine Benito de Peñalosa y Mondragón recorded the 'extreme misery' of the Castilian peasants, their 'simple meals of
garlic, onions, low-grade beef, bread of barley and rye'; their
rough clothes, 'sandals, loose coats, large hoods, coarse collars,
burlap shirts, sheepskin coats preserved with resin'; their miserable dwellings, 'poor cottages and huts with mud walls crumbling
or fallen'; and their pitiful possessions, 'ill-cultivated fields, with
emaciated and starving cattle, deprived of common lands for
pasture'.[57]

The Spanish peasants were hopeless victims of the seigneurial
society in which they lived, a society rigid in its structure and
undeviating in its ideals. No doubt underdevelopment immobilized this society and prolonged its stagnation. Perhaps economic
growth would have raised the living standards of the peasants and
nurtured a native middle class. But social rigidity was a cause as
well as a result of economic depression. The pattern of investment
in Spain reflected the structure of society. When it was not
hoarded or spent in conspicuous consumption, capital tended to
flow into *asientos*, *juros* and *censos*, that is loans destined primarily to finance state and consumer expenditure, rather than into

[54] Quoted in Sureda Carrión, *La hacienda castellana y los economistas del siglo
XVII*, p. 181.
[55] Quoted ibid., p. 194.
[56] Quoted by J. Reglà, 'La época de los dos ultimos Austrias', *Historia social
y económica de España y America*, iii p. 272.
[57] Quoted ibid., pp. 325–6.

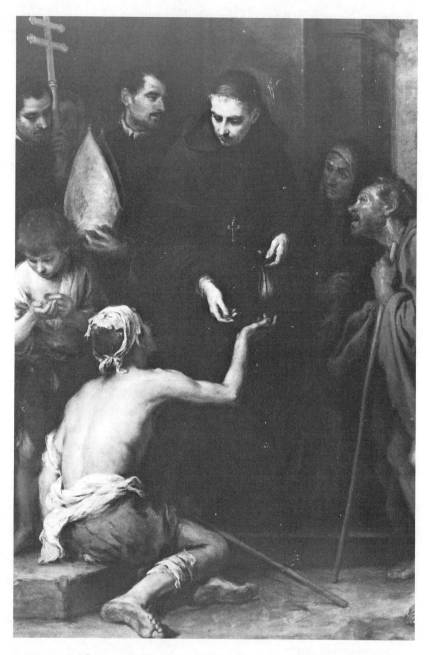

PLATE 4 *St Thomas of Villanueva*, by Murillo (reproduced by kind permission of the Trustees, Wallace Collection, London)

productive enterprises. One of the reasons was the higher rate of return on these investments – 7 per cent on *censos*, much more on *asientos* – than on those in other undertakings; agriculture, according to the *arbitristas*, yielded a return of only 4 per cent. But the basic reason was to be found in deeply rooted social ideals, which placed greater value on honour and status than on entrepreneurial activity. Even if the consumption level of the upper income groups could have been reduced there was no guarantee that the savings would have been invested in agriculture and industry.

Agriculture and Industry

Spain can be divided into two parts, wet and dry. In both these Spains the people had to struggle against adverse topographical or climatic conditions. In the plains of Castile, Extremadura and Andalucía rainfall was erratic and the soil poor; when it rained it rained in torrents on a soil subject to erosion; and in the summer there was drought. The arid terrain of the central plateau discouraged tillage and made it difficult to extend and improve cultivation. In those areas where rainfall was adequate, in Galicia for example, the soil was frequently bad with high acidic content. If there was little investment in agriculture, therefore, one of the reasons was that the land was not good enough to guarantee returns. It would have needed a technical revolution to make it so. Yet while their inheritance was meagre, Spaniards did not endeavour to use it wisely. Although in the course of the seventeenth century there was some extension of new crops, such as the potato and maize, this was not on a scale to produce agricultural change. The area under cultivation did not increase in the course of the century. Land tenure remained inefficient and cultivation backward.[58]

Some parts of Spain had been forced into fertility by irrigation and hard work. Valencia, for example, had been endowed with rich *huertas* (market gardens), and even the arid uplands had been made to yield crops by the industry of the moriscos. The expulsion of the latter adversely affected production, particularly of the

[58] Manuel Colmeiro, *Historia de la economía política en España* (first published 1863; 2 vols, Madrid, 1965), ii, pp. 657–717.

basic crops of the region – sugar, rice and grain – so that Valencia, according to a contemporary chronicler, 'which was formerly the most flourishing region of Spain is now reduced to an arid and neglected desert'.[59] Sugar output had hardly recovered when it was further hit by competition from Brazilian and Caribbean sugar.[60] Rice production no longer yielded a surplus for export, and after 1609 Valencia was dependent on imported grain. Finally, the expulsion of the moriscos caused an even greater concentration of agrarian property, for in the hard times which followed only the biggest and most powerful landowners could survive.

Meanwhile Castile, too, was losing its labour force. The typology of the Castilian peasant differed according to region.[61] In northern Spain a high proportion of the peasantry were independent farmers, sometimes called *labradores*, and were owners of one or more teams of draft animals. In Vizcaya and Catalonia these enjoyed conditions which enabled them to provide a decent living for their families; elsewhere peasant farmers worked little more than *minifundia*, and in Galicia they had to supplement their incomes with work as seasonal *jornaleros* in other parts of the peninsula. Further south the day labourer became more common. In New Castile between 25 and 30 per cent of the rural population were *labradores*, many of them tenant farmers, while some 60 per cent were *jornaleros*.[62] Andalucía, the heartland of great estates, was also the habitat of *jornaleros*, who formed 75 per cent of the rural population. These categories were not absolute and peasants could duplicate roles of farmer and labourer in poor regions or in time of depression. But most sectors of the peasantry were subject to pressures of climate, dearth and disease, and many abandoned the unequal struggle to survive.

Rural depopulation seems to have reached serious proportions from the late sixteenth century. In 1598 the cortes urged the government to take measures to increase farming and stock-breeding: 'The principal cause of decrease in cultivation is the great dearth of people; many places are visibly depopulated and

[59] Quoted by Boronat, *Los moriscos españoles y su expulsión*, ii, p. 329.
[60] Reglà, 'La expulsión de los moriscos y sus consecuencias en la economía valenciana', pp. 221–12.
[61] David Vassberg, *Land and Society in Golden Age Castile* (Cambridge, 1984), pp. 141–7.
[62] Salomon, *La campagne de Nouvelle Castille*, pp. 256–66.

others have lost almost half of their inhabitants.'[63] Observers pointed specifically to the shortage of labourers, blaming wars, emigration to the Indies, sale of common land, pressure of powerful landlords, and above all fiscal inequality which caused people to flee from the tax-collector.[64] The Duero basin was one of the zones particularly affected; it was estimated that in the first two decades of the seventeenth century the number of labourers in the diocese of Salamanca dropped from 8,345 to 4,135, and more than eighty places had been depopulated. It was probably this region that the count of Gondomar, whose home was in Valladolid, had in mind when he wrote of the depopulation, poverty and misery of Spain, the land which foreigners found more distressing and deserted than any other in Europe.[65]

The evidence from government reports and private memoranda are too consistent to be ignored. Lison y Biedma, member for Granada in the cortes of 1621, recorded:

Numerous places have become depopulated and disappeared from the map, in some provinces as many as fifty or sixty, their churches decayed, houses in ruins, property wasted and fields uncultivated. The vassals who formerly cultivated them now wander the roads with their wives and children, searching from district to district for a living and eating herbs and roots to keep alive. Others go to distant provinces which are not so burdened with taxation, with the *millones*, the *alcabalas* and other impositions; for it is the weight of taxation and the oppression of the tax-collectors which are the principal causes of this depopulation.[66]

Other observers attributed rural depopulation to the sale of *tierras baldías*, or common waste lands. Alienation of the commons, authorized by Philip II and his successors, deprived the poor of the plots which they were supposed to receive in rotation, of pasture for their cattle, sheep and goats, and of firewood from the forests, all of which had been of common usage in the villages. In

[63] *Actas*, xv, p. 748.
[64] Reports of corregidores, c.1600, in Viñas y Mey, *El problema de la tierra en la España de los siglos XVI–XVII*, Appendix I.
[65] Gondomar to Philip III, 1619, *Documentos inéditos para la historia de España* (new series, 4 vols, Madrid, 1936–45), ii, pp. 131–46.
[66] Quoted by Domínguez Ortiz, *La sociedad española en el siglo XVII*, p. 119.

1628 the *arbitrista* Barbón y Castañeda remarked: 'If the sale of common land is extended to the rest of Spain then it will experience the same ruin as Old Castile; for it is a truism that the population level of towns and villages depends on the status and treatment accorded to their inhabitants.'[67] By the 1660s, after half a century of war and other adversities, the situation had further deteriorated. According to a memorandum written by a royal minister in 1669:

> This country has now plunged the depths of misfortune and reached a state of prostration unprecedented in our history. In the course of my office I have to visit many places which a few years ago had 1000 inhabitants and now have less than 500, while those which used to have 500 now have barely 100. In all of them there are numerous families who go one or two days without a full meal, and others live on herbs and roots from the fields.[68]

Declarations of this kind, of course, are statistically unreliable, and their authors tend to generalize from a particular district. But their broad conclusions are vindicated by public documents, particularly financial documents. Depopulation reached a point where communities had to request a lowering of the tax quota which they had been set in the registers of 1591–4. The administration only granted a reduction when a community had lost one-half or one-third of its population. Surviving evidence reveals that 156 communities requested, and in most cases procured, a reduction of their tax quota in the course of the seventeenth century, and these communities were only a portion of those which became depopulated.[69] Most of them were in the two Castiles, Extremadura and Andalucía, that is in dry Spain. The zone of maximum depopulation was around Guadalajara and Toledo in New Castile. The inhabitants of these bleak plains and wild *sierras* scraped a living from the cultivation of vines and olives and later from cereal monoculture. Abrupt climatic changes in the second half of the seventeenth century and in particular a series of disastrous frosts ruined this marginal cultivation and

[67] Quoted ibid., pp. 119–20.
[68] Quoted by Duque de Maura, *Vida y reinado de Carlos II* (2nd edn, 2 vols, Madrid, 1954), i, p. 396.
[69] Domínguez Ortiz publishes the details in *La sociedad española en el siglo XVII*, Appendix I, pp. 325–37.

caused the mass exodus of its practitioners, most of whom presumably made their way to nearby Madrid.

Some of the causes of rural depopulation – plague, famine and war – have already been noticed. In addition to these classical adversities, there were certain institutional obstacles to agricultural progress in this period. One of these, though probably the least important, was price control of grain. Throughout the sixteenth century government controls were consistently applied in an effort to counter rising prices. This policy, of course, favoured the consumer against the producer, whose own costs were also subject to inflation, and it was highly unpopular with farmers and peasants. In the first half of the seventeenth century there was a gradual movement towards a free market in grain, in a belated attempt to improve production and alleviate rural distress. Between 1619 and 1628, and again from 1632 to 1650, farmers were free to sell their grain at unregulated prices. By this time agriculture was too stagnant to respond to price de-control alone. But even in its heyday the policy of control had never been fully enforced and farmers had been driven to devise means of exceeding the ceilings. This factor, therefore, was not a major cause of agricultural depression.[70]

Taxation was one of the greatest obstacles to farming in Spain. Burden after burden was imposed on the Castilian peasant, until the weight became more than he could bear. It was a burden, moreover, that was not equitably shared; while unproductive, tax-exempt groups such as nobles, clergy, military officers and officials of the Inquisition proliferated, the peasant producer contributed a disproportionate amount. First he paid dues to his lord, which in New Castile amounted to 5 per cent of his payments. Then he paid tithes to the church, one-tenth of production divided between church and state; these were among his heaviest outgoings, some ten to twenty times higher than seigneurial dues. Next he paid taxes to the crown, the *servicios* and *millones* on basic consumer goods. Finally he paid rent to his landlord and instalments on his mortgage. Rents were high in Castile and rent was the greatest burden, representing for the peasant perhaps as much as four times the amount of the tithe. True, a peasant might be renting only a portion of the lands he worked, and the rest

[70] Hamilton, *American Treasure and the Price Revolution in Spain*, pp. 254–6.

might be common lands or his own property. But tithes were relative to production, whereas rents had to be paid at the same level even in bad years. At such a time a peasant might be forced to take out a *censo*, or mortgage-type loan with interest at 5 per cent, another payment and another threat. At the end of the sixteenth century the accumulated obligations to state, church, and lord consumed more than 50 per cent of a peasant's production in New Castile.[71] In other words more than half the crop so laboriously farmed by the New Castilian peasantry went to enrich non-peasant classes. And from the pittance that remained to him the farmer had to live, support his family, pay his labourers, renew his equipment and buy his seeds. Little wonder that many of them abandoned the struggle in despair, some seeing their mortgages foreclosed, others simply running away from the tax farmer and debt collector.

The peasant farmer was caught between the tax-collector and the big landowner. The concentration of landed property in the hands of the higher nobility was difficult to break and easy to extend. Established in their vast *latifundia*, secured by entail and fortified by seigneurial power, the aristocracy were in an impregnable position which only their own improvidence could subvert. And they were well placed to make further conquests. As they dominated the higher administration and municipal government they could appropriate common land with impunity and without too much expense. They also absorbed farms previously owned by small proprietors who could not keep up with their overheads, their taxes and their mortgage repayments. The *censos*, or mortgage system, offered only a short-term escape for the small farmer and he tended to ruin himself by it.[72] The time came when many of them were forced to redeem their mortgages at the expense of their property and sell out to their more powerful neighbours, who were anxious to round off their estates. Many aristocratic proprietors were absentee landlords who regarded their estates as a status symbol rather than an investment. The great estate was a social, not an economic institution. It was wasteful of land and rarely became an efficient unit of produc-

---

[71] Salomon, *La campagne de Nouvelle Castille*, pp. 212–51; Vassberg, *Land and Society in Golden Age Castile*, pp. 217–18; Kamen, *Spain in the Later Seventeenth Century*, pp. 200–4, 234, 243.

[72] Salomon, *La campagne de Nouvelle Castille*, pp. 245–7.

tion. Moreover, land concentration by the elite imposed other obstacles to change.

Most of Castilian agriculture was self-sufficient in function, but wealth was extracted from it to pay for state spending and for imports. State, church and landlords siphoned off taxes, tithes, seigneurial dues and mortgage payments from a peasantry made dependent by the dominance of the great estate. Much of this income was further concentrated in the hands of the landed elites, who in addition to rent and feudal dues had won possession of tithes, *alcabalas* and other taxes through concession of the crown. In some cases the amount paid by peasant producers to the state was less than that paid to the landed elites, who may have collected as much as 50 per cent of agricultural output. Some of this revenue was in cash, but a large proportion of it was taken in the form of wheat, barley, rye and wine, much of which was difficult to exchange for other forms of wealth.[73] But landlords could divert lands to wool, which was saleable, and store grain and other received products until times of shortage when prices rose and sales were good, a tactic which was beyond the means of small farmers. Thus the rentier groups consolidated their income into cash, which they used not for investing in the rural sector but for buying luxury imports, simultaneously depriving agriculture of capital and industry of protection.

Depressed by taxation and the agrarian structure, agriculture was also frustrated by the traditional bias towards livestock farming in Castile.[74] Pastoral farming, it is true, responded to the market. Flocks of sheep were usually cost-effective and wool was a valuable commodity; for some farmers sheep breeding was an escape from poverty, and for exporters the economy produced nothing better. But the question remains, had Spain got the balance right between plough and pasture?

The Mesta, the organization of migrating herdsmen, had already won the struggle for access to commons, waste lands, fallow strips adjoining tilled fields and other town lands; the notorious law of *posesión*, by which a Mesta member was granted permanent tenancy of any field he had occupied, continued to operate; and Philip II and his successors reinforced previous

---

[73] García Sanz, *Desarrollo y crisis del Antiguo Régimen en Castilla la Vieja*, pp. 382–4.

[74] See Lynch, *Spain 1516–1598*, pp. 21–3, 160–2, 194.

208 SOCIETY AND ECONOMY

legislation in favour of pastoral and against arable farming.[75] The cumulative effect of this policy was to prevent the extension of arable lands in central and southern Castile and to accelerate rural depopulation. Yet in the second half of the sixteenth century the power of the Mesta had begun to wane. Its flocks of sheep and its wool production ceased to expand; its profits were eroded by heavy taxation; and its legal position was gradually subverted. In a series of important lawsuits Mesta members lost a number of pasture privileges. Their opponents were towns and local agrarian interests, fighting for possession of common lands. But this was not a victory for arable farming: the new enclosers were simply the sedentary branch of the pastoral industry, enclosing for ox pastures, swine fields and non-migratory sheep grazing, the latter a much larger sector than the migratory. By the end of the seventeenth century, under pressure of independent landowners, farmers and peasants, the Mesta had further retreated, but so had arable farming.[76] The consequence of this was that Spain continued to suffer periodic subsistence crises and to depend on the import of foreign grain. Valencia needed imports from the Mediterranean area, Andalucía from northern Europe. In 1635, during the war with the United Provinces and France, when trade with the enemy was prohibited, San Sebastian complained that Guipúzcoa was suffering from severe grain shortage, because its normal suppliers, the Dutch and the French, were excluded from Spanish ports.[77]

Thwarted by man and nature, agriculture yielded progressively less in the first half of the seventeenth century and showed no signs of recovery until the years after 1660. Harvests were smaller than those of the sixteenth century, and only half the volume of those in the late eighteenth century.[78] Population loss was obviously a prime factor causing low yields. But in addition there was little technical progress, which might have enabled farmers to expand production, cut costs and absorb labour losses. The increase in agricultural production in sixteenth-century Castile was

[75] J. Klein, *The Mesta. A Study in Spanish Economic History*, 1273–1836 (Cambridge, Mass, 1920), pp. 93–4, 322.
[76] Ibid., pp. 279, 337–43.
[77] A. Domínguez Ortiz, 'Guerra económica y comercio extranjero en el reinado de Felipe IV', *Hispania*, xxiii (1963), pp. 94–5.
[78] Gonzalo Anes, *Las crisis agrarias en la España moderna* (Madrid, 1970), pp. 338–50.

based primarily on extension of area under cultivation rather than
real improvement of existing productivity. The one technological
change – the conversion from oxen to mules for ploughing – was
a mixed blessing. Mules were more adaptable, mobile and econo-
mical, and they could plough more land. But they ploughed
shallower furrows, and this produced lower yields; and they
consumed (in barley) a significant portion of the harvest they
produced.[79] Moreover, extensive agriculture had taken many
farmers into shallower hillside soils, which were easily eroded
and less productive; the ploughing of marginal lands was thus a
further factor in decreasing productivity.

Agricultural depression was general throughout Spain, though
there were regional variations and some chronological movement.
Catalan agriculture escaped the severe crisis afflicting industry
and commerce and continued to respond, if faintly, to the demands of foreign markets. In Valencia on the other hand, agricultural production decreased in the first half of the century and
showed only slight signs of recovery in the decades 1650–80. In
Galicia, tithe income rose from the late sixteenth century to 1615,
then stagnated until 1675, when it began to recover.[80] In Old
Castile agriculture remained in total depression in the first half of
the century and only began to emerge from crisis after 1660, more
strongly perhaps from 1680–90; even so, wheat tithes did not
regain their 1590 level until 1750.[81] Andalucía was a case apart.
Here there was no particular crisis of production, simply a long
stagnation, with minimum changes as production responded to
population trends and the number of mouths to feed; the years
1680–3 showed the first glimmer of recovery.[82] The region of
Cadiz adjusted to changes of this kind, and in the period 1591–
1632 agricultural production showed a slight tendency to rise and
certainly to avoid any great decrease. A significant factor here was
the pull of America: on the one hand producers had the possibility of exporting to the colonial market, and on the other the
consumer population of Cadiz itself increased, as immigrants
moved in for better access to American trade and emigration.

[79] Vassberg, *Land and Society in Golden Age Castile*, pp. 158–9.
[80] Pegerto Saavedra, *Economía, política, y sociedad en Galicia*, pp. 210–12.
[81] García Sanz, *Desarrollo y crisis del Antiguo Régimen en Castilla la Vieja*,
p. 95.
[82] Antonio Miguel Bernal, in Antonio Domínguez Ortiz, ed., *Historia de
Andalucía* (8 vols, Barcelona, 1980), vi, p. 199.

These factors account for an increase in agricultural production particularly in the years 1623–7.[83]

Agriculture was the key which locked the door to economic growth in Spain. Without agrarian change there was no prospect of raising the living standards of the mass of the people, and without this there was no possibility of industrial development. Peasants living at subsistence level were not regular consumers of manufactures; and urban workers had to pay too much for food to have anything left for consumer goods. Inhibited by the mediocrity of the market, industry was also frustrated by the pattern of consumption and investment in Spain. The small luxury market preferred foreign goods, which were a drain on domestic capital; what was left was invested in state and consumer loans rather than risked in industrial enterprise.[84] The example of Madrid was critical. Poor immigrants, forming the service, artisan and construction sectors of the capital, had to use what income they had on the most basic commodities and did not constitute an urban market for regionally produced manufactures. Meanwhile the small elite used its purchasing power on imported products. Thus Castilian manufactures suffered and the regional economy settled for wheat production and sheep; granted the vagaries of urban demand, it was not surprising that rural society moved away from market forces and opted for subsistence and self-sufficiency.[85]

Economic institutions were not propitious for industry. Guild organization, enshrining a defensive mentality and the values placed on hierarchy and seniority, maintained a rigid framework

---

[83] Francisco M. Traverso Ruiz, *Riqueza y producción agraria en Cádiz durante los siglos XVI y XVII* (Cadiz, 1987), p. 171, and the same author's 'La producción agrícola en el Obispado de Cádiz, otra excepción en la decadencia del siglo XVII (1591–1648)', *Hispania*, 47, 165 (1987), pp. 163–201.

[84] For different interpretation of the failure of Spanish industry see E. J. Hamilton, 'American Treasure and the Rise of Capitalism, 1500–1700', *Economica*, ix (1929), pp. 338–57. According to Hamilton, the lag of prices behind wages in Spain gave insufficient profits to manufacturers and deterred investment in industry, while there was no technical progress to reduce costs; but it has still to be shown that wages of industrial workers in Spain were in general higher than those of workers in industrializing countries. See the same author's 'The Decline of Spain', *Economic History Review*, first series, viii (1938), pp. 168–79. An informed and balanced judgement will be found in Antonio Domínguez Ortiz, *El Antiguo Régimen: los Reyes Católicos y los Austrias* (2nd edn, Madrid, 1974), pp. 131–9.

[85] Ringrose, *Madrid and the Spanish Economy*, pp. 88–9, 127.

around production. And even when industry escaped from guild control into artisan and workshop form, as in ironworks and some manufactures, its progress was still inhibited by social attitudes and prejudice against 'low and mechanical' occupations. Industry was also depressed by the fiscal policy of the state which penalized production by heavy purchase taxes and deterred consumption.[86] The negative consequences of taxation in the period 1630–50 could be seen in Ciudad Real, where potential industrial investors were constrained to divert their resources into land and offices, assets which provided more prestige as well as greater security.[87] Thus Castile turned away from urbanization, manufacturing and commerce, and the middle sectors abandoned any pretensions they had ever had to economic vocations. Readjustment of this kind was in effect a retreat from national markets into localized self-sufficiency, a process of survival in times of depression but not a stimulus to growth. The other face of localized economies was isolation. Internal customs barriers impeded the free movement of materials and goods. There were customs posts between Castile, the Basque provinces, Navarre, the Aragonese provinces and Andalucía; and royal customs, usually at 10 per cent, were accompanied by numerous municipal and seigneurial tolls, which further encumbered the transit of goods.[88] It was frequently cheaper to import foreign manufactures by sea than to place orders within Spain. As Gondomar pointed out in 1616:

It would be better for Spain to remove all internal customs and to increase those at the ports, where foreigners would pay and not the natives who trade within the country ... It is more convenient at the moment for consumers in Galicia, Asturias, Vizcaya, Navarre, Aragon, Valencia, Catalonia, Andalucía and Portugal to get their cloth from London than from Segovia.[89]

Virtually every sector of Spanish industry was depressed in the seventeenth century, though the depression was more serious in

[86] Salvador de Moxó, *La alcabala. Sobre sus orígenes, concepto y naturaleza* (Madrid, 1963).

[87] Carla Rahn Phillips, *Ciudad Real, 1500–1750: Growth, Crisis, and Readjustment in the Spanish Economy* (Cambridge, Mass., 1979), pp. 124–6.

[88] J. Carrera Pujal, *Historia política y económica de Cataluña*, ii, p. 459.

[89] Gondomar to Philip III, 1616, in Sureda Carrión, *La hacienda castellana y los economistas del siglo XVII*, pp. 123–4.

the major sectors – textiles, metallurgy and shipbuilding – than in light industries supplying local markets. The worst victim was the once-booming textile industry, embracing the woollen cloth of Segovia, Toledo and Cuenca, and the silks of Granada, Málaga, Seville and Toledo.[90] While none of these centres actually ceased production, all of them suffered severe recession, unemployment and loss of export markets.

In the sixteenth century about 77 per cent of the active population of Segovia was occupied in industry, 65 per cent in the textile industry. Segovia consumed a good part of the raw wool of Old Castile, and its great boom in the years 1570–90 took place to some extent at the expense of Burgos, which owed its prosperity to the export of raw wool. Between 1590 and 1630 Segovia slipped from prosperity into crisis and entered a century of depression during which its population dropped from 25,000 to 8,000, and its economy was reorientated from industry to agriculture.[91] Segovia was a victim of its own success. As urban and industrial growth proceeded apace, so it drew in workers from the countryside and weakened the agrarian sector; a smaller rural work force now had to provide food and raw materials for an expanded urban population. Agricultural production was extended to marginal zones, which yielded poorer returns for higher costs, involved excessive crop fluctuations and ultimately pushed up prices. The higher costs of food and labour were felt in the urban sector; costs of industrial production increased and Segovian textiles became less competitive. And in the countryside peasants plagued by increased rents and higher taxes had less to spend on the products of urban industry. Thus Segovia's industry was decapitalized and the economic boom collapsed. The number of textile looms dropped from 600 operating in 1580, to 300 in the reign of Philip IV, and 159 in 1691. No doubt foreign competition played its part in this demise, and well known handicaps – technical inferiority, guild regulations and price inflation – weakened Segovia's ability to respond. But the Segovian economy

---

[90] On Spanish industry in the seventeenth century see Colmeiro, *Historia de la economía política en España*, ii, pp. 783–97; J. Carrera Pujal, *Historia de la economía española* (5 vols., Barcelona, 1943–7), i–ii; Santiago Rodríguez García *El arte de las sedas valencianas en el siglo XVIII* (Valencia, 1959); Kamen, *Spain in the Later Seventeenth Century*, pp. 71–4.

[91] García Sanz, *Desarrollo y crisis del Antiguo Régimen en Castilla la Vieja*, pp. 53–4, 82–4, 145–6, 216–18.

had already been undermined from within. Segovia now sought a new model of growth. This was found in the agricultural sector, which earned some surplus for Segovia by exporting wheat to the uncertain market of Madrid, and otherwise lapsed into subsistence.

Elsewhere, de-industrialization and ruralization became the common pattern of the Castilian economy. Collapse of international and national markets, contraction of industry, an agrarian escape hatch and regional subsistence economies, this was the economic landscape of seventeenth-century Castile. Population losses were part cause, part consequence of urban and industrial recession. The population of Cuenca fell from 15,000 to 5,000, losses parallel to those of its textile industry. Toledo's failure was even more spectacular. Measured in the number of looms in operation, its woollen output fell by three-quarters in the first two-thirds of the seventeenth century; in the 1660s thousands of silk looms and closed down, and by 1685 there were only 600 in active operation; and its population fell from 60,000 in the late sixteenth century to 20,000 in 1691, by which time Toledo was a town of churches and convents.[92] The depopulation of these industrial centres further reduced the demand for consumer goods, while the loss of skilled labour worsened the prospects of revival; subsequent attempts to rebuild the textile industry invariably involved the employment of foreign craftsmen or management. Spain continued to manufacture textiles, especially for the lower end of the market. Where she could not compete was in high quality textiles, as buyers preferred the foreign article to the national product, which tended to lack variety and style. To some extent Spanish textiles failed to adapt themselves to changes in consumer tastes. When the international market for woollens collapsed in the early seventeenth century, they failed to adapt their products as rapidly as manufacturers in northern Europe. They lost the home market to competition from English cloth: England possessed a quasi-monopoly of long-staple light-weight wool, especially suitable for wear in Mediterranean countries, and it was partly this which enabled English worsted manufacturers to dominate the Spanish market in the seventeenth century.[93]

[92] Domínguez Ortiz, *La sociedad española en el siglo XVII*, pp. 136–9.
[93] P. J. Bowden, 'Wool supply and the woollen industry', *Economic History Review*, second series, ix (1956–7), pp. 44–58.

Spain had formerly possessed a small but active metallurgical industry, centred in the northern provinces of Vizcaya and Guipúzcoa. By the 1550s this consisted of some 300 ironworks, powered by large water-driven hammers, and producing about 300,000 quintals (3,300 tons) of iron and steel goods a year.[94] Two-thirds of this output consisted of arms, ships' parts, and general hardware, while the rest was in the form of ingots. Defence orders obviously provided a stimulus to the metallurgical industry and indeed exceeded its capacity. In the first decades of the seventeenth century Spanish firms were still supplying all types of arms but no longer on the scale with which they had supplied the Armada of 1588. By this time output of iron and steel manufactures seems to have dropped to some 100,000 quintals a year. A report of 1634 estimated that 80,000 quintals of iron and steel a year, about three-quarters in the form of manufactured products, were being shipped through Bilbao for other parts of Spain, for the colonies, and for export abroad.[95] The industry could no longer meet domestic requirements. As early as 1619 the *arbitrista* Sancho de Moncada claimed that although iron ore was exported the country had to import some 2 million ducats' worth of iron and steel manufactures every year. In the late seventeenth century even the production of iron ore slumped. Between 1650 and 1700 the ironworks of Liérganes produced an average of only 4,000 quintals a year, compared with 24,000 in 1639 and 20,000 in 1703.[96] As for manufactures, Spain was now an importer of arms. The most famous centre for swords and daggers had been Toledo, but by the 1650s its forges had almost ceased production; Vizcaya still produced a few but they were extremely expensive.[97] In the second half of the seventeenth century the country depended for its hardware on England and France, who also supplied much of its military equipment. Spain, a military power for so long, no longer even possessed an adequate arms industry.

[94] T. Guiard Larrauri, *Historia del Consulado y Casa de Contratación de Bilbao y del comercio de la villa (1511–1880)* (2 vols, Bilbao, 1913–14); J. Caro Baroja, *Los Vascos. Etnología* (San Sebastian, 1949), pp. 255–71.
[95] Guiard, *Historia del Consulado*, i, p. 526.
[96] José Alcalá-Zamora y Queipo de Llano, *Historia de una empresa siderúrgica española: los altos hornos de Liérganes y La Cavada, 1622–1834* (Santander, 1974), pp. 21–2, 94–6, 238–40.
[97] Ibid., pp. 259–60.

PLATE 5 *View of Zaragoza, 1647*, by J. B. Martínez del Mazo (reproduced by kind permission of the Museo del Prado, Madrid)

The shipbuilding industry had experienced a boom in the six-teenth century, stimulated by orders for the Indies trade and defence requirements.[98] Now orders were less frequent and more difficult to meet. The Barcelona shipyards, rescued from stagnation by Philip II's naval war against Islam, did not sustain their performance in the seventeenth century; shippers tended increasingly to purchase or hire vessels in Italy.[99] The shipyards of northern Spain were more active than those of Catalonia. Although they had come to depend heavily on imports of timber and naval stores from the Baltic, they had so far survived the attempts of Spain's northern enemies to cut these vital supplies. In the best years of the sixteenth century there were orders totalling 15,000 *toneladas* under construction at one time in the shipyards of Bilbao.[100] Production continued, though on a reduced scale, in the first decades of the seventeenth century, and vessels were still built for the navy, the merchant marine, including transports for iron, and the fishing industry. It was reported by the *consulado* of Bilbao in 1630 that forty galleons, many of 600–700 tons, had been constructed in the port's shipyards during the previous twenty years. In 1640 there were four large vessels under construction, and in 1662 there were ten.[101] In 1673 five vessels for the Atlantic fleet ranging in size from about 400 to 900 *toneladas* were constructed in Guipúzcoa and the Asturias.[102] In 1677–9 five vessels were built in the various yards of Guipúzcoa. One of the leading shipbuilders in the first half of the century was Pedro de Colima, who undertook to construct twelve galleons of 800 tons in 1638 and six galleons of 850 tons the following year in the shipyards of San Sebastian, Ubursil and Osorno.[103]

The history of six ships built in Basque shipyards for the royal

[98] See Lynch *Spain, 1516–1598*, pp. 169–71.

[99] Carrera Pujal, *Historia política y económica de Cataluña*, ii, pp. 333–69.

[100] Gervasio de Artíñano de Galdárano, *Historia del comercio con las Indias durante el dominio de los Austrias* (Madrid, 1917), pp. 247–8; see the same author's *La arquitectura naval española (en madera)* (Madrid, 1920).

[101] Guiard, *Historia del Consulado*, i, p. 531; see the same author's *La industria naval vizcaína. Anotaciones históricas y estadísticas* (Bilbao, 1917).

[102] Kamen, *Spain in the Later Seventeenth Century*, p. 115.

[103] José de Veítia Linaje, *Norte de la contratación de las Indias Occidentales* [1672] (Buenos Aires, 1945), p. 667. The price contracted for was 30 ducats a ton.

service in 1625–8 demonstrates that Spain was still a major sea power and possessed the national shipping resources needed to sustain her world role.[104] She could still assemble capital, labour, raw materials and technology to build large vessels. Whether these were of a standard comparable to those of northern Europe is perhaps an open question, but the navy obtained good service from the six vessels under review. If there were economic problems they did not necessarily lie in the shipyards. It was more costly to operate a ship than to build it. While each of the six galleons cost about 15,696 ducats to build, it cost double this amount to provision and operate a galleon for one round trip on the transatlantic run. Yet in spite of the loss of an entire treasure fleet to the Dutch at Matanzas in 1628, Spain displayed great powers of recovery and renewed the Indies sailings with hardly a pause. These six vessels operated actively in the Indies fleets in 1629–35 and in the Atlantic fleets in 1635–9, and some of them played a dramatic role in the Battle of the Downs, evidence indeed of the endurance of Spanish-built galleons and of Spanish sea power.

While the Basque shipbuilding industry survived in the seventeenth century it did so in the face of serious problems. It suffered in the first place from the recession in the Indies trade from the 1620s which seriously reduced investment in new ocean-going vessels.[105] It was, moreover, heavily dependent on foreign-based service industries for the supply of masts, tar, hemp and sail. Spain could not furnish appropriate timber in adequate quantity, and she produced insufficient naval stores; these had to be imported from the Baltic, and as war material they were a particular target of the Dutch blockade. Shortage of naval stores raised their price; shipbuilding costs were also raised by shortage of skilled labour which inflated the industry's wages bill. Tomás Cano, a former captain, calculated in 1612 that a vessel of 500 tons, which in the mid-sixteenth century cost 4,000 ducats, now cost 15,000.[106] Yet adverse conditions were not the only enemy of the Basque shipbuilding industry. It was also a victim of its own

---

[104] Carla Rahn Phillips, *Six Galleons for the King of Spain: Imperial Defense in the Early Seventeenth Century* (Baltimore, MD, 1986), pp. 19–46.

[105] Chaunu, *Séville et l'Atlantique*, viii, 2, 2, pp. 1046, 1520–1, 1597.

[106] *Arte de Navegar*, 1612, quoted in Braudel, *La Méditerranée et le monde méditerranéen*, p. 399.

technical failure. In the period 1614–22 the number of Basque-built vessels in the Indies trade fell dramatically; in the next three decades it fell further, and Basque vessels came to constitute less than one-third of those operating on the transatlantic run, losing place to foreign vessels (more than one-third) and even to American-built vessels (about one-third).[107] These figures seem to have improved later in the century, when a sample of 239 vessels employed in the Indies trade gives 37 per cent as foreign-built, 20 per cent American-built, and 43 per cent built in Spain itself.[108] But the fact remains that shippers at Seville and Cadiz no longer merely tolerated foreign vessels: they chose them, and one of the reasons was their superior quality. In the first quarter of the seventeenth century a series of losses at sea cast serious doubts upon the adequacy of Spanish-built ships and caused many shippers to complain of their technical inferiority. As more and more foreign transports entered the Indies trade the government made several attempts by decree to impose on the Basque industry new standards of construction and new proportions in vessels for the transatlantic run.[109] Yet by 1640 little progress had been made. A treatise published in that year focused on two weaknesses of the industry.[110] It was starved of naval stores and other raw materials, and these were only available at prices well above the general price level. The industry also lacked technical proficiency, and was impervious to change; it still produced huge and ponderous galleons, floating castles which were years behind the vessels of northern Europe in manoeuvrability and adaptability.

While textiles, metallurgy and shipbuilding were all in various degrees of trouble in the seventeenth century, import-substitution industries appear to have fared better. In Barcelona and Valencia the manufacture of ceramics and glass, drawing on local raw materials, maintained its performance, and output was probably

---

[107] Chaunu, *Séville et l'Atlantique*, vi, 1, pp. 114–67; viii, 2, 2, pp. 1563, 1682, 1757–8, 1831.

[108] Kamen, *Spain in the Later Seventeenth Century*, p. 115.

[109] See A. P. Usher, 'Spanish Ships and Shipping in the 16th and 17th centuries', in *Facts and Factors in Economic History. Essays presented to Edward Francis Gay* (Cambridge, Mass., 1932), pp. 189–90.

[110] 'Diálogo entre un vizcaíno y un montañés sobre construcción de naves', 1640, summarized in Chaunu, *Séville et l'Atlantique*, v, p. 369; on the neglect of naval architecture in Spain see Veitia Linaje, *Norte de la contratación de las Indias Occidentales*, p. 665.

adequate for the home market, though this was not large as glass was less used for windows in Spain than elsewhere in Europe. Leather manufacture at Córdoba (shoes), and Ciudad Real and Ocaña (gloves), seems to have diminished but still supplied the home market. Soap manufacturing was continued in establishments at Triana (Seville) and Valencia, and even succeeded in exporting some of its product. Paper mills, on the other hand, while continuing production at Segovia, Gerona and Cuenca, could not meet domestic demand, and Spain depended heavily on paper imports throughout the seventeenth century.[111]

The evidence is too scanty to permit a quantitative assessment of Spanish industry in the seventeenth century, and the most that it yields is a general impression. Two conclusions may be justified. The traditional picture of universal and utter collapse has been overdrawn. A number of light industries, fed by local raw materials and catering for the home market, stayed in business and effectively substituted for imports. But in three of the European growth industries of the period – textiles, metallurgy and shipbuilding – Spain suffered serious recession and lagged far behind her rivals in northern Europe. She lost her export markets, of course, but she also lost a large part of her domestic and colonial markets; she lost them to the English, the French and the Dutch.

Contemporary proposals for remedying the situation were based on mercantilist assumptions.[112] A typical example was the submission made by the University of Toledo in a memorandum drafted by one of its professors, Sancho de Moncada. It was argued that countries which produced only primary products were poor and had a trade deficit, for the unit value of their exports was less than that of countries which exported manufactured goods; it followed that Spain should industrialize, and this was also essential for defence needs and to supply the colonies; and industry should be given protection by outright prohibition of foreign manufactured goods. The policy of import prohibition was frequently canvassed and occasionally adopted. A decree

---

[111] Colmeiro, *Historia de la economía política en España*, ii, pp. 783–97.

[112] On contemporary economic thought see E. J. Hamilton, 'Spanish Mercantilism before 1700', in *Facts and Factors in Economic History*, pp. 214–39; Robert S. Smith, 'Spanish Anti-mercantilism of the Seventeenth Century', *Journal of Political Economy*, xlviii (1940), pp. 401–11; J. Larraz, *La época del mercantilismo en Castilla*, 1500–1700 (2nd edn, Madrid, 1944).

issued in the celebrated *Pragmática de Reformación* (10 February 1623) forbade under pain of fine and confiscation the import of textile, leather and other manufactures for the consumer market, on the grounds that these competed with Spanish products, put Spanish factories and artisans out of work and impaired the balance of payments.[113] Amidst a chorus of protest from foreign exporters and native importers, the government was forced to concede so many exemptions that the decree became irrelevant. Prohibition simply caused a diminution of trade or, more likely, an expansion of contraband, from both of which the treasury suffered. The basic reason for the failure of this policy was that Spain either took foreign imports or went without manufactures altogether. For the removal of competition could not in itself revive Spanish industry. The mercantilists never explained where the factors of production were to come from. Who was to supply the capital, the entrepreneurial skills and the technical expertise for industrial expansion? And would not industrialization simply divert resources which could be better used to expand the production of wool, agricultural and other primary products already assured of export markets? Even as an exporter of raw materials Spain's performance was not impressive.

Foreign Trade

Spain's commodity exports were limited to a few primary products – wool, wine, olive oil, iron and cochineal (a re-export from America). Against these she imported textiles, linens, hardware, naval stores, paper and grain. Large foreign payments also had to be made for defence purposes. The deteriorating balance of payments was bridged by export of gold and silver, when they were available.

Andalucía was a fertile resource base, but not an expanding one. Most of its exports – olive oil, olives, raisins and wine – went to the Indies, little to northern Europe, while its grain production and its textiles were consumed locally. Andalucía was more important as an entrepôt for trade between northern Europe and America, in which French, Netherlands and English merchants

[113] Domínguez Ortiz, 'Guerra económica y comercio extranjero en el reinado de Felipe IV' *Hispania*, xxiii (1963), pp. 71–110.

had a sizeable stake but from which Andalucían merchants also made large fortunes, if only as middlemen. In eastern Spain Alicante was an extreme version of Spain's foreign trade, exporting little beyond a few primary products and importing a wide range of manufactured goods from northern Europe, Baltic products such as timber and iron, fish and occasionally grain, mostly in foreign vessels while local merchants were content to earn commissions as middlemen.[114] The trade of Catalonia expanded by 60 per cent in the period 1664–99, though it was heavily imbalanced, importing textiles, spices and fish against a few regional exports. From its northern coast, where the Basque ports were relatively free from customs duties, Spain exported wool and iron, a trade which was the object of much competition between Bilbao and Santander. In the early seventeenth century the region served only as an entrepôt for Castilian wool and foreign manufactures and was dominated by foreign merchants, leaving only a share of the profits for the local economy. But by the end of the century the native merchants of Bilbao had come into their own.

Wool continued to be the most important Spanish export commodity. By the end of the sixteenth century the quality of Spanish wool in fineness was accepted as superior to English and it was doing much better than its rival in continental wool markets.[115] Spanish wool maintained its reputation until well past the middle of the seventeenth century. In the meantime it had secured a good market in England. English manufacturers began to increase their import of fine Spanish wool from the 1620s; it was this wool which enabled the West Country to develop the production of a new type of cloth, called Spanish or medley cloth, a high quality product which sold well in northern Europe.[116] In 1667, at the time of the Anglo-Spanish commercial treaty, it was estimated that Spain exported 36,000 to 40,000 bags of wool a year, with 8 *arrobas* of wool in each bag; Holland and Hamburg took 22,000 bags, England between 2,000 and 7,000 bags.[117] While Spanish wool was of good quality it was also expensive. This was due not only to inflationary tendencies in

[114] Kamen, *Spain in the Later Seventeenth Century*, pp. 120–1, 123–5.
[115] Bowden, 'Wool supply and the woollen industry', p. 48.
[116] Ibid., pp. 56–8.
[117] Jean O. McLachlan, *Trade and Peace with Old Spain, 1667–1750* (Cambridge, 1940), pp. 8–9.

Spain but also to government taxes on wool exports. By 1667 these had reached a level which caused the *consulado* of Bilbao to complain that they were almost equivalent to the value of the commodity taxed.[118] An English estimate in 1680 claimed that fine Spanish wool was 'always near twice as dear as our finest English wool'.[119]

Following the collapse of Burgos, the wool trade was almost entirely handled by the merchants of Bilbao. Bilbao also exported iron, a high quality ore from its hinterland, for which there was a fairly constant demand. In 1680 it was complained in England that the great increase in the import of Spanish iron was detrimental to native iron works.[120] Between wool and iron Bilbao enjoyed some prosperity in the seventeenth century. While the account books of *consulado* income are not a valid index of trade, they give perhaps a general picture of commercial activity. The *consulado* of Bilbao's average annual income was some 607,000 maravedis in the period 1590–96; 565,000 in 1600–25; 725,000 in 1626–51; 1,850,000 in 1651–77; 2,555,000 in 1677–1701.[121] From this it would appear that Bilbao maintained some activity in maritime commerce, and did not suffer the fate of other commercial centres in Spain. The volume of Bilbao's shipping in this period can be deduced from the evidence of the charity tax on each vessel entering and clearing the port. An average of 209 vessels a year paid the tax in the period 1601–26; 184 in 1626–51; 211 in 1651–75; 213 in 1675–1700.[122]

In the first half of the seventeenth century Spanish foreign trade had to operate in conditions of almost permanent warfare. Yet war never caused a complete cessation of trade, even with the enemy. In the long war with England to 1604, and with the United Provinces to 1609, Spain had to allow her enemies to bring grain and manufactured goods into the peninsula, for she needed these imports and did not have the shipping to handle them; for the rest of her northern trade she had to rely on Hansa shipping. The route between Cadiz and northern Europe, there-

---

[118] Klein, *The Mesta*, p. 46; Smith, *The Spanish Guild Merchant*, pp. 74–5.
[119] 'Discourse of Trade', 1680, in J. R. McCulloch, ed., *Early English Tracts on Commerce* (Cambridge, 1954), p. 322.
[120] Ibid., p. 418.
[121] Smith, *The Spanish Guild Merchant*, p. 89.
[122] Ibid., pp. 89–90.

fore, was still active. Following the renewal of war between Spain and the United Provinces in 1621, the Dutch continued to trade with Spain by various means, inserting their goods via France and Portugal. The trade was so active that the Council of Castile complained in 1624: 'The Dutch buy merchandise from the English, export it here, and take out gold and silver, with which they then finance their rebellion against us.'[123]

The Spanish government attempted to fight back on the commercial front. In October 1624 it created the *Almirantazgo de Sevilla*, a kind of trading company whose function was to provide armed convoys for trade with northern Europe, to attack Dutch shipping, and to keep it out of the peninsula.[124] The company was therefore instructed to maintain an armada of twenty-four warships and merchant vessels, financed from prizes, condemnations and a 1 per cent tax on goods from Andalucía to northern Europe. In view of the difficulty experienced in maintaining armed convoys for the Indies trade, it is not surprising that the *almirantazgo* failed to function in this form. It soon became simply a bureaucratic institution, based on Madrid, which maintained a network of agents for the confiscation of enemy goods entering the peninsula.[125] The English during the war of 1625–30, and the French during the war of 1635–59, suffered from its attentions. And so, until 1648, did the Dutch. Indeed they were the particular target of this type of economic warfare, but they were skilful enemies. They devised various means of evading the embargo; a favoured method, in collaboration with Spanish merchants, was to exchange goods for silver a few miles from the coast.

Spanish merchants complained bitterly against the *almirantazgo*, alleging that it fulfilled none of its positive functions but simply restricted valuable trade. They argued that obstacles to imports not only caused shortages and drove up prices but also harmed Spanish exports, to such an extent that the wine and olive producers of Andalucía were in serious difficulty. Seville merchants were particularly resentful, for they were deprived of their

---

[123] Quoted by Domínguez Ortiz, 'Guerra económica', p. 75; see also Mauro, *Le Portugal et l'Atlantique au XVIIe siècle*, p. 342.

[124] A. Domínguez Ortiz, 'El Almirantazgo de los Países Septentrionales y la política económica de Felipe IV', *Hispania*, xxvii (1947), pp. 272–90.

[125] Domínguez Ortiz, 'Guerra económica', pp. 78–81, 85.

usual supplies for the American trade, and this in turn reduced the sale of re-exports from America; according to the *consulado* of Seville, the price of cochineal, indigo and ginger dropped by 25 per cent.[126] Yet the government of Olivares continued to prohibit trade with the enemy, in the belief that prohibition deprived the enemy of wealth. A decree of 16 May 1628 further defined illegal trade: it included enemy and neutral goods carried in enemy vessels, and enemy goods carried in neutral vessels. The list of prohibited goods indicates the type of imports on which Spain normally relied: textiles headed the list, followed by furniture, watches, books, pictures, needles, combs and musical instruments.

Although these measures ceased to apply against England after the Anglo-Spanish peace of 1630, they were intensified against France, especially from the outbreak of full-scale war in 1635. But total closure was never effected. French linens always found a ready market in Spain, chiefly for re-export to the Indies; and shippers relied on the import of French sails for equipping the Indies fleets.[127] The frontier provinces of north-east Spain were also dependent on trade with France, in their case for food imports as well as consumer goods. In these circumstances prohibition was evaded by various devices, ranging from outright contraband to the use of neutral vessels – mainly Hansa and English – which endeavoured to conceal the origins of their cargo. The government itself recognized the need for French imports, from which it could also derive a revenue. It therefore sold licences: in 1638 revenue from licences yielded 255,460 ducats, indicating a substantial trade with France, for the licencees usually exceeded their quotas. In any case, the government could not control climatic conditions and it had to allow the entry of French grain. The Cantabrian region continued to import French grain, and in 1647, a year of poor harvests, Andalucía was allowed to do the same. In 1648 the government believed that peace with Holland would enable it to tighten up on the French trade, as it now had an alternative trading partner. In fact the Dutch simply took the opportunity to carry French merchandise into Spain, as the English were already doing.

[126] Memorandum of the consulado of Seville, 1627, ibid., pp. 85–6.
[127] In the years 1636–7 there was a spurt of demand in the Indies trade which reinforced the need for French goods; see Chaunu, *Séville et l'Atlantique*, v, p. 237; viii, 2, 2, p. 1757.

By 1650 it was appreciated even in official circles that measures against French trade were ineffective. Yet the policy of prohibiting trade with the enemy continued to be applied, and by decree of 8 April it was extended to a new enemy, Cromwell's England. In 1657 the Council of Castile debated its efficacy. A minority group argued that the policy was ineffective and harmful, ineffective because corrupt customs officials connived at evasion, harmful because it deprived the treasury of revenue. Yet the majority of councillors favoured prohibition as a weapon of war and believed that it could be made effective if the Portuguese lessees were removed from the customs houses. In the event the weapon was as harmless against England as it had been against France. English goods continued to reach Spain, frequently in Dutch vessels, and to be re-exported to the Spanish Indies.

During war Spain was a target as well as a market for her enemies. Normally the Indies fleets were too strongly defended to offer easy prizes to privateers, and by this time there were very few Spanish vessels on the trade routes of western and northern Europe. Enemy privateering, therefore, was directed essentially against neutral vessels trading in war commodities to Spain. The English took a much stricter view of war contraband than the French and the Dutch, who were prepared to deal in most commodities, including naval stores. English privateers crowded the Channel and sought to cut communications between Spain and northern Europe, at least in respect of vital war supplies. During the war of 1625–30 they were particularly active off the north-west coast of Spain and kept Galicia virtually in a stage of siege.[128] In the war of 1655–60, on the other hand, the privateers tended to trade with the enemy, and it was the English navy that conducted operations against Spanish shipping. Spain herself did not develop a privateering industry: there were very few Spanish candidates for licences, and foreign captains could not be trusted. When, after 1648, a number of Dutch captains procured Spanish privateering licences for use against French shipping, they simply traded with France, took the merchandise to the Spanish Indies and sold it as an alleged prize of war. Basque captains did the same. In 1651 it was alleged that twelve to fourteen were operat-

[128] Domínguez Ortiz, 'Guerra económica', pp. 96–8.

ing in this way.[129] Normally, however, Spain did not issue privateering licences, for she was fearful of massive retaliation.

By the mid-seventeenth century Spain's balance of payments difficulties had worsened. Her export performance was poor: wool output was not increasing, and wine, oil raisins and other agricultural products were earning little. Bullion had to be expended on Portuguese sugar and spices, on grain from northern Europe and the Mediterranean and on manufactured goods, arms and naval stores from England, France, Holland, Denmark and Sweden. As an English observer remarked in 1680, 'The exporting of treasure [is] prohibited in Spain under the highest penalties; and yet because Spain is overbalanced by consumptive importations, foreigners continually carry it away.'[130]

Yet peace was hardly more propitious than war. As Spain did not win her prolonged war against Holland, France and finally England, she was forced to concede favourable trading terms to her former enemies, to the Dutch in 1648–50, to the French in 1659, and to the English in 1667. The Dutch were acknowledged to have complete freedom to transport merchandise of all countries, including those at war with Spain. By the Treaty of the Pyrenees France procured a most-favoured-nation clause, giving her all the privileges the Dutch had already acquired; and French merchants spent the rest of the century exploiting the treaty.[131] Customs duties were limited; merchants' accounts and warehouses were free from inspection; consuls were appointed in Andalusian towns; and eventually a Judge Conservator was appointed to hear cases involving Frenchmen. Under favourable conditions French trade to Andalucía – chiefly Rouen linens and Lyons silks – expanded rapidly and acquired a large stake in the Indies trade.

The pattern of Spanish trade with England was already established.[132] The chief import was cloth, especially the new worsted

[129] Ibid., pp. 99–100.

[130] 'Discourse of Trade', 1680, in McCulloch, *Early English Tracts on Commerce*, pp. 390–1.

[131] A. Girard, *Le commerce français à Séville et Cadix au temps des Habsbourgs. Contribution à l'étude du commerce étranger en Espagne aux XVIIe et XVIIIe siècles* (Bordeaux, 1932), pp. 133–86.

[132] See Ralph Davis, 'English Foreign Trade, 1660–1700', *Economic History Review*, second series, vii (1954–5), pp. 150–66.

fabrics. Fish was another important item, worth perhaps £500,000 a year to England. Spain also took lead, tin, wax, wheat, butter and cheese. She exported oil, wine, dried fruit, iron ore and above all two basic commodities for the English cloth industry, wool and dyeing materials, the latter chiefly American cochineal.[133] England's considerable exports to Spain, and her command of the carrying trade between the two countries, earned her a surplus in bullion with which she financed her trade to other parts of the world. As English merchants wryly remarked, the only advantage Spain possessed was the ability to place an embargo on English property in the event of war: 'In time of free trade with Spain the subjects of England have seldom less in that country than one million pounds sterling besides the great number of ships . . . and in England the Spaniards have no estate to answer such an adventure.'[134]

The Anglo-Spanish treaty of 1667 improved the conditions of trade between the two countries, to the greater benefit of the more powerful partner.[135] It gave the English advantageous terms for important branches of their trade, including the carrying trade and the fishing industry. Without abolishing customs duties, it limited the number of customs officers who might visit an English ship and left the actual level of duties vague enough to enable English merchants to negotiate with compliant officials. And individual merchants came to enjoy the protection of a Judge Conservator who, among other things, prevented inspection of their books. Armed with this treaty, the English developed their trade to Spain in the last decades of the seventeenth century. Spain, on the other hand, continued to suffer a large trade deficit. In 1697–8 the value of Spanish imports from England totalled £580,499 and her exports to England £354,165; in 1698–9 imports totalled £574,628 and exports £469,903; in 1699–1700 imports

---

[133] McLachlan, *Trade and Peace with Old Spain*, p. 10.

[134] The Humble Complaint of Merchants, 1660–64', in J. O. McLachlan, 'Documents illustrating Anglo-Spanish trade between the commercial treaty of 1667 and the asiento contract of 1713', *Cambridge Historical Journal*, iv (1932–4), pp. 299–311; see particularly p. 303.

[135] On the treaty of 1667 see ibid., pp. 304–8, and the same author's *Trade and Peace with Old Spain*, pp. 20–2.

totalled £610,912 and exports £545,056. The balance against Spain was normally in the region of £100,000 to £200,000.[136]

In the eighteenth century Spanish economists and officials blamed the commercial treaties for Spain's trading adversities.[137] But the treaties did not create economic conditions; they simply reflected Spain's inferiority in manufactures, capital resources and shipping. Contemporaries were particularly impressed by the 'drain' on Spain's bullion supplies. Ultimately these supplies were the returns which Spain earned from her investment in the Indies, an integral part of the Spanish economy. They were normally re-invested not in domestic production – shipbuilding perhaps excepted – but in foreign trade. Yet as long as Spain earned sufficient profits in America to bridge her trade gap in Europe she could be said to be paying her way. In the middle of the seventeenth century, however, returns from America dwindled to a trickle. The crisis in the Indies trade caused severe dislocation in the Spanish economy and contributed to its notorious depression; the Indies trade was also a victim of that depression.

[136] McLachlan, 'Documents illustrating Anglo-Spanish Trade', pp. 310–11, and *Trade and Peace with Old Spain*, graph 1.

[137] A. Christelow, 'Great Britain and the trades from Cadiz and Lisbon to Spanish America and Brazil, 1759–1783', *Hispanic American Historical Review*, xxvii (1947), pp. 2–29, and the same author's 'Economic Background of the Anglo-Spanish War of 1762', *Journal of Modern History*, xviii (1946), pp. 22–36; see also Reglà, 'La época de los dos últimos Austrias', *Historia social y económica de España y América*, pp. 348–50; Girard, *Le commerce français à Séville et Cadix*, pp. 115–34.

7

American Trade: Recession and Revival

The Monopoly: Seville and Cadiz

After a century of almost unbroken expansion Spain's American trade first contracted then collapsed. The great upswing of 1562–92 was followed by a plateau from 1593 to 1622 and a downward swing from 1623 to 1650; the trade then recovered, confidence less so. This profound crisis in the *carrera de Indias* had its roots within the trade itself and the colonial economies which fed it; but it was aggravated by challenge and violence from without which relentlessly eroded the Seville monopoly.

The ideal of a Castilian and more particularly an Andalusian monopoly survived into the seventeenth century.[1] It drew its strength from the capital resources of the Seville merchants, seconded by foreign colleagues, first the Genoese and Portuguese, then the French, Dutch and English; from the network of interests which bound together the merchants and shippers of the *consulado* of Seville and the officials of the *Casa de la Contratación*, the government body which regulated the trade; from another network, more obscure but no less powerful, between these same merchants and the great territorial magnates of Andalucía, of whom the Count Duke of Olivares was the most striking representative; and from the slavish devotion to routine of the Spanish bureaucracy which, having devised an effective means of delivering goods to America and receiving silver in return, was

[1] On the monopoly and its organization see Lynch, *Spain 1516–1598*, pp. 231–9.

content to maintain the apparatus even when circumstances changed and even when foreign interests began to appropriate it.

The doors of American trade were more effectively closed to Spanish nationals than to foreigners. Yet the exclusion of Aragonese and Catalans from the *carrrera de Indias* was due less to Castilian prejudice than to the facts of economic life. The peoples of eastern Spain did not have the resources to contribute to trade and colonization in America; and had they been allowed to do so they might well have become yet further agents of foreign penetration. In any case we have to distinguish between emigration and trade. In law non-Castilians were free to enter America; this was made clear by the decree of 1596 which stated that Aragonese, Catalans and Valencians were not classified as foreigners and could reside in the Indies.[2] In 1619 the ordinances of the *consulado* of Lima, describing the qualifications needed by the guild's thirty electors, specifically included subjects of the crown of Aragon.[3] The great jurist, Juan de Solórzano, writing probably under the influence of the Catalan revolt of 1640, remarked in his *Política Indiana* (1647) that subjects of the crown of Aragon 'appeared' to be classified as foreigners in relation to the Indies; but he also admitted that force of custom allowed them in.[4] The *Recopilación* of 1680, the general coding of the Laws of the Indies, had no such doubts; it simply repeated the decree of 1596. Castile therefore possessed no monopoly of emigration. If few Aragonese and Catalans actually went to America it was for other reasons than legal ones.[5]

[2] *Recopilación de leyes de los reinos de las Indias* [1680] (3 vols, Madrid, 1943), IX, xxvii, p. 28. The law of 1596 simply legitimized existing practice and echoed similar enactments of 1564 and 1591; see Artíñano, *Historia del comercio con las Indias*, p. 118.

[3] '...y no han de ser extranjeros de los Reinos de España, y se entiende no serlo los de la Corona de Aragon...' See R. Konetzke, *Colección de documentos para la historia de la formación social de Hispanoamérica 1493–1810* (3 vols, Madrid, 1953–62), ii, p. 294; María E. Rodríguez Vicente, *El tribunal del consulado de Lima en la primera mitad del siglo XVII* (Madrid, 1960), p. 319.

[4] F. Rahola, *Comercio de Cataluña con América en el siglo XVIII* (Barcelona, 1931), p. 13.

[5] C. Bermúdez Plata, *Catálogo de pasageros de Indias durante los siglos XVI, XVII, y XVIII* (2 vols, Seville, 1932–40) gives the official figures for the first few decades, inadequate though they are: in 1509–38 out of a total of 13,399 there were eighty-nine Aragonese, forty-eight Valencians and thirty-eight Catalans; see J. Rodríguez Argua, 'Las regiones españoles y la población de América (1509–1538)', *Revista de Indias*, viii (1947), pp. 698–748.

Commerce was a different matter. Andalucía was better endowed for transatlantic trade than any other region of Spain.[6] In the first years of colonial enterprise the Catalans showed not the slightest interest in America. Belatedly, in 1522, they requested permission to trade and were refused.[7] But every businessman in Europe knew that you did not need to cross the Atlantic to get your hands on American treasure. All you needed was a foothold in Seville or Cadiz. These ports were as open to Catalans as they were to foreigners, and in the sixteenth century they were to be found there. A series of Catalan merchants traded to America via Seville and the Canary Islands, not simply as isolated individuals but as participants in a continuous tradition of Catalan trade which gradually established a network of interests for Catalonia in the Spanish Atlantic.[8] From 1513, but especially from the 1530s, a number of Catalan merchant dynasties forged trading links with Tierra Firme and New Spain, while other Catalans were proprietors, captains or pilots of vessels in the *carrera de Indias*. By mid-century three-quarters of Catalan textile exports to Castile were probably exported to the Indies.[9] While these gains were not abandoned in the years after 1600, nor were they expanded. Aragon was hampered by its economic recession and stagnation which culminated in the expulsion of the moriscos.[10] Catalonia spent its commercial energies, before and after the revolt of 1640, in attempting to restore its first life-line, the Mediterranean trade. It was not until the last decades of the century, especially from 1680, that modest economic recovery brought Catalonia within striking distance of transatlantic operations.[11] Its merchants then evinced a new interest in America and advocated the formation of a trading company; and in the first half of the eighteenth century their economic resources

---

[6] Lynch, *Spain 1516–1598*, pp. 232–3.

[7] Carrera Pujal, *Historia política y económica de Cataluña*, i, pp. 298–9, 303–4.

[8] Carlos Martínez Shaw, 'Sobre el comerç català amb Amèrica al segle XVI', *2nes Jornades d'Estudis Catalano-Americans. Maig 1986* (Barcelona, 1987), pp. 33–9.

[9] Carrera Pujal, *Historia política y económica de Cataluña*, i, pp. 321–4; Vilar, *La Catalogne dans l'Espagne moderne*, i, p. 537.

[10] Chaunu, *Séville et l'Atlantique*, viii, 1, pp. 249–50.

[11] Carlos Martínez Shaw, *Cataluña en la Carrera de Indias 1680–1756* (Barcelona, 1981), pp. 80–2.

enabled them to overcome the law and break into the colonial trade. The Basques, too, sought permission for direct trade with America, especially after the independence of Portugal prevented them from using Lisbon as an entrepôt.[12] But it was 1728 before they proved their point and procured for the Basque-financed Caracas Company the privilege of trading with Venezuela.

Seville's desperate defence of its monopoly in the seventeenth century reflected shift of power as well as depression of opportunity in the transatlantic sector. Seville, of course, had never possessed the entire monopoly. It was an Andalusian monopoly of which Seville was the commercial, financial and administrative centre. Between 1506 and 1650 Seville had 60 per cent of registered trade to America, and was followed in order of importance by Cadiz, San Lúcar de Barrameda, the Canaries and Lisbon.[13] In the course of the seventeenth century, however, Seville suffered an accumulation of adversities which weakened its economy. Its population was ravaged by plague and dropped from a peak of 150,000 in 1588 to 85,000 a century later.[14] Its merchants bore the brunt of royal taxation and forced loans. And its location became a serious liability. For Seville was an inland port, access to which steadily deteriorated in proportion to the heavy increase in tonnage of transatlantic vessels–the average size rose from seventy tons in 1504 to 391 tons in 1641–5. From the early seventeenth century navigation of the Guadalquivir and the bar at San Lúcar became increasingly hazardous. Seville's loss was Cadiz's gain. As a sea port Cadiz was more accessible and more successful in procuring foreign vessels at a time, especially from the 1630s, when Indies shipping, like its contents, became less Spanish.[15] Cadiz, moreover, was preferred by foreigners who wished to evade the administration in Seville and found the bay of Cadiz more suitable for contraband than the riverine port. Finally, Cadiz had advantageous customs rates, as its customs lessees purposely sought to attract foreign merchants to their constituency. By 1650 Cadiz had successfully challenged the supremacy of

---

[12] Guiard Larrauri, *Historia del Consulado y Casa de Contratación de Bilbao*, i, pp. 445–50.
[13] Chaunu, *Séville et l'Atlantique*, viii, 1, pp. 228–33.
[14] Domínguez Ortiz, *La sociedad española en el siglo XVII*, pp. 140–2.
[15] Chaunu, *Séville et l'Atlantique*, viii, 1, pp. 294–329; Domínguez Ortiz, *Orto y ocaso de Sevilla*, p. 89.

its rival, and in the second half of the century its victory was complete. As trade moved towards Cadiz so did people: its population grew from some 2,000 in 1600 to 40,000 by 1700.[16]

The rivalry between Seville and Cadiz in the seventeenth century was symptomatic of the growing crisis in the Indies trade. The days of peace and plenty were over, and the remnants of prosperity were bitterly contested. The crown too fought for its share of dwindling returns. While the policy of the state was to encourage trade in order to gain maximum tax revenue, the policy of the *consulado* was to restrain the flow of merchandise in order to control prices in America, which in some cases could be 300 or 400 per cent higher than in Spain. On some points, however, the interests of the state and merchants concided; both wanted to exclude foreign competitors. Although these were a permanent presence, it was only from about 1620 that they really began to undermine the monopoly. Up to that time the rule of Seville was supreme, and Spain preserved for itself the major share of returns from America.

There was, then, a state monopoly and a private monopoly. In the sixteenth century the state, represented by the *Casa de la Contratación*, was the dominant partner. In the seventeenth century the merchants of the *consulado* altered the balance of power and it was they who now arranged many of the rules of the game. Although trade was organized in *ferias* at fixed trading points, the organization broke down in the years after 1600. As trade by-passed the Portobello fairs, so the official monopoly was eroded and the state lost revenue. The strengthening of the merchant monopoly at the expense of the state was also seen in the changing roles of the *Casa de la Contratación* and the *consulado* of Seville. The control of trade established by the *Casa* in the sixteenth century was gradually taken over by the *consulado*. And the *consulado* controlled not only the trade with America but also many fiscal functions of the state, for it came to administer the *avería*, to appoint key officials of the fleets, to admit foreigners, and eventually to organize payments of *indultos* to compensate for fraud. The monopoly, therefore, came to form a whole complex of royal laws, public agencies, private interests and defence mechanisms. The model can be described in legal terms, but it did

[16] Domínguez Ortiz, *La sociedad española en el siglo XVII*, pp. 142–3.

not function according to the law. There was a real monopoly, as distinct from the formal monopoly, and the real monopoly represented a compromise between various interests. It was the interplay of these interests which opened gaps in the official system. A monopoly is usually a stimulus to alternatives, and one of the alternatives was fraud, a whole range of fraud involving merchants, officials, foreigners and contrabandists.

Fraud: the Response to Taxation

A monopoly trade was an easy trade to tax. All traffic between Spain and America was subject to registration, and the outgoing register was checked at destination. Taxation was directed at the trade itself and at the colonial economies. On the former there were two major impositions, the *avería* and the *almojarifazgo*.

The *avería*, an *ad valorem* duty charged through the register, was paid by the trade to procure its own defence. It was therefore governed by two factors, the cost of defence and the value of cargo, and it varied from year to year according to the size of the fleets and of their escorts.[17] From 1562 the *avería* was let out by contract to the *consulado* of Seville; it eventually became a millstone round its neck. Enemy attack, or more often simply threat of attack, forced the convoys to increase their naval escorts, especially from 1621 when the Dutch mounted a new offensive. The gross tonnage of the escorting *armadas* increased from 20,128 tons in 1601–5 to 30,362 in 1636–40; it then plunged to 16,575 in 1640–5, to 16,560 in 1646–50.[18] During the crisis years of 1620-30 the tonnage of the *armada de la guardia* amounted to 37 per cent of the total tonnage of the fleets, compared with 12 per cent in 1601. The *avería* thus became a tax which devoured the trade it was designed to defend. The rising cost of defence, of naval stores and of shipbuilding, coincided from 1608 with the contraction and depression of transatlantic trade. As defence costs rose and the trade became less capable of meeting them, merchants took refuge in fraud, and the *avería* disintegrated. Fraud was less a

[17] Guillermo Céspedes del Castillo, *La avería en al comercio de Indias* (Seville, 1945); Chaunu, *Séville et l'Atlantique*, i, pp. 169–237.
[18] Chaunu, *Seville et l'Atlantique*, i, p. 204; vi, tables 183–4.

cause than a consequence of crisis. For the *avería* penalized those who obeyed the law. Spanish merchants suffered in relation to foreign contrabandists who shipped their goods on the fleets unregistered and untaxed. Inevitably Spanish merchants too sought to save their returns from a diminishing trade by evasion and fraud. The development of fraud further restricted the taxable material, reduced the yield of the *avería*, weakened the escorting *armadas* and invited further enemy attack. This was the vicious circle in which the transatlantic trade was entrapped. Between 1602 and 1630 the *avería* was levied at the rate of 6 per cent; in 1631 it rose to 35 per cent, clear evidence of the absolute fraud which killed the system. Although the *consulado* renewed the contract on various occasions up to 1628, in fact it cut down on effective defence and used the *armadas* as merchant vessels. Between 1628 and 1660 the *ad valorem* duty was gradually abandoned; from 1641 the *consulado* refused to renew the contract; the state had now to administer the *avería* itself, make good its deficiency, and in effect subsidize defence of the trade.

The *almojarifazgo* was an *ad valorem* customs duty charged on merchandise at Spanish and American ports. Up to 1660 total customs on outbound traffic (exit and entry) amounted to 15 per cent, on the eastbound trade 17.5 per cent.[19] The duties exacted in America were based on prices in the American market. Merchandise shipped from Spain to Peru, for example, paid *almojarifazgo* first on appraised value at Portobello, and on arrival at Callao 5 per cent of the increase in value which had accrued in transit from the isthmus. This rule held good for all the Indies, covering European commodities reshipped from one colonial port to another. Some commodities received special fiscal attention. By 1616 cochineal imported into Spain was taxed at 50 ducats an *arroba*, its selling price being 126 ducats. Taxation on this scale simply diverted the trade into contraband: registered imports of cochineal fell from 7,673 *arrobas* in 1607, to 2,000 in 1614, to 859 in 1615, though it was known that in the latter year 4,000 *arrobas* left New Spain alone.[20]

The colonial economies themselves were subject to a variety of

[19] C. H. Haring, *Trade and Navigation between Spain and the Indies in the time of the Hapsburgs* (Cambridge, Mass., 1918), pp. 83–6.
[20] Chaunu, *Séville et l'Atlantique*, iv, pp. 571–2.

taxes, the *quinto* (a royal fifth on bullion), proceeds of the sale of mercury, Indian tributes (a personal assessment of 6 pesos), the *cruzada* and the *alcabala*. Out of these the treasuries of Mexico and Peru had to defray local administrative and defence costs, subsidize their dependent colonies and remit the surplus to Spain. At the end of the sixteenth century the surplus from Mexico amounted to about 1 million pesos a year, a peak from which it subsequently fell; Peru provided greater returns, for its superior silver production yielded a greater *quinto*.[21] To supplement this revenue the crown levied various extraordinary taxes. One of these was the Union of Arms imposed in 1627 as part of Olivares's call for assistance from all provinces. America was assessed at 600,000 ducats a year for fifteen years, 250,000 from New Spain and 350,000 from Peru, on the understanding that it would be applied to naval defence of the transatlantic route. The contribution was raised by doubling the *alcabala* from 2 to 4 per cent, and it was subsequently renewed so that it became a permanent tax with little relevance to its declared object.[22]

Further sums were raised from merchants on both sides of the Atlantic in the form of *servicios*, *donativos* (voluntary gifts) and *préstamos* (loans), often overtly for imperial defence but invariably diverted to expenditure in Europe. It was the peninsular merchants who bore the greater share. Between 1613 and 1655 the *consulado* of Lima raised 277,000 pesos in *donativos*, and in the whole century the Lima merchants contributed one million pesos in *donativos* and *préstamos*, compared to 2.3 million from Spanish merchants in *donativos* alone.[23] A merchant group capable of providing 11.2 million pesos was obviously not as financially pressed as it claimed to be. There were powerful reasons for these advances: to gain favour, to compensate for deceit, to buy off the attentions of the crown at such times as the notorious frauds of 1624 and 1651. While colonial merchants rarely obtained the naval defence they were promised, they received other valuable

---

[21] Domínguez Ortiz, 'Los caudales de Indias y la política exterior de Felipe IV', *Anuario de Estudios Americanos*, 13 (1956), p. 314.

[22] Ibid., pp. 317–19.

[23] Rodríguez Vicente, *El tribunal del consulado de Lima*, pp. 144–7; María Encarnación Rodríguez Vicente, 'Los cargadores a Indias y su contribución a los gastos de la Monarquía, 1555–1750', *Anuario de Estudios Americanos*, 34 (1977), pp. 211–32.

concessions, such as 'pardons' for past fraud and above all honours and titles of nobility. The *donativo* was one of the ways by which colonial merchants improved their social status. Another means of acquiring security and respectability was by purchase of office. This too the crown exploited as a money-raising device; sale of office had been practised in the sixteenth century, but in the reign of Philip IV, especially in the 1640s and 1650s, it acquired new dimensions, and was extended to financial and judicial offices, with pernicious results.[24]

By extending imperial taxation the crown sought to squeeze the last drops from an empire whose mineral wealth was either drying up or being diverted to other channels. In spite of increased fiscal pressure the crown's revenue from America showed a tendency to fall or to fluctuate in the reign of Philip IV. To counter the downward trend the crown resorted increasingly to a further expedient, confiscation of private bullion returns. Silver sent from Mexico and Peru to pay for last year's merchandise and gain credit for the next was taken over by the crown, and merchants were compensated in vellon currency or in *juros* at 10 per cent, later reduced to 6.3 per cent. In 1620 Philip III took one-eighth of registered private treasure. Philip IV took much more – in 1629 1 million ducats, in 1635–7 2 million ducats (forcibly exchanged for vellon), in 1637–8 500,000 ducats, in the 1640s varying amounts culminating in 1 million ducats in 1649.[25] This was the most harmful of all fiscal devices. Its immediate effect was to deprive the trade of vital capital, for merchants reacted by consigning less bullion in the following year. They were also driven to large-scale fraud to protect their investments. The combined result of withdrawal and fraud was to reduce registered trade to the point where the crown's own customs revenue was seriously damaged. But the greatest victim was the *avería*, which was assessed on registered returns. As the latter decreased, the *avería* rate increased and became a further incitement to fraud; the time came when the crown had to subsidize the *averías* in order to maintain a semblance of transatlantic defence. By its new

[24] J. H. Parry, *The Sale of Public Office in the Spanish Indies under the Habsburgs* (Berkeley and Los Angeles, 1953), pp. 48–58.
[25] Domínguez Ortiz, 'Los caudales de Indias y la política exterior de Felipe IV', pp. 342–52; Rodriguez Vicente, *El tribunal del consulado de Lima*, pp. 149–50.

folly, therefore, the crown not only undermined long-term confidence and investment in the Indies trade but also subverted its own financial position.

The consequences were most apparent in the 1640s. In 1642, with the connivance of the fleets' commanders, the greater part of private silver returns was not declared, thus evading not only confiscation but also the *avería* and other taxes.[26] The Council of the Indies regarded confiscation of private treasure as one of the greatest abuses afflicting the transatlantic trade, and it recommended in 1643 'that on no account and for no reason should Your Majesty lay hands on private silver consignments from the Indies, but should give orders that in future when the fleets arrive from Peru and New Spain their consignments should be immediately handed to their owners'. The crown remained unrepentant. In 1649 it confiscated 1 million pesos of private returns. At the beginning of 1652 government agents descended on Seville to compute sequestrations in advance of the fleets, and in addition to buy up merchandise (tobacco, cochineal and indigo) then held by the merchants of Seville at imposed prices and in vellon for immediate shipment to Flanders.[27] This was the last straw. In the face of acute resentment and opposition the government was forced to cancel the projected confiscation, and indeed made no more. But by now it was too late; the habit of fraud was too deeply engrained and the trade too depressed to respond to official reform.

The crown was not the only parasite on the American trade and colonies. The wealth of the New World was regarded as fair game by hordes of place and pension seekers, many of whom had never crossed the Atlantic. *Mercedes* to courtiers and favourites, pensions to widows and orphans, dowries to ladies-in-waiting, grants of various kinds were frequently charged on the colonial treasuries, especially in the second half of the seventeenth century. Many *mercedes* were granted on *indios vacos*, that is on *encomiendas* (grants of Indians who paid tribute in labour and/or money) which had fallen vacant. Viceroys and colonists protested in vain that *encomiendas* which should have been reserved for

---

[26] Domínguez Ortiz, 'Los caudales de Indias y la política exterior de Felipe IV', p. 362.
[27] Ibid., pp. 370–2.

descendants of the conquerors were going instead to people who had never left Castile. Some of these *encomiendas* were granted in anticipation of their becoming vacant and meanwhile the grants were charged on the colonial treasuries. The recipients were usually courtiers and higher nobility. A few examples will suffice.[28] To Doña Leonor Moscoso on the occasion of her marriage in 1653 a grant of 3,000 ducats a year on a vacant *encomienda*, valid for two lives; to Juan de Palafox y Cardona, son of the Marquis of Ariza and nephew of Bishop Palafox, 2,000 ducats a year on vacant *encomiendas* in Guatemala; to Doña Antonia de Mendoza, Countess of Benavente and lady-in-waiting to the Infanta, 6,000 ducats in 1665 on vacant *encomiendas*; to Doña Antonia María de Toledo, widow of the Count of Priego, 2,000 ducats in 1666 on vacant *encomiendas* to imrove her financial position. Many a wretched Indian scraping a living in the Peruvian *sierra* was working in fact for distressed gentlefolk in Castile.

Plunder and parasitism made fraud and contraband a way of life. The monopoly system and high prices induced market conditions propitious for contraband; taxes and confiscations incited it; impecunious officials connived at it; naval authorities co-operated in it. The close alliance between the merchants of Seville and officials of the *Casa de la Contratación* made customs control one of the weakest points of the monopoly.[29] Contents of merchandise were assessed at their declared not their verified value, and volume was declared in general categories; naturally they were falsely declared and undervalued in order to evade customs.[30] On the outward voyage the object was to avoid displaying the Seville register at the port of entry in the Indies, on the return voyage to avoid registration on leaving the Indies so that there would be no check on the accuracy of declarations at Seville. Both ways meant underpayment of taxes. Another device was to use the warship escorts for merchandise and thus avoid registration altogether, in connivance with the naval commanders who might also permit vessels to unload at unauthorized ports. In this way, through family networks, bribery of officials or sheer deceit, Seville and Cadiz became active centres of fraud, and it was here that avoid-

---

[28] Domínguez Ortiz, *La sociedad española en el siglo XVII*, pp. 246–7.
[29] See Lynch, *Spain 1516–1598*, pp. 235–6.
[30] Chaunu, *Séville et l'Atlantique*, i, pp. 88–121.

ance of taxes began. In the Portobello fleet of 1624 only 14.8 per cent of the 9.3 million pesos of merchandise carried in the fleet had been registered in Seville, and an even smaller percentage, 11.5, actually changed hands in the fair, the rest by-passing the fair and going directly to Peru.[31]

Contraband in silver returns from the Indies was also highly developed and took two main forms, evasion of the royal *quinto* at the mining base, and evasion of registration at port. Again, the methods were various, ranging from suborning ships' captains, to declaring ingots under their real weight, to loading at the last minute and thus avoiding close inspection. A favoured device in Peru was to consign registered silver to non-existent persons in Panama, where the consignment nominally remained and was marked off the register; this silver would then be transferred across the isthmus to the fleet waiting in Portobello for the return journey to Spain. The object of fraud in silver consignments was not merely to avoid paying the *averia*, but also to have free silver to trade with, for this was a much more valuable trading commodity than registered silver. In the first place it was not in danger of confiscation; secondly it was easier to re-export abroad from Spain to buy the foreign goods so much in demand in the Indies trade. At Portobello Spanish merchants would lower the prices of their goods by 10 or 15 per cent in order to get their hands on unregistered silver.[32] There is, of course, no way of measuring the volume of contraband; but in 1651 a Peruvian estimate, for what it is worth, claimed that 25 per cent of the silver shipped from Callao was unregistered.[33] In any case fraud was not constant throughout the history of the Indies trade: it increased from 1590 and even more from 1620.[34] Both sides, crown and commerce, were deeply involved in deceit. It was for this reason that avoidance of registration was regarded not as fraud but as a form of collusion with the government, which imposed its own malpractices on the merchants of Seville, in particular the sequestration of private silver, the appropriation of

[31] Enriqueta Vila Vilar, 'Las ferias de Portobelo: apariencia y realidad del comercio con Indias', *Anuario de Estudios Americanos*, 39 (1982), pp. 275–340, especially p. 321.
[32] Rodríguez Vicente, *El tribunal del consulado de Lima*, pp. 262–3.
[33] Ibid., p. 259.
[34] Chaunu, *Séville et l'Atlantique*, viii, 2, 1, p. 398.

ships and the plundering of fleets for the needs of war. Between a collaborating *consulado* and a permissive crown the system was well understood. Officials in Panama marked up the value of registered goods coming in, on the assumption that they were underdeclared; and the level of mark-up was a compromise between conflicting interests. Thus fraud was sanctioned by the crown, and on the return of the fleets compensatory payments, the so called *indultos*, were charged. The size of the fraud and the amount of the *indulto* varied according to the state of the game and the power of the players. For all these reasons it is difficult to estimate accurately silver returns from America, public and private.

Total treasure receipts fell from the peak of 78.4 million pesos in 1595–9, to 55.5 million in 1600–4, to 51.8 million in 1605–9, and to 43.1 million in 1610–14. Then followed a period of fluctuation, an upswing to 47.4 million in 1615–19 and 50 million in 1620–4, down to 42.2 million in 1625–9 and 39.8 million in 1630–4, and up again to 68.8 million in 1635–9. After this date receipts diminished steadily, from 45.2 million in 1640–4, to 36.6 million in 1645–9, and 39 million in 1650–4. In 1655–9 receipts moved up again, to 51.6 million, and signs of recovery began to appear. Meanwhile the share due to the crown in the first half of the seventeenth century was also subject to fraud and fluctuations; it constituted perhaps between 8 and 20 per cent of total receipts, averaging out at 14 per cent.[35]

What were the causes of the decrease in American treasure? Economic depression, or shift, in the colonies between the late sixteenth and mid-seventeenth centuries lowered their returns to the metropolis.[36] The fall in the Indian population reduced the yield of *encomiendas* and of silver mines and made Mexico in particular much less profitable to Spain. Moreover the colonies were absorbing more of their own revenue in administrative and

[35] These figures are derived from Morineau, *Incroyables gazettes et fabuleux métaux*, pp. 247–8, 250, 262, who bases his calculations on a range of non-official sources; these give more realistic and usually higher quantities than those of Hamilton, *American Treasure and the Price Revolution in Spain*, pp. 34–8, which are official figures based on registered imports and fail to account for treasure which evaded control at the mining centres and for unregistered treasure. On the recovery of American trade and treasure after 1660 see below, pp. 277–86.

[36] See below, pp. 288–9, 303–10, 329–33.

defence costs; appropriations for garrisons, fortifications and naval forces progressively reduced public returns to the crown. Enemy action accounted for very few losses among the treasure fleets; but the convoys always needed escorts, and the mere threat of attack was enough to swell defence expenditure, raise the *avería* and thus augment fraud. These were the reasons why the actual amount of royal treasure from the Indies rarely equalled its reputation. It never represented more than one-tenth of Philip IV's total revenue, and in many years not even one-twentieth. But this income had an importance beyond its quantity. The very fact that it was a fortuitous income, both in the date of its arrival and in its volume, prevented it from suffering the fate of other royal revenues which were assigned in advance to bankers and *juristas* and permanently lost to the treasury. When it arrived it was ready cash, immediately available for use; and in a period of debased currency an income in silver was particularly valuable to the crown for its overseas payments and to businessmen for foreign trade. If the silver fleets were delayed the premium on silver soared, foreign trade was hit, and supplies for the armed forces abroad were unobtainable.

While much bullion escaped official channels before it could reach Spain, much also was syphoned off after it arrived. Although the export of bullion was prohibited by law, the law was ignored, because the Spanish market and the Indies trade itself needed foreign manufactures. The amount of bullion smuggled out of Spain is a matter of speculation. Between 10 and 30 per cent of *registered* bullion, which was supposed to be transferred directly from the fleets to the *Casa de la Contratación* before being distributed to its owners, in fact left Spain illegally.[37] Unregistered bullion, of course, was designed precisely for smuggling. Professional smugglers, the *metedores*, acting on behalf of the owners, took it from the Indies fleets and loaded it on the foreign ships waiting in Cadiz bay to convey it northwards.[38] Unable to prevent the loss of bullion the Spanish government, as has been seen, sought to compensate itself by selling *indultos*, or pardons, to those who admitted to bullion frauds. The proceeds from *indultos*, however, did not satisfy the government's own

---

[37] Hamilton, *American Treasure and the Price Revolution in Spain*, p. 37.
[38] Haring, *Trade and Navigation between Spain and the Indies*, p. 112.

need for precious metals in an age of rising defence expenditure and falling silver returns. It was at this point that it reached out to take possession of private silver consignments, and thus completed the vicious circle of further fraud and loss of revenue.

Foreign Penetration

Fraud within the monopoly did not in itself destroy the system. The greater danger lay in penetration from without. This took various forms – the foreign presence in Seville and Cadiz, European expansion in the Americas and direct trade in the Caribbean, the South Atlantic and the Pacific. Direct trade by foreigners outflanked the monopoly. From the Antilles English, Dutch, and French merchants opened trading contacts with the Spanish Caribbean and these gradually extended to Cartagena and Portobello. Northern textiles, exported directly into the Spanish Caribbean, undersold those brought from and via Seville, paying no taxes and bringing benefits to consumers and sellers alike.[39] And this competition, directed at the very heart of the Spanish trading system, was a permanent thorn in Spain's flesh, for it was based on rival colonial possessions held by major European powers.

Direct trade to Buenos Aires first developed from Brazil and to a lesser extent from Europe in the 1590s, reaching a high point in 1611–15, and declining thereafter to a low level in 1640–5.[40] But the Atlantic trade of Buenos Aires recovered in the second half of the seventeenth century, now dominated by the Dutch, Portuguese, English and, unofficially, the Spanish too. This was a trade from Europe, not from within America; it was another sector of foreign penetration, reflecting a general expansion of European trade along the unexploited perimeter of the Spanish American economy. Trade through Buenos Aires was attracted by Potosí. But it was the regional economy, and the consequent interregional

[39] Among an extensive bibliography see in particular K. R. Andrews, *The Spanish Caribbean. Trade and Plunder 1530–1630* (New Haven, Conn., 1978), and Enriqueta Vila Vilar, *Historia de Puerto Rico 1600–1650* (Seville, 1974), pp. 131–56.

[40] Raúl Molina, *Las primeras experiencias comerciales del Plata: el comercio marítimo, 1580–1700* (Buenos Aires, 1966), pp. 134–45.

trade, which first opened the Río de la Plata to the Atlantic by earning a surplus in Potosí to pay for European imports, and by establishing the infrastructure of people and transport necessary for circulation. The regional economy linked Potosí to the trans-atlantic trade through complex mechanisms of exchange, in which silver, mules, slaves, European manufactures, yerba mate and textiles were all involved.[41]

Foreigners had further ways of penetrating the Indies trade and appropriating its returns. They could actually settle in America. The law stated that emigrants had to be Spaniards or naturalized Spaniards, and they had to have a licence. By decree of November 1607 ships' captains were threatened with the death penalty and generals and admirals of fleets with loss of rank if they carried unlicensed passengers. By the 1670s, however, the punishment had been reduced to a fine and the order was widely dis-regarded. Forging passports was a profession in Seville. Fore-igners travelled on the official fleets, or they entered by the back door, the Río de la Plata. In Peru three groups could be iden-tified. A number of foreigners had settled in the interior and acquired modest property holdings. Others were to be found in maritime occupations, as pilots and seamen, profiting from the shortage of skilled personnel; in 1619 foreigners – Italians, Frenchmen, and above all Portuguese – were owners and in many cases masters of eighteen vessels in the Peruvian merchant marine.[42] But the biggest group were merchants, officially tran-sient but in fact resident, in the ports and towns. By 1630 the Portuguese dominated the retail trade of Lima. Others were ac-tive in the transatlantic trade itself, using Spanish agents as front men as was done in Seville; they had contacts with contrabandists in Andalucía who exported goods without paying duties and undersold their rivals. Following its normal practice the Spanish crown taxed what it could not prevent: foreigners were granted permission to trade if they had twenty years' residence in Peru, were married to a Peruvian, had property valued at not less than

[41] Carlos Sempat Assadourian, *El sistema de la economía colonial. Mercado interno, regiones y espacio económico* (Lima, 1982), pp. 72–5; Zacarias Mou-toukias, *Contrabando y control colonial en el siglo XVII* (Buenos Aires, 1988), pp. 119–33, 142–8.
[42] Rodríguez Vicente, *El tribunal del consulado de Lima*, p. 71.

4,000 ducats and paid a composition tax to the crown.[43] The Portuguese also favoured Cartagena, an important staging post in the Indies trade. So numerous did they become there after 1610 that they even acquired administrative offices; they also received the attentions of the Inquisition, for they included a number of Jews, and from 1640 of course they were harassed and in some cases expelled.[44]

It was common knowledge, however, that a foreign merchant could tap the American trade without going to America; he could concentrate on its metropolitan base in Andalucía. Here too the law was explicit enough. To engage in transatlantic commerce a merchant had to be a native Spaniard; this precluded foreigners from trading with the colonies either on their own account or through Spanish intermediaries.[45] But the law could be evaded, either by simple contraband, or by use of Spanish cover-men, or by acquiring naturalisation. The latter gave the greatest security, but there were certain legal requirements: the successful applicant had to have twenty years' residence in Spain, at least ten of them in a furnished house, he had to be married to a Spanish wife, and he had to possess at least 4,000 ducats' worth of property. More and more foreigners began to take advantage of naturalization. In the last quarter of the sixteenth century only twenty-five foreigners acquired naturalization rights to trade with the Indies – seventeen Portuguese, five Flemings and three French.[46] During the reign of Philip III (1598–1621) the number rose to fifty-nine comprising twenty-one Flemings, seventeen Portuguese, eleven Italians, four French and, among the small groups, one Englishman. In the first decade of Philip IV's reign naturalization rights for trade with the Indies were given even more liberally: between 1621 and 1630 there were seventy-seven successful applicants. Many of these did not possess the legal qualifications, but they made up for this by handsome payments to the crown; in effect the crown sold certificates of naturalization, again making money

[43] Ibid., pp. 73–4; Boyajian, *Portuguese Bankers*, pp. 122–4.
[44] Manuel Tejardo Fernández, *Aspectos de la vida social en Cartagena de Indias durante el seiscientos* (Seville, 1954). On the Portuguese in Mexico, see above, pp. 153–4.
[45] Haring, *Trade and Navigation between Spain and the Indies*, pp. 107–8.
[46] A. Domínguez Ortiz, 'La concesión de "naturalezas para comerciar en Indias" durante el siglo XVII', *Revista de Indias*, xix (1959), pp. 227–39.

out of lawbreakers. The scale on which Philip IV's government issued certificates caused such resentment among Spanish merchants and their allies in the *Casa de la Contratación* that the policy was strongly attacked in the 1630s and 1640s.[47] For the growing demand from foreign merchants was essentially an attempt to eliminate Spanish intermediaries in order to sell direct to the Indies from their own merchant houses in Andalucía. Under pressure from monopolist interests in Seville the crown began to tighten up on eligibility from about 1645. Later in the century, however, particularly from the early 1680s, naturalization policy was again relaxed. By the end of the century the majority of the merchant aristocracy of Cadiz, with legal status in the Indies trade, consisted of foreigners, without counting the many foreigners who traded through Spanish intermediaries.[48]

The use of intermediaries was well developed. They are often called mere commission agents, and perhaps some of them were, passing foreign goods through inspection and registration, loading them under their own name and watching the returns going direct to the owner.[49] But some of them were more than agents. They were part of the triangular trade between Europe, Andalucía and the Indies. The foreigners brought their manufactures to Andalucía and there they bought Andalusian products, wine, oil and fruits. This left the Spaniards with a large trade gap which had to be bridged by the Indies trade. Many Seville merchants shipped to America on their own account Spanish and foreign goods, and from the returns they balanced their foreign payments, making very good profits, or commissions, from all these transactions. In the course of the seventeenth century it became less necessary for foreigners to use the official channels as more of the actual loading and unloading of the fleets was transferred from Seville to Cadiz and its satellite ports.[50] Here, away from the immediate surveillance of the *Casa de la Contratación*, the *metedores* could load merchandise direct from foreign vessels on to the fleets after the last inspection had been completed.[51]

[47] Chaunu, *Séville et l'Atlantique*, v, p. 413.

[48] Raimundo Lantery, *Memorias de Raimundo de Lantery, mercader de Indias en Cádiz, 1673–1700*. Publícalas Alvaro Ricardo y Gómez (Cadiz, 1949).

[49] Girard, *Le commerce français a Séville et Cadix au temps des Habsbourgs*, p. 87.

[50] See above, pp. 232–3.

[51] Chaunu, *Séville et l'Atlantique*, iv, p. 536; v, p. 368.

Foreign merchants could thus escape registration, customs duties and the *avería*, and undersell their Spanish competitors in the American market. So Spaniards too had to smuggle to survive. The government reacted by applying its classic seventeenth-century formula: it sanctioned lawbreaking and taxed the offenders; foreigners were included in the sequestrations imposed on Andalusian merchants and in the fines levied for past frauds.

Foreigners supplied not only merchandise for the American trade but also capital and shipping. As the Dutch, the French and the English came to earn increasing returns from the Indies, they also began to plough back some of their profits. In the first half of the seventeenth century the trade did not depend entirely on foreign capital; it also received large injections of American capital. But its dependence on foreigners was enough to alarm some Spanish merchants. At the prompting of the *consulado* of Seville the crown issued a decree in 1608 prohibiting foreign merchants from selling their goods on credit to Spanish shippers against payment in the Indies.[52] But this decree, like many others, was a mere formality. As Spanish merchants rarely possessed sufficient capital for their purchases they were forced to rely on a degree of foreign finance to keep the trade going.

The law closed the Indies trade not only to foreigners but also to foreign shipping. But again what the law forbade conditions encouraged. The growing impoverishment of the Spanish merchant marine forced the government to accept the need for foreign vessels in the Indies trade. It tried to insist that these should be owned by Spaniards and should carry Spanish crews.[53] But in the reign of Philip IV, especially from the 1630s, even this became a formality; the government had to allow the hiring of foreign-owned vessels and to accept the fact that their crews contained aliens as well as Spaniards.[54] The freighting of foreign vessels, of course, increased the opportunities of fraud; it was also resented by the owners and builders of Spanish ships. Under their pressure foreign-built ships were excluded from the Indies trade by decree of July 1642. The decree, which was intended to stimulate Spanish shipbuilding, simply revived previous prohibitions; the only

[52] Ibid., iv, p. 393.
[53] Girard, *Le commerce Francais à Séville et Cadix*, p. 21.
[54] On the number and origin of foreign vessels see Chaunu, *Séville et l'Atlantique*, v, pp. 342, 364, 390, 404–8, 432–7.

difference was that the condition of the Spanish shipbuilding industry in the 1640s made its application even less likely than before.[55] In any case foreign vessels were particularly vital for carrying specialized cargoes such as naval stores, for which there was constant demand from Spain's other competitors, the ship-yards of the New World. In the circumstances the most that the *Casa de la Contratación* could do was to give preference to Spanish vessels when they were available.

The extent of foreign penetration of the American trade is impossible to compute, granted its devious ways.[56] In 1628 the *consulado* of Seville – an interested party prone to exaggeration – explained to the government that the Indies trade needed each year more than 6 million ducats' worth of foreign goods; American and Spanish products sold in return covered barely half of this; it was therefore impossible to comply with a recent decree insisting that foreign payments should be met entirely by merchandise and not by bullion.

> Foreign imports to the value of even 6 million ducats are barely adequate to satisfy demand; shortage and high prices are notorious, especially in woollen goods.... The New Spain fleet which sailed from Cadiz on 15 July this year is a good example. Its cargo would have been confined to wines, had not the French vessels arrived in time with their merchandise; and although they provided cloth it was only half the amount required by New Spain. It is to be feared that if the Indies are not supplied in the normal way then our enemies will supply them illegally and the colonists will admit them out of necessity.[57]

Throughout most of the seventeenth century relations between foreign merchants and the Indies trade were regulated more or less by the free play of supply and demand. In spite of differences over details, the interests of the *consulado* of Seville basically coincided with those of foreign merchants. Throughout the second

---

[55] Haring, *Trade and Navigation between Spain and the Indies*, pp. 258–61; see above, pp. 216–18.

[56] Some of it moreover was based on the Portuguese trade to Brazil and its re-export through the Río de la Plata.

[57] Quoted by Domínguez Ortiz, 'Guerra económica y comercio extranjero en el reinado de Felipe IV', *Hispania*, xxiii (1963), pp. 92–3; the decree in fact was suspended.

half of the seventeeth century the *consulado* invariably protected foreigners from investigations of their cargoes and returns, and arranged *servicios* or *indultos* in preference to an application of the law, because foreigners were closely involved in Spanish business deals.[58] For fiscal reasons the state colluded with the *consulado* to keep foreigners in the game through payments of compensation. In effect foreign and Spanish merchants in Andalucía collaborated in bribing Madrid to tolerate illegal practices in return for *donativos* of 3.5 million pesos and *indultos* of almost 6 million in fifty years (1650–1700). The process culminated in the transfer of the headquarters of the Indies trade from Seville to Cadiz, where the opportunities for foreign intervention were greater. In this way certain privileged foreigners became part of the monopoly, enjoyed its fruits and paid its penalties. Most foreigners found conditions in Andalucía suitable for their operations. But some, as the *consulado* of Seville implied, were tempted to tap the wealth of the Indies nearer its source, in the Caribbean and the Pacific.

Imperial Defence: the Atlantic

In the course of the sixteenth century Spanish seamen perfected the technique of maintaining regular communications between Andalucía and America by means of two large fleets a year, each sailing in convoy, one to Tierra Firme, the other to New Spain.[59] They sailed from Cadiz or San Lúcar, the New Spain fleet in May (if it was ready) and the Tierra Firme fleet in August. First they headed southwest to the coast of Africa and then proceeded to the Canaries; from the Canaries the route was west by southwest until they caught the trade winds which took them due west to Deseada or one of the other Leeward islands. From there the

[58] On foreign participation in the late seventeenth century see below, pp. 283–5.
[59] There are two classical 'institutional' accounts of the *carrera*, both valuable repositories of source material: José de Veitia Linaje, *Norte de la contratación de las Indias Occidentales* [1672] (Buenos Aires, 1945) by a treasurer of the *Casa de la Contratación*; Rafael Antúñez y Acevedo *Memorias históricas sobre la legislación y gobierno del comercio de los españoles con sus colonias en las Indias Occidentales* (Madrid, 1797). Fernando Serrano Mangas, *Los galeones de la carrera de Indias, 1650–1700* (Seville, 1985), is a well-researched modern study.

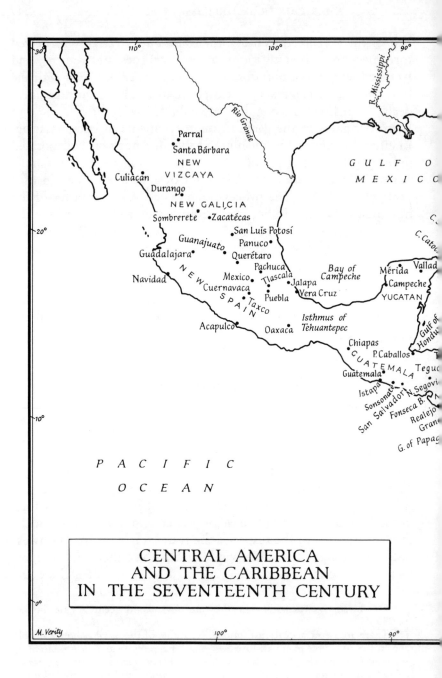

30°   110°   100°   90°

Parral
Santa Bárbara
NEW
VIZCAYA
Culiacán

Durango

NEW GALICIA

Sombrerete   •Zacatécas

20°   San Luís Potosí
Guanajuato   Panuco•
Guadalajara•   •Querétaro
Pachuca   Bay of   Mérida   Vallad
Navidad   Mexico•   Tlascala   Campeche   •Campeche
Cuernavaca   •Jalapa   YUCATAN
Taxco   Puebla   Vera Cruz

Acapulco•   Oaxaca   Isthmus of
Tehuantepec

Chiapas
P.Caballos
GUATEMALA   Tegu
Guatemala•

Istapa•
Sonsonate•   N.Segovi
San Salvador   Fonseca B.
Realejo
Gran
10°   G. of Papag

P A C I F I C

O C E A N

GULF   O
M E X I C   C

C.

C. Cato

Gulf of
Hondu

R. Mississippi

Rio Grande

NEW
SPAIN

CENTRAL AMERICA
AND THE CARIBBEAN
IN THE SEVENTEENTH CENTURY

M.Verity   100°   90°

ATLANTIC

OCEAN

St. Augustine

FLORIDA

Bahama Channel

BAHAMA ISLANDS

na Matanzas

C U   S. Espíritu B A   P. Principe

JES   C. de la Cruz

Windward Passage

TORTUGA   P. de Plata

AYMAN

Santiago de Cuba

HISPANIOLA

JAMAICA   Port Royal   Saint-Domingue

Santo Domingo

Beata Pt.

San German

Mona Passage   PUERTO RICO   San Juan

MONA

SANTA CRUZ

VIRGIN ISLANDS

ANGUILLA   ST. MARTIN   ST. BARTHOLOMEW   BARBUDA   ANTIGUA

SABA   EUSTATIUS   ST. KITTS   MONTSERRAT   GUADELOUPE

DOMINICA

MARTINIQUE

ST. LUCIA

ST. VINCENT   BARBADOS

CARIBBEAN   SEA

Mosquito Coast

STA. CATALINA (Old Providence)

Río de la Hacha

ARUBA   CURAÇAO   BUEN AYRE

GRENADA   TOBAGO

MARGARITA

Coro

La Guaira   P. Araya   Cumana   TRINIDAD

Nombre de Dios
Portobello   Chagres

RICA   VERAGUA   Panama

Nata   Gulf of Panama

Sta Marta

Maracaibo   P. Cabello   Caracas
Valencia

Cartagena

Gulf of Darien   Tolu   Gibraltar   Trujillo

Mompos   Mérida

R. Magdalena   Pamplona

R. Cauca

Antioquia

N E W   Tunja

Santa Fe de Bogotá

G R A N A D A

V E N E Z U E L A

R. Orinoco

Popayán

P. de la Galera

Quito

R. Negro

R. Amazon

80°   70°   60°   30°

20°

10°

0°

galeones, as the Tierra Firme fleet was called, steered southwest to Cartagena and Portobello (4,300 miles and eight weeks from Cadiz), while the *flota* took a northwesterly direction to Hispaniola, Cuba and Vera Cruz (4,860 miles from Cadiz). The return course for Spain was via Cuba and through the Bahama channel, the most dangerous passage of the whole voyage; having negotiated its hurricanes and reefs, the fleets headed northeast to pick up strong northerly winds, then east to the Azores and so to San Lucar.[60]

Predictable though the route was, the fleets suffered few losses from enemy action. They drew strength from the convoy system; the merchantmen carried armament; and they had their naval escort, usually eight galleons for the Tierra Firme fleet (the famous *armada de la guardia de la carrera de las Indias*) and two for the Mexican. These defences may not have been completely adequate, but the enemy could rarely assemble anything more powerful. In September 1628 a numerically superior Dutch fleet – thirty-one vessels, 700 cannon, 3,000 men – attacked the Mexican *flota* of some twenty vessels off Matanzas in Cuba, destroyed it and took its enormous treasure, some 6 million pesos according to the Dutch. This disaster was due in part to an unwonted failure of intelligence about the enemy's movements, but above all to failure of leadership; the Spanish commander, General Juan de Benavides, paid for his negligence on the gallows.[61] In 1656 an English squadron from Blake's fleet took the *capitana* and another galleon of the Tierra Firme fleet as it approached Cadiz, capturing some 2 million pesos. The English then sought out the Mexican fleet which had taken refuge in the Canaries; there, in April 1657, they almost completely destroyed it, and the Spaniards managed to save only a portion of its treasure.

These were the only major disasters to the *carrera de Indias* at the hands of enemies. The fleets suffered much more from the elements. Harassed by the close schedule of the turn-round, delays to trade and silver supplies, the expense of wintering in the Indies, and a government impatient for its bullion, fleet commanders often took excessive risks in sailing out of season. In 1622 five merchantmen and three galleons of the Tierra Firme

---

[60] Haring, *Trade and Navigation between Spain and the Indies*, pp. 201–30.
[61] Fernández Duro, *Armada española*, iv, pp. 97–106.

fleet sank in storms with heavy loss of treasure. In 1624 the same fleet lost three galleons through shipwreck, with 433,770 ducats of the crown's silver and 1 million belonging to private merchants. In 1631 the New Spain fleet left Veracruz late in the season and was struck by hurricane off the coast of Yucatán; the *almiranta* went down with all its silver, and most of the merchantmen were sunk or ran aground, a disaster which Olivares lamented as 'beyond words'.[62] In 1641 the New Spain fleet, again sailing late in the season, was devastated by hurricane on leaving the Bahama channel; the *almiranta* made its way to Santo Domingo where it sank; and the *capitana*, having survived the crossing, went down at the bar of San Lúcar; between them they lost 770,000 pesos for the king and 1,070,000 for merchants, though most of the *capitana*'s cargo was subsequently salvaged.[63]

The activities of pirates and privateers were puny compared to hurricanes in the Bahama strait. An international pirate community infested the Caribbean from bases like Tortuga, attacking local trade and pouncing on undefended Spanish settlements. But these were petty operations, even after their increase from the early seventeenth century. Nor was privateering particularly successful, confined as it was to the less prosperous and less defended parts of the Spanish empire. The returns from English privateering were so low that they hardly covered investment. Englishmen preferred contraband to privateering, though even this was second in importance to trade with Seville. From about 1625, however, the French, English and Dutch came to the lesser Antilles as settlers as well as interlopers, trading with Venezuela and the offshore islands, selling cloth and Negroes against tobacco and cacao, and syphoning off much of the local trade.[64]

The opportunities for contraband trade in the Caribbean, called by the Spaniards *rescate*, were becoming more numerous. Constant surveillance of the whole area was out of the question. The fleet system was geared to the supply of large markets in Mexico and Peru. Smaller settlements remote from the main routes were starved of trade. They were allowed *permiso* vessels which detached themselves from the fleets and made their way unescorted

---

[62] Domínguez Ortiz, *Política y hacienda de Felipe IV*, p. 283.
[63] Artíñano, *Historia del comercio con las Indias*, p. 346.
[64] Haring, *Trade and Navigation between Spain and the Indies*, pp. 118–22.

to a few ports of call; but these single vessels were favourite targets of corsairs and they tended to be withdrawn. Jamaica was one of the victims of such neglect; direct links between the island and Spain had virtually ceased by 1634, twenty years before its loss to England.[65] Settlements like Jamaica and Venezuela were also low on the list of Spanish defence priorities, preference being given to Hispaniola and Cuba which had greater strategic importance. The poor relations of the Indies trade were thus extremely vulnerable to commercial penetration by foreigners and less amenable to Spanish trade on the rare occasions when it arrived. The main zone of contraband was the coast of Tierra Firme from Trinidad to Maracaibo.[66] Here the economy was based on tobacco and cacao; as these had insufficient outlet in the annual fleets the trade fell into the hands of foreigners, the English, Dutch and Portuguese, who also supplied the Negro slaves needed on the coastal plantations. This trade, of course, was on the periphery of the Spanish empire and it did not tap the major sources of wealth, Mexico and Peru. But it was yet another breach of the monopoly, and it was conducted from bases which threatened Spain's imperial communications.

The foreign colonies which proliferated in the lesser Antilles from 1625 were dangerously close to the route by which the fleets entered the Caribbean. Even more dangerous were the English settlements in the islands of Santa Catalina and Tortuga. This movement towards the heart of the Spanish empire, closer to the routes of returning silver fleets, was regarded as a grave threat to security. No power could possibly have provided military and naval defence for every part of this vast empire. Spain's first reaction to foreign aggression, therefore, was to establish an order of priorities, abandoning those settlements regarded as of little value and concentrating defence on Mexico and Peru and on the staging posts thereto. This might be called a strategic withdrawal, first from the lesser Antilles, later from Jamaica. It was a rational enough policy and in pursuing it Spain lost nothing of value. She also devised certain substitutes for defence. Occasionally the warships escorting the trade fleets were diverted from convoy

    [65] Chaunu, *Séville et l'Atlantique*, viii, 1, p. 570; see also Francisco Morales Padrón, *La Jamaica Española* (Seville, 1952).
    [66] Chaunu, *Séville et l'Atlantique*, viii, 1, p. 626.

duty to eject foreign intruders. In 1629 the galleons of Don Fadrique de Toledo were used to expel English and French settlers from the islands of Nevis and St Kitts.[67] The risk attached to these operations – the fleets were left exposed – meant that they were confined to those foreign bases which were potential threats to the main trade routes and ports. One of these was the Dutch stronghold of St Martin which was cleared in 1633. Another was Santa Catalina, occupied by the English from 1630 and called by them Providence; after the failure of two small expeditions from Cartagena in 1635 and 1640, the galleons of Don Francisco Díaz Pimenta overcame the settlers in 1641 and left a Spanish garrison.[68] Finally, as a substitute for defence from the metropolis, the colonies themselves were encouraged to take the initiative. Their resources were usually adequate for immediate self-defence: the Dutch were repulsed at Puerto Rico in 1626, the English at Santo Domingo in 1654. But they were incapable of taking the offensive against intruders.[69] An expedition from Santo Domingo cleared the island of Tortuga in 1635, but the English and French soon returned, as they had already returned to St Kitts. These mopping-up operations did not succeed in stemming the tide. A permanent naval force was needed. This was recognized by the metropolis, though the latter short-sightedly preferred to channel resources to northern Europe.

At the eastern end of the transatlantic route defence was provided by the *Armada del Mar Océano* which operated out of home waters, protecting the Atlantic approaches for the returning fleets and performing general defence duties in western Europe. Its strength fluctuated considerably: in the early 1620s it consisted of forty-six vessels, but it gradually diminished in the course of the century and by the last decade it was down to about twenty. For Caribbean defence there were sporadic attempts to maintain an *Armada de Barlovento*, or Windward Squadron,

[67] Fernández Duro, *Armada española*, iv, p. 109.
[68] D. Rowland, 'Spanish Occupation of the Island of Old Providence or Santa Catalina, 1641–70', *Hispanic American Historical Review*, xv (1935), pp. 298–312; Fernández Duro, *Armada española*, iv, p. 338.
[69] R. D. Hussey, 'Spanish Reaction to Foreign Aggression in the Caribbean to about 1680', *Hispanic American Historical Review*, ix (1929), pp. 286–302; Andrews, *The Spanish Caribbean*, pp. 234–6; Enriqueta Vila Vilar, *Historia de Puerto Rico (1600–1650)* (Seville, 1974), pp. 137–50.

PLATE 6 *Recovery of San Juan de Puerto Rico*, by Eugenio Caxes (reproduced by kind permission of the Museo del Prado, Madrid)

charged on the colonial treasuries.[70] This was first dispatched – six frigates and other craft – in 1598, but it was soon diverted to convoy duty; from 1606 it was kept in Spanish waters and the money provided by the colonies for its maintenance was absorbed in European expenditure. In 1640, after five years' discussion, a new *Armada de Barlovento* consisting of eight galleons was assigned to anti-corsair operations and escort duties in the Caribbean.[71] In 1641 it escorted the New Spain fleet from Havana to Vera Cruz, back to Havana and from there to the Bahama channel. Again, however, it was soon diverted to transatlantic convoy duty: in 1643 it escorted the New Spain fleet from Vera Cruz to Spain, and also provided the escort for its outward voyage in 1644. From then until 1647 it continued to perform escort and transport duties across the Atlantic, becoming in effect a substitute for the *armada de la guardia*, evidence that defence of the fleets was now being subsidized by the colonies themselves. Yet they were not even getting value for their money, for in 1648 the *Armada de Barlovento* was incorporated in the *Armada del Mar Océano*, and between then and 1667 there was no permanent defence squadron in the Caribbean. In 1665 the *Armada de Barlovento* was re-formed; it consisted of eight vessels, four of them specially built in Holland, and was immediately assigned to European duties. Two years later five of its units were dispatched to the Indies; two were quickly diverted to transatlantic duties, and the remainder were destroyed by Henry Morgan and his buccaneers at the entrance to Lake Maracaibo. In 1672 a revived *Armada de Barlovento* entered service; it consisted of five vessels with subsequent additions from Caribbean resources, and in more or less this form it survived for the rest of the century.

Meanwhile military fortifications had also received some attention. In the 1620s and 1640s defence installations in Cuba and other major bases were reconstructed and extended. The English capture of Jamaica in 1655 stimulated further defence programmes. 'By the last quarter of the seventeenth century most harbors important for trade or military strategy possessed strong forts and fair garrisons.'[72]

[70] Veitia Linaje, *Norte de la contratación*, pp. 540–56; Artíñano, *Historia del comercio con las Indias*, pp. 103–6; Bibiano Torres Ramírez, *La Armada de Barlovento*, (Seville, 1981).
[71] Chaunu, *Séville et l'Atlantique*, v, pp. 409–12.
[72] Hussey, 'Spanish Reaction to Foreign Aggression in the Caribbean', p. 295.

This defence record was not unimpressive. No major possession was lost and no foreign colony was allowed to remain a
danger. Had the metropolis properly used all the funds which the
colonies appropriated to defence, instead of diverting them to
Europe, even more could have been accomplished. As it was,
resources were not sufficient to recover Jamaica and Curaçao, or
to defend the most desirable islands in the Antilles against foreign
occupation. From the mid-seventeenth century, with a growing
sense of realism, Spain began to accept the inevitable. Foreigners,
too, wanted peace in order to consolidate their possessions and
extend their trade. There resulted a series of treaties recognizing
the existing situation in terms of effective occupation. In 1648 the
Treaty of Munster gave the Dutch all the territory they actually
occupied in America – this was not very much – in return for a
promise not to trade with Spanish domains. In 1670 the Treaty of
Madrid sanctioned Britain's retention of its existing possessions in
the West Indies and America, against a promise to refrain from
illegal trade. Meanwhile the hordes of independent pirates, the
buccaneers, had also become an international nuisance, and by
1680 the English, French and Dutch, as well as the Spaniards,
were taking action against them. Defence policy in the Caribbean
therefore lost its urgency. And Spain could not reverse the economic trend which made contraband trade, in spite of treaty pro-
mises, an extensive and lucrative practice, widening the breach of
the monopoly which had already been made at Cadiz.

Pacific Defence

The fleet system was designed to supply all the southern contin-
ent by way of the isthmus of Panama, thence down the Pacific to
Peru and Chile, and inland to Upper Peru and the Río de la Plata.
The Tierra Firme fleet transferred its cargo at Portobello; it was
then transported in mule trains across the isthmus to Panama
where the Pacific fleet, which had already brought up the silver
consignments from Peru, was waiting to ship it to the southern
markets.

To preseve this monopoly route and prevent the escape of
Potosí silver the Spaniards closed the Río de la Plata to trade and
shipping. For the same reason they also had to maintain Buenos
Aires, fortified and populated, as a key defence point. But how

could they attract settlers to this distant possession and at the same time enforce a closed-port policy which made it impossible for settlers to survive? To solve this dilemma Spain tried to do two things at once, to maintain her trade system and to relax it in the smallest possible degree in favour of Buenos Aires. A decree of 1618 redefined the restrictions on the maritime trade of Buenos Aires; the port was allowed two licensed vessels a year to Seville and back, though the licences became ever more irregular and insufficient. And to seal off Buenos Aires from the silver province of Upper Peru an inland customs house was established in Córdoba, at the foot of the eastern cordillera; operating from about 1622, it charged 50 per cent duties on goods moving inland.[73] This policy restricted the economic prospects of the Río de la Plata without greatly restricting contraband trade. Through the pampa route to Upper Peru the Portuguese directed a traffic which at its peak in 1600–20 may have taken returns amounting to 20 or even 25 per cent of Potosí's silver production.[74] Spanish counter-measures reduced this traffic but did not eliminate it.

The Portuguese 'route to Potosí' was successful not because it was a superior route but because Potosí was an insatiable market. The Pacific provinces of the subcontinent were best supplied via Panama. This was the shortest route to the heart of Spanish South America, which, because of the location of silver deposits and labour supply, was nearer to the Pacific than the Atlantic. The transfer of merchandise at the isthmus was economically much less onerous than would have been the routing of trade across the vast and empty pampas of the Río de la Plata, devoid of inhabitants, water and defences against marauding Indians. And navigation across the South Atlantic was extremely vulnerable to attack from Brazil, especially from the 1620s when the Dutch had a base there and from 1640 when the Portuguese were enemies of Spain. Pacific trading routes, on the other hand, had certain built-in advantages.

[73] Ricardo Levene, *Investigaciones acerca de la historia económica del virreinato del Plata* (1st edn, 1927–8, 2nd edn, 1952, reprinted by Academia Nacional de la Historia, *Obras de Ricardo Levene 2*, Buenos Aires, 1962), pp. 141–84; Mario Rodriguez, 'The Genesis of Economic Attitudes in the Río de la Plata', *Hispanic American Historical Review*, xxxvi (1956), pp. 171–89; Raúl A. Molina, 'Una Historia Inédita de los primeros ochenta años de Buenos Aires. El "Defensorio" de D. Alonso de Solórzano y Velazco, Oidor de la Real Audiencia (1667)', *Revista de Historia de América*, 52 (1961), pp. 429–97.
[74] Chaunu, *Séville et l'Atlantique*, viii, 1, p. 1182.

The principal trading route in the Spanish Pacific was that between Panama, Callao (the port of Lima) and Arica (the port of Potosí), which was simply an extension of the transatlantic route. There were also two secondary routes, Acapulco–Callao for trade between Mexico and Peru, and Acapulco–Manila for trans-Pacific trade. The targets most favoured by the enemies of Spain were the silver fleets from Arica to Panama and the Manila galleons. Yet the Pacific was effectively sealed to large-scale enemy penetration without too much effort by Spain. After the severe lessons taught by the English marauders in the late sixteenth century, the isthmus complex was now a focus of defence which could not easily be breached. Access to the Pacific by sea round the Horn was limited by the navigational possibilities of the time. Spain never dominated the Straits of Magellan; shipping found it difficult to survive the unpredictable winds and the shallow waters of the narrowest straits, and the victims of shipwreck were likely to die of hunger and exposure in this cruel region. The same conditions prevented Spain's enemies from maintaining constant pressure via Cape Horn, and in the seventeenth century it remained an exceptional rather than a regular route.

In these circumstances the defence problem in the Pacific was not to stem a continuing wave of intruders but to have sufficient force to repulse rare attacks when they occurred. This did not require constant patrolling of the coast from Acapulco to the Straits. All that was needed was an efficient early-warning system and an *armada* based on Callao. The former was supplied by intelligence from Spain, which usually identified all hostile expeditions leaving Europe, and from warnings relayed up the Pacific coast once the enemy had navigated the Straits of Magellan. Naval power was provided by the *armada del mar del Sur* operating out of Callao. From the late sixteenth century this consisted, when at full strength, of five galleons, built in the shipyards of Guayaquil from funds supplied by the *alcabala* revenue.[75] Its purpose was to transport silver, guard the silver

---

[75] Marie Helmer, 'Le Callao (1615–1618)', *Jahrbuch für Geschichte von Staat, Wirtschaft und Gesellschaft Lateinamerikas*, ii (1965), pp. 145–95; Chaunu, *Séville et l'Atlantique*, viii, 1, p. 1107; and now the definitive study of Pablo Emilio Pérez-Mallaína Bueno and Bibiano Torres Ramírez, *La Armada del Mar del Sur* (Seville, 1987).

route and escort merchant convoys between Arica, Callao and Panama. It was divided into two flotillas, each consisting of two galleons and a patache, one operating to the south, the other to the north, if necessary as far as Mexico, while the fifth galleon was held in reserve in Callao.[76]

For some years after the English intrusion in the sixteenth century the Spanish Pacific enjoyed a period of calm. This was disturbed by the coming of Dutch raiders, known to Spaniards as *Pechelingues*, a word corrupted from the name of the island port of Flushing. The Dutch offensive was heralded by two minor expeditions (1598–1600) in search of trade, bases and a route to the East Indies. The first major expedition was dispatched by the Dutch East India Company in August 1614, during the period of truce with Spain. It consisted of four large and heavily armed warships and two smaller vessels, and it was commanded by Admiral Joris van Speilbergen, a German in the company's service. Its ultimate object was to trade and reinforce Dutch naval power in the Moluccas, but it was equally intended to attack the Spanish empire on the way.[77] The expedition entered the Pacific through the Straits of Magellan in May 1615 and as it moved up the coast warnings went ahead. Just south of Callao the way was barred by a Spanish squadron of seven ships (the southern flotilla reinforced by merchantmen) under Rodrigo de Mendoza; but in a sharp engagement on 17–18 July the Spaniards were soundly defeated, losing two warships and 450 men. With the whole west coast lying open, the Dutch ignored Callao, missed the northern *armada* and sailed to Acapulco where they obtained provisioning facilities in exchange for return of Peruvian prisoners. In December they left Mexican waters to cross the Pacific and missed the Manila galleon.

After this uncomfortable experience the Spaniards began to look to their defences. The viceroy of New Spain began the construction of a fortress at Acapulco, and in Peru naval defences

---

[76] The Peruvian convoy system was never as rigorous as the transatlantic one; merchants preferred to trade out of convoy, as the danger from pirates was intermittent and they wished to evade registration; see Helmer, 'Le Callao', pp. 174–6.

[77] See Peter Gerhard, *Pirates on the West Coast of New Spain* 1575–1742 (Glendale, 1960), pp. 108–21, a work which goes beyond its title; for the latest research see Peter T. Bradley, *The Lure of Peru. Maritime Intrusion into the South Sea, 1598–1701* (London, 1989), pp. 32–46.

were improved. These were in the capable hands of viceroy the prince of Esquilache; he constructed three forts at Callao, established a new military unit with duties divided between service in Callao and the escort of silver to Panama, and brought the *armada* up to strength, increasing its firepower and manpower. But his programme was highly expensive and ate into imperial revenue, including the royal *quinto*; remittances to Spain were reduced, which was thought to be extremely inconvenient on the eve of the Thirty Years War, and so Esquilache was recalled. Colonial defence was sacrificed to policy in Europe.[78]

Yet Esquilache was right. In 1616 the Dutchman Jacob Lemaire discovered a new though hardly less dangerous or shorter passage into the Pacific south of Tierra del Fuego through the strait which still bears his name. This heralded a new series of raiders. In April 1623 the so-called Nassau fleet left Holland; consisting of eleven vessels, heavy armament and 1,637 men under the command of Admiral Jacques l'Hermite, its object was not only to attack Spanish ports and shipping and impose contraband trade but also to challenge Spanish sovereignty in the Pacific by establishing a Dutch military and trading post in Peru or Chile in alliance with disaffected Indians.[79] The expedition entered the Pacific through the Lemaire Strait in February 1624 and arrived off Callao on 8 May, just five days after the viceroy, who had been forewarned, had dispatched to Panama the treasure fleet carrying two years' crown silver, some 9 million pesos.[80] At this point l'Hermite died and his successor, the young and inexperienced Hugo Schapenham, lost his chance through indecision. An ill-managed attack on Callao was repulsed, and the Dutch then spent over four months on the coast of Peru, accomplishing little apart from the destruction of Guayaquil and acquiring a bad reputation for killing prisoners. The expedition reached the coast of Mexico in October; but now Acapulco had its fortress and it refused provisions; at other points on the coast the Dutch were harried, and in November they abandoned their wait for the Manila galleon and left to cross the Pacific. This expedition was a failure, and the Spaniards had now evened the score.

The Spanish authorities held a searching inquest into the de-

[78] Helmer, 'Le Callao', pp. 153–7; Bradley, *The Lure of Peru*, pp. 47–8.
[79] Gerhard, *Pirates on the West Coast of New Spain*, pp. 123–9; Chaunu, *Séville et l'Atlantique*, v, pp. 74–9.
[80] Bradley, *The Lure of Peru*, pp. 51–2, 55–6.

fence implications of the Nassau fleet, and decided in principle to give priority to land rather than sea defences. But in the event they rested on their laurels. Viceroy Esquilache had tried to create a new and larger *armada del mar del Sur* to patrol the coasts of Mexico, Central America, Peru and Chile. From 1624 to 1635 the idea was shuttled back and forth between Peru and Spain, based on a requirement of ten galleons and 7,000 men at an estimated cost of 1 million pesos.[81] The idea was eventually abandoned, not because Peru lacked the money but because the crown wanted that money in Europe. Apart from a hunt for informers, some minor naval improvements and the increase of fortresses surrounding Callao, Spanish authorities continued to rely on the natural invulnerability of the Pacific. For the moment they were probably justified. After the fiasco of 1624 the Dutch confined their hostilities to the Atlantic side of America. Their last serious effort to penetrate the Spanish Pacific was the expedition of Hendrick Brouwer under the auspices of the Dutch West India Company. This was another attempt to establish a trading colony. The Dutch squadron arrived off the island of Chiloe in May 1643. Although Brouwer died a few months later, his men stayed on at Valdivia, built a fort, and attacked the Spaniards. But they found the land inhospitable and the Indians aloof; and they left in October 1643. So in the event the Dutch made little impact in the Spanish Pacific. The chief consequence of their intervention was to force the Spanish authorities to reappraise defence needs and to raise the defence expenditure of the Lima treasury: 200,000 pesos in 1624, 948,000 in 1643. Viceroy the Marquis of Mancera (1639–48) undertook an extensive and costly programme of defence from north to south of the viceroyalty. A maritime expedition was organized to refound and fortify Valdivia; when the Englishman John Narborough sailed to Valdivia in 1669 on a reconnoitring expedition he found it occupied, defended and closed to foreigners. The wall of Callao was built to encircle the whole town. New galleons were constructed, military forces expanded and equipped. The 1.5 million pesos shipped to Spain in 1644 might have been twice that amount, it was reported, but for the costs of defence.[82]

[81] Chaunu, *Séville et l'Atlantique*, v, pp. 75–9.
[82] Bradley, *The Lure of Peru*, pp. 85, 86–100; Kenneth J. Andrien, *Crisis and Decline: the Viceroyalty of Peru in the Seventeenth Century* (Albuquerque, NM, 1985), p. 67.

In the second half of the seventeenth century, however, new enemies penetrated the Pacific, this time from the Caribbean. These were the buccaneers, the international gangsters of the Indies. From the 1640s to the 1670s, in alliance with the Indians of the Mosquito Shore, the buccaneers asserted control over the largely uncolonized east coast of Central America and made periodic raids inland. The San Juan River of Nicaragua offered access to the Pacific coast in spite of Spanish fortifications. In 1660 Henry Morgan led a raid on Costa Rica, though he was driven off. He returned to capture Portobello, which he held for a while in the summer of 1668. In January 1671 Morgan led an expedition across the isthmus of Panama, defeated a Spanish force 2,000 strong, held the city for a month, attacked other coastal settlements and departed in March with substantial booty.[83] This was a pointer to his colleagues.

The isthmus of Panama was the vital link between the silver route from Peru and the transatlantic route from Spain. It had always been protectd by distance. Now, after the English capture of Jamaica in 1655, its protection was removed. It needed military and naval security. After Morgan's raid Portobello and Panama were refortified, their garrisons were increased, and the silver route across the isthmus was strongly guarded. But a few miles east of Panama, in the province of Darien, swamp and jungle country inhabited by Indians hostile to the Spaniards offered another means of access to the Pacific. This jungle route became 'an inter-oceanic highway for the buccaneers'.[84]

In April 1680 English pirates launched a major invasion of the Pacific. First they took all the shipping in the Gulf of Panama. Then, after raiding, pillaging and capturing a silver transport in the vicinity, they sailed south along the Pacific coast under the command of Bartholomew Sharp; for over a year they raided the west coast of South America, including the silver port of Arica, and took two valuable prizes loaded with bullion. Eventually they left via Cape Horn and reached Barbados in February 1682. This was the most serious attack yet on the Spanish Pacific, motivated not by desire of conquest or colonization but by pure

---

[83] Gerhard, *Pirates on the West Coast of New Spain*, pp. 139–41.

[84] Ibid., p. 146; see also G. Céspedes del Castillo, 'La defensa militar del istmo de Panamá a fines del siglo XVII y comienzos del XVIII', *Anuario de Estudios Americanos*, ix (1952), pp. 235–75.

plunder. Merchant shipping, remoter settlements and security in general were directly threatened. The Spaniards were forced to spread their defence resources more thinly over the ground at a time when their naval strength in the Pacific was again run down, incapable of aiding ports, protecting merchantmen or confronting pirates. The old dilemma reappeared: was it to be warships, arms or fortifications? And which was the cheapest?[85] The Spaniards estimated the damage to shipping and ports at over 4 million pesos; their merchant marine lost twenty-five ships; and they suffered more than 200 fatal casualties.[86] And there was more to come.

The largest buccaneer invasion of the Pacific began in March 1684 with the entry of three English ships, two through the Straits of Magellan, the third round Cape Horn.[87] They made their way to Central America where they were joined by other pirate gangs who had crossed the isthmus of Panama. In June 1685 in the Gulf of Panama they awaited a Spanish silver fleet from Callao, a 'fleet' which in spite of its duties consisted only of two crown galleons, one of which subsequently blew up, and a patache; even so the Spaniards first landed their treasure and then beat off the pirates. The invaders escaped to create immense havoc up and down the coast. They attacked coastal settlements in Nicaragua, careened in the Galápagos Islands, took a few prizes off Peru, raided and looted along the Peruvian coast, raided Central America and Mexico, looted Guayaquil, but missed the Manila galleon. Eventually the raiders left in the course of 1686–9, some by way of the East Indies, others via Cape Horn or across Central America, having effected landings at some thirty sites, captured twenty-eight prizes at sea, taken booty worth over 400,000 pesos, and killed twenty-nine opponents.[88] This was the last large-scale invasion of the Pacific. In May 1690 Captain John Strong entered through the Straits of Magellan on a contraband mission and disposed of most of his cargo in Peru; but this, like one or two other foreign incursions of the time, was a trading, not a piratical, expedition, and it heralded the French break-through into the Pacific in the early eighteenth century.

[85] Bradley, *The Lure of Peru*, pp. 126–7.
[86] Artíñano, *Historia del comercio con las Indias*, p. 225.
[87] Gerhard, *Pirates on the West Coast of New Spain*, pp. 154–94.
[88] Bradley, *The Lure of Peru*, pp. 140–1, 159–60.

In the last decades of the seventeenth century viceroys of Peru found their exiguous forces overstretched in a struggle to defend coastal zones, offer resistance at sea and maintain vital commercial links with Chile, Panama and the ports supplying Lima, in addition to protecting the treasure routes between Arica, Callao and Panama. Spanish defences were heavily handicapped by the inability of viceroys and merchants to agree on the division of responsibility and costs for defence against the buccaneer incursions. As the Spaniards were reluctant or unable to meet the pirates at sea, in effect they had to fight land battles to defend their coastal possessions, as at Guayaquil in 1687 when a band of 300 buccaneers struck inland, terrorized the city and escaped with their booty intact. In the same year, despairing of official action, a group of private merchants in Peru invested in a company of armed vessels to sweep the Pacific clear of pirates. The *armada del mar del Sur* had been allowed to run down to two galleons and a patache. It was adequate for carrying silver, as it showed in 1685, but for nothing more. From 1692 it acquired new vessels and was brought up to a strength of three galleons and two pataches, with 144 cannon and 1238 men.[89] But this was only possible because the *consulado* paid most of the bill. Peruvian sources also funded two new works of fortification at Trujillo and Lima.[90] Meanwhile the viceregal government refused to invest in defences at Guayaquil, though garrisons at Valdivia, Callao and Panama were strengthened. The defence of the Pacific, therefore, was indebted to local resources and initiative, and if the viceroyalty had to provide men, materials and finances for its own protection, it was increasingly private enterprise rather than the state which provided them, further evidence of the growth of local economic resources and their deployment in America.

The cost of Pacific defence – basically the protection of the silver route to Panama and the mercury route to Arica – was high. On three occasions the defence of Peru against foreign incursions consumed a greater proportion of the Lima treasury's revenue than that remitted to Spain. In 1624, when l'Hermite interrupted normal silver operations, defence costs soared to their

[89] Céspedes, 'La defensa militar del istmo de Panamá', pp. 250–1.
[90] Lawrence A. Clayton, 'Local Initiative and Finance in Defence of the Viceroyalty of Peru: the Development of Self-Reliance', *HAHR*, 54, 2 (1974), pp. 284–304; Bradley, *The Lure of Peru*, p. 164.

highest point of the century, over 1.5 million pesos, or almost 38 per cent of crown revenue. In 1658 the defence budget consumed nearly 29 per cent of revenue. These were single years. But in the last decades of the century, particularly during the buccaneer years of 1680–90, the unmistakable trend of expenditure was towards higher defence costs at the expense of remittances to Spain. During the first fifty years of the seventeenth century silver bullion exported to Spain accounted for about 41 per cent of revenue, and defence costs some 14 per cent. But in 1650–90 defence costs averaged 21 per cent and remittances to Spain dropped to about 25 per cent of revenue. The real trouble began about 1680. In 1681–90 the Lima treasure remitted to Spain a mere 7 per cent of its revenue, or 1.8 milion pesos, while 33 per cent, or 8.3 million pesos, was consumed in defence.[91] Viceroys grasped at any pretext and used any argument to cut defence costs. Viceroy Salvatierra even found consolation in the wreck of the great galleon *Jesús María* off Guayaquil in 1654, because it saved the crippling costs of ship maintenance and repair. Empire had become a burden without benefit.

The Course of American Trade

In the sixteenth century the Indies trade underwent two long phases of expansion, from 1504 to 1550 and from 1562 to 1592, separated by a mid-century recession of twelve years. This was followed by a reversal of the major trend between 1593 and 1622, and a long depression from 1623 to 1650.[92] The movement of

---

[91] Peter T. Bradley, 'The Cost of Defending a Viceroyalty: Crown Revenue and the Defence of Peru in the Seventeenth Century', *Ibero-Amerikanisches Archiv*, 10, 3 (1984), pp. 267–89, and *The Lure of Peru*, pp. 192–4; John J. TePaske, 'The Fiscal Structure of Upper Peru and the Financing of Empire', in Karen Spalding, ed., *Essays in the Political, Economic and Social History of Colonial Latin America* (Newark, Delaware, 1982), pp. 69–94, esp. pp. 76–80; Pérez Mallaína and Torres, *La Armada del Mar del Sur*, pp. 130–3, 286–8.

[92] The trends have been identified and the estimates computed by Chaunu. Valuable reviews of this great work are provided by H. G. Koenigsberger, *English Historical Review* (1961), pp. 675–81; C. H. Haring, 'Trade and Navigation between Spain and the Indies: a Re-view – 1918–1958', *Hispanic American Historical Review*, xl (1960), pp. 53–62; Robert S. Smith, 'Seville and the Atlantic; Cycles in Spanish Colonial Trade', *Journal of Economic History*,

vessels between Spain and America quadrupled between 1506 and 1620, from 226 sailings (outbound and inbound) in 1506–10 to 867 in 1616–20. The number of sailings reached three quinquennial peaks, 874 in 1546–50, 886 in 1586–90, and 965 in 1606–10; but they dropped to 366 in 1646–50, and the average in 1641–50 was practically the same as in 1521–5. Gross tonnage (outbound and inbound) increased from 15,680 tons in 1511–15, to 273,560 in 1606–10; between then and 1646–50 it suffered a 60 per cent drop to 121,308 tons. The whole period may be divided into (a) a long wave of expansion, culminating in 1608, and (b) a prolonged period of contraction, interrupted by short upturns.

Until the seventeenth century the trade of Tierra Firme (mainly Peru) and New Spain was more or less balanced, rather more than 40 per cent of the trade going to Tierra Firme, rather less than 40 per cent to New Spain, the remainder to the Caribbean islands. Until about 1570–80 exports to America were dominated by grain, oil and wine. But from then, when the colonists had settled for home-produced meat, wheat and maize, and their own wine production had increased, foodstuffs gave way to textiles and hardware. To about 1580–90 Spanish products dominated the trade; subsequently the products of northern Europe and France eroded the Spanish monopoly. Imports from America were dominated by precious metals; in value they constituted more than 90 per cent of returns.

At the beginning of the seventeenth century the outbound fleets carried wine, oil, mercury, iron and hardware, textiles,

xxii (1962), pp. 253–9. It has received a more critical reception from W. Brulez, 'Séville et l'Atlantique: quelques réflexions critiques', *Revue Belge de Philologie et d'Histoire*, xlii (1964), pp. 568–92. Lacking production statistics, Chaunu assumes that tonnage statistics – the carrying capacity of vessels leaving and returning to Seville – measure general economic activity. Doubtless there are margins of error caused by fraud, arrivals and departures at other ports than Seville-Cadiz, the failure of some vessels to fill their cargo capacity and the tendency of others to overfill, and the loss of vessels on voyage. But Chaunu is aware of almost every possible contingency, and in particular he has anticipated criticisms concerning the relation between tonnage and the volume of merchandise carried, by showing that shippers bought or chartered vessels of a particular tonnage according to the state of the trade; Spanish shippers were not so devoid of economic instincts as to underutilize their vessels over a long period. Finally, Chaunu does more than measure an exclusively Spanish commercial activity; his Atlantic is the European Atlantic, for it is incontrovertible that most European merchants preferred to trade via Seville rather than in the Indies themselves.

books and paper. But the export pattern of the colonies was changing, evidence of a shift in the American economies. In 1594 precious metals formed 95.62 per cent of total imports from America.[93] In 1609 they were down to 84 per cent the remainder being agricultural and colonial products, mostly Mexican. In this period Mexico sent back silver, cochineal, hides, indigo, wool, dyes, dye-woods, medicinal plants and, especially in the years 1600–20, Chinese silks, re-exports from Manila.[94] In 1609 Mexico exported to Spain 3.3 million pesos of precious metals (public and private); non-treasure exports totalled 1.8 million pesos, or about 35 per cent of the value of cargo.[95] Mexico's non-treasure exports became progressively more important as the colony diversified its economy. The Peruvian economy on the other hand, more 'colonial' in its structure, was more closely tied to mining, and Peru exported little but silver to Spain.

The years 1592–1622 form a plateau between expansion and contraction, a high plateau to be sure, with continuing signs of prosperity but equally distinct signs of hesitation which indicate a reversal of the previous trend.[96] At the end of this period sailings (outbound and inbound) dropped by 10 per cent, from 867 in 1616–20 to 775 in 1621–5. The relative roles of Tierra Firme and New Spain also began to fluctuate. Between 1581 and 1590 Tierra Firme had contributed the major part in trade and in silver to the great expansion of those years. But between 1596 and 1620 the high plateau was sustained by increasing contributions of trade from New Spain. After 1620 New Spain flagged again, leaving Tierra Firme to sustain the plateau. Prices and the Indies trade fluctuated in more or less regular periods, and did so in statistical correlation. The end of expansion corresponded to the reversal of the major trend of prices about 1605, followed by the depression of real prices in 1609–12. Subsequent inflation was artificially induced by monetary debasement, especially from the 1620s, which was not healthy for the Indies trade or for any trade.

The great inflation of the sixteenth century had been engendered in large part by treasure imports. These now began to drop,

---

[93] Hamilton, *American Treasure and the Price Revolution in Spain*, pp. 33–4.

[94] François Chevalier, 'Les cargaisons des flottes de Nouvelle Espagne vers 1600', *Revista de Indias*, iv (1943), pp. 323–30.

[95] Ibid., p. 329.

[96] Chaunu, *Séville et l'Atlantique*, viii, 2, 2, pp. 852–1525.

from 58.2 million pesos in 1591–5, to 40.3 million in 1601–5, and 44.2 million pesos in 1631–5. Crown receipts dropped almost 40 per cent from 10.9 million pesos in 1596–1600 to 6.5 million in 1601–5; there was a long plateau from 1616 to 1645 when they scarcely rose above 4 million in any quinquennium, followed by a further drop to 1.6 million in 1646–50, to 606,524 in 1656–60.[97] The depression of public treasure receipts was a further sign of a changing empire, for it represented to some degree an increase in the cost of colonial administration and defence, a kind of state investment in the Indies. The reversal of the major trend of private treasure receipts occurred rather later than that of public receipts, but in spite of fluctuations the trend was downwards until 1651–65.

What was the relation of treasure, prices and trade? What was the effect of the vast amounts of silver and gold delivered from America to Spain between 1501 and 1650? This massive importation of treasure directly affected prices, which in turn stimulated trade or, when imports levelled off and fell, depressed it. Treasure returns gave merchants the capital for further investment; when treasure diminished, trade was starved of finance. But the more the American trade expanded in the second half of the sixteenth century, the greater the amount of treasure it needed to keep it going. For treasure induced inflation, which meant that the yield of mining in effect progressively diminished: the very success of American mining caused the value of its yield to decrease.[98] In the course of the sixteenth century prices in Spain quadrupled; in the

---

[97] Hamilton, *American Treasure and the Price Revolution in Spain*, pp. 34–8; Morineau, *Incroyables gazettes et fabuleux métaux*, Table 42, p. 250. It is difficult to correlate treasure receipts and trade performance, for treasure was the commodity most susceptible to fraud, and fraud itself took various forms: contraband, under-estimates in the register and trade outside the register. Hamilton suggests a 10 per cent margin of error through fraud, but this is too low; others have argued for 50 per cent or more of treasure escaping control of the *Casa de la Contratación* in the decades after 1630, which is probably too high. A recent estimate suggests 15 per cent. Unregistered bullion was most likely to go abroad as immediate returns to foreigners, while most of the re-gistered bullion remained in Spain and was re-invested in the Indies trade. The statistics therefore have some value. See Chaunu, *Séville et l'Atlantique*, viii, 2, 2, p. 902; Morineau, *Incroyables gazettes et fabuleux métaux*, pp. 238–50. Hamilton expresses his quantities in *pesos de mina* (450 maravedis), Morineau in *pesos de a ocho reales* (272 maravedis).

[98] See the acute analysis by Chaunu, *Séville et l'Atlantique*, viii, 2, 2, p. 917.

same period the value of gold and silver, as merchandise, decreased by about three-quarters. To prolong the expansion, to sustain the purchasing power of gold and silver, mining production had to grow faster than prices and trade. This could only be done by constant extension of the mining area or great improvement of technology. By about 1590, however, the Spaniards had exhausted the immediately available mineral wealth of America without renewing their methods. With the primitive production techniques of the colonists, the Spanish American economy had reached the limits of its expansion; it was also seriously affected by labour shortage caused by the depopulation of the Indian sector. Simultaneously the colonists were beginning to supply their own needs and becoming less dependent on European imports; the growing self-sufficiency of the empire was a basic factor in the crisis of the Indies trade. Up to 1622 the curve of prices and trade remained roughly level. But in the meantime Spain's own economy had been seriously weakened by an extraordinary rise in wages caused by acute labour shortage after the plague of 1599–1600 and the expulsion of the moriscos in 1609.

Even in this period, however, the Indies trade was still capable of striking performance. The year 1608 was the 'year of all the records'.[99] The previous year had seen the worst recession yet; outward sailings dropped from ninety-eight in 1606 to thirty-seven in 1607 (62 per cent), and tonnage from 23,286 tons to 9,783 (57 per cent).[100] In 1608 massive convoys totalling 202 ships and 54,093 tons were dispatched to America, an increase of 445.9 per cent in vessels and 452.9 per cent in tonnage. This was 50 per cent better than the previous peak in 1596, and it was never equalled again. Indeed 1608 was a flash of lightning out of surrounding gloom, a year of fragile prosperity made at the expense of subsequent years. In 1609 the trade returned to the secular norm – 138 ships and 32,536 tons outwards.[101] There were serious fears in Seville that that Mexican market had reached saturation point. And there were other signs of trouble. The Tierra Firme fleet of this year brought to Seville a horde of *Peruleros*. These, as

[99] Ibid., viii, 2, 2, p. 1276.
[100] Ibid., viii, 2, 2, p. 1236.
[101] Ibid., viii, 2, 2, p. 1299.

their name implies, were factors of creole business houses in Peru. They were not to tied to monopolistic trading practices as were the merchants of Seville; they brought with them large supplies of capital for use in Europe; and they were, if anything, even more serious competitors than the foreigners.[102] The presence of the *Peruleros* in Seville, their employment of American capital in a trade which was theoretically the monopoly of Spain, was a further sign of the reorientation of the empire and of its growing economic independence. The normal reaction of the monopolists to crisis was to restrict trade, induce shortage and raise prices. The *Peruleros* resisted this practice. In 1610, in opposition to the *consulado* of Seville, they insisted on dispatching a fleet. Peru itself was advancing and demanding more trade, including naval stores for its shipyards; the growth of American shipping and its competition with Spanish trade and navigation were yet further signs of the shift of power from Andalucía.

In 1611 recession was manifest. Traffic (outbound and inbound) fell from 201 to 159 sailings (21 per cent), tonnage from 65,713 to 41,684 tons (36.6 per cent). The volume of traffic to New Spain in 1611 was almost 50 per cent less than in 1609, and by 1620 outbound traffic was down to forty-seven vessels; the colony's withdrawal into itself was now irreversible.[103] Many of the vessels in the transatlantic fleets were no longer Spanish. From 1614 Biscayan predominance in Indies shipping became a thing of the past. Instead of replacing stock by new orders from Basque shipyards, Spanish shippers relied more and more on foreign, Portuguese and American vessels.[104] Difficulties were aggravated by the shortage of seamen and the high level of wages. Seville's response to recession was to reduce tonnage and ship only the most expensive and lucrative goods; these were necessarily foreign manufactures, a development which favoured the drift of trade from Seville to Cadiz, the port preferred by foreigners. The crisis of 1619–23 was all the more ominous as it was not a war-induced crisis of a type familiar to Spanish trade – the years 1609–21 were ones of exceptional peace – but a crisis caused by structural failings within the Indies trade.

[102] Ibid., viii, 2, 2, pp. 1330–2; see below, pp. 291–3.
[103] Ibid., viii, 2, 2, pp. 1336–45, 1499.
[104] Ibid., viii, 2, 2, pp. 1415–17.

From 1623 the trend was sharply and irretrievably downwards, both in prices and in the volume and value of trade. The great depression had begun, and it continued until, by 1650, the American trade in its classical form and dimensions was almost totally destroyed. In traffic and tonnage the depression was in the order of at least 50 per cent: sailings (outbound and inbound) dropped from 965 in 1606–10 to 366 in 1646–50; gross tonnage dropped from 273,560 tons in 1606–10 to 121,308 in 1646–50.[105] The depression gathered momentum between 1621–5 and 1626–30, total sailings dropping from 775 to 588 (about 24 per cent). The trend was most evident in the outward traffic to New Spain; its portion of total trade moved from 43.19 per cent in 1621–5, to 28.58 per cent in 1626–30, to 29.82 per cent in 1631–5, while Tierra Firme climbed up to 51.23 per cent.[106] Peru was now the most important sector of the transatlantic economy and it attracted relatively more trade. The balance in favour of Peru can also be seen in the origin of treasure imports.[107] Between 1586 and 1625 Mexico supplied 36 per cent of total treasure imports, Peru 64 per cent, evidence not only of serious depression of Mexican mining but also of the fact that Mexico was diversifying its economy more rapidly than Peru. Mexican consignments decreased to 21 per cent of total treasure receipts in 1626–30, while those from Peru rose to 79 per cent. And while the actual amount of registered treasure from Mexico fell from 10.8 million pesos in 1621–5 to 5 million in 1626–30, Peru's contribution rose from 16.2 million pesos in 1621–5 to 19.5 million in 1626–30. There was therefore some correlation between the recession in trade and treasure. It was evidently in the 1620s that the pause in New Spain's first economy became most pronounced. This was the major factor behind the crisis in the American trade.

New Spain was the sick man of the transatlantic economy from the 1620s to the 1650s. Depopulation of the Indians deprived the colony of a sufficient labour force to keep its economy at its former level, and it was not until the middle decades of the seventeenth century that there were signs of demographic

[105] Ibid., viii, 2, 2, pp. 1541–3.
[106] Ibid., viii, 2, 2, pp. 1534–5.
[107] Again these are the official figures of registered treasure, but assuming that contraband was roughly the same for both sectors they give the relative position.

recovery. In the absence of significant technological change or the discovery of new mineral resources, there was no possibility of Mexico's renewing its contribution to transatlantic trade before the later decades of the century.[108] Basic change in the Mexican economy, therefore, disrupted the Atlantic trade and the Pacific trade between Acapulco and Manila, which also suffered recession in the 1620s.[109] But the crisis was aggravated by other factors. The correlation between treasure, prices and trade was again significant. The precipitous drop in royal treasure returns was one of the reasons why the crown had recourse to monetary inflation by debasement, which was highly damaging to commercial transactions, especially from the 1620s. The slump in Spanish shipping was another factor. In the course of the depression of 1623–50 Biscayan shipping dropped to less than one-third of the vessels employed on the transatlantic run. More than one-third were now foreign vessels, principally English and Dutch; while American vessels, the products of Havana shipyards, contributed the remaining third.[110] In terms of shipping, therefore, Spain was losing control of her imperial communications. Here the state also played a part, for it preferred large galleons for war-time *armadas* and convoys. This again favoured Cadiz against Seville, and had further repercussions on the other side of the Atlantic. It meant that many of the island and coastal settlements of the Caribbean, where navigation was difficult for heavy galleons, were virtually abandoned; this neglect of the poor relations of the empire precipitated their economic independence and widened the breach for foreign interlopers; these increased their pressure from 1620, still further from 1630.[111] Finally, the Indies trade, stripped of its resources, was all the more sensitive to renewed warfare; the enemy was now a constant menace, especially the Dutch who from the 1620s obtained a foothold in Brazil. In 1628, at the hands of the Dutch, the *carrera* suffered a crushing defeat at Matanzas, its first real defeat. Apart from the loss of vessels and the grievous loss of seamen, the trade was deprived of almost a year's returns from New Spain, estimated at 36–40 per cent of

---

[108] For a more detailed discussion of Mexico's crisis see below, pp. 298–315.
[109] Pierre Chaunu, *Les Philippines et le Pacifique des Ibériques* (Paris, 1960), pp. 96–7, 100–1, 202–3, 222–3.
[110] Chaunu, *Séville et l'Atlantique*, viii, 2, 2, p. 1563.
[111] Ibid., viii, 1, pp. 224–8.

its working capital.[112] Matanzas was also a profound psychological shock which heightened the nervous tension within the *carrera*
and hastened its breakdown.

The American trade paid for Matanzas in the period immediately following. The years 1629–31 were catastrophic.[113] The
presence of the Dutch in Brazil undermined the confidence of
investors. It also forced the *carrera* to increase its defences, a
burden which the enfeebled trade could not bear. The *avería* was
no longer sufficient to finance even minimum defence requirements, and could only cover 50 per cent of the cost of the *armada
de la guardia*. The ever growing shortage of seamen, and their
cost, reached a point where the navy was reduced to augmenting
crews with slaves. Traffic (outbound and inbound) fell from
143 sailings in 1630 to seventy-nine in 1631 (44 per cent), gross
tonnage from 59,025 tons to 22,367 (60 per cent).[114] In 1635 the
war with France caused the government to divert some of the
transatlantic galleons to the home fleet; their places were taken by
more foreign vessels, together with their crews and masters.[115] In
the years 1637–8 Spanish vessels almost disappeared from the
Indies trade and those that remained were old and unseaworthy.
Altogether this was a depressing decade for Seville and Cadiz.

The catastrophe of 1629–31 was repeated in 1639–41.[116] In the
period 1632–41 the annual average of sailings (outbound and
inbound) was ninety-four; in 1639–41 it dropped to sixty-nine.
The trade was starved of capital: receipts of American silver;
which had totalled 49.8 million pesos in 1616–20, fell to 44.2
million in 1631–5, and 45 million in 1636–40. In 1639 the fleet to
New Spain was cancelled in order to concentrate available resources on that to Tierra Firme. From now the cost of the *armadas* fell more and more on the royal treasury, for the *consulado* of
Seville, which in 1640 undertook a three-year *avería* contract, was
forced to declare itself bankrupt. The weakened fabric of trade
was further torn by the political crisis of 1640. True, the revolt of
Catalonia had no direct repercussions in Seville, nor did it visibly

[112] Ibid., viii, 2, 2, p. 1645.
[113] Ibid., viii, 2, 2, pp. 1653–84.
[114] Ibid., viii, 2, 2, p. 1677.
[115] Chaunu refers to 'l'importation massive de navires anglais et hanseates' in
1635–8, ibid., viii, 2, 2, pp. 1757, 1796.
[116] Ibid., viii, 2, 2, pp. 1793–1851.

affect the Indies trade.[117] But the revolt of Portugal was a different matter. Portugal was an important sector of the Spanish Atlantic; its alienation from Spain was a consequence of economic depression and of the attendant restraint on Portuguese in the Spanish empire; and its revolt heightened the sense of uncertainty in Seville and directly affected investment.[118] Military conflict in the peninsula, moreover, forced up the government's defence budget and launched the wildest vellon inflation to date, a severe handicap for any trade to bear. On top of everything came a major calamity at sea in 1641 which revealed in microcosm the whole Atlantic crisis. The returning New Spain convoy was shattered by hurricane in the Bahama channel and lost ten vessels totalling 5,000 tons.[119] This was not a random disaster. The ships themselves were in a pitiable state to start with; they had been further impaired when the sluggishness of the market caused them to be immobilized at Vera Cruz for more than a year, exposed in the warm seas of the tropics to the *broma*, that deterioration of hulls and cordage dreaded by seamen; and the fleet did not command the financial resources to refit. It then left Havana over three weeks after the last date (20 August) set by meteorological observation as the margin of safety before the hurricane season. To ignore the experience of a century and a half of Atlantic navigation was inviting disaster, for the sake moreover of a cargo which was at best mediocre. The whole episode was a sign of the times.

The depression continued unabated for the rest of the decade. In 1650 traffic (outbound and inbound) totalled only fifty-one sailings, gross tonnage 14,022 tons.[120] The convoys were sailing without their full complement of escorts, as European defence needs diverted warships to other duties. American vessels now outnumbered those built in Spain, a further stage in demonopolization and a further shift towards American control of the trade, first heralded by the appearance of the *Peruleros*. The Mexican sector continued to contract; its contribution to total colonial exports fell from 40 per cent in 1636–40 to 22 per cent in

[117] Ibid., viii, 2, 2, pp. 1831–2.
[118] On the reaction against the Portuguese in the Spanish empire see above, pp. 154–5.
[119] See above, p. 253.
[120] Chaunu, *Séville et l'Atlantique*, viii, 2, 2, pp. 1867–8, 1876, 1952.

1646–50, while that of Tierra Firme rose from 60 to 78 per cent. Silver returns from Peru thus maintained themselves, while those of New Spain diminished.

After 1650 the Atlantic trade decayed even further. The golden days of Seville were now over and Cadiz took the remnants of former prosperity. English naval operations in 1656–7 brought a new period of insecurity, accounting for a substantial part of the Tierra Firme fleet at Cadiz in 1656 and the New Spain fleet in the Canaries in the following year.[121] In 1659 the Tierra Firme fleet carried copious remittances, the accumulation of three years. It was diverted to Santander to avoid a repetition of 1656, but Santander lacked even the modest machinery of control possessed by Seville and Cadiz, and the opportunities for fraud were unlimited. The New Spain fleet of 1661 was diverted to La Coruña, with similar results. A *consulta* of the *junta de guerra* testified to the Spaniards' helplessness.[122] It reported that numerous foreign vessels lay in wait at Cadiz to syphon off the silver from the returning fleets. In 1659 and 1661 they simply transferred to Santander and La Coruña in the company of the fleets and there continued operations. It was thought too dangerous to take rigorous counter-measures, for fear of provoking armed attack which Spain did not have the means to repulse. The report even justified the situation by arguing that foreigners had legitimate rights to bullion in return for their considerable exports to America.

Yet the fleets continued to sail, and after the exceptional reverses of 1650–9, a consequence of the hostile international situation, there were signs of revival of trade and treasure returns. The government itself contributed to recovery by suppressing the *avería* and signalling a new commercial policy. The times called for desperate remedies. The government had no credit abroad; to procure warships for the convoys from foreign sources it had to make expensive contracts each year with private merchants whose credit was better than its own. When it tried to recoup its losses by raising the *avería* it simply encountered more fraud. The point was eventually reached when the government preferred to demand from merchants a fixed contribution and to abandon the

---

[121] See above, pp. 169, 252.
[122] September–October 1661, cited by Domínguez Ortiz, 'Los caudales de Indias y la política exterior de Felipe IV', p. 376.

system of taxation. By decree of 11 March 1660 it was declared that private treasure and merchandise shipped from the Indies would no longer be subject to the formalities of registration nor the payment of *ad valorem* taxes of *almojarifazgo* or any other import duty. Instead a fixed quota was imposed on the fleets, to be paid by the merchants of Andalucía and the Indies, for the expenses of convoys and *armadas*. The new system was designed to raise 790,000 ducats, a quota shared between Peru, New Spain, New Granada, Cartagena and the royal treasury, and calculated to meet the costs of an *armada de la guardia* for the Tierra Firme galleons and two armed escorts for the New Spain fleet.[123] This arrangement, too, underwent vicissitudes in the course of the century, but it was better than an unrealistic *avería*. Although Andalucía was not apparently assessed, in fact it paid the New Spain quota. The *consulado* of Seville, therefore, suggested a re-assessment which was accepted in 1667: royal treasury 150,000 ducats; Peru 350,000; Andalucía 170,000; New Spain 90,000, Cartagena and New Granada 30,000; total 790,000.

Trade continued. Sailings were less frequent: between 1650 and 1699 there were only twenty-five *flotas* and eighteen *galeones*, an average of one convoy to New Spain every two years, and one to Tierra Firme every three years. But in these fleets copious exports were concentrated, and the accumulated returns were the more abundant. Merchants continued to employ Spanish ships and Spanish shipyards to build them. In the period 1650–99 national vessels in the *carrera* numbered 289, or 31 per cent of the whole; Spain's American shipyards supplied a further 211 vessels 22.6 per cent); 275 (29.5 per cent) were foreign-built, and 155 were of unknown origin. The use of Spanish vessels rose especially in the 1670s and 1680s, coinciding with a period of improved export performance. Does this mean that the depression was halted, perhaps reversed?

The official records show that the Indies trade dropped from 6573 vessels in 1600–50 to 1835 in 1650–99, leaving the last fifty years with only 22 per cent of the century's traffic.[124] No doubt the downward trend slowed from the 1650s, but by now the

---

[123] Chaunu, *Séville et l'Atlantique*, v, pp. 415–16; Céspedes, *La avería en el comercio de Indias*, pp. 89–96.

[124] Lutgardo García Fuentes, *El comercio español con América, 1650–1700* (Seville, 1980), pp. 164, 203–7, 230–1, 232–6.

depression was so deep that the upward spasms of the 1660s and 1670s were of minor significance. Numbers of vessels and tonnage values from 1650 demonstrate that the downward trend which had begun in 1620 continued and even worsened up to 1715. The moving average of ships and tonnage descended inexorably in these years. In terms of gross tonnage of outbound trade, the negative trend can be seen in the ten-year averages: 1641–50, 7345 tons; 1651–60, 4559 tons; 1661–70, 4511 tons; 1671–80, 4797 tons; 1681–90, 3898 tons; 1691–1700, 3481 tons; 1701–10, 1729 tons. This points to a 76.5 per cent loss of traffic between 1641–50 and 1701–10, and indicates a sustained depression in the Indies trade after 1650, reaching a low point in 1685–1700, with worse to come in 1700–15. Are we to conclude, then, that the signs of recovery in 1660, 1662, 1675, 1678 and 1695 were no more than isolated fluctuations, flickers in a gloom of depression?

The total evidence is not so negative. Modern research suggests that the suppression of the *avería* in 1660 inaugurated a new commercial policy and a steady recovery of transatlantic trade which could be seen in the growth of exports to the Indies, higher fleet valuations, the remittance of increased silver returns, the imposition of larger *indultos*, and the commercial growth of Cadiz.[125] Lutgardo García Fuentes maintains that shipping is not the only, and perhaps not the truest, gauge of the Indies trade in this period. It is true that statistics of official trade in the years 1650–1700 show a fall to exactly 22 per cent of the century's total.[126] But official figures of shipping movements and tonnage do not tell the whole story. While, on the margin of the fleets, there was much illegal shipping, within the official convoys fraudulent returns were substantial. In theory fleets should have sailed annually. But over a period of time there were more and greater gaps, most of them arranged by the *consulado* of Seville to prevent further saturation of the American market with European goods. In the second half of the century only 60 per cent of the theoretical total number of annual fleets were sent to New Spain

---

[125] Morineau, *Incroyables gazettes et fabuleux métaux*, p. 249; García Fuentes, *El comercio español con América*, pp. 230–3, and 'En torno a la reactivación del comercio indiano en tiempo de Carlos II', *Anuario de Estudios Americanos* 36 (1979), pp. 251–86. The figures for shipping origins differ slightly from the source cited above, p. 218.

[126] García Fuentes, *El comercio español con América*, p. 218.

and only 40 per cent to Tierra Firme.[127] Is the evidence conclusive? Antonio García-Baquero suggests that a 76.5 per cent loss of traffic between 1641 and 1710 cannot be ignored and argues that the negative trend begun in 1620 endured and kept the Indies trade in a state of depression.[128]

Exports from Spain to America provide yet another guide. While the volume of exports measured in tonnage and number of ships was diminishing, the value of exports was increasing.[129] After 1660 there was a long-term upward trend in colonial trade, most of the exports to America consisting of non-Spanish manufactured goods. Exports of olive oil, spirits, textiles, hardware and paper all rose significantly, with the most pronounced rise from the 1670s. The valuation of the convoys for fiscal purposes also rose, the *flotas* from 150 million maravedis in 1662 to 299 million in 1695, the *galeones* from 86 million in 1665 to 206 in 1695, further confirmation of the positive trend of exports and of the recovery of the Indies trade in these years.[130] In 1673 the *Casa de la Contratación* calculated that the value of goods sent to New Spain oscillated between 4 and 8 million pesos, and of those to Tierra Firme between 10 and 20 million. The growth of European exports to America in the period 1650–1700 would help to explain the copious returns of precious metals revealed by the research of Michel Morineau. Such trends may also correspond to sustained economic activity and consumer expansion in the colonies themselves, which were drawing in rising quantities of European goods. These events preceded Bourbon reforms by many years and reinforce the view that *comercio libre* of the eighteenth century reflected rather than created a long period of growth in the Atlantic economy.

The revival of American trade was reflected in treasure returns. These are difficult to measure because of fraud, contraband and direct trade, infringements which were covered to some extent

[127] Ibid., p. 164.
[128] Antonio García-Baquero González, *Cádiz y el Atlántico (1717–1778)* (2 vols, Seville, 1976), i, p. 150; ii, graphs 3, 4, 6, 7, 13; and the same author's 'Andalucía y los problemas de la carrera de Indias en la crisis del siglo XVII', Coloquio de Historia de Andalucía, 1980, paper kindly provided by the author.
[129] García Fuentes, *El comercio español con América*, pp. 229–36.
[130] Ibid., pp. 239–326; García Fuentes, 'En torno a la reactivación del comercio indiano', pp. 263–6.

by *indultos*. Declared returns for the entire period 1650–1700 amounted to only 43.6 million pesos, of which 45 per cent came in the New Spain fleets, 54 per cent in those of Tierra Firme; 49 per cent went to the royal account, 51 per cent to the private sector. Compared to 366.2 million pesos declared in the first half of the century, this was a decrease of 88 per cent.[131] But the official returns registered in the *Casa de la Contratación* are not realistic, at least for the private sector, and the level of *indultos* would seem to imply higher returns. Between 1684 and 1700 in particular *indultos* rose extraordinarily over those of the previous three decades, reaching 500,000 pesos in 1684 and 1695. In 1698 the crown demanded a substantial *servicio* from the *consulado* of Seville, estimating that in that year the *almirante* of the *galeones* had carried illegally 11 million pesos, and that of the *flota* 10 million.[132] But the most spectacular *indulto* was that of 1692. On the departure of the *galeones* from Spain in 1690 a payment of half a million pesos was demanded, a modest compensation for the great quantity of cargo carried outside the register. On their return the *galeones* were threatened with an official inspection; to avoid this the *consulado* promptly offered a payment of 2.5 million pesos, a sum which the crown accepted.

Amidst the storm of protests against the subsequent allocation of the *indulto*, which inevitably favoured the principal culprits, the powerful Seville merchants and their French colleagues, the Peruvian merchants stated that Peru produced each year about 6 million pesos in silver and gold; so in five years without a fleet it could have accumulated some 30 million pesos. Of these, two-thirds, or 20 million pesos, were employed in Portobello purchasing French, Genoese and English merchandise, Spanish goods being 'fewer than ever'.[133] It is logical to assume that the silver was flowing abroad. In fact in the *galeones* of 1690 36 million pesos left Peru, and 27 million were accounted for in purchases in Portobello and Cartagena; thus the Peruvian merchants travelling on the *galeones* carried 9 million pesos. In the event, 40 million pesos were unloaded from the fleet. Figures of this magnitude are not signs of depression, and the evidence from export values and

---

[131] García Fuentes, *El comercio español con América*, pp. 381, 388–9.
[132] Ibid., p. 383.
[133] García Fuentes, 'En torno a la reactivación del comercio indiano', pp. 269–70.

treasure returns confirms the conclusion that 'in the last three decades of the century, the Indies trade went through a period of relative optimism and prosperity.'[134]

Silver remittances were still copious, if measured from non-official sources.[135] These indicate that after a fall in American treasure receipts around 1650, caused simply by wartime disruption of trade which held back precious metals in America, the quantities not only recovered in the second half of the seventeenth century but were considerably higher than those of the supposed peak of 1580–1620. Moreover, the returns of precious metals in the second half of the seventeenth century were 50 per cent higher than those in the first half of the century and more impressive than those in the first half of the eighteenth century, except for the years around 1730.[136] The distribution of these sums was no less significant than their quantity. The foreign nations concentrated in Seville and Cadiz, awaiting and watching the returns on their exports, received the major share of treasure, while Spain was reduced to an inferior position in a trade which theoretically she controlled.

The period began well. The galleons of 1659 (to Santander) brought some 25 million pesos (3.5 million for the crown), followed by a further 10 million in other vessels, the best returns in one year since 1595. This was a foretaste of things to come. The figures for individual years indicate abundant returns: 10 million pesos in 1666, 1671, 1672 and 1683; 18 million in 1682; 25 million in 1663 and 1693; 29 million in 1673; 30 million in 1670 and 1697; 36 million in 1686 and 1692; 41 million in 1698; 42 million in 1676; and 46 million in 1679. These receipts, from both Tierra Firme and New Spain, easily outstrip the record annual returns

---

[134] Ibid., p. 267.

[135] Morineau, *Incroyables gazettes et fabuleux métaux*, 249; Morineau relies exclusively on non-official sources, that is Dutch and other European gazettes and French consular reports, which he presents as reliable, accurate and professional records, more realistic than official Spanish statistics.

[136] Ibid., pp. 39, 117, 249. There remains the question, how can increased flows of treasure be reconciled with the seventeenth-century recession in American mining production, or interlude between mining booms? There are two possibilities, suggested here as hypotheses: (1) the fall in output in Upper Peru and New Spain may be exaggerated in the official figures; (2) treasure remittances may have been drawn from accumulated resources preserved from more prosperous times.

Table 1 American treasure returns by quinquennia in million pesos 1580–1699

1580–4	48	1620–4	50	1660–4	65
1585–9	43.2	1625–9	42.2	1665–9	61.3
1590–4	30.4	1630–4	39.8	1670–4	87
1595–9	78.4	1635–9	68.8	1675–9	84.5
1600–4	55.5	1640–4	45.2	1680–4	51.5
1605–9	51.8	1645–9	36.6	1685–9	78
1610–14	43.1	1650–4	39	1690–4	81.8
1615–19	47.4	1655–9	51.6	1695–9	65.5

Source: Morineau, *Incroyables gazettes et fabuleux métaux*, pp. 250, 262, who revises the pre-1660 figures of Hamilton.

of the sixteenth century; the 1595 peak of 35 million pesos was superseded at least six times.[137] Of course there was no longer the annual regularity of former times; poor years were followed by years of plenty, and some were empty. Fluctuations were caused by a combination of international, economic and American factors; the decrease of 1680–4 was occasioned by European war which interrupted the rhythm of the convoys. Treasure returns, therefore, have to be grouped in quinquennia and calculations made in averages.

The structure of the Spanish American trade in the last decades of the seventeenth century differed from that of the earlier period. By law one-third of cargo space was reserved for Andalusian agricultural exports; these were almost exclusively wines and brandies, and in the period 1680–99 there was a decrease of wine volume, counterbalanced by a rise in brandy shipments. The key export items of course were not agricultural products but expensive linens, silks and woollens, which came to form the bulk of exports by value, and a high proportion of which were French. The destination of returns had also changed. Theoretically the new structure could have included Spanish merchants from others regions of Spain. But these were slow to take advantage of the breakdown of the monopoly. When the Catalans began to export from Cadiz, from about 1680, trading their wines, spirits and dried fruits against Venezuelan cacao, Cuban tobacco and Central

[137] Ibid., p. 237.

Table 2 Structure of Spanish American trade in 1686 in million livres

	Linens	Woollens	Silks	Haberd.	Wax	Hardw.	Misc.	Total	%
France	10,004	2,740	1,440	2,359	500			17,043	39.3
Genoa			5,366	1,590			375	7,331	16.9
England	380	3,700		868	1,332			6,280	14.5
Holland	570	2,120	1,000	260	666	160	400	5,176	11.9
Flanders	320	347		1,980	160			2,807	6.4
Spain			1,200				1,200	2,400	5.5
Hamburg	2,186					80		2,266	5.2
Total	13,460	8,907	9,006	7,057	2,658	240	1,975	43,303	

Source: Morineau, *Incroyables gazettes et fabuleux métaux*, p. 276; quantities revised and adjusted.

American cochineal, they offered little competition to Andalusian and foreign interests already established in Cadiz.[138] The French were the clear leaders, followed by the Genoese, English, Dutch, Flemish, Spanish and Germans.

The figures are a commentary on the collapse of the Seville monopoly. In the period 1660–75 the French earned receipts amounting annually to 12 million livres, the Genoese 7.5 million, the Dutch 6 million and the English 4.5 million. In the period 1675–1700 the quantities increased: the French 13.14 million, Genoese 11–12 million, Dutch 10 million and English 6–7 million.[139] If the proportions received by the Seville merchants were decreasing, so were those of the crown. At the beginning of the period, around 1660, the crown returns amounted to 10–15 per cent of the total. This was more or less maintained in 1670–80, though with large fluctuations caused by essential expenditure in America itself. Between 1680 and 1690 the royal percentage frequently dropped to 2–3 per cent, as public expenditure within Spanish America eroded the surplus available for Spain.[140]

The growth of foreign participation in the monopoly was closely paralleled by the growing importance of Cadiz. Seville did not easily accept this, and the contest for primacy in the Indies trade was bitterly fought.[141] Already in the 1650s Cadiz was the preferred port of return from the Indies. Between 1679, when the dispatch of fleets from Cadiz was authorized, and 1717, when the transfer was formally confirmed, Cadiz moved into first place and became the effective headquarters of the *carrera*. The growth of Cadiz at the expense of Seville was seen in changing export patterns. The export of Seville's local products, especially wine and olives, decreased, while those of Cadiz increased. Cadiz was now the principal point of exports of textiles within the monopoly, 71 per cent, compared to Seville's 24 per cent. In the 1670s

---

[138] Martínez Shaw, *Cataluña en la carrera de Indias*, pp. 80–2.

[139] Morineau, *Incroyables gazettes et fabuleux métaux*, p. 302; Girard, *Le commerce français á Séville et Cadix*, pp. 323, 414, 445–55; John Everaert, 'Le commerce colonial de la "Nation Flamande" á Cadix sous Charles II', *Anuario de Estudios Americanos*, 28 (1971), pp. 139–51.

[140] Morineau, *Incroyables gazettes et fabuleux métaux*, pp. 288–9.

[141] Antonio Domínguez Ortiz, *Orto y ocaso de Sevilla* (Seville, 1946); Chaunu, *Séville et L'Altantique*, viii, 1, pp. 191, 320; García-Baquero, *Cádiz y el Atlántico*, i, pp. 104–7, and 'Andalucía y los problemas de la carrera de Indias', pp. 9–15.

Seville had less than one-third of the official trade, and by the end of the century less than one-fifth. By 1722 the participation of Seville in the Indies trade was less than 10 per cent, and its monopoly had become a thing of the past.[142]

The abundant treasure shipments revealed by modern research are not easily reconciled with the recession, or pause, or interlude, whatever it is called, in American mining production in the second half of the seventeenth century or with the argument that this was a time when the colonial economies suffered depression and collapse. But these economies did not collapse: consumer imports were maintained and so was mining production. If the evidence proves anything it is that depression was the fate of Spain rather than America. Although the mines of Mexico and Peru could not sustain their great peak of the 1620s, they continued to produce silver in abundance for the rest of the seventeenth century. A small portion of this went to Spain. Some went to the Far East through the trade with Manila. A much larger percentage went to Europe. And an unknown but sizeable amount stayed in America. There the historical process was one of change rather than collapse. If the colonies no longer fed the trade as of old, it was largely because they were employing their capital at home, in public and private investment. More than this, they even absorbed Spanish and European capital. By the 1640s more and more merchants were leaving their bullion returns in America, especially in Peru, either as loans or investments, thus avoiding the risk of sequestration in Spain. Even if this was only a temporary expedient, it suggests that there was a profitable use for capital in America and is evidence of economic vigour and autonomy. The crisis in the *carrera de Indias* occurred not because the American economies were collapsing but because they were developing and disengaging themselves from their primitive dependence on the mother country. This was the first emancipation of Spanish America.

[142] García Fuentes, 'En torno a la reactivación del comercio indiano', p. 281.

8

Spanish America: a Changing Empire

The Hispanic World: a New Balance of Power

In the prime of empire Spain held her colonies in leading strings.[1]
Spanish bureaucrats supplied their government, Spanish merchants their material needs. Manufactures, equipment, even foodstuffs were so apportioned from Spain as to yield the maximum
return for the minimum outlay. Payment was demanded in precious metals, virtually the only commodity of interest to the
metropolis. The foci of empire were therefore the silver colonies
of Mexico and Peru, whose societies and economies were orientated around mining production. Other settlements were assigned
inferior status and given the minimum support compatible with
imperial defence. The system was paternal, benevolent, but essentially exploitative. And the balance of power was firmly weighted
towards the metropolis.

This primitive imperialism could not endure. Mineral wealth
was a wasting asset, and invariably engendered other activities.
American societies gradually acquired an identity and a life of
their own, developing further sources of wealth, reinvesting in
production, improving their subsistence economies in foodstuffs,
wine, oil and cloth. As the first mining cycle came to an end in
Mexico, the colony rebuilt its economy around agriculture and

[1] On the Spanish empire in America consult Lyle N. McAlister, *Spain and
Portugal in the New World 1492–1700* (Oxford, 1984), an expert modern
account; see also the relevant chapters in Bethell, ed., *The Cambridge History of
Latin America*, i and ii; James Lockhart and Stuart B. Schwartz, *Early Latin
America* (Cambridge, 1983).

livestock and began to supply some of its own needs in manufactured goods. Peru still had considerable mining capacity and remained less 'developed' than Mexico; but Peru, too, diversified its economy, exploited its natural resources and absorbed its own wealth. As the inequity, shortages and high prices of the Spanish monopoly system became more flagrant, the colonies extended economic relations between themselves, and inter-colonial trade developed a buoyancy of its own, independent of the transatlantic network. Economic growth was accompanied by social change, by the formation of a creole elite of landowners and merchants whose interests did not always coincide with those of the metropolis, least of all in their pressing claims to property and labour. The colonists were also ambitious for office, a right defended by the distinguished Spanish jurist, Juan de Solórzano, who argued that creoles were qualified for appointment by their talents and experience, and were entitled to preferment in their own country.[2] While the colonial elite never acquired formal political power, they were a powerful group whom bureaucrats could not ignore. Spanish colonial government became in effect a compromise between imperial sovereignty and regional interests; viceroys diluted the demands of the crown, persuaded the creoles to collaborate and negotiated obedience rather than imposed it.

The new balance of power between metropolis and colonies was reflected in the distribution of treasure output, as has been seen. The diminution of returns to the crown and to Spanish merchants was a consequence not merely of recession in the mining industry, or even of the growing dominance of foreign merchants, but also of redistribution of wealth within the Hispanic world. It meant that the colonies now appropriated more of their own production, and employed their capital in their own administration, defence and investment. Living more for itself, America gave less to Spain and shared less in Spain's European commitments. Spain's recession was America's growth.

Shift of power from the peninsula was also noticeable outside the mining colonies. This was not a universal trend, for there is no doubt that some parts of America suffered real recession or worse. Central America experienced absolute depression in virtually every sector of its economy in the seventeenth century,

---

[2] Brading, *The First America*, pp. 224–5.

when the area became 'rural, self-contained, and isolated', though not necessarily less dependent on outside economies.[3] Elsewhere it was different. At the beginning of the seventeenth century, particularly towards 1620, new plantation economies appeared, self-sufficient in their development, outside the *carrera de Indias*, and beyond the control of Spain. Unlike the mines, the plantations did not work for Spain; they sold their products directly to foreigners or to other colonies; and they employed a type of shipping which the monopoly trade no longer possessed – small, mobile vessels, plying singly or in flotillas, with a rapid turn-round. Tobacco plantations brought modest prosperity to the forgotten coasts of eastern Tierra Firme and its adjacent islands, to Trinidad, Cumaná, Caracas, Río de la Hacha, Maracaibo and Margarita.[4] By 1621 Trinidad was producing 6,000 arrobas of tobacco a year, Cumaná 12,000. An active contraband trade developed; the Portuguese, English and Dutch were soon involved; and slave ships were found to serve a double purpose, taking labour in and products out. Many of these slave cargoes, licensed by the Spanish crown for Peru and Mexico, were in fact diverted from their official markets by growing demand in the new plantations, ready to expand their investment and compete for labour with the older colonies. By the early 1620s the Portuguese virtually monopolized the tobacco trade, shipping the commodity direct to Europe. When, in 1621, the Spanish government was alerted and tried to impose a state monopoly in tobacco, it was too late; producers preferred the more regular traffic and the better prices of the contrabandists. The tobacco cycle was succeeded by cacao. Plantations of cacao were developed in the central valleys of Venezuela towards the end of the sixteenth century, and by 1630 there were half a million trees in the various centres of production. Cacao gave rise to a creole aristocracy of plantation owners, the *grandes cacaos*, who invested in Negro slaves, extended their holdings and grew rich from a lucrative export trade. Cacao was exported not to Spain but to Mexico, earning for Venezuela a growing share of Mexico's silver.

The expansion of economic activity in the colonies denoted an

[3] Murdo J. MacLeod, *Spanish Central America. A Socioeconomic History*, 1520–1720 (Berkeley and Los Angeles, 1973), pp. 341, 388–9.
[4] Chaunu, *Séville et l'Atlantique*, viii, 1, pp. 602–12.

investment pattern – American capital in the American economy
– which though modest in its proportions was outside the transatlantic sector. American merchants began to diversify their operations and to vary their options. The creation of the *consulado*
of Lima in 1613 was the reply of the merchant class of Lima to
the drawbacks of commerce with Spain through the fleets and
other agencies of monopoly.[5] The objective was to control, regulate and Americanize the import trade of Peru and to impose
new rules of the game on the Seville monopolists. There was now
open conflict between the two groups, and the hitherto docile
agents of Seville in America became to their former masters
'Peruvian traitors'.

During the sixteenth century the Portobello fairs were the
point of exchange between European products and Peruvian silver. In the first decades of the Indies trade, when the 'merchants
of Peru' were simply the agents of Seville houses, the goods were
sent to Portobello where an agent received them and paid for
them in silver. These agents did not settle in Peru; after making a
fortune they returned to Spain, and from there they sent their
own agents to Peru. The ideal was that the father should remain
in Seville while his sons were posted to Panama or Peru. While
these early merchants did not settle in Peru, nor were they
allowed by their houses in Seville to make any long-term investment in the colony.[6] But when the merchants of Peru eventually
began to establish roots in the country, they found the Spanish
monopoly too restrictive and sought ways to evade it. One way,
as will be seen, was to trade with Mexico for Chinese goods: this
was beyond the control of Seville, it did not pay *avería*, and
prices were low. Intercolonial trade of this kind did not directly
challenge Seville but other pressures were building up. From the
early seventeenth century lower returns and changing patterns of
transatlantic trade meant that Seville and Lima merchants were

---

[5] Rodríguez Vicente, *El tribunal del consulado de Lima*, pp. 26–30; Javier
Tord and Carlos Lazo, *Hacienda, comercio, fiscalidad y luchas sociales (Perú
colonial)* (Lima, 1981), pp. 45–56.

[6] James Lockhart and Enrique Otte, *Letters and People of the Spanish Indies.
The Sixteenth Century* (Cambridge, 1976), pp. 88, 109. Merchants and emigrants
without sons sought to recruit nephews; otherwise, as Pedro García Camacho
explained from Lima in 1580, 'I have to rely on servants and slaves who waste
my property and cannot be trusted.' See Enrique Otte, ed., *Cartas privadas de
emigrantes a Indias, 1540–1616* (Seville, 1988), p. 403.

in dispute over their share of the profits. The intervals between fleets became longer, with consequent delay to returns on investments. The purchasing power of silver was diminishing.[7] And finally the Peruvian market itself needed careful management, as it was now self-sufficient in some products, yet often saturated with luxury imports.

The growing difficulties of transatlantic trade had a number of consequences. Only those merchants with large capital resources could survive; this tended to concentrate trade in fewer hands, mainly the merchants of the Lima *consulado*.[8] Moreover, there was now a tendency to diversify investments into internal trade, transport, loans and even local production, often through groups of merchants acting in consortium. At the same time there was an increase of contraband and direct trade outside the Portobello fairs, as in 1610 when the *Casa de la Contratación* reported that Peru was 'so full of merchandise from the Canary Islands and from the ships contracted for the slave trade that when the fleet arrived the goods sold for prices as cheap as those in Spain'.[9] As unregistered trade within the fleets and direct trade outside them increased, so Seville lost its ability to manipulate prices and became itself the victim of excess supply and lower profits. Cartagena complained to the *Casa* in 1620 that it was so full of 'merchandise, linens, silks and cloths' that imports were selling for less than in Spain.[10] When Seville used its influence with the crown to fight these trends, the Peru merchants moved their offensive into the centre of the Indies trade, into Seville itself.

The *peruleros* were first noticed in Seville in 1607 and again in 1609. Who were these newcomers? They were of Spanish origin, beginning as itinerant merchants operating between Seville and Lima, and then settling in Peru. It was in Peru, and not in Spain, that they had their families, properties and principal investments. Before they began to trade on their own account they were often agents of Lima merchants, making the Atlantic crossing in charge of 4 or 5 million pesos to be spend in Europe rather than at the American end of the *carrera*, and competing with the Spanish

[7] Chaunu, *Séville et l'Atlantique*, viii, 2, 2, p. 197.
[8] Tord and Lazo, *Hacienda, comercio, fiscalidad y luchas sociales*, p. 110.
[9] Quoted by Chaunu, *Séville et l'Atlantique*, iv, p. 316.
[10] Casa de la Contratación to Consejo, 15 July 1620, in Chaunu, *Séville et l'Atlantique*, iv, p. 566.

monopolists on their home ground. In Seville they bought directly from foreign suppliers, and on the return voyage they by-
passed the Portobello fair and took their cargoes via Panama
straight to Peru. Soon the *peruleros* graduated to higher status and
greater ambitions.[11] In 1610, against the wishes of the *consulado*
of Seville, they obtained permission for the dispatch of a fleet to
Tierra Firme in that year. For the first time American, not Spanish, merchants decided whether a fleet should sail, whether there
should be restriction or abundance of trade, whether prices
should be high or low. Now each returning fleet brought its
peruleros with silver to employ in Seville and an interest in deciding when the next fleet should depart. The *peruleros* traded both
inside and outside the fleets; they engaged in unregistered and in
direct trade. They were linked inevitably with foreign interests in
Seville. They traded personally with foreigners, paying silver for
goods and arranging deals for the American market; this enabled
them to cut out the Seville merchants even in their role as middle
men, and to divert considerable earnings from commissions into
their own hands. Foreign merchants would more readily give
credit to American merchants for sales in America, because they
received returns directly and, of course, illegally.

The Seville merchants complained to the crown, but the
peruleros survived. They had immediate access to silver produced
in Peru, which was superior to the debased Spanish coinage and
was valued at 20–50 per cent higher in Europe than in America. It
was this asset which enabled them to negotiate directly with
foreign merchants and guaranteed their immunity from excessive
fiscal demands. The fact was that no one wished to frighten off
the *peruleros*, except perhaps the *consulado*. The monopolists'
resentment bore more than a trace of anti-Americanism. The
contador, Antonio de Rojas, reported on the intruders to Olivares
in 1623:

> There ought to be a law against the so-called *Peruleros* who come
> from Tierra Firme to do business in Spain and cause notorious

---

[11] On the *peruleros* see particularly Margarita María Suárez Espinosa, *Las
estrategias de un mercader: Juan de la Cueva, 1608–1635* (Pontificia Universidad Católica del Perú, Memoria para obtener el grado de bachiller, Lima 1985),
pp. 15–16, 21–34, who clearly identifies them as a force for Peru's economic
autonomy; see also Chaunu, *Séville et l'Atlantique*, viii, 2, 2, pp. 1330–2.

damage to our own trade.... They are the drones in the hive of
Spanish commerce with the Indies; they devour it and deprive
Spaniards of profits. They are not the owners of the capital they
employ but merely factors. They assemble all the silver from Peru,
silver which ought to be employed in purchasing from the fleet at
Portobello; but they do not in fact employ it there, with the result
that there are no buyers for Spanish merchandise and it has to be
sold off at a loss. Instead the *Peruleros* bring their capital to Spain
and buy up merchandise here, sending up prices and ruining the
market.[12]

The Seville merchants could not compete with these American
capitalists, who made direct contact with foreign suppliers and if
necessary employed their capital outside of Spain. They represented the determination of Peruvian merchants to dictate the
terms of trade, to break the grip of Spanish monopolists on the
most valuable market in America and to give the developing
colony the supplies it wanted. And the Peruvians operated from a
position of strength, for the *carrera* needed their capital; this was
why they received preferential treatment from the crown, especially in the matter of sequestrations, from which they secured
either exemption or repayment in silver.

The transatlantic trade came to rely not only on American
capital but also on American shipping. By the 1640s American-
built vessels comprised at least 30 per cent of the fleets; they
shared first place with foreign vessels, and were much more
numerous than Spanish. This new inroad into the Spanish monopoly tipped the balance still more towards America. It was made
possible by the development of a shipbuilding industry in America, one of the soundest growth industries in the New World and
another outlet for American and Spanish capital.

Havana was the greatest centre of American shipbuilding, producing about 75 per cent of American vessels employed in the
transatlantic trade.[13] Cuba was favoured by local abundance of
raw materials, including excellent timber; the island was also a
strategic base of Caribbean defence and of the homeward-bound
silver fleets, for which it offered repair facilities. The first major
stimulus to Cuban shipbuilding was the conquest and occupation

---

[12] Domínguez Ortiz, *Política y hacienda de Felipe IV*, p. 294 n. 6.
[13] Chaunu, *Séville et l'Atlantique*, viii, 1, p. 667.

of Florida (1565–74), for which it provided most of the vessels; between 1572 and 1590 Cuba built a great number of frigates. It then graduated to heavy galleons, and in the period 1608–30 orders multiplied, placed partly by Spanish merchants for their transatlantic fleets and partly by the state for the escorting *armadas*. From about 1620 Cuba had to import timber from neighbouring islands and the mainland to supplement its own resources. For naval stores – iron, nails, rigging, pitch, tar and hemp – its shipyards relied on imports from Europe via Seville. In the course of the seventeenth century, however, Cuba came to procure these supplies direct from northern Europe.[14] The Spanish government, now relying more on American than on Spanish shipyards, had to open breaches in the monopoly to expedite the supply of naval stores to America. In 1608, for example, having placed orders in the Havana yards for galleons for the *Armada de Barlovento*, it concluded a contract with prominent Antwerp businessmen, Denis and Jacques l'Hermite, for the supply of naval stores direct from the Baltic to Havana; in return for this they received the right to trade with Havana, from which apparently they profited beyond all permission.[15]

While other American shipyards did not achieve the Atlantic stature of Havana, they built for local trade and navigation and thus contributed to the growth of an independent American economy. Maracaibo developed a shipbuilding industry precisely because its shores were neglected by transatlantic shipping, which found them difficult to navigate; local shipyards were established in the sixteenth century to cater for local needs, producing small vessels suitable for coastal navigation in the Caribbean. Maracaibo had good access to supplies of pitch in its hinterland and to timber in the hills of Mérida. It profited from the growth of the tobacco and cacao trades, which brought in further capital for investment in a merchant marine. Its vessels increased in size and by the late 1630s it was building up to 180 tons, specializing in a Dutch rather than a Spanish type of vessel, one which was extremely navigable and combined great cargo capacity with shallow draught. Cartagena was another secondary centre of shipbuilding. Its yards developed in the second half of the sixteenth

---

[14] Ibid., viii, p. 566 n. 3.
[15] Ibid., i, pp. 205–6; v, p. 1622 A, n. 2.

century primarily for repair work on the Tierra Firme fleet and small defence contracts, such as construction of galleys for anti-corsair patrols. But its real growth began in the early seventeenth century, again in response to the recession in Spanish shipyards. It now built large galleons for the transatlantic run, and by mid-century was producing vessels of over 600 tons.[16]

These developments did not go unnoticed. In Spain there was considerable prejudice against American shipbuilding, and jaundiced comments on its high costs, its poor quality, and above all its danger as an instrument of economic independence. The first criticism was exaggerated, the second untrue. But the third was accurate enough – the balance of Atlantic ship-building had now moved decisively from east to west, from Spain to America.

Isolated from transatlantic shipping, Pacific navigation necessarily depended on local shipyards. These built vessels of a Spanish Atlantic type, generally smaller but including galleons – three-masted vessels with high sides and seaworthy features. Panama had shipyards almost from its foundation, and by the 1530s the industry had reached sizeable proportions, profiting from local supplies of timber and the demand of the Pacific coastal trade. At the beginning of the seventeenth century it was building small vessels between 45 and 130 tons. Realejo in Nicaragua had even better reserves of raw materials. It could draw on a variety of suitable timber from forests near the coast; it had access to adequate deposits of *brea* (pitch); and local *pita* and *cabuya* fibres were manufactured into cables and cordage on the nearby island of Puna.[17] By the mid-sixteenth century Realejo had outstripped Panama and was producing vessels up to 700 tons for the trans-Pacific run to Manila.

But the best, the largest and the most numerous vessels on the Pacific coast came from Guayaquil. By the beginning of the seventeenth century the yards on the River Guayas became one of the most active shipbuilding centres in the Hispanic world, stimulated by defence contracts, the needs of the Pacific coastal trade and the demand for galleons for the trans-Pacific route. Guayaquil, a town of about 200 Spaniards, had exceptional resources. In

---

[16] Ibid., viii, 1, pp. 1033, 1037–8.
[17] Woodrow Borah, *Early Colonial Trade and Navigation between Mexico and Peru* (Berkeley and Los Angeles, 1954), pp. 5, 65–6.

the tropical forests of its hinterland there were vast reserves of timber, linked to the coast by a labyrinth of navigable rivers; at nearby Piura deposits of *copey* yielded tar and pitch to supplement imports from Nicaragua; at Porto Viejo the *cabuya* fibre provided a good substitute for hemp; from the inland river port of Chimbo came sail cloth; and copper was imported from Chile. At Guayaquil therefore Spanish technique worked almost entirely on American material. The only supplies which its yards had to import from Spain were hardware, nails and anchors, for no iron-ore deposits were then exploited in America; these were a major item in the industry's costs but one which it could afford.[18] The work-force consisted largely of blacks and mulattos, who provided the essential pool of skilled labour, while the finances of the industry were in the hands of creoles and Europeans.

Orders came from both the colonial state and the private sector. From about 1610, in response to Dutch penetration of the Pacific, Peru increased its defence expenditure, and Guayaquil received a series of substantial contracts for large warships. In the course of 1616–20 the Lima treasury placed orders amounting to 25.8 million maravedis, the equivalent of 12.3 per cent of government funds remitted to Spain; from that date the figures remained fairly constant; in 1641–5 naval orders amounted to 36.2 million maravedis, 8 per cent of remittances to Spain.[19] In 1644 the *Jesús María*, a monster of 1,000 toneladas and forty-four canon and the largest galleon of the Pacific fleet in the seventeenth century, left Guayaquil for service on the Callao-Panama route, now adding high maintenance expenses to the costs of production. Ten years later, undermanned and overloaded, and carrying 9 million pesos in contraband silver, she was wrecked in the shallows off the Guayaquil coast, a loss to the navy but a gain to the treasury.[20] In the second half of the century Peruvian investment in defence increased still further and ate more ruthlessly into remittances to Spain.

[18] The difficult task of calculating construction costs has been performed by Lawrence A. Clayton, *Caulkers and Carpenters in a New World: The Shipyards of Colonial Guayaquil* (Ohio University, Center for International Studies, Latin America Series No. 8, Athens, Ohio, 1980), pp. 88–94. Vessels of 600 to 1,000 tons cost at least 125,000 pesos in the 1640s, 200,000 pesos in the 1670s.

[19] Chaunu, *Séville et l'Atlantique*, viii, 1, pp. 1089, 1168–9.

[20] Pérez-Mallaína and Torres, *La Armada del Mar del Sur*, pp. 44–5, 200, 281–2.

It is difficult to assess how much of the later investment made its way directly to the shipyards of Guayaquil; the construction costs of royal vessels were beyond the resources of the Lima treasury alone and had to be shared with the *consulado*. Nor is the relation between owners and builders of merchant ships known in any detail, though it is likely that they were sometimes the same party. The Castro family, a commercial dynasty founded in the 1570s by Toribio de Castro Grijuela, built ships for the crown as well as for themselves, traded in Spain and the Far East, and protected their interests through their presence or their influence in the bureaucracy.[21] By the end of the seventeenth century, however, the orders and the finance for Guayaquil's shipyards were coming less from local entrepreneurs and more from the shipowners and merchants of Lima. Nevertheless, the whole enterprise was still American. As such it had a triple significance. In the first place, shipbuilding at Guayaquil had become a major industry, absorbing state as well as private capital, and stimulating the local economy. Second, the shipyards formed an important link in the chain of imperial communications and defence. Third, they were another example of the Americanization of the colonial economy in the seventeenth century.

Investment in shipbuilding, however, was only one aspect of America's self-sufficiency in defence. Military and naval defence in Mexico and Peru were financed out of the local treasuries; this involved heavy expenditure on fortifications, garrisons, warships and crews. In addition these two vice-royalties were responsible for the defence costs of the rest of America, in the form of *situados* (subsidies, primarily for defence) assigned to those parts of the empire which were strategically important but lacked the resources to provide for themselves. Peru was responsible for defence in the *mar del Sur*, and also subsidized Chile, Panama and distant Cumaná. New Spain provided the *situados* for the coasts and islands in the Caribbean from Florida to Paria, and also for the Philippines. In 1664, for example, Lima was instructed to provide 105,150 pesos a year for the military defences of Panama; in 1673 this was raised to 275,314 pesos. A subsidy of 212,000 ducats a year for the army in Chile was also charged on the viceroyalty. New Spain had equally heavy obligations; by the

---

[21] Clayton, *Caulkers and Carpenters*, pp. 141–57.

mid 1630s it already supported defence charges of more than 400,000 pesos, and this steadily increased in the course of the century.

America was more than self-sufficient in defence. It also contributed to Atlantic defence. The *Armada de Barlovento*, overtly a Caribbean squadron, was charged on the New Spain treasury and subsidized by the *consulado* of Mexico. But in fact, as has been seen, it was invariably diverted to convoy duty between Spain and America, and on more than one occasion was assigned for long periods to the home fleet.[22] This simply meant that Seville would not or could not provide the revenue for convoy defence, and America had to come to its rescue, paying three-quarters of the cost of defending transatlantic communications.[23] This was further evidence of the shift of economic power within the Hispanic world. The merchants of America, who already controlled the Pacific trade between Acapulco and Manila, were becoming increasingly dominant in the Atlantic route.

Defence expenditure is not normally regarded as an instrument of great economic growth. But it can have vital importance for developing countries; it amounts in effect to a form of economic aid from the metropolis to its dependencies. This is roughly what happened in Spanish America: imperial defence contracts went to the colonies not to Spain. These contracts, of course, had a peculiar feature, for they were financed from capital which America itself created through its bullion production. They were another example of American capital being invested in the American economy. And they were a stimulus to growth, activating not only shipyards, copper-foundries and arms workshops, but also secondary supply bases servicing these industries. They provided increased employment in the various sectors, and indirectly they gave a boost to agriculture, for workers, crews and garrisons had to be fed as well as clothed and paid.

Mexico: from Mining to Agriculture

The Mexican economy was never exclusively orientated towards mining. The colony began a balanced economic development with

---

[22] See above, pp. 255–7.
[23] Chaunu, *Séville et l'Atlantique*, v, p. 420.

the first generation of settlers, and by 1540–60 it was enjoying a boom in the rapid expansion of European agriculture and the growth of industry. European-type production, especially in raising sheep and silk, weaving of textiles and manufacture of furniture and clothing, gave the colony a wide base of prosperity. Production was modest in its proportions, but it met much of the local demand and helped to keep prices low by competing with imports from Spain. There was even a surplus for export in sugar, textiles, clothing, furniture and household articles, and other manufactures. Compared with other colonies, including Peru, this development involved a much larger Spanish population, with more farmers and craftsmen, and it brought more of the Indian population into European-type production. Between 1531 and 1580, for example, silk raising, especially in the Mixteca, expanded rapidly and gave rise to a silk manufacturing industry in centres like Mexico City, Puebla and Antequera, producing for the home market and for export to Peru.[24] By the early seventeenth century, however, silk raising, like other sectors of the Mexican economy, was in severe recession, hit by competition from Chinese silks, by the government's policy of restricting competition and economic independence in the interests of Spain, and above all by the decrease of the Indian population.[25]

The white population of Mexico steadily increased, from 63,000 in 1570 to 125,000 in 1646.[26] In Mexico City the growth was relatively greater, from 18,000 to 48,000; whereas in 1570 the capital's white population comprised 28.5 per cent of that of the whole colony, by the 1640s it was 38.4 per cent, evidence of the growth of a great European-style city, a centre of production but above all of consumption. The upper ranks of the white population formed a colonial aristocracy which was drawn from two groups, *encomenderos* and merchants. The *encomenderos* were descendants of the conquerors and others who had earned royal favour; they lived on the income from tribute or labour supplied by the Indians who had been commended to them. By the end of

[24] Woodrow Borah, *Silk Raising in Colonial Mexico* (Berkeley and Los Angeles, 1943), pp. 32–8.
[25] Ibid., pp. 85–101; see below, pp. 339–40.
[26] Woodrow Borah, *New Spain's Century of Depression* (Berkeley and Los Angeles, 1951), p. 18; Sherburne F. Cook and Woodrow Borah, *Essays in Population History* (3 vols, Berkeley and Los Angeles, 1974–9), ii, pp. 197–8.

the sixteenth century many of them had begun to supplement possession of Indians with the other great mark of nobility, possession of land, and to associate their *encomiendas* with haciendas. These were the classical aristocracy. They were joined by many who made their fortunes in Atlantic and Pacific trade, men like Simon de Haro, prior of the *consulado* of Mexico in 1650, whose fortune was estimated at 600,000 pesos.[27] Capital earned in commerce was often invested in agrarian property, for the Mexican merchant, like his Spanish counterpart, sought social status in landowning. And some capital found its way into mining. The actual mining proprietor was not normally a wealthy capitalist or at the summit of the social hierarchy. There was wealth in mining, of course, but this wealth did not go exclusively to mineowners and prospectors; much of it went to those who supplied labour and finance, and who were to be found among the colonial aristocracy, once or twice removed from actual operations.

While the white population was increasing, the Indians were vanishing. The Indian population of central Mexico, which may have been as high as 25.2 million in 1518, decreased from 16,871,408 in 1532, to 2,649,573 in 1568, to 1,372,228 in 1595, to 1,069,255 in 1608.[28] In the Valley of Mexico alone the native population fell from 1,500,000 on the eve of the conquest to 325,000 in 1570, to 70,000 in the mid-seventeenth century.[29] This demographic calamity, 'one of the great catastrophes in the history of the human race', was the result of a number of factors, chief among which was epidemic disease, particularly the scourges of 1545–8 and 1576–81. The Mexican Indians were

[27] Chaunu, *Séville et l'Atlantique*, viii, 1, p. 733; on the social structure of the colony see L. N. McAlister, 'Social Structure and Social Change in New Spain', *Hispanic American Historical Review*, xliii (1963), pp. 349–70.

[28] Woodrow Boràh and Sherburne F. Cook, *The Aboriginal Population of Central Mexico on the Eve of the Spanish Conquest* (Berkeley and Los Angeles, 1963), pp. 4, 88; Cook and Borah, *The Indian Population of Central Mexico 1531–1610* (Berkeley and Los Angeles, 1960), p. 48; Borah and Cook, *The Population of Central Mexico in 1548: A Critical Analysis of the Suma de visitas de pueblos* (Berkeley and Los Angeles, 1960). For a succinct survey of the state of research on Indian demography in colonial Spanish America see Linda A. Newson, *Indian Survival in Colonial Nicaragua* (Norman, Oklahoma, 1987), pp. 5–14.

[29] Charles Gibson, *The Aztecs under Spanish Rule. A History of the Indians of the Valley of Mexico 1519–1810* (Stanford and London, 1964), pp. 136–41.

victims of imported diseases against which they had no immunity; the greatest killers were smallpox, measles, typhus and typhoid, though malaria and influenze also took their toll. Indian resistance to disease, however, was weakened by the shock of conquest and subjugation, by ecological changes attendant on the disruption of their economy and by deteriorating food supplies. The native inhabitants lost some of their land and water resources to the Spaniards; the latter imported cattle and sheep which swarmed over the land left vacant by the diminishing Indians, and often invaded the reserves of land needed by the native system of field rotation; finally the diversion of scarce water supplies to Spanish farms, ranches and flour mills greatly handicapped Indian agriculture.[30] If the Indians abandoned the land to seek a livelihood elsewhere, in mines and *obrajes* (factories), inhuman conditions wrought havoc on bodies and spirits already enfeebled by destitution. Leaderless and increasingly landless, the Indians were reduced to a subordinate position, payers of tribute and suppliers of labour. They sought refuge in alcohol: 'few peoples in the whole of history were more prone to drunkenness than the Indians of the Spanish colony.'[31] Conditions improved but slowly. After the great demographic tragedy, the low point was reached in 1620–5, when the Indian population of central Mexico was approximately 730,000, or 3 per cent of its size at the time the Europeans first landed.[32] Allowing for regional variation, it seems that at some point between 1625 and 1650 the population of Indian towns began to increase.

Human losses on this scale were bound to affect the economic structure of the colony. A growing settler population encountered fewer Indians to work for its needs, especially after the precipitous population fall during the epidemic of 1576–81. Labour shortage affected all sectors of the economy – agriculture, mining and manufacture. Fewer hands meant harder work and

[30] Lesley Byrd Simpson, *Exploitation of Land in Central Mexico in the Sixteenth Century* (Berkeley and Los Angeles, 1952).
[31] Gibson, *The Aztecs under Spanish Rule*, p. 409.
[32] Cook and Borah, *Essays in Population History*, iii, pp. 95–102, compute a total of 702,929 from a revenue list of 1646 referring to an average date between 1620 and 1625. Previous estimates favoured a low point of 1650, though José Miranda, 'La población indígena de México en el siglo XVII', *Historia Mexicana* 12 (1962–63), pp. 182–9, had already conjectured that the reversal of the downward trend began in the 1620s and 1630s.

ruthless competition for those who remained; and new forms of labour recruitment had to be devised. Meanwhile, from the 1570s to about the middle of the seventeenth century, while the colony adjusted itself to its profound labour crisis and until the Indian population began to increase, New Spain endured a prolonged economic crisis.[33]

Mexico can be broadly divided into two parts, the humid south and the dry north, with the frontier between the two some 100 miles north of Mexico City. This was also more or less a demographic division: the south had a relatively dense population of mild and sedentary Indians, while the tribes of the north were scattered, nomadic, wild and indomitable. Northern Mexico was the mining zone; the south was agricultural.

The Puebla region specialized in production of grain and maize, supplying the transatlantic fleets and the Mexico City market. Cuernavaca was one of the principal sugar zones; sugar production in Mexico never attained the importance of the industry in Hispaniola, but two cycles can be identified, the first to 1570, followed by recession induced by the diversion of diminishing labour supply to the mining boom, and a second period of growth from about 1618.[34] Cuernavaca was also the centre of indigo production, radiating to other parts of Mexico. The Mixteca, with its relatively large Indian population, produced salt, cotton and maize. But it was also the chief centre of raw silk, and of cochineal which, after silver, was the second most important export of the colony. Further south still, in Oaxaca, was the territory of the Marquesado del Valle, the immense fief granted to Cortés. European crops and livestock had been quickly introduced by the agents of the Cortés estate, and maize was also cultivated. Oaxaca, like the Mixteca, produced cochineal for export. This, in brief, was the economy of the south. It was severely disrupted by the Indian depopulation. Shortage of labour caused a steady fall in food production; the urban centres, foci of the growing white population, suffered decrease in supplies and, from the 1570s, serious shortage.[35] In 1595 Viceroy Velasco reported

[33] This is the brilliantly argued hypothesis of Woodrow Borah, *New Spain's Century of Depression*.

[34] François Chevalier, *La formation des grands domaines au Mexique. Terre et société aux XVIᵉ–XVIIᵉ siècles* (Paris, 1952), p. 96.

[35] Borah, *New Spain's Century of Depression*, pp. 22–6.

gloomily to Philip II: 'All supplies are becoming scarce and are rising in price so fast that before many years this land will experience as great a dearth and want as now exists in Spain.'[36] The measures adopted to meet the crisis constituted in effect an attempt to impose a system of rationing. After 1595 the failure of crop production to keep pace with a still rising white population brought down living standards and reduced the poor whites to the margin of subsistence. And agriculture had to compete for labour with mining.

Mexico's mining zone lay substantially in the north, in New Galicia, which included the most important mines of all, notably Zacatecas and San Luis Potosí, and New Viscaya, whose principal settlements were Durango and Santa Barbara, supplemented by a later strike at Parral.[37] These settlements were remote islands in a sea of hostile and rebel tribes. The mining zone was a frontier, whose expansion promoted pacification and colonization, it is true, but only with great difficulty and at heavy cost. For the further north the mining frontier advanced the more hostile the Indians became. San Luis Potosí, the richest strike of all after Zacatecas, was only worked relatively late, in 1591, after the viceroy had negotiated a truce with the Chichimecs; this permitted the establishment of a colony of friendly Tlaxcalans to begin operations. When, after 1600, northern expansion opened up new mines, these were expensive to sustain, and they invariably suffered from shortage of troops and arms. In the northernmost mining district of Parral a case of cannibalism was reported in 1652 when the rebellious Chichimecs were alleged to have eaten a Jesuit missionary.[38]

Mexican silver production reached its peak in the 1590s. After this many mineowners found returns insufficient to cover labour and equipment costs, and they were forced to cut back on investments. But boom was not followed immediately by depression. In Guanajuato mining production did not decrease until 1632.[39]

[36] Ibid., p. 23.
[37] Robert C. West, *The Mining Community in Northern New Spain: The Parral Mining District* (Berkeley and Los Angeles, 1949), pp. 10–14.
[38] Chaunu, *Séville et l'Atlantique*, viii, 1, p. 776.
[39] D. A. Brading, *Miners and Merchants in Bourbon Mexico 1763–1810* (Cambridge, 1971), pp. 8–12; D. A. Brading and Harry E. Cross, 'Colonial Silver Mining: Mexico and Peru', *Hispanic American Historical Review*, 52, 4 (1972), pp. 545–79.

Zacatecas sustained its output even longer. Zacatecas provided about one-third of Mexican silver, so its performance was important. Production rose steadily from 1570 to the 1620s, and continued to increase until 1636 before falling back to levels not much lower than those registered in the 1580s and 1590s.[40] The depression was caused not by labour shortage, for the 5,000 workers needed by Zacatecas were supplied from Indian migrants, and production here rose precisely in the years when demographic depression was at its worst. It was caused in part by mercury shortage, when the crown diverted Almadén mercury to Peru and then stopped supplying mercury on credit. The slump, when it came was severe but not catastrophic. After the mid-1630s the days of the great mining fortunes were past, and silver output fell until the 1660s. At that point output recovered and profitable times returned. There were new strikes and even a few bonanzas; areas with high-grade ores, where operations could economize by converting to smelting and also avoid the shortage of mercury, continued to produce in large quantities and to attract commercial interest, thus offsetting the depression of older mining zones such as San Luis Potosí. Financiers, or *aviadores*, continued to extend credit for supplies and loans for new works, and even to invest in mining production themselves. It is possible that far from receding, silver output increased in the second half of the seventeenth century. Judging by the figures of treasury income from Mexican silver, the mines were producing more at the end of the century than at the beginning.[41] This was due in large part to the revival of smelting at Zacatecas, to new silver strikes at Guanajuato and Pachuca, and to the performance of a few places like Parral, which enjoyed a late boom from 1630. No doubt the weaker mining operators were driven out, some to retreat into rural estates, some to seek alternative income from purchase of office.[42] But others remained to wrestle with the problems of the industry.

[40] P. J. Bakewell, *Silver Mining and Society in Colonial Mexico: Zacatecas 1546–1700* (Cambridge, 1971), p. 226.

[41] TePaske and Klein, 'The Seventeenth-Century Crisis in New Spain: Myth or Reality?', pp. 116–35, esp. p. 128; West, *The Mining Community in Northern New Spain*, pp. 12–14; on the impact of smelting on production, see Peter Bakewell, 'Mining in Colonial Spanish America', in Bethell, ed., *The Cambridge History of Latin America*, ii, pp. 119, 145.

[42] Chevalier, *La formation des grands domaines au Mexique*, pp. 178–80.

The key to mining performance was manpower. The recruitment and feeding of workers, in a zone which was largely semi-desert, were perennial problems for Mexican mining, and account for the relatively small labour force employed in the industry.[43] But mining was a heavy consumer of labour. The appalling conditions of work, lack of safety precautions, foul air, high temperatures, heavy carrying tasks and mercurial poisoning, all caused the physical deterioration of workers – or absenteeism. The crown acceded to the colonists' demands for Indian labour by sanctioning *repartimiento* (forced wage labour), which was applied to mining as well as agriculture. But this could only supply a rotating and unskilled labour force, whereas from the 1570s the industry was confronted by greater technical problems associated with drainage, deeper shafts and the amalgamation process, all of which required skilled and permanent labourers. Moreover, the richest mines – Zacatecas, San Luis, Durango, Guanajuato, Parral – were situated in northern territory where the nomadic and hostile Indian population was quite unadaptable to *repartimiento*. The northern mines, therefore, always tended to prefer free labour, tempted from central and southern Mexico by higher wages and then frequently held to employment by debt peonage.

These difficulties were worsened by the demographic catastrophe which overtook the Indians, especially from the 1570s. The depleted task force was now spread more thinly over the various sectors of the economy, and subjected to relatively greater demands. The mines at Pachuca in central Mexico, for example, which before the great epidemic of 1576 had a *repartimiento* quota of 1,108 Indians a week, had only fifty-seven in 1661.[44] The crown was forced to impose a policy of labour curtailment and rationing, with priority to essential sectors such as agriculture and mining.[45] Decrees of the late sixteenth century prohibited the use of Indians in certain industries considered particularly detrimental to their health, notably sugar processing and cloth production. And attempts were made to prevent the transfer of Indians over

[43] Even Zacatecas in 1570 only had 300 Spaniards, 500 slaves; in 1605 it had about 1,000 Europeans; see J. H. Parry, *The Audiencia of New Galicia in the Sixteenth Century* (Cambridge, 1948), p. 186.

[44] Borah, *New Spain's Century of Depression*, p. 26.

[45] Ibid., pp. 34–6.

long distances, which ruled out the northernmost areas. The policy was not entirely consistent and could be circumvented, and mining simply competed as best as it could with the labour demands of agriculture, public works and building.

The poor technical performance and now the utter decrease of *repartimiento* labour forced miners to turn to other sources of supply. One of these was Negro slaves. Between 1519 and 1650 Mexico imported at least 120,000 slaves, two-thirds of all the Africans shipped to Spanish America.[46] The Negro population grew from 20,000 in 1570 to 35,000 in 1650 with 100,000 mulattos and zambos. This was in direct response to Indian depopulation. The Negroes were directed to plantations and ranches, to sugar refineries and textile factories (where Indian labour came to be prohibited), and to the service sector of the towns. Some of them also went to the northern mines, though not in great numbers. Slaves were a heavy capital investment; at the beginning of the seventeenth century a Negro slave cost 400 pesos, the equivalent of about eight months' wages for a *repartimiento* Indian.[47] They had already suffered physical deterioration since leaving Africa, and they were unfitted for work in the dry, cold climate of the northern plateau; in any case they hated mining and fiercely resisted it.[48] For these reasons Negro slaves never formed more than a moderate percentage of the mining labour force: at the beginning of the seventeenth century they composed only 6 per cent of the total labour force at Zacatecas, and 10 per cent at Pachuca.[49] There were other slaves, too, the so-called *gente de guerra*, rebellious Indians captured in war, and these probably outnumbered Negroes in the mining industry, though again they were not numerous.

The mines, therefore, relied more and more on free labour, Indians from central Mexico, mulattos and mestizos, attracted by the high salaries and even more perhaps by assurance of food and clothing. Free labourers were more expensive – 4 reales a day

[46] Gonzalo Aguirre Beltrán, *La población negra de México*, 1519–1810 (Mexico, 1946), pp. 199–222; see also Rolando Mellafe, *La esclavitud en Hispanoamérica* (Buenos Aires, 1964).

[47] Gibson, *The Aztecs under Spanish Rule*, p. 244.

[48] David M. Davidson, 'Negro Slave Control and Resistance in Colonial Mexico, 1519–1650', *Hispanic American Historical Review*, xlvi (1966), pp. 235–53.

[49] West, *The Mining Community in Northern New Spain*, p. 53.

compared with the 1 real paid to *repartimiento* Indians – but their technical performance was better and the miners preferred them, frequently holding them by debt peonage. By 1600 they outnumbered *repartimiento* Indians in most mines, and by 1650 they had almost displaced them. At Zacatecas the entire Indian labour force consisted of free workers, and at Parral almost all wage earning workers were freely hired.[50] Around 1600 the total number of workers employed in silver production in New Spain was 9,143, slightly smaller than the 9,900 working in Potosí (not counting the other mines of Upper Peru). The Mexican force included 1,263 black slaves (13.8 per cent), whereas in Potosí few blacks were mine workers. In New Spain just over two-thirds of the labour force in silver mining (68.5 per cent) were Indians working for wages; these were concentrated in the west and the north, where the Indians were resistant to labour recruitment. *Repartimiento* workers were concentrated in the centre and south, where the Indians were more sedentary and already accustomed to draft work.[51] The employment of free labour, of course, could not solve the problem of diminishing labour supply. It merely meant that the mines were competing more keenly for what labour was available, particularly against agriculture, which had to feed a growing white population and also drew heavily on the free labour market.

The effects of labour shortage were more pronounced as they coincided with other difficulties besetting the mining industry, particularly the upward trend of costs. Whereas miners received a fixed price for their bullion – 1 peso an ounce – they were faced with rising costs for labour, food and equipment. They had campaigned successfully to get the *quinto*, the royal tax on silver, reduced to a tenth; they then sought to evade even the reduced taxation. To get their profits quickly and to avoid taking their product long distances to the nearest *caja real* for stamping and assaying, miners adopted the practice of selling their silver at the mine direct to merchants, often under price. With the product in their grasp merchants kept back a portion from registration and taxation and so retained a highly valuable trading commodity.

[50] Ibid., pp. 48–51; Bakewell, *Silver Mining and Society in Colonial Mexico*, pp. 121–9.
[51] Peter Bakewell, *Miners of the Red Mountain. Indian Labor in Potosí, 1545–1650* (Albuquerque, 1984), pp. 183–4.

Outside capitalists thus came to exert a powerful control over the industry, for they also handled supplies to the mines and frequently advanced loans to the miners against future yield. In the mid 1630s the crown ceased to distribute mercury on credit, and many miners who had accumulated debts were unable to meet their obligations and abandoned mining. This development also favoured financiers in Mexico City and strengthened their hold over the industry. Once credit for mercury was controlled from Mexico City, it was allocated only to the most productive mines and the marginal producers were forced out. The profits from mining, therefore, were largely escaping the control of the miners themselves, with the result that they had insufficient margin for reinvestment at a time when operations were posing new problems.

By the beginning of the seventeenth century, the amalgamation process of refining silver, which had first been adopted in the 1550s, was employed in most mines, and about two-thirds of the Mexican product were thus processed. Amalgamation revolutionized mining, for it forced a yield from low-grade ores, precisely when these were becoming more frequent.[52] But amalgamation needed additional equipment and labour, and it depended on a number of ingredients, particularly mercury, which were scarce and expensive. The exhaustion of rich ores near the surface led to deeper mining – down to 400 feet – for lower-grade ores, a development encouraged by the amalgamation process. Larger and deeper mines became more common in the seventeenth century. In Parral, which began its boom in the 1630s, the deepest shaft reached 130 yards, and in Real del Monte a shaft reached 200 yards by the end of the century. But as mining went deeper costs increased, and so did technical difficulties. Shaft reinforcement, illumination, ventilation and haulage operations all became more complicated and more expensive. The greatest problem was flooding, for drainage technique was primitive in the extreme; and some miners found drainage so expensive that they preferred to abandon their mines. Finally, amalgamation demanded finely ground ores; grinding machinery, and the numerous mules needed to drive it, became an additional expense. In short, mining now required heavy capital investment for an end product whose

[52] Modesto Bargalló, *La minería y la metalurgia en la América Española durante la época colonial* (Mexico, 1955), pp. 107–33, 203–14.

yield was steadily diminishing. This in itself persuaded many miners to revert to smelting in the late seventeenth century, though this in turn depended on new strikes of rich ore.

Costs were further inflated by the expense of procuring supplies. To some degree mining settlements were self-sufficient units, for the industry stimulated local stock ranching and grain farming as proximate bases of supply.[53] The northern plateau provided a favourable environment for livestock, which multiplied enormously in the period 1560–1620. Local ranches, sometimes owned by miners as an additional investment, supplied mules for motor-force, hides and tallow for mining operations, and meat for the labourers.[54] But farming did not keep pace with ranching, and some settlements had to import grain supplies. And they all relied on imports for tropical products such as sugar, for wine, textiles, hardware and other manufactures. Trade between Mexico City, the entrepôt for European imports and locally produced goods, and the northern mining settlements was one of the principal commercial activities of the colony. According to an estimate of 1673, some 600,000 pesos' worth of merchandise was sent annually from the capital to Parral.[55] The mines had to compete at a long distance with other sectors for these supplies, not all of which were abundant; and they were faced with heavy transport costs, for the northern settlements were two to three months' journey from the capital.

But it was mercury which posed the greatest supply problem. World sources of mercury were – and remain – few in number. Through a striking coincidence of circumstances Spain possessed not only the greatest silver mines in the world but also two rich and workable deposits of mercury, the mines at Almadén in the peninsula and Huancavelica in Peru. The Mexican mines required about 5,000 to 6,000 quintals of mercury a year; consumption grew from 263 quintals a year in 1559, to 1,387 in 1569, to 6,557 in 1589, and varied between 3,000 and 3,700 in 1597–1606.[56] Up to about 1580 they were supplied from the total production of both Almadén and Huancavelica; subsequently, owing to the increasing demand of Peru's own silver mines, Mexico had to rely on the sole product of Almadén. In some years Mexico even had

[53] West, The Mining Community in Northern New Spain, pp. 57–91.
[54] Chevalier, La formation des grands domaines au Mexique, pp. 167–8.
[55] West, The Mining Community in Northern New Spain, p. 85.
[56] Chaunu, Séville et l'Atlantique, viii, 2, 2, pp. 1958–80.

to compete for Almadén's exports with Peru; yet Zacatecas alone, in 1612–18, when its output was still forging ahead, consumed, 1,180 to 2,330 quintals of mercury a year.[57] Mexico's mining fortunes were linked to Almadén at a time when the latter's production had passed its peak of sustained growth. Output fluctuated from 4,526 quintals in 1622, to 6,936 in 1624, to 4,797 in 1631; by the 1670s it was averaging only 2,000 a year.[58] According to miners, the high price of mercury – its distribution and sale were a state monopoly – was a major item pushing up their costs. The shortfall in mercury production and the need for more revenue caused the crown in 1643 to cease granting credit for its mercury sales and to demand cash and the payment of old debts. For many smaller miners this was one burden too many. Chronologically, however, the problem of mercury supply was a relatively late factor in the mining depression; it simply placed an additional burden on an already enfeebled industry.

As Mexico's first mining cycle paused in its progress, the colony's economy was reorientated towards agriculture and production for subsistence or regional consumption. And Mexican society was reintegrated around an institution which was to dominate it for three centuries to come, the hacienda, the great landed estate producing grain and livestock for the market, the characteristic base of a new colonial aristocracy. The hacienda emerged in a period of economic crisis when the Indians could no longer support the *encomenderos* or the towns. It was a means of escape from direct dependence on the weakened Indian communities for food supplies. The estates, of course, still relied on the Indians for labour, but the Indians could be better organized for commercialized food production on estates under Spanish supervision than when they were left to produce food in their own communities.[59]

The origin of the hacienda can be traced back to the land grants which the Spanish crown made to the conquistadores and their offspring for services rendered. These grants were limited in size, but the grantees tended to ignore the limitations. From the 1570s they began to occupy land vacated by the vanishing Indians, with

[57] Bargalló, *La minería y la metalurgia*, p. 273.
[58] Chaunu, *Séville et l'Atlantique*, viii, 2, 2, p. 1973; on the reasons for Almadén's difficulties, linked to the waning fortunes of the Fuggers, see Domínguez Ortiz, *Política y hacienda de Felipe IV*, pp. 144–6.
[59] Borah, *New Spain's Century of Depression*, p. 32.

or without title from the crown; they also began to encroach on areas still being worked by Indian communities, and to add to their territorial wealth by Indian land procured through extortion or purchase.[60] The process was hastened by the demands of the mining settlements for food supplies; each *real de minas* needed its tributary stock ranches and grain farms in close proximity, and the ranch-mine complex became the typical unit of settlement in northern Mexico. Then, when the first mining cycle ended, the miners themselves were forced to look to the land for a living, and many of them became hacendados. The formation of great estates was further promoted by the tendency of *encomenderos* to transfer their *encomiendas*, which were strictly speaking not land grants, into farms, especially when their income from tribute decreased with the depopulation of the Indians.[61] Finally, the growth of the great hacienda was stimulated by a motive which lay deep in the Iberian mentality: Spaniards and creoles alike wanted large estates for the sake of size alone and the social prestige that accrued therefrom, for landownership was linked with nobility and 'purity of blood'.[62] Landed wealth alone did not guarantee elite status but it played a large part. Capital usually flowed from commerce and mining into agriculture, not the reverse. Yet the size of estates, which varied from region to region, was determined not only by social factors but even more by geographical, climatic and demographic conditions, and their value depended not on mere size but on the quality of soil, availability of water and proximity to the market. Smaller estates in land of good quality had greater capital value than *latifundia* in deserts.

The growth of the large estate, of course, could not in itself solve the basic question of labour. The progression from *encomienda* to *repartimiento* to wage labour was a response to the

---

[60] Gibson, *The Aztecs under Spanish Rule*, pp. 274–6; Chevalier, *La formation des grands domaines au Mexique*, pp. 113, 127–8.
[61] Lesley Byrd Simpson, *The Encomienda in New Spain: The Beginnings of Spanish Mexico* (Berkeley and Los Angeles, 1950).
[62] Chevalier, *La formation des grands domaines au Mexique*, p. 231. This fine and readable work on the formation of the *latifundia* has also been published in English; *Land and Society in Colonial Mexico. The Great Hacienda*, trans. Alvin Eustis, Lesley Byrd Simpson, ed. (Berkeley and Los Angeles, 1963). For subsequent research and conclusions see Eric Van Young, 'Mexican Rural History since Chevalier: The Historiography of the Colonial Hacienda', *Latin American Research Review*, 18, 3 (1983), pp. 5–61.

shrinkage of the labour pool. So fierce was the competition from agriculture and other sectors for the diminishing supply of *repartimiento* labour that employers turned to another means of securing workers – free, or ostensibly free, wage labour.[63] Under this system the worker hired himself out to an employer for wages and could leave at any time. In practice such labour had a tendency to turn into debt bondage, the worker being bound to serve by advances of money, food and clothing, and unable to leave the employer until he had worked out his debt. But debt peonage was not the only option. Wages were the largest single cost of a hacienda, and many workers were attracted and retained by wages, not indebtedness. Moreover, the new labour system also had compensations from which the Indians benefited. Competition for labour in a free market resulted in higher wages and better living conditions; this accounts perhaps for the higher survival rate among the remnants of the Indian population in the later seventeenth century, and for the eventual reversal of the demographic trend.[64] Moreover, in some aspects the hacienda was a benevolent institution, a refuge, a means of livelihood and an instrument of credit. In later colonial times debt peonage in the Valley of Mexico affected fewer than half the workers on haciendas, and there was relative freedom of movement among workers as they went in search of yet bigger advances, attempting 'not to escape but to enlarge the indebtedness'.[65]

The hacienda involved not only increasing white domination over land and labour but also over agriculture.[66] On their own land the Indians preferred maize. But Spaniards wanted wheat, and Indian resistance to wheat cultivation simply accelerated the Spanish acquisition of land. In the Valley of Mexico the transition to large-scale enterprise in wheat occurred in the late sixteenth century. Between 1563 and 1602 the number of wheat farms increased about four times and the amount of grain sown about twelve times. In its next stage of advance, between 1580 and 1630, Spanish agriculture moved into Indian crops; large-scale enterprises began commercial production of maize and *pulque* (an intoxicating drink obtained from maguey), competing with Indian

[63] Borah, *New Spain's Century of Depression*, pp. 36–42.
[64] Lesley Byrd Simpson, 'Mexico's Forgotten Century', *Pacific Historical Review*, xxii (1953), pp. 113–21, especially p. 120.
[65] Gibson, *The Aztecs under Spanish Rule*, p. 255.
[66] Ibid., pp. 323–34.

production and acquiring control of the markets. Mixed livestock and farming haciendas emerged, concentrating on cereal production by irrigation, and linked to the market of Mexico City. Not all haciendas, therefore, conformed to the stereotype of backward and unproductive estates, with low levels of investment, technology and labour utilization. Some were models of a market economy.

In tropical Mexico the hacienda quickly adapted itself to its environment. Indigo production, especially in Yucatán, made great strides and was an important export commodity in the seventeenth century. Sugar cane was even more important. In the sixteenth century the sugar industry underwent an excessive boom, eating into land needed for other crops and ruthlessly consuming Indian labour.[67] Government policy added its weight to natural restraints to cut back the industry. Official preference granted to Caribbean sugar virtually closed the Spanish market to the Mexican product by the end of the sixteenth century. And pressure to restrict the use – or abuse – of Indian workers culminated in a decree (24 November 1601) forbidding even free Indian labour in the refineries and permitting it only in the fields. By the seventeenth century the majority of workers were mestizos, mulattos and *gañanes*, resident workers who were paid higher than hacienda peons. Although Mexican sugar did not develop into a good export commodity, its domestic performance was highly successful in the seventeenth century and provided further evidence of the colony's self-sufficiency. The principal zones of production were the Cuernavaca basin, Michoacán, the Marquesado del Valle and Jalapa. Sugar was an industrial as well as an agricultural enterprise. In needed large tracts of fertile land, ample water supply, and expensive equipment. Each hacienda employed hundreds of peons and labourers, to be fed as well as employed, and they became in effect self-contained units of production. Sugar therefore required heavy capital investment; normally it attracted an ample flow of capital, from private sources and religious institutions, usually in the form of mortgage-type loans at 5 per cent interest,[68] an indication of the successful linkage of sugar estates to regional and colonial markets.

Yet the typical Mexican hacienda was not the farm, nor the

[67] Fernando B. Sandoval, *La industria del azúcar en Nueva España* (Mexico, 1951), pp. 23–44, 45–51.

[68] Ibid., pp. 114–23.

sugar estate, but the cattle ranch. In the vast, unpopulated and semi-arid territories of the north, stock farming was obvious adaptation to environment. To some extent, as has been seen, it expanded with the advance of the mining frontier, and new ranches were established along highways to silver mines, particularly in the environs of Zacatecas and Querétaro.[69] By the early 1580s some 200,000 sheep, 100,000 cattle and 10,000 horses were grazing on ranges a few miles south of Querétaro. Stock raising was cheaper and needed less Indian labour than crop raising. And it needed vast estates: certain stockmen in the region of Valles had 150,000 cattle, and 20,000 were considered a mere trifle. Each hacienda aimed to be self-sufficient. As well as pasturage for their herds and flocks, the cattle barons would try to acquire fertile valley land for raising subsistence crops, and further extend their estates to control water supply from rivers or streams. Stock raising on this scale could be risky for there was always a danger of glut. But normally the rancher had two principal outlets – hides were a good export commodity, and wool was in demand by the colony's own textile industry.

With the slowing of the silver boom, therefore, land became a more important source of income in Mexico. The hacienda became a microcosm of Mexico's economic self-sufficiency and of its growing independence. Workers on a hacienda, of course, living at subsistence level, did not constitute a consumer market; and the majority of Mexico's peasants did not produce agricultural surpluses or consume urban products. But the seventeenth-century hacienda was not necessarily a retreat from the market into subsistence. The hacienda could generate further activity, for it needed to import some consumer goods and it provided raw materials for the colony's own production, and for export to urban or to overseas markets. At the next level the hacienda activated and responded to regional and intercolonial trade, both of which were expanding in the seventeenth century. Finally, the hacienda was the core of local self-sufficient economies with their own urban centre; these could survive independently of the transatlantic trade, dealing with other localities in particular

[69] William H. Dusenberry, *The Mexican Mesta. The Administration of Ranching in Colonial Mexico* (Urbana, Illinois, 1963), pp. 35–9, 174–91; Chevalier, *La formation des grands domaines au Mexique*, p. 141.

commodities, and trading especially with Mexico City, a market, an entrepôt, a source of capital, a new metropolis.[70]

Economic change should not be mistaken for economic depression. Allowing for moderate cyclical fluctuations, the income of the Mexican treasury was sustained throughout the seventeenth century at a higher level than that of the late sixteenth century.[71] While government revenue is not a proof of economic performance, over a long term it is a valid indicator. The rising revenue of the central treasury in Mexico from taxes and other sources creates a presumption in favour of sustained economic activity which is not easy to reconcile with a hypothesis of absolute depression. Moreover, an increasing proportion of government income in Mexico remained in the colony or its dependencies for administration, defence and public works, which meant that Mexico's wealth now sustained Mexico rather than Spain. Whereas in 1611–20 55 per cent of public revenue was sent abroad, only 21 per cent went abroad in 1691–1700. An increasing proportion of Mexican revenue was allocated to the Philippines: in 1601–1610 Spain received 90 per cent of Mexican remittances, and the Philippines only 10 per cent; in 1691–1700 the proportion for the Philippines rose to 38 per cent. Thus, although the income of the colonial treasury increased throughout the century, the remittances to Spain fell from 10 million pesos in 1601–10 to 2.7 million in 1691–1700. These official indices of activity point to a transition from one economic structure to another, from a mining economy to one more widely based. The period of transition was a critical one for the Mexican economy, but it was a crisis of change rather than stagnation.

Peru: Silver Colony, Silver Metropolis

Peru, a wealthy and powerful kingdom, with rich mines of silver, gold, mercury, lead, tin and copper. A land endowed with every kind of food, abundant in livestock, agriculture, birds and fish. A

[70] William B. Taylor, *Landlord and Peasant in Colonial Oaxaca* (Stanford, Calif., 1972), p. 19.

[71] John J. TePaske, *La Real Hacienda de Nueva España: La Real Caja de México (1576–1816)* (Mexico, 1976); TePaske and Klein, 'The Seventeenth-Century Crisis in New Spain: Myth or Reality?', pp. 116–35; on revenue increase see also Chaunu, *Séville et l'Atlantique*, viii, i, pp. 753, 759–67, 799–802.

land of moderate climate, free of poisonous snakes and wild beasts. A land of many herbs and medicinal plants.'[72]

The anonymous Iberian Jew, writing in the early seventeenth century for his Dutch masters, was aware of his priorities and their implications. In the eyes of the world Peru was a producer of silver, virtually its only export commodity, the monopoly of Spain, the envy of other powers. Yet this was not the whole story. Peru also possessed the resources to service its mining sector and to achieve a high degree of autonomy. And the colony's developing economy began to absorb more of the mining product. In the course of the seventeenth century, as silver output decreased and imports became more expensive, there was a shift from a mining and export economy to a more diversified resource base; conditions for local production improved, and agriculture and industry began to absorb more capital, chiefly from clerical and merchant groups, than mining and imports. Peruvian wealth was at last being invested in the Peruvian economy. The same was true in the public sector. An increasing proportion of silver in Peru, as in Mexico, was absorbed by the viceroyalty in its own administrative and defence costs, and therefore indirectly in its own economy.

Economic development was accompanied by population growth. Peru's white population increased more rapidly than that of Mexico but remained much smaller – 25,000 in 1570, 70,000 in 1650.[73] In the same period the colony's Negroes, mestizos and mulattos increased from 60,000 to 130,000. Meanwhile the Indian population suffered a catastrophe hardly less severe than that in Mexico. The Peruvian Indians, who numbered some 9 million in 1520, decreased to slightly over 1 million by 1570, and to about 670,000 by 1620, a decrease of some 93 per cent.[74] Along the coast, especially in the south, the Indian population was almost completely wiped out, to be replaced by Spanish colonists and

[72] Descripción del Virreinato del Perú. Crónica inédita de comienzos del siglo XVII. Boleslao Lewin, ed. (Rosario, 1958), p. 19.
[73] These figures exclude Upper Peru, for which the same source gives 7,000 in 1570, 50,000 in 1650: Angel Rosenblat, La población indígena y el mestizaje en América (2 vols, Buenos Aires, 1954), i, pp. 59, 76–7, 88, 225. A more recent estimate for the European population gives 25,000 in 1619 and 80,000 in the early 1680s: Kenneth J. Andrien, Crisis and Decline: The Viceroyalty of Peru in the Seventeenth Century (Albuquerque, NM, 1985), pp. 29–30.
[74] Noble David Cook, Demographic Collapse: Indian Peru, 1520–1620 (Cambridge, 1981), pp. 113–14, 246.

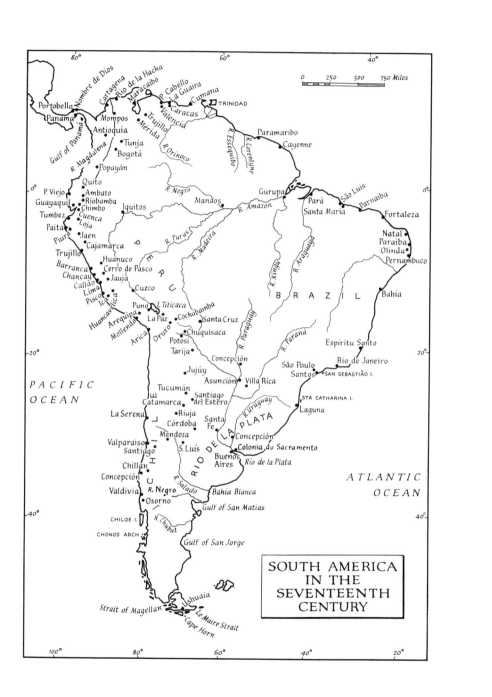

SOUTH AMERICA
IN THE
SEVENTEENTH
CENTURY

African slaves; and it fared little better in the low-lying areas of the northern sierra. Peru, too, suffered relentless and devastating epidemics in the sixteenth century, as well as droughts, famines, and earthquakes. To these may be added other explanations for the Indian demographic collapse – the social disruption caused by the conquest, the heavy mortality suffered in rebellion in the 1530s, the subsequent massive dispersals, especially after 1570, and the *mita*, the forced recruitment for mining and other tasks which, although it affected relatively few Indians, caused many more to flee from Spanish jurisdiction.[75]

Was the shock of conquest less traumatic for the Peruvian Indians than for their Mexican counterparts? They were already conditioned to imperial domination and to working for sovereign masters; and they had a well-developed agrarian economy capable of sustaining workers. It is difficult to measure the relative demands of the Incas and the Spaniards on the working population.[76] Work in the mines was new, at any rate on the scale demanded by Spaniards. It was also very punishing. But so had been the almost superhuman architectural tasks imposed by the Incas. Whereas before the Peruvian Indians had toiled to build temples of the Sun, now they laboured to satisfy the bullion demands of the world economy. Whatever the contrast, the Indians of the central and southern highlands survived disease and exploitation, and managed to retain their structure and culture; here too there was decrease but not catastrophe, and in 1620 there were 350,000 Indians living in the southern sierra, about 50 per cent of the Indian inhabitants of Peru. In the central and southern highlands the labour demands, especially the *mita* of Huancavelica and Potosí, contributed to Indian mortality and even more perhaps to flight from labour conscription.[77]

---

[75] On the 'destructuration' of Indian society, see Nathan Wachtel, *The Vision of the Vanquished. The Spanish Conquest of Peru through Indian Eyes 1530–1570* (Hassocks, 1977), pp. 86–98.

[76] See however John Howland Rowe, 'The Incas under Spanish Colonial Institutions', *Hispanic American Historical Review*, xxxvii (1957), pp. 155–99, a key, though perhaps partial, study, which concludes that Spanish rule over the Peruvian Indians carried 'economic exploitation and personal degradation ... to an extreme'; for a good account of Spanish government over the Indians at district officer level see Guillermo Lohmann Villena, *El corregidor de indios en el Perú bajo los Austrias* (Madrid, 1957).

[77] Cook, *Demographic Collapse*, pp. 222–6, points to further health hazards caused by the methods and environment of coca cultivation in Los Andes.

The conquerors and their descendants, as in Mexico, were assigned Indians in *encomienda*, which gave them title to tribute and in effect to labour. The *encomienda* conferred, if not nobility, social status and prestige, and it was regarded as a mark of natural aristocracy, to be secured if possible in perpetuity. By the late sixteenth century the institution was in decay, both as a system of labour and as a means of easy wealth and power, partly because of the collapse of the Indian population, partly because of the competing demands of other sectors, especially mining, for scarce labour supplies. In the course of the seventeenth century, the Peruvian *encomenderos* entered a period of crisis. To counter the feudal implications of the institution, the crown tended to refuse requests for grants in perpetuity to seek the reversion of *encomiendas*, and to diminish their economic benefits by heavier taxation.[78] Far from keeping up with inflation, income from *encomiendas* decreased in value and in security. The *encomenderos* were driven to seek an alternative source of income, in land, office or even commerce.

Business enterprise had never been despised in America. Conquerors, officials, *encomenderos*, emigrants, all were ready to invest in mining, agriculture and overseas trade, and to make profits in a new world where land and labour were abundant and could be made to work for Spaniards and creoles alike. Commerce, as long as it was wholesale, was no more an obstacle to social status in Peru than it was in Spain. The *consulado* of Lima, unlike that of Seville, extended its jurisdiction to retail as well as wholesale merchants; but it was the latter who provided the prior and consuls and monopolized voting rights.[79] An income acquired from large-scale maritime trade was socially respectable. It could also be invested in further advancement. Such was the crown's need for money, especially in the reign of Philip IV, that it sold *hábitos* and titles of nobility for hard cash; in the late

[78] Manuel Belaunde Guinassi, *La encomienda en el Perú* (Lima, 1945), pp. 218–49; Marvin Goldwert, 'La lucha por la perpetuidad de encomiendas en el Perú virreinal, 1550–1600', *Revista Histórica* (Lima), xxii (1955–6), pp. 336–60; xxiii (1957–8), pp. 207–45; Guillermo Céspedes del Castillo, 'La sociedad colonial americana en los siglos XVI y XVII', in J. Vicens Vives, ed., *Historia social y económica de España y América*, iii, pp. 388–578, especially pp. 518–24; the latter work is a fine synthesis of the economic and social history of Spanish America to 1700.
[79] Rodríguez Vicente, *El tribunal del consulado de Lima*, pp. 40–1, 51, 56, 69, 75–6.

seventeenth century the price of title was 30,000 pesos, somewhat less if it was for one life only.[80] Merchants were more likely
to have this amount of capital than were *encomenderos* or landowners. According to an observer in the early seventeenth century, 'There are merchants in Lima who have fortunes of a
million pesos, many with 500,000, and very many with 100,000.
Very few of these wealthy people have retail shops. They export
their capital and employ it abroad, in Spain, Mexico and other
places. Some of them trade with China. And many merchants
have an income from land.'[81] In Potosí, Antonio López de
Quiroga, a Galician who successfully invested in silver refining,
exploration, land and trade, confidently followed his entrepreneurial instincts and never considered himself as anything but a pillar
of colonial society.[82] Wealth of this kind broke through social
barriers and promoted further fusion between landed and merchant clases in Peru by means of marriage alliances, which was
another way for descendants of rich merchants to ennoble themselves and for the aristocracy to revive its fortunes.

The ultimate source of merchant wealth, as of all wealth in
Peru, was silver mining: this was the market merchants supplied
and the industry they financed. But the Peruvian economy also
had to provide for the sustenance of mining and its secondary
industries. And it had to feed Lima, capital of Peru and of the
mining industry, a city of 10,000 whites, 10,000 Negroes and
5,000 Indians.[83] North and south of Lima, in the valleys of
coastal Peru, a Mediterranean-type economy was created as the
region developed its centres of food production, commercial
crops and raw materials. In the immediate vicinity of Lima some

[80] Richard Konetzke, 'La formación de la nobleza en Indias', *Estudios Americanos*, iii (1951), pp. 329–57; Guillermo Lohmann Villena, *Los americanos en
las órdenes nobiliarias, 1529–1900* (2 vols, Madrid, 1947); on the entrepreneurial
activities of the colonial aristocracy, see Hans Pohl, 'Zur Geschichte des adligen
Unternehmers im spanischen Amerika (17./18. Jahrhundert)', *Jahrbuch für
Geschichte von Staat, Wirtschaft und Gesellschaft Lateinamerikas*, ii (1965),
pp. 218–44.
[81] *Descripción del Virreinato del Perú*, p. 59.
[82] Peter Bakewell, *Silver and Entrepreneurship in Seventeenth-Century Potosí. The Life and Times of Antonio López de Quiroga* (Albuquerque, NM, 1988),
pp. 151, 172–7.
[83] Helmer, 'Le Callao (1615–1618)', p. 151 n. 12; Rosenblat, *La población
indígena y el mestizaje en América*, i, p. 225, gives much higher figures for
Lima's population in 1630, taking perhaps a wider district – 25,000 whites,
30,000 Negroes, 5,000 Indians.

200 well-irrigated *chacras* (farms or small estates) supplied the capital with wheat, maize and animal fodder. These were supplemented by supplies brought down the coast by sea. The region to the north of Lima – Guanbacho, Lasma and La Barranca – sent the products of the fertile valleys of Callejón de Huaylas, where many Lima residents had landed property, producing wheat, maize, wine, vegetables, fruits, poultry, goats, pigs, mules, tallow, hides, charcoal and firewood. The coastal plantations supplied cotton and sugar, products which at Chancay, where the Jesuits had property, were developed on a highly commercial basis. Everywhere along the coast labour was in great demand; there were complaints that *mita* Indians (*mita* being the Peruvian form of *repartimiento*) were diminishing, further evidence perhaps of an expanding agricultural economy. Further north the region of Trujillo also had its irrigated valleys, worked by Negroes and Indians and rendered more productive by the use of guano as a fertiliser. Here wheat and maize were excellent investments, yielding returns of 500 per cent and 200 per cent respectively. Trujillo also produced cotton and sugar, wines and olives, as well as a variety of fruits; it had a number of flour, sugar and cotton mills; and it exported its products north to Panama and south to Lima.

To the south of the capital the outstanding product was wine, which became second in importance to silver – though well behind – as a motor of the Peruvian economy. In the sixteenth century vines from Andalucía, notably from Málaga, were exported with official blessing to Peru, where they were cultivated by Negro slave labour in the valleys of Pisco, Ica and Nozca, producing high quality wines and a local variant known as *pisco*. Output was abundant and sold beyond the confines of Peru: it was exported to Chile, New Granada, Tierra Firme, Central America and Mexico, where it was traded against Mexican silk. Soon the days when the Tierra Firme fleet brought 150,000 casks of wine from Andalucía were a thing of the past. The metropolis became anxious. From about 1569 it was official policy to restrict the Peruvian wine industry, not merely because it competed with imports from the peninsula but also because it engendered economic independence.[84] In the 1590s Viceroy Cañete reported that

[84] Borah, *Early Colonial Trade and Navigation between Mexico and Peru*, p. 124.

Peru was peopled with Spaniards, born in the colony who had no attachments to the mother country; that the colony was virtually self-sufficient in foodstuffs, including wine and sugar, and in coarser textiles; that the Philippine trade supplied it with silks and linens; all this to the ruin of Spanish trade and to the detriment of colonial dependence on the metropolis.

Agricultural development was associated with the formation of great estates, comparable in formation if not in scale to those of Mexico. The decrease of the Indian population combined with rising demand for food from Spanish towns to cause a transition from *encomienda*-type indirect agrarian exploitation to Spanish-directed agriculture. Spanish land tenure developed from *chacras* to haciendas with approximately 359 acres as the border line. Where agricultural activity was high, small-scale, more intensively cultivated units of production continued to prevail, as in the wine-growing areas of the Ica Valley. But where productivity was low, adverse factors such as depressed prices and shortage could cause the ruin of *chacra* agriculture and its take-over by larger estates, a process more typical of the north.[85]

In Peru as in Mexico, the formation of haciendas did not signify a withdrawal into self-sufficiency but the creation of large-scale commercial enterprises to provide agricultural products for the regional markets developing around mining and administrative centres. As the market for agriculture expanded so the great landed estate expanded, especially where land was readily available – as in depopulated Indian regions – and property prices were low. The main incentive of landowners in acquiring more land was to prevent competition from other landowners, and to create a pool of cheap labour among Indians already deprived of their own lands.[86] For the large estates were formed through encroachments on lands of neighbours, often Indians, as well as by means of purchase or *mercedes de tierra*. The legalization of this informal land concentration was facilitated by the financial needs of the crown from the 1590s onwards. After due inspection, landowners were confirmed in doubtful property

[85] Robert G. Keith, *Conquest and Agrarian Change: The Emergence of the Hacienda System on the Peruvian Coast* (Cambridge, Mass., 1976); Manuel Burga, *De la encomienda a la hacienda capitalista. El Valle de Jequetepeque del siglo XVI al XX* (Lima, 1976).

[86] Rowe, 'The Incas under Spanish Colonial Institutions', pp. 179–83.

rights after payment of a composition fee.[87] The process can be observed in the growth of haciendas in Ollantaytambo, near Cuzco, an area of early settlement and colonization by creoles and mestizos. The first haciendas were acquired by various means: donations by governors and *cabildos*; effective occupation in agreement with Indian *caciques*; presentation of fraudulent documents; the 'reduction' of Indians into communities thus leaving the land free for Spaniards; and even by purchase, often from people in debt.[88] Labour was drawn from the *mita agraria*, the agrarian equivalent of the mining draft; capital from merchant activities and the fruits or spoils of office; market stimulus from Cuzco and the mining towns of the sierra. In response to market growth, especially for maize, and in the interests of a family or a religious community, new hacendados acquired smaller estates from owners in difficulties, at the same time taking over the various labour forms and agricultural resources that went with the property; some of these, such as community mills, were often of Indian origin. In this way a whole complex of landed properties and usages were integrated into larger commercial enterprises, as was the Porras property in Olantaytambo, taken over by the powerful *señores* and religious communities of Santa Clara and San Agustín.[89]

Estancias de pan llevar (wheatland), relying on native labour services and sometimes associated with *encomiendas*, made their appearance from the late sixteenth century. The origins of these medium-sized estates were varied: some were granted to settlers by *cabildos* from Inca government land; others were based on land bought or usurped from Indians fleeing *mita* service; and periodic government reviews of land titles, notably that of 1634, provided good opportunities for consolidating or extending land claims. As the possibilities of agriculture became more appreciated – it sometimes yielded 500 per cent and rarely less than 50 per cent returns – and as commercialized products like sugar

---

[87] Magnus Mörner, 'The Rural Economy and Society of Colonial Spanish South America', in Bethell, ed., *The Cambridge History of Latin America*, ii, pp. 192–3.

[88] Luis Miguel Glave and María Isabel Remy, *Estructura agraria y vida rural en una región andina: Ollantaytambo entre los siglos XVII y XIX* (Cuzco, 1983), pp. 80–7, 94–6.

[89] Ibid., pp. 146, 150–1.

and wine assumed more importance, there was a tendency to accumulate land and to group *estancias* into great haciendas. These depended on much greater labour and water supplies; so hacendados had to be influential enough to acquire *mita* or *encomienda* Indians, wealthy enough to invest in slave labour and powerful enough to usurp precious water resources. This tended to force out small proprietors or to reduce them to dependency on larger units.

Products like wine and sugar, for which there was a wider market throughout Spanish South America, lent themselves to commercialized production. Not all Peruvian estate owners responded to this challenge. Among those who did were the Jesuits, and they set the pace of commercial farming in Peru. Jesuit estates were units of large-scale production, employing a skilled and unskilled labour force, with processing plants and established market outlets. They were acquired not for status or a way of life, but as profit-making enterprises, earning income for the Society, its colleges and missions. Jesuit estates were distributed between the coast and the *sierra*, and were managed according to strict specialization, grain and livestock in the central *sierra*, sugar and wine on the coast. Property was accumulated from a number of sources – gifts of land from friends and devotees, purchases with funds donated to the Society, reinvestment of profits from existing enterprises, mortgage borrowings, and in some cases usurpation of marginal land.[90] The Jesuits tended to buy neglected haciendas and develop them, rounding off their boundaries, building sugar mills, investing in Negro slave labour and making the whole into an efficient unit of production. The sugar hacienda of Vilcahuaura, for example, purchased by the Jesuits in 1640 from money left in a will and subsequently expanded by additional purchases, started with eight cane fields and others for wheat, corn and beans, together with eighty-seven slaves. The principal estates of the first Jesuit college in Lima were sugar plantations, but in the course of the seventeenth century the college acquired vineyards in the valleys of the southern coast of

[90] Pablo Macera, *Instrucciones para el manejo de las haciendas jesuítas del Perú (ss. XVII–XVIII)* (Nueva Corónica, vol. ii, fasc. 2, Lima, 1966), pp. 16–23; this is a collection of instructions to managers of Jesuit estates, preceded by an expert editorial introduction; Nicholas P. Cushner, *Lords of the Land. Sugar, Wine and Jesuit Estates of Coastal Peru, 1600–1767* (Albany, N.Y., 1980), pp. 28–9.

Peru through purchase or donation, a model followed by other Jesuit colleges. Sugar plantations comprised about 50 per cent of Jesuit holdings, and these were the nucleus of the colony's export industry in sugar. Production was concentrated in coastal Peru, principally in the valleys of Santa and Rímac.[91] It was a demanding enterprise and depended on several concurrent factors. It needed abundant water supply for irrigation and for driving the *ingenios* (water-driven mills). It required extensive land, for the plantations were worked on a rotation system to avoid soil exhaustion; land was also needed to service sugar production, particularly for the provision of *alfalfa*, the fodder for the oxen that ploughed the fields and drove the *trapiches* (animal driven mills), and for transport animals. Sugar also demanded heavy capital investment, in mechanical installations and above all in slaves, the latter representing 25–40 per cent of total capital outlay. The high cost of slave labour meant that it was reserved almost exclusively for the commercialized plantations of coastal Peru. General agriculture, livestock and grain, which the Jesuits practised in their *sierra* estates, employed servile Indian labour and frequently developed debt peonage.

The greatest markets for the produce of the plantations, for sugar, wine and cotton, were the mining settlements of Upper Peru. In one way or another the whole of Peru worked for Potosí and profited from its wealth. To supply the mining settlements, the colony created an agricultural economy which developed parallel to the mines. If its returns were less spectacular than those from mining, it was more stable and more durable. Peru never became so self-sufficient in manufactures as it did in agriculture. It had its European craftsmen, of course, but their operations were on a small scale; and Indian manufactures did not appeal to Europeans.[92] Nevertheless, numerous work-shops, the notorious *obrajes*, employing forced *mita* labour and owned by the state or by individual Spaniards, produced for the lower-class market or for particular needs. *Obraje* operations underwent some expansion in the seventeenth century, at the expense of the sweated

[91] Macera, *Instrucciones*, pp. 32–49; Cushner, *Lords of the Land*, pp. 113–34.

[92] There was, however, a distinct Peruvian class of craftsmen and artisans in the colonial period, including Indians, mestizos and Negroes; these have been well documented by Emilio Harth-Terré, *Artifices en el virreinato del Perú* (Lima, 1945), *El indígena peruano en las bellas artes virreinales* (Cuzco, 1960), and, with Alberto Harth-Terré, *Márquez Abanto. Perspectiva social y económica del artesano virreinal en Lima* (Lima, 1963).

labour employed there, and maintained a fairly high level of output in woollen and cotton cloth, cordage, sandals, leather goods and gunpowder.[93]

In all these ways Peru developed an internal market. While cities like Cuzco and La Plata, and mining centres like Potosí, became considerable centres of consumption, they were also sites of regional production and exchange, trading in the coca of Cuzco, the wine of Arequipa, the sugar of the coast. All roads led to Potosí and all transport depended on Indian labour. The Andean trade routes were maintained by Indian carriers and their teams, a service which drew the Indians into the internal market not only as producers (of coca, for example) and consumers (as their numbers recovered) but also as workers on the highland transport system, or *trajines* as it was known.[94] When, in the late sixteenth and early seventeenth centuries, agrarian production and marketing became increasingly commercialized, so competition for transport from the various sectors of the economy made carriers more difficult to find and exploitation of Indian workers more severe. Conflict developed between Indian communities, who wished to maintain – and market – their own traditional *trajines*, and the Spanish *corregidores*, who sought to mobilize Indians for forced transport service on roads and trade routes. Inexorably the Spaniards took over the Indian system of communications, transformed it for their own commercial needs and exploited the Indians and their animals in the process, many *corregidores* failing to pay for services rendered.[95] Thus the colonial authorities used the Indian *trajines* to extract yet another quota of resources from the ethnic communities. As agriculture and agricultural transport were increasingly commercialized, so the Indians were drawn into the market, where they were treated as mestizos not as communities, and were paid advances or wages to hold them under control for two years or more under a hacienda mayordomo or a Spanish manager of mule trains.

While all sectors where drawn into the internal market, not all needs could be satisfied there. Peru was still part of a wider economic world, though this was not focused exclusively on the

[93] Rowe, 'The Incas under Spanish Colonial Institutions', pp. 177–9; F. Silva Santisteban, *Los obrajes en el virreinato del Perú* (Lima 1964).
[94] Luis Miguel Glave, *Trajinantes: caminos indígenas en la sociedad colonial, siglos XVI/XVII* (Lima, 1989), pp. 37, 84.
[95] Ibid., pp. 161, 174–5, 275–6.

metropolis. The colony had surplus capital and a merchant marine, and it could satisfy many of its consumer needs within America, particularly from Mexico, and from the Far East.[96] The Peruvian merchant marine consisted of fifty-two vessels plying the longer distances to Panama, Mexico and Chile, and twenty-three working the local coastal trade.[97] Their owners were Lima merchants, Jesuits, Potosí miners, and in some cases the Spanish, Genoese and Portuguese captains. These seventy-five vessels were in active operation; at least one vessel left or entered Callao every day, linking some twenty ports along the Pacific coast. They carried copper, tallow and hides from Valparaiso, wine from Pisco, grain and sugar from Trujillo, tropical woods, cotton and cacao from Guayaquil.[98] At Arica they unloaded supplies and merchandise for Potosí and collected its silver exports; at Panama they linked up with transatlantic traffic. The whole of this trade, local and transatlantic, was controlled by the merchants of Lima, who supplied the *avio* (advances) to cover mining overheads in Potosí and there sold most of their merchandise. And it reflected the increasing development of Peru: coastal and intercolonial trade was much more buoyant than the traffic to Panama, a sign of the colony's gradual disengagement from transatlantic trade. The Peruvian economy was self-sufficient; it expanded independently of the Spanish economy in the seventeenth century, and it was able to survive without the massive production of silver demanded by Spain. It possessed its own motors of trade, of which silver was only one; and even in the mining sector, Peru was beginning to keep more of the product for itself.

Potosí was a Spanish not an Inca creation. Situated high in the Andes, its extraordinary elevation made mining at once possible and tragic, possible because it obviated the difficulties of flooding and draining, one of the greatest problems in New World mining, tragic because the effort of labour in an atmosphere rare in oxygen – the *cerro* of Potosí rose to a height of 16,000 feet above sea level – was too great even for the plateau Indians, who were forced to work at altitudes beyond their physical capacity. On the foundations of its dearly extracted silver Potosí became the greatest city in America and in the whole Spanish world, with

[96] See below, pp. 238–43.
[97] Helmer, 'Le Callao (1615–1618)', pp. 160–2.
[98] Ibid., pp. 171–2.

a population which grew from 120,000 in 1580 to 160,000 in 1650.[99] In the eyes of moralists Potosí was a monstrous Babylon of the New World, catering for large-scale vice as well as for Europe's bullion demand. And many of its people were indeed parasites, living on credit and on their wits: as one observer wrote to Philip II in 1595, 'there are 3,000 Europeans, including Spaniards, Portuguese and other nationalities, 2,000 of them idle delinquents, who have no other occupation than gambling, drinking, fornication, robbery and assassination.'[100] Here, as in Mexico, the greatest profits from mining went not so much to actual mineowners as to those who could finance labour and operational costs, and these were mainly the capitalists of Lima.

Unlike Mexico, where the *real de minas* was a closely knit complex of mines, farms and ranches, the Peruvian mining settlements, owing to their high elevation, cold climate and arid soil, lacked the natural basis for the growth of satellite supply bases in the immediate vicinity. Food and supplies had to be brought in from outside, often over great distances. The *mita* Indians brought their own staples, *chuño* (dried frozen potatoes) and coca. For the rest, food supplies and mine timbers had to be transported from the distant Yungas valleys, especially Cochabamba, or from agricultural areas on the western slopes of the Andes such as Arequipa. Mules for work in the mines were driven from north-western Río de la Plata; Tucumán and Santa Cruz de la Sierra also sent wheat, fruits and cotton; from the distant pampas came hides and tallow, which were also supplied by Chile and northern Peru. For the import of Peruvian, American and European products, including vital mercury supplies, Potosí relied on the port of Arica, 400 miles away, and on the

[99] Lewis Hanke, *The Imperial City of Potosí. An unwritten chapter in the history of Spanish America* (The Hague, 1956), pp. 1, 3; on Potosí see also the monumental chronicle by Bartolomé Arzáns de Orsúa y Vela, *Historia de la Villa Imperial de Potosí*. Lewis Hanke and Gunnar Mendoza, eds (2 vols, Providence, RI, 1965), with important introductory studies by the editors.

[100] Quoted by Marie Helmer, 'Luchas entre vazcongados y "vicuñas" en Potosí', *Revista de Indias*, xx (1960), pp. 185–95, an expert analysis of social conflicts in Potosí through review of Alberto Crespo Rodas, *La guerra entre vicuñas y vascongados, Potosí, 1622–1625* (Lima, 1965), and Gunnar Mendoza, L., *Guerra civil entre vascongados y otras naciones de Potosí. Documentos del Archivo Nacional de Bolivia, 1622–1641* (Potosí, 1954). See also Gwendolin B. Cobb, 'Supply and Transportation for the Potosí Mines, 1545–1640', *Hispanic American Historical Review*, xxix (1949), pp. 25–45.

transport controlled by Arica – 2,000 mules and 12,000 llamas, on whose backs were carried the incoming mercury and merchandise and the outgoing silver; and Arica developed in its vicinity a thriving agricultural sector providing fodder for the pack animals.

Potosí's silver production reached its peak towards the end of the sixteenth century. Helped by cheap forced labour and new methods of processing ore with mercury, production surged upwards from the mid-1570s. Registered exports to Spain quadrupled from 4.6 million pesos in 1571–5 to 19.1 million in 1581–5, and in 1591–5 they reached 23.9 million. Silver output excelled itself in 1592, when the Potosí's Cerro Rico yielded a record 7.7 million pesos, equalling about 44 per cent of the crown's annual expenditure in Spain and Europe in the mid-1570s. From the early 1590s the trend of production was downwards, though the slope was not precipitous; silver production fell from 4,753,179 pesos in 1600 to 2,952,562 in 1650. There was a levelling off in 1660–90, when a fairly stable platform of production was maintained, reaching 1,319,420 by 1700, and it was only around 1710 that the amount of silver registered in the Potosí treasury dropped to the levels typical of the early 1570s. Meanwhile, even in the second half of the seventeenth century, there were still profits to be made in mining and refining, as was proved by Antonio López de Quiroga, whose activities produced between a seventh and an eighth of the silver output of Potosí, and who owed his success to perseverence, managerial talent, and ability to reduce costs, invest wisely and integrate his operations.[101] After 1590 silver production levelled off, though the level was fairly high, until about 1650. López de Quiroga showed that even in times of mining problems operations continued and maintained output and profitability. In the second half of the century, while output certainly dropped, the general trend was one of gradual recession rather than absolute collapse. Mining recession in Peru occurred later, caused fewer failures and remained much less severe than in Mexico. The factors affecting production were similar in both colonies, but less oppressive in Peru. First, operational problems and costs were mounting. Exhaustion of

[101] Bakewell, 'Registered Silver Production in the Potosí District, 1550–1735', *Jahrbuch für Geschichte von Staat, Wirtschaft und Gesellschaft Lateinamerikas*, 12 (1975), pp. 67–103, and *Silver and Entrepreneurship in Seventeenth-Century Potosí*, pp. 16, 154–5, 164.

accessible deposits led to deeper mining, presenting greater technical problems which the industry was not equipped to solve; from the deeper galleries came a type of ore which needed more sophisticated treatment to make it yield all its silver, and this was beyond the geological competence of the Peruvian miners. In conditions of technical stagnation output could only be maintained by extension of the mining area; discovery of rich deposits at Oruro in 1608 compensated for Potosí's performance, until the new mines too were overtaken by similar problems. Potosí's downward trend was subsequently countered by new strikes at Chocaya and Caylloma in the 1630s and also at Carangas and Chucuito, but these, like Oruro, soon exhausted their richest and most accessible ores. Deeper mining meant rising costs for fewer returns. To this was added the problem of mercury supply.

The great expansion of silver production at the end of the sixteenth century was made possible by the adoption of the *patio*, or amalgamation, process at Potosí about 1580, an innovation which was itself stimulated by the successful performance of Peru's own mercury mine at Huancavelica.[102] Between 1559 and 1660 Huancavelica produced 21.8 million tons of mercury, compared to 15.1 million tons imported into America from Europe (principally from Almadén).[103] Only in its crisis years of 1606–10, 1621–5, 1626–30, 1631–5, did Huancavelica's output fail to surpass European imports, and even on these occasions it was not far behind. But the silver mines of Upper Peru needed at least 6,000 quintals of mercury a year, 5,000 for Potosí, the remainder for small mines. And from about 1595 production at Huancavelica began to fluctuate. Some of its problems were peculiar to mercury mining: the miners were small operators who depended on prompt payment for their product; purchase and sale of mercury was a state monopoly, and the state was sometimes years in arrears in its payments, which forced miners to cut back on production. Otherwise the industry's problems simply mirrored those of silver mining – mounting technical difficulties, rising costs and, inevitably, the erosion of labour supply by mortality, absenteeism and competition from other sectors. Work at Huan-

---

[102] Guillermo Lohmann Villena, *Las minas de Huancavelica en los siglos XVI y XVII* (Seville, 1949).
[103] Chaunu, *Séville et l'Atlantique*, viii, 1, p. 118.

cavelica had special hazards, notably mercurial poisoning, and a *mita* Indian was lucky to be alive after a stint in its subterranean galleries.[104] Brutal exploitation of Indian workers occasionally drew the attention of officials, churchmen and humanitarians. Although their interventions were transitory and, on the whole, unsuccessful, they sometimes affected short-term production, as they did in 1591–1610, when, largely as a result of Viceroy Velasco's reforms, output dropped by 50 per cent.[105] In the second decade of the seventeenth century production revived; and although it dropped again in 1626–30, it subsequently maintained itself. With the exception of the years 1651–60, however, it never repeated the peak of the late sixteenth century, and after the 1650s it further diminished; by the end of the century it was stagnant again with output showing a tendency to drop. Huancavelica remained a great scourge of Andean communities. And the Indians were also hunted by Potosí, another exploiter of scarce labour.

Until the 1560s Peruvian mines were worked by labour which was more or less free, drawn by easy takings and large profits. In some cases Indians were sent by their chiefs to earn enough silver to pay the tribute of the community. As the high-grade ore diminished, and the mines ran deeper for inferior yield, the work became more exigent and the wages lower, and the Indians departed. To revive the industry, take advantage of a new process of refining by amalgamation and salvage the royal revenue, Viceroy Francisco de Toledo instituted the *mita* in the early months of 1573. This was a system of draft Indian labour, by which quotas were forcibly sent each year to labour in the mines. The *mita* had the effect of reviving the mining industry and encouraging the *azogueros*, or mineowners, to renew operations. But the cost was heavy. In the first place, by giving the *azogueros* a guaranteed forced labour supply, the crown created a privileged class in Potosí, agreeing in effect to share the costs and the profits with

---

[104] Whereas 1,300, *mita* Indians were employed at the face at Huancavelica in 1596, there were scarcely 620 a century later, indicating considerable depopulation; see Bargalló, *La minería y la metalurgía*, p. 257, and Arthur P. Whitaker, *The Huancavelica Mercury Mine. A Contribution to the History of the Bourbon Renaissance in the Spanish Empire* (Cambridge, Mass., 1941), p. 15.

[105] Lohmann Villena, *Las minas de Huancavelica*, pp. 180, 207, 354–60; see also Carlos Contreras, *La ciudad del mercurio: Huancavaelica, 1570–1700* (Lima, 1982).

them: the crown would contribute mercury and the administration of the *mita*, while the *azogueros* would build and operate the mines and mills. Second, the Indians had to pay for increased production in labour: crown revenue and private profits came first, Indian welfare second. Draft labourers provided the unskilled labour, especially of carrying ore to the surface, for meagre reward, while wage workers, the *mingas*, performed the more skilled and more profitable tasks.

Potosí's mineworkers were forcibly recruited from 119 Indian villages in the highland area between Cuzco and Tarija. This, the notorious *mita de Potosí*, provided (according to the model) some 4,500 labourers who worked for four months at a time, or some 13,500 a year, out a reserve of 86,000.[106] It was a crushing burden on the designated area, and played its part in depopulating the Indian communities. True, it affected only a limited part of the total Indian population, and it required from a given individual only four months work once in seven years. But it was a traumatic experience while it lasted, ravaging bodies already weakened from malnutrition. Toiling underground – where they were sometimes kept continuously from Monday to Saturday and often forced to work on Sunday – in an atmosphere rare in oxygen, rich in carbonic gas, hot and humid, the Indians were whipped by foremen into filling their quotas, and eventually staggered sweating into outside temperatures below freezing point.

The Indians developed their own mechanisms of resistance and survival and many fled from the designated villages to take refuge in the 'free' provinces or in the towns. But many stayed at home and earned enough silver from other economic activities to buy their way out of the mining draft, in effect paying the employer the equivalent of the wage of a free worker. Thus in many cases the *mita* was delivered to the *azogueros* not in the form of Indian conscripts but in silver – 7 pesos a week for each *mitayo*, or 112 pesos for his annual quota – which could then be used to employ substitutes from the free labour market or simply as an alternative to mining. In a period of rising costs and diminishing returns many owners preferred to leave their mines unworked and to live

[106] There are two authoritative works on the *mita*: Bakewell, *Miners of the Red Mountain*; Jeffrey A. Cole, *The Potosí Mita 1573–1700: Compulsory Indian Labor in the Andes* (Stanford, Calif., 1985).

on the income from their *indios de faltriquera* as they were called. By 1660 *mita* deliveries in silver amounted to 587,000 pesos a year, while the royal share of production in Potosí was no more than 300,000.[107] Thus the Potosí *mita* was transformed into a money tax for the benefit not of the crown but of the *azogueros*. The key agents in effecting this transfer were the Indian leaders, the *kurakas*, who were responsible for collecting the money and organizing their communities to earn it; to some extent the *kurakas* were co-opted into the system of exploitation, though they were also subject to extortion and torture if they failed to deliver money to the mineowners. But the Indians were not passive victims of Spanish colonization: they learnt how to exploit the fierce competition for their labour and would seize the opportunity to choose their masters, preferably in other economic activities than mining.

As the original *mita* failed to supply the labour required and ever fewer Indian draft workers actually arrived in Potosí, so the mineowners turned to Indian wage labour, the *mingas*, to fill the gap, to such a degree that by 1600 over one-half of the Indian work force producing silver in Potosí was contracted wage labour. Around 1600 the total native labour force in mining in Potosí was about 10,000 men. Of these roughly 5,500 were *mingas*; the other 4,500 were *mitayos*, the original figure but now maintained only by making the fewer *mitayos* extend their period of work from four to six months.[108] The free labour, of course, had to be paid for and paid sufficiently to fill the gaps in the ranks of the conscripts. Ultimately they were paid for by the Indian communities, who had to raise the money to buy themselves out of *mita* labour. Thus Indian villages in the *mita* area found themselves supplying not only draft labourers to Potosí but large sums of money too. These sums provided the mineowners with the means to employ *minga* workers, giving them in effect a free supply of labour, which was moreover more skilled than that of the *mitayos*. The beneficiaries, therefore, were the mineowners and the *mingas*, the victims the *mitayo* communities.[109]

Spanish officials, too, adapted to changing demographic and

[107] Cole, *The Potosí Mita*, pp. 39, 44–5, 148–9 n. 54.
[108] Bakewell, *Miners of the Red Mountain*, pp. 27–8.
[109] Ibid., pp. 134–5.

economic conditions in the *mita* region and to the peculiar features of Potosí mining. They accepted the fact that the *azogueros* profited more than the crown from the resulting distortion of the system. While the crown theoretically had the power to abolish the *mita*, it was reluctant to exercise it out of fear that the whole mining economy might collapse and that reform might provoke resistance and rebellion. When in 1659–60 Fray Francisco de la Cruz, provincial of the Dominicans in Peru and bishop elect of Santa Marta, was appointed 'superintendent of the mita' with a commission to investigate the abuses, he took a strong stand in favour of the Indians and against the mineowners, tried to impose controls on the *mita* system and ordered all *mita* deliveries in silver to be halted. The chronicler Arzáns recorded that 'the rich *azogueros* assembled and agreed that it was not advisable to discredit the *mita*'; one night Cruz was murdered in his bed, the victim of poison in his hot chocolate.[110] It did not pay to alienate the local oligarchy or to disturb the colonial consensus. Although the abolition of the *mita* was mooted from time to time, the most that was accomplished (1692–97) was a reform of conditions and a prohibition of deliveries in silver. The mining guild of Potosí was not the only pressure group in colonial society, but it was one of the more striking examples of the growing power of local elites.

The distortion of the *mita* in favour of mineowners was accompanied by other manifestations of regional compromise and of the 'Peruvianization' of the colonial regime. A second example was the persistance of fraud in the Potosí mint. The cost of extracting and refining silver was met by a simple device, the adulteration of the silver used to make coins by the addition of excessive amounts of copper. This was noticed as early as 1633 – it was difficult not to notice a 25 per cent reduction in silver – and official warnings were given by the crown to the assayers at Potosí. The reaction of the viceroy, the Marquis of Mancera, was one typical of a consensus official: he preferred not to press local interests too hard. He advised that to stir up trouble in Potosí might frighten off those who sold adulterated silver to the mint, often the same people who advanced credit to the mines; this

[110] Arzáns, *Historia de la Villa Imperial de Potosí*, ii, pp. 188–90; Cole, *The Potosí Mita*, pp. 92–3, 126–30.

would bring operations to a halt and cause riots in the streets. But the Council of the Indies, faced with a rejection of Potosí coins in Spain and by Spain's creditors in Europe, insisted on pursuing the perpetrators. A new president of the *audiencia* of La Plata, Francisco de Nestares Marín, priest and former inquisitor in Spain, took measures to restore the value of Potosí coinage and imposed punitive fines on three guilty silver merchants. In 1650 he had the leading coinage criminal, Francisco Gómez de la Rocha, author of the *pesos rochunos*, executed by garrotting. The Spanish crown could not afford to jeopardize its financial credibility in Europe, but in Upper Peru many local interests were alienated by this unusual rejection of consensus.[111] President Nestares Marín died the same night as Francisco de la Cruz, in equally suspicious circumstances.

A third area of colonial conflict and compromise concerned public office. The pressure of Peruvians for a presence in the administration and government desire for revenue found a solution in the sale of office. From the 1630s Americans had the opportunity to obtain offices, if not by right then by purchase or in *beneficio*: the crown began to sell treasury offices in 1633, *corregimientos* in 1678 and judgeships in the *audiencias* in 1687.[112] Peruvians took advantage of these openings, with obvious effects: purchase of office gave the incumbent a measure of independence within the administration, and tended to bypass that isolation from local society which the crown sought for its colonial bureaucracy. And while the Peruvianization of the bureaucracy may have been a victory for the creole elites, it was a further setback for the ethnic communities and those who had to supply tribute and labour, increasingly defenceless under the new alignment. The sale of fiscal offices from 1633 diluted royal authority where it most counted. In Peru treasury officials came to act not as executives of the imperial government but as mediators between the financial demands of the crown and the resistance of

---

[111] Arzáns, *Historia de la Villa Imperial de Potosí*, ii, pp. 190–1; Guillermo Lohmann Villena, 'La memorable crisis monetaria de mediados del siglo XVII y sus repercusiones en el virreinato del Perú', *Anuario de Estudios Americanos*, 33 (1976), pp. 579–639; Bakewell, *Silver and Entrepreneurship in Seventeenth-Century Potosí*, pp. 36–42; Glave, *Trajinantes*, pp. 182–91.

[112] Alfredo Moreno Cebrián, 'Venta y beneficios de los corregimientos peruanos', *Revista de Indias*, 36, 143–4 (1976), pp. 213–46.

tax payers. An informal alliance of regional officials and local interests – merchants, mineowners, and other entrepreneurs – came to dominate the treasury, with the result that imperial control relaxed, opportunities for fraud and corruption increased, and remissions of revenue to Spain diminished.[113]

The fall in silver output and the recession of transatlantic trade in the first half of the seventeenth century led to a reduction in the income of the Lima treasury. There was now a fairly continuous downward trend in public remittances to Spain, from 379 million pesos in 1601–10, to 33.7 million in 1641–50, to 24 million in 1681–90, halted from time to time only by exceptional fiscal extorsion.[114] The colonial government's search for revenue devices which would not alienate local taxpayers led to a precarious reliance on borrowing, a cutback on funds normally sent to Spain, sale of *juros*, land titles and public offices, while the clergy, landowners, merchants and other elites largely escaped new taxes. These desperate measures were not necessarily signs of economic depression. The *azogueros* still took their slice from the *mita* payment in money, the *corregidores* from defrauding the tribute revenue; and *encomenderos* turned themselves into hacendados, consolidating and rationalizing their estates into commercial enterprises. Falling prices were a sign not of stagnation but of strong agricultural production fuelled by market demand.[115] As for merchants, Lima was still a centre of overseas trade, a place where profits could still be made and investments decided. In short, local elites, long capable of accumulating capital, were now concerned to protect it, especially from the tax collector; and they were more interested in government consumption and public spending within Peru than in payments to Spain.

The fiscal crisis, therefore, derived not from economic depression but from fiscal failure and administrative weakness.[116] The crown sabotaged its own financial bureaucracy when, in 1633,

[113] Kenneth J. Andrien, 'The Sale of Fiscal Offices and the Decline of Royal Authority in the Viceroyalty of Peru, 1633–1700', *Hispanic American Historical Review*, 62, 1 (1982), pp. 49–71.

[114] Andrien, *Crisis and Decline*, p. 34. Silver taxes were the chief source, some 55 per cent, of crown revenue at Potosí: TePaske, 'The Fiscal Structure of Upper Peru and the Financing of Empire', pp. 69–94.

[115] Glave and Remy, *Estructura agraria y vida rural en una región andina*, pp. 140–60; Glave, *Trajinantes*, pp. 207–13.

[116] Andrien, *Crisis and Decline*, pp. 74–5.

under pressure from Philip IV and Olivares for quick money, it approved the systematic sale of all high-ranking treasury appointments, thus permitting corrupt, inexperienced officials with strong local connections to dominate the treasury.[117] This was the reason why the colonial state faltered in Peru, as creoles bought treasury offices, established family and political networks, and became part of local interest groups. The process also had implications for Indian society, now confronted by an alliance of bureaucrats, *corregidores*, and mining and landed interests. While viceroys were caught between concern for revenue and the fear of rebellion, local officials were left to maintain a consensus, placate those wanting labour and surpluses, ignore the pressure on Indian resources and line their own pockets. They avoided confrontation and conflict, but at the cost of imperial control; and by resorting to sales of land, *juros* and offices they kept some revenue flowing, but at the cost of solvency and good government. Following gradual decrease of royal revenue in the first half of the century, there was severe reduction from about 1660, and remittances of silver from the Lima treasury to Seville fell from 14.8 million pesos in 1631–40 to 1.2 million in 1681–90.[118]

Remittances to Spain were conditioned not only by Peruvian revenue but also by Peruvian expenditure. Despite the gradual fall of silver production in Potosí after 1640, it remained high enough to keep significant sums flowing into the royal treasury.[119] Between 1561 and 1700 the treasuries of Upper Peru remitted over 200 million pesos to Lima, which were used by the viceroy for local expenditure and remittance of the surplus to Spain. About 1650 remittances from Upper Peru began to fall, first slowly then substantially, as mining production fell and local expenditure rose. The fall was serious for Lima, but more so for Spain. In 1591–1600 shipments to Spain from Lima amounted to 20 million pesos, an average of 2 million pesos a year. In 1600–1650 over 70 million pesos were remitted, at a rate of little less than 1.5 million pesos annually. 'But 1650 was a watershed at which shipments of crown silver from Peru began to drop drastically.'[120] In 1651–

---

[117] Ibid., pp. 103–4, 115–16; Glave, *Trajinantes*, pp. 193–4.
[118] Andrien, *Crisis and Decline*, p. 67.
[119] TePaske, 'The Fiscal Structure of Upper Peru and the Financing of Empire', p. 75.
[120] Ibid., p. 79; John J. TePaske and Herbert S. Klein, *The Royal Treasuries of the Spanish Empire in America*, (3 vols, Durham, NC, 1982), ii, pp. 322–32.

1700 only 16 million pesos were shipped from Peru to Spain, an average annual flow of about 320,000 pesos a year, less than a quarter of what had been remitted in the previous half century. The reasons were twofold: Lima received less surplus from Upper Peru, and at the same time administrative and defence costs in the viceroyalty underwent exceptional growth. In the seventeenth century the need to reinforce imperial defence brought sharp increases in military and naval expenditures. In the period 1601–1650 some 40 million pesos were spent within the viceroyalty on defence, an average of 800,000 pesos a year, or 20 per cent of total revenues. But remissions to Spain survived and, at 1.5 million annually, almost doubled the amounts spent on military expenditure. In 1650–1700 defence costs in the viceroyalty rose by only 6 million pesos to 45 million pesos over fifty years, but they rose at the same time as remittances from Upper Peru bagan to drop. And whereas remittances into the Lima treasury from other treasuries fell by 47 per cent compared to the previous fifty years, remittances to Spain fell by 79 per cent.[121] Defence, moreover, was not the only item of local expenditure: further sums were spent on viceregal administration, salaries, pensions, grants, and above all purchase of mercury. In spite of the fall in government receipts from the 1660s, the viceregal treasury spent an increasing share of its income within Peru. Whereas between 1591 and 1600 the treasury retained 36 per cent of its income within the viceroyalty, in 1681–90 95 per cent of government revenue was spent within the viceroyalty, most on defence and *situados*, such as the Pacific fleet, shipbuilding and fortifications at the Straits of Magellan, Valdivia, Lima, Callao and above all Panama, which was the focal point of corsair activity in the last decades of the century.[122] The bulk of Peruvian public revenue, therefore, was spent in Peru. The colony had become in some degree its own metropolis.

Inter-American Trade

The shift of the Spanish American economy and its mounting independence of Spain, the decrease of remittances to the metro-

[121] TePaske, 'The Fiscal Structure of Upper Peru and the Financing of Empire', pp. 76–80.
[122] Andrien, *Crisis and Decline*, 33–4.

polis and the growth of investment in the colonies themselves, all gave rise to a flourishing trade between the various parts of Spanish America, which further stimulated independent growth. The main routes of inter-American trade and navigation were between Mexico and Peru, and between Mexico and Venezuela.

By the beginning of the seventeenth century the Peruvian economy had begun to turn away from Spain towards Mexico. Transatlantic trade was too rare and too expensive to meet the demands of the growing colony. The Peruvian cycle of production and export, depending as it did on the seasonal activity of the mining industry, was difficult to synchronize with the arrival of the annual fleet at Portobello. The Spaniards too found it impossible to maintain the official timetable; transatlantic navigation became increasingly irregular, and between 1600 and 1650 Tierra Firme received only twenty-nine fleets.[123] To the inconvenience of transatlantic trade was added the insecurity of the capital invested in it. Sequestration of private silver remittances to Seville simply encouraged Lima merchants to divert their capital to intercolonial trade, which was in any case less heavily taxed; it was also less subject to enemy attack and therefore less burdened with defence costs.[124] For all these reasons merchants' shipments from Peru to Spain moved from 14 million pesos in the two-year consignment of 1626 to 3,680,000 in 1635, to 5 million in 1645, to 4.3 million in 1650.[125]

Trade between Mexico and Peru began in the sixteenth century, and consisted in the movement of manufactured and luxury goods from Mexico, whose economy was more developed, and the return of silver from Peru, where mining was more productive and prices higher. Peru thus imported textiles, clothing, furniture, jewelry, toilet and household goods, leather goods and books from Mexico, and paid for them in silver, later also in wine and in some years mercury.[126] By the end of the sixteenth century the trade was buoyant and never short of finance. The drift of capital from Spanish to colonial trade was reported by the viceroy

---

[123] Manuel Moreyra y Paz-Soldán, *Estudios sobre el tráfico marítimo en la época colonial* (Lima, 1944), pp. 67–87.

[124] Borah, *Early Colonial Trade and Navigation between Mexico and Peru*, p. 125.

[125] Rodríguez Vicente, *El tribunal del consulado de Lima*, pp. 227–8.

[126] Borah, *Early Colonial Trade and Navigation between Mexico and Peru*, pp. 80–95.

of Peru in 1592; he attributed it to the shortage and delays of shipments from Spain, the slow returns on capital, taxation and sequestration; whereas trade in Peruvian products and the import of goods from Mexico enjoyed a quick turnover and steady prosperity in safer conditions.[127]

From the 1570s the trade received a new injection – Chinese goods, procured in the Philippines, shipped across the Pacific in the Manila galleons and sold for silver in Mexico.[128] Chinese damasks, satins, silks, chinaware, porcelain, perfumes and jewelry began to pour into Acapulco and found a ready market. For the Philippine trade offered a supply of luxury goods, and even vital necessities such as spices, iron and copper, at prices far below imports from Spain or even the cheaper – and cruder – products of the Mexican *obrajes*. In the 1590s Chinese textiles sold for perhaps one-ninth of the price of Spanish cloth in Peru. The opening of the Manila–Acapulco trade coincided with the steep rise of Potosí's silver output, which immediately acted as a magnet. Peruvian merchants were forbidden direct access to the Orient. With their greater silver resources, however, they could outbid the Mexicans for Chinese imports in the Acapulco market, and these they re-exported to Peru in enormous and increasing volume. By the 1590s the value of the Mexico–Peru trade, including re-exports of Chinese goods, amounted perhaps to 2 or even 3 million pesos a year.[129] It had grown even larger by 1602 when the *cabildo* of Mexico City claimed that 5 million pesos a year went from Acapulco to the Philippines and thence to the Chinese. Most of this money came from Peru, which took the greater part of the cargoes and supplied perhaps some 3 millions of the returns. By this time Mexico was merely an entrepôt for the re-export of Oriental goods to Peru, and Mexican manufactures – many of which Peru could now produce for itself – amounted to no more than about one-tenth in value of the trade. Indeed one Mexican activity, silk raising and manufacture, was a victim of Chinese competition, which, combined with Indian labour shortage and crown policy, helped to ruin the industry.[130]

[127] Ibid., pp. 95, 121.
[128] William Schurz, *The Manila Galleon* (New York, 1939).
[129] Borah, *Early Colonial Trade and Navigation between Mexico and Peru*, pp. 116–24.
[130] Borah, *Silk Raising in Colonial Mexico*, pp. 85–101.

The very prosperity of the new trade brought retribution. The imperial government was conscious of Peru's economic independence and alarmed at the escape of silver to the Far East. Spanish monopolists resented the competition and the shrinking market. Peninsular interests therefore combined to curtail the Philippine trade and to stop re-export to Peru.[131] Their reaction was part of the desperate attempt of Spanish merchants, in a period of contracting trade, to preserve Peru, the most valuable market, for themselves. Simultaneously they were also attempting to close another gap in the monopoly's defences, Buenos Aires and the pampa route to Peru.[132] In 1593 shipment of Chinese goods to all colonies other than Mexico was forbidden. Trade between Mexico and the Philippines was restricted to two ships; Chinese goods from Manila could be imported to the value of 250,000 pesos a year, and returns in silver to Manila up to 500,000 pesos. This legislation simply diverted the Mexico–Peru trade to contraband channels. These flowed so freely that the crown tried to impose further restrictions. In 1604 it reduced the size of the two Manila galleons from 300 to 200 tons; trade between Mexico and Peru was limited to three ships of 300 tons each year; these might carry products of Mexico and Peru for exchange, but no specie, and they were restricted to the ports of Acapulco and Callao.[133] Further decrees reduced navigation between Mexico and Peru to two vessels a year, then to one a year, and in 1620 the export of Peruvian wine to Mexico was forbidden. Finally, the logical conclusion of this policy was reached in 1631 when, under pressure of the *consulado* of Seville, the crown forbade all trade and navigation between Mexico and Peru, a prohibition which was renewed in 1634 and endured for the rest of the century and beyond.

These prohibitions were not taken seriously. Peruvian ecclesiastics argued that they were unjust and not binding in conscience; and local officials could not resist the pressure, or the temptation, to turn a blind eye.[134] In any case there were too many contraband outlets to permit strict control. One loophole

---

[131] Borah, *Early Colonial Trade and Navigation between Mexico and Peru*, pp. 124–7.

[132] See above, pp. 258–9.

[133] Chaunu, *Séville et l'Atlantique*, viii, 1, p. 759.

[134] Rodríguez Vicente, *El tribunal del consulado de Lima*, pp. 244–52, 270.

was Peru's legal trade with Nicaragua, a source of vital supplies of pitch; this provided cover under which Chinese goods, transported from Mexico to Realejo and Sonsonate, could be loaded on Peruvian vessels. Another method was to divert to Acapulco silver consignments nominally registered to Guatemala and Nicaragua; returning shipments could be landed at Paita or other minor ports north of Callao. And there was always the well-tried device of rendezvous and transfer of silver off the Peruvian coast. Guayaquil was a favourite base of contraband, for it possessed weaker customs machinery than Callao; and vessels from Central America coming to its shipyards for repair did not normally arrive empty. The source of contraband, the Philippine trade itself, outgrew its legal confines; the value of shipments varied between 200,000 and 1.5 million pesos at Manila, worth two or three times that amount in Mexico and Peru; and contraband trade sometimes raised the final value to more than 10 million pesos.

The other great route of intercolonial trade was that linking Venezuela and Mexico. Venezuela's chief product and export commodity was cacao, and its principal market was Mexico, where returns were quick and secure. Chocolate was in wide and popular demand; it was a favourite creole beverage, and Venezuela's product had a reputation for quality.[135] In the course of the seventeenth century production in the province of Caracas expanded strongly, and by the 1690s there was an exportable surplus of some 13,000 fanegas a year.[136] Regular traffic between Venezuela and Mexico began in 1622 when one vessel shipped sixty fanegas of cacao; in Mexico it earned good prices, paid in silver, which enabled producers to invest further in cacao production. From then onwards the Mexican market became far more important to Venezuela than that of the metropolis, both in the regularity of traffic and its value. In the period 1620–50 Venezuela exported to Mexico 35,512 fanegas of cacao, to Spain only 289. In 1651–1700 the Mexican market consumed 322,264 fanegas

[135] Eduardo Arcila Farías, *Economía colonial de Venezuela* (Mexico, 1946), pp. 87–98; see also Antonio Arellano Moreno, *Orígenes de la economía venezolana* (Mexico, 1947), and Federico Brito Figueroa, *La estructura económica de Venezuela colonial* (Caracas, 1963).

[136] Eduardo Arcila Farías, *Comercio entre Venezuela y México en los siglos XVII y XVIII* (Mexico, 1950), pp. 51–61, 72–3.

of Venezuelan cacao, while Spain took only 71,306. Up to about 1670 Spain provided a modest market for Venezuelan hides and tobacco, but these were trifling in value compared to cacao. Venezuela lived on colonial trade and had decreasing contact with Seville. By 1630 Mexican purchasees had risen to 112,560 reales, while Spain's purchases (all products) stood at 136,177. In 1640 Mexican purchases of cacao amounted to 321,792 reales, and those of Spain (all products) dropped to 44,400. In 1660 Venezuelan exports to Mexico were valued at 572,720 reales, those to Spain only 61,650. Although after this date cacao exports to Spain increased, they increased even more to Mexico. In the period 1661–1700 Mexico imported 273,763 fanegas of Venezuelan cacao, a 200 per cent increase over the previous forty years.[137] Between 1684 and 1720 Mexico was virtually the only market for Venezuela, for trade with Spain dwindled to a trickle, not only in cacao but also in hides and tobacco, which the Dutch were now carrying direct to Europe. In the last decade of the seventeenth century, while Mexico consumed 108,801 fanegas of Venezuelan cacao valued at about 17 million reales, Spanish purchases in all products hardly reached 2 million reales.[138]

The only competition for Venezuela could come from Guayaquil, whose cacao production expanded about the same time. But Venezuela won the struggle for dominance in the Mexican market, thanks in part to the support of Spain. It was the policy of the crown, within the limits of its actual power, so to regulate intercolonial trade that there was an apportioning of activities and markets and no monoculture colony was left completely out. Just as it deterred sugar exports from Mexico, which had alternative activities, in order to protect the Carribean islands, so it discouraged cacao exports from Guayaquil in order to favour Venezuela.[139] In so doing the crown furthered Venezuela's growth until it had little need of Spain. The colony then developed its modest economy independently of the metropolis, earning Mexican silver for reinvestment in its plantations and merchant marine, and generating enough public revenue to pay for its own administration and defence.

[137] Ibid., pp. 106, 134–5.
[138] Ibid., p. 56.
[139] Ibid., pp. 195–216, 249–78.

Colonial Autonomy

The growth of intercolonial trade in the early seventeenth century presupposed the development of the colonial economies in agricultural products, viniculture and local manufactures, activities which generated sufficient surplus for export to other colonies and established a form of intercolonial division of labour. Capital was also accumulated and exported for purchases in other colonies; Peru, for example, exported capital to pay for imports from Mexico and through Mexico for Chinese goods. The Spanish monopoly had to reckon with these developments; the growth of independent economies in America was a permanent threat to Seville and it was forced to modify the monopoly; that was why some Spanish merchants sought to participate in intercolonial trade and thus diversify their investments. Finally, intercolonial trade was a consequence of demographic growth in the colonies, the increase of mestizization, and the recovery of the Indian population from about 1630. The Indians, moreover, were now more closely integrated into the colonial economy as sellers of labour and consumers of merchandise, and they had to adjust their own production in order to pay tribute and fulfil their other obligations.

The growth of direct trade, the expansion of intercolonial trade, and the penetration of the very headquarters of the *carrera* by American merchants, all indicated the growing freedom of America from monopoly control and a significant degree of colonial autonomy in economic matters. Economic change should not be mistaken for economic depression. Mining production in Mexico and Peru did not collapse, and if the days of the first boom were over there were still valuable yields to be obtained.[140] Agriculture did not slide into subsistence; both in Mexico and Peru commercialization and production for regional markets stimulated land use and investment in haciendas. In the public

---

[140] For a useful survey of the state of research on mining see Rosario Sevilla Soler, 'Minería americana y la crisis del siglo XVII. Estado del problema', *Suplemento de Anuario de Estudios Americanos. Sección Historiografía y Bibliografía*, 47, 2 (1900), pp. 61–81.

sector tax returns indicated growth rather than depression.[141] No doubt fiscal extortion rather than economic growth can explain increases from taxation in the short term. But revenue expansion over a long period, comprising taxes based on production, can only take place if the economy is capable of sustaining it. At the same time the destination as well as the quantity of colonial revenue was changing. A colony without a revenue surplus for the metropolis, or with a diminishing surplus, need not be depressed but could possibly be undergoing a degree of autonomous growth and freedom from monopoly control. There was a period between 1650 and 1750 when Spanish America experienced conditions of this kind, when colonial revenue was employed on colonial administration, defence and services, and when major colonies allocated subsidies to lesser dependencies whose economies were linked to those of the donor rather than directly to the metropolis. The fact that revenues were spent in client colonies rather than in their place of origin does not weaken the argument for colonial autonomy, any more than the expansion of inter-regional trade weakens it.[142]

While it may be true that the recession of mining production and the costs of local administration and defence in the seventeenth century cut back the colonial surplus, and that the colonies had reached a degree of self-sufficiency in agriculture and manufactures and through investment of silver in their own economies, does it follow that the colonies were less dependent on their metropolis? In the first place, it is obvious that public revenue was only a fraction of the income from mining and commerce; the greatest capital resources were in private hands and their destination is more problematical. Second, it is also clear that the essential link across the Atlantic was established by quality textiles, hardware, paper, slaves and the commercial credit and cap-

---

[141] The figures of TePaske and Klein in *The Royal Treasuries of the Spanish Empire in America*, although subject to criticism and revision in recent years, especially for the eighteenth century (see *Hispanic American Historical Review*, 64, 2, 1984), remain an important guide to relative trends and continue to yield fruitful results.

[142] Misconceptions of this kind can be found in J. I. Israel, 'The Seventeenth-Century Crisis in New Spain: Myth or Reality?', *Past and Present*, 97 (November 1982), pp. 144–56.

ital supplied by merchants in Seville, on all of which colonial life depended.[143] These were the high-price commodities most valued in colonial trade and they were supplied only from outside; so Seville continued to extract silver from Peru and Mexico in monopoly form. Many of these commodities, of course, were produced or distributed not by Spaniards but by foreigners, and profits were accordingly diverted abroad. Therefore, although Seville continued to dominate the Indies trade as an intermediary, the former metropolis no longer received exclusive profit from its colonies. If self-sufficiency was limited and dependence continued, this was not the primitive dependence of the sixteenth century but one in which the colonies had more options, a partial dependence. To some extent conditions were reversed and the Indies trade depended on American capital. The Peruvian merchants, for example, adjusted to change; protected by mining production, they continued to invest in the transatlantic trade but outside the official fairs.

Spanish America, moreover, was not simply an Atlantic economy; it also had a strong internal market. The colonies lived by regional circulation of merchandise.[144] They produced local agricultural products and some manufactures, and sold them from region to region. The mining markets of Potosí and Zacatecas were important consumers, circulators and generators of growth. By the seventeenth century these regional markets were primarily consumers of colonial products, compared to which European manufactures were relatively few.[145] The greater proportion of

---

[143] Carlos Sempat Assadourian, 'La producción de la mercancía dinero en la formación del mercado interno colonial. El caso peruano, siglo XVI', in Enrique Florescano, ed., *Ensayos sobre el desarrollo económico de México y América Latina, 1500–1975* (Mexico, 1979), pp. 232–5, 281–2.

[144] Carlos Sempat Assadourian, *El sistema de la economía colonial. Mercado interno, regiones and espacio económico* (Lima, 1982), pp. 85–8; Juan Carlos Garavaglia, *Mercado interno y economía colonial* (Mexico, 1983), pp. 20, 382–3.

[145] The trend towards inter-regional trade in the seventeenth century has been questioned. It has been argued that there was a decline in such trade between the 1630s and 1670s, including the trade between Peru, Mexico and the Philippines, as the mining economies became depressed and the colonies suffered shortage of capital; see Murdo J. Macleod, 'Spain and America: the Atlantic trade 1492–1720', in Bethell, ed., *The Cambridge History of Latin America*, i, pp. 373–6. This may be true in the case of minor colonies in Central America, prone to depression in the best of times; but it does not necessarily apply to Mexico or Peru, whose 'depression' has been exaggerated.

goods consumed before the eighteenth century – textiles, tobacco, foodstuffs – were produced by the colonies themselves. Peru achieved a high degree of self-sufficiency and regional integration; in 1603 Potosí took only 9.5 per cent of its consumption from non-American sources, a proportion which grew but slowly in the next 150 years.[146] The growth of internal markets, of course, was not inconsistent with the entry of the colonies into the Atlantic economy. Spanish America had a dual economy: on the one hand, it was an internal market; on the other, it was a producer of precious metals and a consumer of European goods. These were complementary functions, and they were not under the exclusive control of the Spanish monopoly.

The seventeenth century was a time of transition in the Hispanic world, when imperial controls were diluted, colonial government began to compromise, regional economies worked for themselves and the creoles came into their own. In the process Mexico, Peru and the lesser colonies helped to create a second Spanish empire, whose societies and economies had emancipated themselves from their primitive dependence on Spain.[147]

[146] Sempat Assadourian, *El sistema de la economía colonial*, pp. 112, 278–93.

[147] In a recent study, *Conjonctures opposées: La "crise" du XVIIᵉ siècle en Europe et en Amérique ibérique* (Geneva, 1992), Ruggiero Romano argues that the seventeenth-century crisis in Europe enabled the Iberian colonies to obtain more autonomous forms of growth and government.

9

Government and Society
in the Reign of Charles II

Privilege and Power: the Rule of Aristocracy

Charles II was the last, the most degenerate and the most pathetic victim of Habsburg inbreeding. When, on 17 September 1665, he succeeded his father Philip IV, he was only four years old, a sickly child, retarded by rickets and mentally subnormal. During the whole of his thirty-nine years he suffered chronic ill-health, serious psychological disturbances and frequent attacks of acute melancholia; these he tried to exorcise by spiritual means, which earned him the name of *el Hechizado*, the bewitched. Living his life under the shadow of death, he was incapable of exercising government. He was also incapable of producing children, and his two marriages remained, if not unconsummated, at least unfruitful. Monarchy therefore now suffered from two mortal afflictions – a weak incumbent and a succession problem.[1]

Yet Spanish government owed its weakness not to any one monarch or single event but to a long process of neglect during which absolute power and central authority had been allowed to

---

[1] The traditional work on the reign of Charles II is by the Duque de Maura, *Vida y reinado de Carlos II* (2nd edn, 2 vols, Madrid, 1954). This year-by-year chronicle of the political events of the reign is almost unreadable, but it is based on a lifetime of study, and on original documentation described in the preface. The peculiar form in which the work is cast is due in part to the fact that the author's entire collection of books, transcripts and notes was destroyed in the Civil War. Two previous works on the reign are much inferior: Julian Juderías, *España en tiempo de Carlos II el Hechizado* (Madrid, 1912); Ludwig Pfandl, *Carlos II* (Madrid, 1947). All these have been superseded by Henry Kamen, *Spain in the Later Seventeenth Century, 1665–1700* (London, 1980).

wither and decay. At the end of the reign of Philip II central government began to divest itself of various functions – financial, military, even judicial – in an attempt to compensate for lack of competence or scarcity of resources in particular fields. The new instinct of government was to delegate. If revenue was urgently required, farm it out. If military forces were needed, make contracts with local lords. If litigants were queuing for justice, send them to lower courts. Abdication of responsibility was accompanied by alienation of property, as the crown mindlessly sold its patrimony for immediate income. These various forms of privatization led to loss of royal authority and resources, and to the consolidation of regional oligarchies and prerogatives.[2] The attempt of Olivares to reverse the trend and to recover for the monarchy the absolute powers it had once enjoyed led to the explosion of 1640 and the crisis of government that followed, yet a further stage in the retreat from absolutism. Thus between the ineptitude of the crown and the ambition of local oligarchies, royal power receded and kings ruled not by exacting obedience but by negotiating with powerful interest groups. The defection of central government was completed by the flow of litigation away from the royal courts of justice, condemned by their cost, inefficiency and corruption, and by the withdrawal of the council of Castile and the royal chancelleries from the public life of Castile.[3] The winners were municipal and other local courts, where justice could be done but where a multiplicity of customs and *fueros* flourished and alternative power groups prevailed. Devolution of justice had been accepted by the governments of Philip III and Philip IV, and in some cases actively encouraged by monarchs who also sold jurisdiction to private lords. By the late seventeenth century a large part of the authority of the state had slipped from the king's control into the hands of regional aristocracies, and municipal and rural oligarchies.

Charles II was not the king to halt the eclipse of royal sovereignty or arrest the progress of the aristocracy. He was no

[2] The process has been identified by I. A. A. Thompson, *War and Government in Habsburg Spain* (London, 1976), and further reviewed in his 'The Rule of Law in Early Modern Castile', *European History Quarterly*, 14 (1984), pp. 221–34.

[3] Richard L. Kagan, *Lawsuits and Litigants in Castile 1500–1700* (Chapel Hill, NC, 1981), pp. 220–30.

more than a cipher, a shadow king. Government was first controlled by his mother, the queen regent, and then by a succession
of favourites and ministers, the former destroyed, the latter created by the aristocracy. Orders and decrees were issued in the
king's name, but they were seldom submitted to him for signature, and official documents of the reign usually bore only a
facsimile of the royal hand. In the unhappy, neurotic person of
Charles II Spanish monarchy was reduced to a mockery of its
former grandeur. Into the vacuum moved the aristocracy, who
now reached their greatest – and their final – fulfilment. The only
challenge to them came from the church. While the aristocracy
deposed royal favourites and promoted their own leaders, the
church provided the royal confessors who moved assiduously
along the corridors of influence if not of power. Premier and
priest, these were the two manipulators of power in the reign of
Charles II. But if there was any conflict between the two estates it
was an argument between allies, not between alternatives. They
had much in common. They were the privileged sectors of society;
between them they virtually monopolized land; and the hierarchy
of the church was almost an aristocratic preserve.

Against the general demographic trend of the seventeenth century, the ecclesiastical population seemed to be increasing. In the
absence of exact statistics, estimates are largely guess-work; contemporary guesses varied between 100,000 for the 1620s and
180,000 for the 1660s.[4] Most of the *arbitristas* complained of the
excessive number of clergy. According to Sancho de Moncada, 'a
third of the Spanish population is made up of ecclesiastics, if we
include religious and nuns, secular clergy, tertiaries, hermits and
people who have taken a vow of chastity.' While the ecclesiastical
population grew in numbers, it did not grow in wisdom, knowledge or even piety. No doubt there was much anonymous sancti-
ty and charity in the Spanish church, but for many of its clergy it
was simply a career. The higher clergy, sons of the aristocracy,
shared the ideals and the background of their class. The mass of
the lower clergy, the majority of humble origin, had little hope of
preferment; but many of them had entered the priesthood in

---

[4] Reglà, 'La época de los dos últimos Austrias', in J. Vicens Vives, ed.,
Historia social y económica de España y América, iii, p. 267. Domínguez Ortiz
suggests 150,000 for the end of the century.

order to escape the winds of destitution outside the cloister, and in this at least they succeeded. The church drew its wealth essentially from its own land and from other people's labour, that is from rents and from tithes. The extent of landed property controlled by ecclesiastical institutions is difficult to determine; in the mid-eighteenth century it amounted perhaps in Castile to 15 per cent of land and 24 per cent of total agricultural income.[5] In addition to land owned directly in mortmain, the church also possessed *señorío eclesiástico*, which gave it seigneurial jurisdiction and revenue in the towns and lands under its lordship. Finally, as a last line of defence, the church possessed its own *fuero*; this endowed the clergy with substantial immunity from civil jurisdiction and enabled them to defend their interests – and their property – by reference to ecclesiastical law and in ecclesiastical courts.[6]

The omnipresence of the clergy, their economic security and their extensive *fuero*, all engendered a certain anti-clericalism in the rest of society and provided material for conflict with the state. In the cortes of 1621 Mateo Lison, deputy for Málaga, denounced the 'disadvantages of so many religious foundations and chantries and the excessive accumulation of landed property by the ecclesiastical estate'. In 1626 the cortes complained of ecclesiastics who 'by endowments, confraternities, chantries or simple purchase, are gradually possessing themselves of the whole kingdom', and it requested the crown to halt the accumulation of property in mortmain, particularly as it was exempt from taxation. Criticism of this kind became even more common in the reign of Charles II. Reporting on the state of Valladolid, in 1683, at a time of great economic difficulty, a minister of the crown claimed that

the most important part of the inhabitants consists of the ecclesiastical chapters and other clergy, infinite in number, from the University, College, Chancellery and Inquisition, and from the 53 convents of religious that there are, besides 17 parishes and other oratories, all of which employ people solely for the service

[5] John Lynch, *Bourbon Spain 1700–1808* (Oxford, 1989), p. 269.
[6] See Quintín Aldea, S. J., *Iglesia y Estado en la España del siglo XVII (Ideario político-eclesiástico)* (Comillas, 1961).

PLATE 7   *Charles II*, by J. Carreño de Miranda (reproduced by kind permission
of the Museo del Prado, Madrid)

of their ministers . . . . It seems that this city is made up principally of consumers only.[7]

Valladolid of course was an exceptional centre of ecclesiastical activity; and it was easy to blame the church for problems which the administration could not solve. Nevertheless, the number of clergy in a country which notoriously lacked producers inevitably drew the attention of ministers seeking solutions to economic distress. In its concern the government of Charles II took an unprecedented step and in 1689 addressed a circular letter to all the bishops of Spain asking them temporarily to suspend ordinations to the priesthood:

> The number of those admitted to minor orders in recent years is so great that many places have hardly a batchelor left who is not a cleric. And many older men, now widowers, also enter orders. The object of most of them is to procure clerical immunity, to live with greater ease, to enjoy exemption from taxes and other worldly motives.[8]

The church in fact was not completely exempt from taxation. Its services were indispensable for raising the *cruzada*, whose annual yield in the peninsula alone was 800,000 ducats in silver. And the church itself paid the *tercios reales*, a portion of its income from tithes; the *subsidio*, an annual tax on real property, yielding 420,000 ducats; and the *excusado*, a type of tithe, producing 250,000 ducats.[9] The papacy also conceded a number of special taxes on the Spanish clergy, the *décimas eclesiásticas*, assigned to defence needs from time to time and amounting to some hundreds of thousands of ducats. Finally, the clergy were liable, much to their resentment, to the *millones*, though this too was subject to the periodic permission of the papacy, not always granted with enthusiasm. In 1656 there was a kind of clergy revolt led by Archbishop Pedro de Tapia of Seville and Bishop Juan de Palafox of Osma, aroused by constant demands for revenue and by government accusations that the clergy were not

---

[7] Quoted by Henry Kamen, 'The Decline of Castile: the last crisis', *Economic History Review*, second series, xvii (1964–5), pp. 63–76, see especially p. 70.
[8] Quoted by Maura, *Vida y reinado de Carlos II*, i, p. 510.
[9] Domínguez Ortiz, *Política y hacienda de Felipe IV*, pp. 193–232.

contributing to national needs. In the reign of Charles II the Archbishop of Toledo utterly refused to allow his clergy to be taxed for the *millones*. By this time the church was even better positioned to defend itself, for the Archbishop of Toledo and the royal confessors occupied important positions in the counsels of government.

Yet the church could not compete in privilege and power with the secular aristocracy, who now reached their political majority, if not maturity. The monarchy of Charles II was a kind of aristocratic republic, where the grandees assembled to make or break a government regardless of the royal will. Numerically the higher aristocracy expanded in this reign, as more and more nobles, some of them recently created, were promoted to the ranks of the *grandeza*. Charles II doubled the size of the Castilian titled aristocracy, creating twelve new viscounts, eighty new counts, and 236 new marquises. Moreover twenty-six nobles were raised to the rank of grandee, and whereas in 1627 there were only forty-one grandees, in 1707 there were 113. Most of the new titles were sold for money, the prices rising as the government's need increased.[10] In the crown of Aragon, too, honours and prizes were subject to sale and inflation. This movement upwards served to heighten the intolerance and exclusivism of the older aristocratic houses, but it also augmented the power and the wealth of the group as a whole. For the new grandees were wealthy men who openly bought their rank. Wealth, after all, was the ultimate test of *grandeza*. The grandees had the greatest fortunes in the kingdom, some of them 100,000 ducats a year, most of them not less than 40,000 to 80,000. At the beginning of the seventeenth century the income of grandees and *titulos* in the whole of Spain was computed at 5 million ducats, not counting the value of their property; at mid-century it was estimated at 7 million ducats, compared to 1.7 million received by eleven archbishops and fifty-five bishops. To some extent the landed aristocracy benefited from economic depression. The agricultural crises of the seventeenth century ruined many small farmers and

---

[10] Domínguez Ortiz, *La sociedad española en el siglo XVII*, pp. 219–21; Kamen, *Spain in the Later Seventeenth Century*, pp. 249–53; I. A. A. Thompson, 'The Purchase of Nobility in Castile, 1552–1700', *Journal of European Economic History*, 8, 2 (1979), pp. 313–60, places more emphasis on grants than on sales of titles.

favoured property concentration. The large Andalusian estates grew from an original unit by successive additions of small areas of land, often maintaining their identity in spite of changes of ownership. The owner was usually a noble, a prosperous merchant with noble pretensions or an ecclesiastical institution.

The aristocracy possessed great wealth in terms of fixed assets, but were restricted in cashing in on these by entail. And the extravagant expenditure of many nobles far outstripped their capital resources. For them the rule of Charles II came as manna from heaven. The heavy financial demands of Philip IV and Olivares had wounded the pride and hurt the pockets of numerous noble families and alienated them from the crown; further resentment was caused when older houses, struggling with creditors, saw upstart *hidalgos*, well placed in the higher ranks of the administration, getting rich and buying *senoríos* and titles. Political power could be employed in defence of property. In the reign of Charles II the crown was too weak to stand up to the nobility; they could divert taxation away from their class, refuse with impunity to give *donativos* and increase their demands for *mercedes*. The request for a *donativo* in 1667 drew only paltry returns from some and a curt refusal from others; many nobles stated quite firmly that they had already given more than enough to Philip IV. In the last decades of the century the administration had to reconcile itself to requesting only limited *donativos* from the nobility. By then severe economic depression had affected even big estates. To a decree of 1680 conceding four months' delay to cattle owners for payment of the *hierbas* tax, the Duke of Béjar replied that the rent from his pasture land was 'almost the only capital he has, so depopulated are his estates; he has lost a fortune in the Portuguese wars; he has to pay 30,000 ducats a year to run his house in Valladolid, and 6,000 for other establishments; he has lost 30,000 ducats through devaluation, and he owes 120,000 to his creditors'.[11] If this was the situation of one of the greatest magnates in Castile, the middle and lower ranks of the nobility were even worse off, for they could expect less by way of *mercedes*.

Lacking entrepreneurial instincts or experience, the nobility were incapable of remedying their fortunes by economic methods

[11] Quoted in Domínguez Ortiz, *La sociedad española en el siglo XVII*, p. 231.

alone. In the second half of the seventeenth century the financial affairs of some of the greatest families of Castile were in
chaos.[12] The estates of the Enríquez, the Admirals of Castile,
were encumbered by vast debts and besieged by creditors; the
Dukes of Osuna, the house of Pastrana, the Constables of Castile
and many other members of the higher nobility were in similar
difficulties. Nevertheless they continued to live up to their rank
and to remain the largest spenders in the community. How did
they do it? Partly by mortgaging their property. The crown was
reluctant to allow this, regarding it as almost as bad as disentail-
ing. But permission could be procured, especially under Charles
II, and especially for pretexts such as dowries; this explains the
immense dowries of the time – they were a means of freeing
property and getting hands on liquid capital. By one means or
another the nobility maintained their personal income. And one
of the means was royal grants.

The aristocratic reaction which followed the fall of Olivares,
combined with the indolence and generosity of Philip IV, opened
the gates for a new outflow of pensions and grants. This became a
deluge in the reign of Charles II. Access to *mercedes* was at once
a motive and a consequence of aristocratic dominance. Indeed, so
accessible did public funds become, including colonial *encomiendas* and revenue, that the treasury virtually ran a welfare service
for the aristocracy, and many nobles regarded an income from
mercedes as a convenient alternative to working their estates. It
was estimated that *mercedes* and other benefits consumed some 3
million ducats a year, an enormous burden for a treasury already
tottering under its many obligations. The Council of Finance
attempted to stem the flood, not out of principle but because it
could not find the funds. It did not have much success. In some
cases, perhaps, royal grants were justified because of services
rendered. Embassies were financial tombstones for their incumbents; and they were only given to those who had personal
fortunes, for cost-of-living allowances only covered part of the
heavy outlay. But these were not the appointments most sought
by the aristocracy. The richest prizes were the viceroyalties in
Italy and the Indies. These were so profitable that even after

---

[12] See above, pp. 188–9, and Jago, 'The "Crisis of the Aristocracy"',
pp. 60–90.

living in extraordinary splendour and making princely gifts to the king, viceroys still had enough to restore their estates and build great mansions. Nobles like the Marquis of Mancera brought back immense riches from the Indies. These viceroyalties were so valuable that the ministers of Charles II auctioned them off to the highest bidder. In 1695 the viceroyalties of Mexico and Peru were so disposed of; the former went to the Count of Cañete for 250,000 escudos.[13]

Offices, court appointments and *mercedes* were all supplementary to the nobles' basic income which came from land, *señoríos* and royal revenue alienated to them. This complex of property rights enabled the aristocracy to monopolize power at a local level, and gave Spanish provincial life an essentially feudal character. The rot set in under previous monarchs, who had alienated their own private estates through the sale of jurisdiction over their vassals, their rents and other services, and of local offices within the *realengo* (lands under authority of the crown). In addition to seigneurial dues, therefore, *señorío* gave a lord the right to name judges and local officials, and in some cases to possess the revenue from *alcabalas*. In the reign of Philip IV some 200,000 royal vassals were transferred to the control of mainly noble purchasers, nearly 4 per cent of the total Castilian population. In the provinces of Burgos, Soria, Segovia and Avila, some 43 per cent of the towns were owned by nobles. In the province of Salamanca only 30.5 per cent of territory and 33.7 per cent of population came under royal jurisdiction; 63 per cent of territory and 60.4 per cent of population lay within secular *señoríos*; and the rest belonged to *señorío eclesiástico*.[14] Other provinces of Old Castile presented similar features, the chief cities being in royal jurisdiction but the major towns and villages – 500 out of 700 in Castile by 1710 – in the hands of the aristocracy. Over the whole of Spain the crown came to control less than half the centres of population. This did not amount, of course, to a privatization of sovereignty. Subjects in the *señoríos* were just as subject to laws, decrees and other orders emanating from king and councils as

---

[13] Domínguez Ortiz, *La sociedad española en el siglo XVII*, p. 249.
[14] See María Dolores Mateos, *Salamanca*, in Miguel Artola, ed., *La España del Antiguo Régimen* (Salamanca, 1966), p. 14; Kamen, *Spain in the Later Seventeenth Century*, pp. 29, 159–60; Stradling, *Philip IV*, p. 235.

were citizens in the *realengo*. But it did mean that in many parts of Spain the king was not wholly master of functions and resources that should have been in the public domain.

This primitive feudalism seriously inhibited royal administration. For the territorial preponderance of the nobility was paralleled by their control of political and social life. The greatest cities of Castile – Toledo, Avila, Ciudad Real, Seville – were dominated by aristocratic families, who spread out a network of influence throughout the land. Vassals served them, corregidores deferred to them; and delinquents, if they were relatives or clients, could shelter under their protection. A chronicler of Jérez recounts that in 1664, after violent riots in the town, a special judge, Sebastian Infante, was sent to restore law and order; one of his first actions was to initiate proceedings against the corregidor, Rodrigo Dávila Ponce de León. At this point the Duke of Arcos arrived one night in his coach outside the lodgings of the judge, and seeing the latter's clerk in the porch called out from his coach, 'Listen, where is Don Sebastian?' 'He is inside sir, I'll call him.' 'Just tell him that the corregidor of Jérez belongs to my family, that's all.' The clerk immediately informed the judge, who came rushing out, pulling on his clothes and running after the coach, but the duke, although he heard him calling, did not stop.[15]

The territorial power of the aristocracy in the *señorío* was complemented by their political power in the *municipio*. The Castilian nobility tended to live in towns rather than on their uncomfortable estates, the higher aristocracy in Madrid, the rest in the provinces. Excluded by the earlier Habsburgs from a political role at the centre, the majority of the nobles had made their base of influence in the towns. The sale of municipal offices enabled them to control the municipalities. In the course of the seventeenth century most towns came to be dominated by proprietory *regidores*; these were almost always nobles of the middle rank, the *caballeros*. In some of the principal towns of Castile– Valladolid, Avila, Toledo, Alcalá de Henares, Plasencia, Ciudad Real, Trujillo, Córdoba, Seville, Madrid itself – the nobility had a legal monopoly of municipal offices, which they often exercised through deputies or rented out for money. But the majority of

---

[15] Domínguez Ortiz, *La sociedad española en el siglo XVII*, p. 221.

Castilian towns practised the system of *mitad de oficios*, that is an equal distribution of offices between nobles and commoners, a system still favourable to the nobles as they were a minority. In this way local oligarchies of powerful men came into being, combining traditional nobles and newly-rich commoners. These rural oligarchies greatly profited from their position, administering public property to their own advantage, such as the official granary, the royal and municipal taxes and other local institutions. This urban alliance between nobles and wealthy commoners tended to replace the primitive stratification of society based on estates by another based on wealth. In a sense it also strengthened the defences of the aristocracy.

What did commoners think of government by aristocracy? In Valencia, where seigneurial jurisdiction was particularly savage, anti-aristocratic feeling exploded into rebellion.[16] In Castile, on the other hand, there was virtually no challenge to the existing structure. The larger cities had long lost the right to elect their representatives; and provincial interests saw some advantage in having proprietory *regidores*, independent of the central government. In smaller towns the system of *mitad de oficios* was a compromise solution, though it did not entirely preclude conflict between nobles and commoners. The towns of northern Castile were so prolific in *hidalgos* that there could be no successful challenge from below. In the south the nobles were a small minority, but of greater substance, and urban opposition movements simply substituted one noble leader for another. But in the towns of central Castile there was a balance of estates and fierce competition for power, issuing sometimes in popular revolt on a small-town scale. Violence was ruthlessly suppressed; in the absence of a police force the nobility itself controlled the enforcement of order and dominated the local militia. Yet there is no evidence of basic anti-aristocratic sentiments in society at large or of any real threat to the social structure. The close and mutual alliance between crown and aristocracy presented a united front to the rest of society.

For most of the Habsburg period the relation between aristocracy and crown was based on a compromise: the nobles were left undisturbed in their provincial strongholds, while the king

---

[16] See below, pp. 387–91.

exercised undisputed sovereignty at the centre. Under a strong monarch like Philip II the equilibrium was tipped towards the crown. Under Charles II the equilibrium was destroyed, and the aristocracy showed its power. The grandees first made it clear that they would not tolerate ministers who came from outside their ranks; they then assessed the weakness of the queen mother and her son and decided they were amenable to force; and they finally ousted plebeian *validos* and replaced them by aristocrats. But in spite of its power the aristocracy was a flawed ruling class, usually split into interest groups along family or factional lines and rarely capable of combining for political action. Moreover, their interventions were purely destructive, and embodied no political programme. The nobles failed to co-operate with their own chief ministers or even to sustain them. As soon as they entered politics they exposed their ineptitude and parasitism. It is not surprising that under a new dynasty they were quickly demoted.

The Last *Validos*

Spanish government needed a prime minister: this had now been recognized by kings and political theorists alike. Unfortunately the office emerged in association with the *valido*, the favourite, who monopolized the king's confidence and patronage as well as his political duties. It therefore attracted the prejudice of moralizers and the suspicion of the aristocracy, who regarded the *valido* as a barrier between themselves and the crown. In his last years Philip IV succumbed to these prejudices and ruled without a prime minister. And he so disposed in his will that there would be no place for a *valido* after his death. He appointed the queen mother, Mariana, regent and guardian of the heir to the throne, the young Charles, until he should reach the age of fourteen. She was authorized to deal with state papers and to remit them to the deliberations of a *Junta de Gobierno*, formed under the terms of Philip's will. This was to be composed of the president of the Council of Castile, the vice-chancellor of Aragon, the Archbishop of Toledo, the Inquisitor General, a councillor of state, and a grandee to be nominated. Thus although the queen mother was in a sense the chief executive she did not have a sovereign power, for she had to act with the advice of the Junta, which was instructed to assemble daily.[17] The thinking behind Philip's will is clear enough. Mariana was an unstable, ignorant and obstinate woman, unfitted to rule a vast and complex empire. On her own she was ready-made for recourse to a *valido*. The solution as Philip saw it was to assign power in advance not to a single person – admittedly there were few outstanding candidates for a premiership – but to an institution representing the higher bureaucracy, the church and the grandees. This was intended to take the place of a *valido* and prevent one emerging. But in the event the Junta was not incompatible with favouritism, for there was nothing to prevent it being subverted from within.

And subverted it was.[18] At first the queen worked exclusively with her official advisers. But she soon began to prefer more personal support. As she was weak of character and scrupulous of conscience she inevitably took counsel of her confessor, not only on faith and morals but also on matters of government. Her confessor was John Everard Nithard (or Neidhard), an Austrian Jesuit who had accompanied Mariana to Spain on her marriage to Philip IV. He was a good divine, pious and ascetic, but inexperienced in politics and unqualified for office. Mariana trusted him and now promoted him. From the confessional he moved to the Council of State, the office of Inquisitor General, membership of the Junta de Gobierno, and finally in effect prime minister. Like all previous *validos*, Nithard was first friend and confidant of his royal patron, then, with the latter's total support, head of government. Observers watched the process with incredulity. As an anonymous memorial said of the new favourite: 'From favour he passed to confidence, then to arrogance, and from all this to command of a universal empire'.[19]

Yet Nithard was unlike any previous *valido*. An essential difference lay in his personal qualifications. As these did not conform to the social structure of power in Spain they virtually ruled him out as a serious candidate for leadership. He was not a

---

[17] Valiente, *Los validos*, p. 21.

[18] For a contemporary account of Spanish politics, 1665–75, see 'Relación histórica de la menor edad de Carlos II y estado de la monarquía durante este período', *Colección de documentos inéditos para la historia de España*, lxvii, pp. 3–68.

[19] Quoted by Valiente, *Los validos*, p. 23.

member of the Castilian aristocracy. He was moreover extremely unpopular, being regarded as an obscure Jesuit of modest origins, and a foreigner to boot. As if this were not enough there were two political impediments to his progress, the will of the dead king and the opposition of Don Juan José de Austria. The will of Philip IV was difficult to ignore, for it possessed a kind of 'constitutional' appeal. The queen did not dare to flout it openly. She sought instead to preserve the appearance of constitutionalism by preserving the Junta de Gobierno, and then included Nithard in it at the first opportunity. It was not enough to appoint him to the Council of State, for there he was simply one of its members, with no more status or voting power than the others. In the course of 1666, therefore, the queen procured Spanish naturalization for Nithard; this she did by appeal to the votes of the cities represented in the cortes, though five of them, under the influence of a hostile aristocracy, abstained from voting. She then got the necessary papal permission for Nithard as a Jesuit to accept high ecclesiastical office, and on 22 September 1666 appointed him Inquisitor General.[20] He was now *ex officio* member of the Junta de Gobierno, and it was at this point that the settlement of Philip IV was subverted. The Junta itself, representing different factional interests, was not homogeneous enough to resist the placing of a *valido* within its ranks. And opinion at court was divided: some wanted to reinforce the power of the Junta, others wanted to give power to Don John of Austria.

This dark, handsome prince, the illegitimate son of Philip IV and the actress María Calderón, was deeply sensitive of his second-class status in the royal family. Touchy and conceited, he seemed to attract the extremes of admiration and aversion. His father was frankly outraged by his blatant political ambition and in his last years refused to have him in his presence. Don John attributed the estrangement to the malice of his stepmother, and his distrust of Mariana gradually hardened into hatred. He enjoyed some popularity of a demagogic kind. He had fought in every theatre of Spain's recent wars – Naples, Catalonia, the Low Countries and Portugal. Although his various commands had not been crowned with conspicuous success, he embodied what military virtues existed in Spain at the time; and his patriotic career, com-

[20] Maura, *Vida y reinado de Carlos II*, i, pp. 87–9.

bined with a reputation as a womanizer, gave him some place in popular estimation. At all events he contrasted vividly with the sombre Nithard. The political vacuum left by Philip IV sharpened Don John's political ambitions. Now aged thirty-seven, he resented his exclusion from the Junta de Gobierno, and refused to be fobbed off with peripheral assignments. In his own eyes at least, he was no longer a mere general.

In 1667 Louis XIV launched the War of Devolution to enforce his spurious claim to the Spanish Netherlands. Amidst the political uncertainties of the time, war at least was a familiar landmark, and the Spanish government went through the well-tried motions of raising money and troops for dispatch northwards. Don John was appointed commander-in-chief and governor of the Netherlands. He had previous experience of a similar appointment; and now, as an inducement to leave Spain, he was given unprecedented powers – authority to make war and peace, to confer titles of nobility, to dispose of 1 million pesos in cash and 780,000 escudos in letters-of-credit. He was assigned a personal emolument of 600,000 escudos; reinforcements were ready and a naval squadron was waiting at La Coruña. Anxious for a confrontation with Nithard, Don John declared all this insufficient and raised his demands impossibly high, including the right to sell commercial privileges to the English and to enter into financial arrangements with the Dutch. When these terms were inevitably rejected, he claimed that the government had 'closed all roads for employing my life in the service of the crown'; and he declined the appointment.[21] The Junta recognized the latent threat to their own position, and so did the administration. With unwonted vigour they abandoned the traditional procedure of posting opponents to lucrative offices in the periphery, and instead went on the offensive. Don John was replaced as governor of the Netherlands by the Constable of Castile and was ordered to be confined at Consuegra in New Castile, where he was prior of the military order of San Juan. And a number of his partisans, such as the Duke of Pastrana and the Count of Castrillo, were removed from office.

Yet the unity of the Junta and the councils which advised it was more apparent than real. Don John had his supporters within

[21] Ibid., i, pp. 111–12.

their ranks, nobles who referred to him as 'the son of our lamented monarch' and who thought he embodied the qualities of monarchy, at a time when there was no Infante and the shadowy figure of the boy king inspired little confidence for the future. Meanwhile the rule of Nithard, if such it was, earned little credit from its handling of the war. The Triple Alliance of England, the United Provinces and Sweden brought Louis XIV to the peace table in 1668, but Spain, after heavy defeats in the Netherlands, had no cards to play. In return for recovering Franche-Comté she had to give up a number of strategic points in the Low Countries. At home, whatever his qualities of integrity and dedication, Nithard was totally lacking in credibility and the kind of prestige which counted in Spain; he was not a noble, he had no faction or political following, and his position depended solely on the support of the queen, whose own power was not sovereign. Mariana might regard Nithard as prime minister, but the administration refused to view him as anything other than a *valido* whose influence on the queen was secret and sinister. In 1668 the Council of Castile addressed a *consulta* to the queen requesting her to choose 'a person through whose hands would pass matters of government'. The 'person' tacitly proposed was undoubtedly Don John. But the Council was not unanimous: four councillors expressed a minority view arguing that Philip IV knew what he was doing in establishing the existing form of government and purposely avoided giving total power to one man. This of course was an argument against Nithard as well as against Don John. And on this occasion the queen leaned towards the minority report and sought to maintain more of an equilibrium between the Junta and the *valido*.

The lowest common denominator among government opinion was opposition to Nithard. Was this enough to win power for Don John? He thought it was. In October 1668 he resumed his conspiratorial activities with more determination. The Junta got wind of these and ordered his arrest. But the military were reluctant to co-operate and a leak from the Junta forewarned Don John. He was able to escape to Aragon and Catalonia, denouncing 'the tyranny and execrable evil of Father Nithard', and rallying some support in the eastern kingdoms. In Barcelona he was respectfully received by the viceroy, the Duke of Osuna, and even more cordially by local officials. From there he conducted a campaign of political propaganda against Nithard and called for his dismissal. Outside Catalonia his demands were cautiously received by public authorities, who agreed with him about Nithard but did not like his crude pressure on the crown. Outside the ruling groups his campaign flourished and received much popular support.[22] Even at the top there was apparently a split in Junta solidarity and evidence of support for Don John within its ranks. The Council of Castile refused to initiate legal proceedings against him, and by the end of 1668 the other councils were moving away from the queen and her *valido*. The tendency within the administration was not so much to back Don John as to wait and see. What they saw was threat of violence. In January 1669 Don John moved out of Aragon towards Madrid and refused to disband his forces until the queen dismissed Nithard. The menace was sufficient – some 400 horse – to persuade the Junta de Gobierno and the Council of Castile to advise compliance; and the queen, reluctantly but with no alternative, dismissed the *valido* and sent him out of the country.[23]

The programme of Don John and his aristocratic faction, as expounded by an assiduous propaganda machine, was impeccably reformist – reorganization of the treasury and fiscal relief; just distribution of *mercedes*; improvement of the army, 'the right arm of monarchy'; good administration of justice; careful education of the king; replacement of Nithard's creatures; and a promise that never again would the royal confessor have control of government.[24] This sounded more like a charter for the aristocracy than a new deal for the common people. In any case it remained no more than a promise. Having removed Nithard, the only point on which there was unanimity, Don John did not reach the premiership. He professed not to want it: 'I have never had civil ambition or thought of seizing power; indeed I would expect to be regarded the most unworthy of creatures the day I was seen to seek or procure it.'[25] In fact he could not get it. Political

---

[22] Kamen, *Spain in the Later Seventeenth Century*, pp. 333–5.

[23] Ibid., i, 139–50; Valiente, *Los validos*, pp. 25–6, 61–2; Antonio Cánovas del Castillo, *Bosquejo histórico de la Casa de Austria* (Madrid, 1911), p. 337.

[24] Maura, *Vida y reinado de Carlos II*, i, pp. 153–4.

[25] Quoted ibid., i, p. 151.

opinion was not yet ready for a military *golpe de estado*, nor did Don John know how to implement one. After a few months of uncertainty he seemed to lose his nerve and took the easy way out, accepting appointment as vicar-general of Aragon and Catalonia and taking up residence in the archiepiscopal palace in Zaragoza. As for his supporters they did not form a compact opposition capable of replacing the senior ministers and the conciliar personnel, so these continued to serve their constitutional superiors. From mid-1669 to 1673 the queen mother governed under the advice of the Junta de Gobierno and with its collaboration. The will of Philip IV appeared to have been vindicated.

Yet this system of government was still as vulnerable as before. The semi-coup of 1669 had shaken the queen mother but not changed her. Don John had failed to follow up his negative success. And the aristocracy, while they could agitate, had not yet grouped themselves into an opposition capable of controlling government developments. So by 1673 political observers had identified a successor to Nithard. The new *valido*, Fernando Valenzuela, proved at least that in seventeenth-century Spain success was open to a certain type of talent. Valenzuela was an adventurer. Born in 1636, the son of an obscure army officer, he began life in the service of the Duke of Infantado. After an unsuccessful military career in Italy he returned to Madrid at the age of twenty-three, an elegant, uneducated young man, hanging around the fringes of the court, without office or prospects.[26] In 1661, through marriage to a maid of honour at the palace, he obtained an appointment as equerry to the queen, and acted unofficially as a kind of factotum in the night life of Philip IV. He survived in the new court in the service of the queen and Nithard, and was rewarded with the *hábito* of Santiago in 1671. Rumours began to circulate, chiefly from the pen of the Archbishop of Toledo, that Valenzuela's relations with the queen were sexual; this was certainly untrue and, in Mariana's case, out of character. What she needed was a government adviser to lean on. She was an ill-informed and bewildered woman, unable to cope alone or to confront an institution like the Junta de Gobierno without personal support; so she relied on Valenzuela for information about people and affairs and for reassuring advice. In 1673 he

[26] On Valenzuela see ibid., i, pp. 185–90, 194–201, 225–42, 244–52, 257–61.

was appointed chief equerry and superintendent of works at the palace; this gave him unrestricted access to the royal household. In 1674 he was promoted to the Council of Italy, though this was an income rather than an office. In fact Valenzuela, unlike Nithard, received no major political appointment at this stage. He was simply the closest confidant of the queen; while this made him influential, it did not enable him to handle matters of government directly. But he reinforced his position by self-advertising activity in the realm of patronage: he was associated with a number of court hand-outs, bread and bull fights for the populace of Madrid, *mercedes* and offices for the aristocracy, contracts for bankers and merchants.[27]

Influence over the queen and in matters of patronage were not the only factors in Valenzuela's meteoric rise. He was also helped by the poor performance of the Junta de Gobierno, an effete and supine body both collectively and, with the possible exception of the Archbishop of Toledo, individually.[28] The Count of Peñaranda was decrepit, the Count of Villaumbrosa indolent, Don Melchor de Navarra incompetent, the Constable semi-illiterate and as lacking in scruple as in ability, and Don Diego Sarmiento de Valladares was one of the worst presidents of Castile in recent memory, solely concerned with keeping himself in office. If the aristocracy were to be judged by these representatives they had already failed the country. In these circumstances it was not surprising that a clever, bold and self-confident creature like Valenzuela should have come to monopolize the counsels of the queen. And new developments soon gave him a more positive political role.

On 6 November 1675 Charles II attained his majority at the age of fourteen. His reign lasted another twenty-five years, during which he was always ailing, often close to death, and increasingly neurotic in his behaviour. Now that the king had come of age the Junta de Gobierno should have automatically terminated. This was probably one of the reasons why Don John had withdrawn from political activity, in the expectation of being

---

[27] For contemporary material on Valenzuela see 'Documentos referentes a D. Fernando de Valenzuela, primer marqués de Villasierra', *Collección de documentos inéditos para la historia de España*, lxvii, pp. 135–457.

[28] Maura, *Vida y reinado de Carlos II*, i, pp. 178–82.

called to power by constitutional means. He now returned to court, confident that his time had come. And again he was disappointed. As Charles II was obviously incapable of ruling alone, the existing team of ministers sought to share power by retaining the previous system, ignoring its obvious vulnerability to favouritism. On 7 November the Councils of State and Castile advised in *consulta* that the king should now sign decrees, but these should be supervised for two more years by the Junta de Gobierno under the presidency of the queen; Don John should be sent to Italy, and Valenzuela banished from court.[29] Don John left to re-think his tactics. As for Valenzuela he only went through the motions of complying. As a gesture he was nominally appointed ambassador to Venice; but the queen was only waiting for the dust to settle. Within a few months, in April 1676, he returned to court and, as Charles was dominated by his mother, soon became *valido* of the king as well as of the queen. Under their joint patronage he was loaded with appointments. He acquired offices such as master of the horse, governor and general of the coast of Andalucía, the title of Marquis of Villasierra, and in particular the two things he most sought, elevation to the *grandeza* and appointment as *primer ministro*, with authorization to lodge in the royal palace. If Valenzuela was not the first *valido* to be described as prime minister, he was the first to receive specific appointment as such. As a consequence of this a decree was issued in September 1676 dissolving the Junta de Gobierno; Valenzuela was given the right to attend all sessions of councils; and the presidents of councils were ordered to present themselves before him for regular conference on matters of government. Valenzuela was now at the height of his power, prime minister as well as *valido*.[30]

In a sense this was constitutional development. The prime minister had at last acquired a single public title, with unequivocal superiority over the presidents of councils and other ministers. But it was a frustrated development. In the first place, Valenzuela did not do much actual governing: he was more interested in patronage than policy. Secondly, his position was politically

[29] Ibid., i, pp. 211–26.
[30] Ibid., i, pp. 235–42; Valiente, *Los validos*, pp. 28–30, 103–5; Cánovas, *Casa de Austria*, p. 347.

untenable. The higher nobility were outraged, regarding this as the last straw. As their existing representatives in the government were manifestly incapable of controlling events, the aristocracy began to plan concerted action outside the government.

The Revolt of the Grandees

Most of the royal ministers complied with the decree ordering them to confer with Valenzuela; but they did so reluctantly, and two of them, the Duke of Osuna and the Count of Peñaranda, refused to conform and openly joined the faction of malcontents. These were the higher nobility of Castile, offended in their social values by the dominance of the upstart Valenzuela; to them it was intolerable that their interests should be at the disposal of a vulgar outsider. Their candidate for office was Don John, a man of royal blood, acceptable on class grounds and popular at large. And Don John became their spokesman. The aristocracy now met together, grouped themselves into a solid opposition, and declared themselves.

On 15 December 1676 they issued a manifesto signed by twenty-four leading nobles, among them Don John, the Dukes of Alba, Osuna, Medina Sidonia, Arcos, Gandia, the Duchess of Infantado, and the Counts of Benavente and Monterrey. This *documento de la grandeza* attributed the country's disorder and discontent to 'the evil influence of the queen mother ... and particularly the abominable promotion of don Fernando Valenzuela'.[31] It demanded that the king 'remove the queen mother totally and permanently from his presence, imprison Don Fernando Valenzuela, and establish permanently at his side the Lord Don John of Austria.' The signatories undertook upon their 'honour, faith, and word as *caballeros*' to employ all effective means to secure these objectives 'without any reserve whatso-ever', and to serve with their 'persons, houses, estates, rents and retainers'. The grandees were not completely unanimous. One of their number, Pedro de Aragon, refused to sign because he had been promised high office; others, like the Duke of Medinaceli

---

[31] For a summary of the text see Maura, *Vida y reinado de Carlos II*, i, pp. 244–5.

and the Count of Oropesa, held aloof because they did not like the political implications of the document. And in the event the persons, estates and retainers of the grandees were not sufficient, or not sufficiently mobilized, to make a civil coup d'etat. It also needed the intervention of the army, the conspiratorial activity of Don John and the support of the regions.

Don John had a base of power in Aragon, a region which he had cultivated for some time, posing as the defender of its *fueros* and the representative of its interests. Aragon was behind him and ready to move. He also had much support in Catalonia. There he was remembered as the general who had helped to drive out the French, the negotiator of favourable terms after the Catalan revolution, the viceory who had mediated between Catalonia and Madrid. Following his subsequent visit in 1668 Don John had patronized the principality and built up a following. Catalans who believed in economic growth and saw their hopes frustrated by Madrid looked upon Don John as a champion who would win further victories for their *fueros* and open new channels for their trade.[32] Although he did not have a specifically regional support elsewhere in Spain, he had the aristocracy behind him. From Andalucía and the two Castiles the government received news that the grandees were arming their vassals and preparing to join Don John. Finally, in addition to regional and aristocratic support, Don John had the sympathy of two important institutions. The military regarded him as one of their own, a patron who would look after their careers; and his friends among the senior officers of the royal army stationed in Catalonia placed 600 cavalry at his disposal. The church, too, was well disposed, seeing him as a saviour who would restore traditional Spanish virtues to public life after the corruption of recent decades.

At this point there was a chance of civil war, for Valenzuela, unlike Nithard, was not responsible to a Junta de Gobierno, and he could have decreed the use of force to defend his regime. But he lacked the nerve. He did his best to secure his wealth and fled to the Escorial for asylum. Now isolated among aristocratic advisers, Charles wrote to Don John inviting him to 'come without delay to assist me in this crisis'. Don John did not need

[32] Ferran Soldevilla, *Història de Catalunya* (3 vols, Barcelona, 1935), ii, pp. 345–50.

inviting. He was inciting the country to violence, giving heated instructions to his partisans:

> Make known to people of every sort that what the grandees and other subjects have recently effected at court has been done with the knowledge, influence and approval of the Lord Don John; and that His Highness is now moving to take issue with any Spaniard, good or bad, who, failing God, king and country, tries to undo it. Incite all honourable and faithful men to oppose these people, and to employ themselves only in their destruction.[33]

On 11 January 1677 Don John crossed from Aragon into Castile at the head of an army 15,000 strong, with most of the Aragonese aristocracy, and from Castile eighteen grandees and a flock of other nobility. The few ministers and nobles still around Charles II began to edge away; the Madrid garrison was disbanded; and Don John and the grandees entered the capital on 23 January virtually unopposed. They immediately secured the dismissal and banishment of Valenzuela, forced him out of his monastic asylum, and sent him as a prisoner to Consuegra. They were not satisfied until the king had stripped him of all his property and titles, including of course that of grandee, and exiled him to the Philippines. There he served a prison sentence of ten years. And he never saw Spain again. Waiting in Mexico for permission to return, he died from a horse-kick in January 1692. The rebels completed their work by insisting on the banishment of the queen mother to Toledo and the promotion to power of Don John.[34]

As an exercise in removing a prime minister this was one of the most peremptory in Spanish history. In its use of violence and terrorism the revolt of Don John and the nobility was a genuine *golpe de estado*. It was the first time a modern Spanish king had a government imposed upon him.[35] For this reason Don John is not to be classified as a *valido*, or even a prime minister. He did not advise the king, he coerced him. He was able to do this because he now had what he lacked in 1669 and 1675, the backing of almost all the aristocracy. No doubt Don John was cheered by

[33] Maura, *Vida y reinado de Carlos II*, i, p. 254.
[34] Ibid., i, pp. 246–62.
[35] Maravall, *Teoría española del estado en el siglo XVII*, pp. 305–6, with some exaggeration, describes Don John as a forerunner of the modern dictator.

the mob and carried along by popular support. But the popular sectors did not form a power base. What counted was the support of nobles who could provide soldiers for his *golpe* and defend it afterwards. On this occasion the grandees of Spain shed their political diffidence, if not their ineptitude, and acted together for the first time. The event which moved them was the formal promotion of Valenzuela to the premiership. Regarding Spain as an extension of their own estates, they were provoked in their honour, exclusivism and elitism when the king took his chief minister not from the natural ruling class but from the ranks of commoners or poor *hidalgos*. The savage sentence on Valenzuela was meant to be a warning against any further subversion of the social structure. The grandees did not revolt in order to re-establish personal monarchy, or to revitalize conciliar government, or to erect any institutional barrier against the absolute power of a prime minister. On the contrary, they sought to impose the personal rule of Don John, whom they regarded as their representative, a man who could be trusted to defend their group interest. This was not a political programme. As for Don John, he was seeking personal power, the power which had escaped him on two previous occasions.

The new leader was hailed as a political messiah.[36] In fact he was a *caudillo*, a strong man, a distributor of patronage, a ruler who improvised as he went along, living from day to day.[37] He rewarded the 'ins' and punished the 'outs'. Friends and creatures of Valenzuela were cruelly persecuted; and any leading noble who had not signed the grandees' manifesto was suspect. Other people were promoted, not on their merits, but on their record as rebels. The Duke of Alba, for example, in spite of his notorious incompetence, was appointed president of the Council of Italy. To satisfy his Aragonese supporters Don John insisted that the king visit Zaragoza. There the cortes voted a minimal grant – 56,000 libras a year for eight years to support 1,500 troops – in return for cancellation of all previous debts to the crown and a

---

[36] For a contemporary account of events in 1677–8 see 'Diario de Noticias de 1677 a 1678', *Colección de documentos inéditos para la historia de España*, lxvii, pp. 69–133; see also Kamen, *Spain in the Later Seventeenth Century*, pp. 340–1.
[37] Maura, *Vida y reinado de Carlos II*, i, pp. 271–315, regards Don John as a *cacique*, or political boss.

promise not to request any further subsidy for the next twenty years. Indeed the price of Don John's success was aristocratic immunity. From the grandees of Castile he received little financial support. When in 1678 he requested a *donativo*, one after another of the higher aristocracy, their rents and estates now removed from service, declined to contribute. As usual, it was the bankers, merchants and *asentistas* who had to dip into their pockets, and the common taxpayers who had to increase their quota.

As fast as money was raised it was devoured in war. Louis XIV was perhaps Don John's worst enemy, for it was he who caused Spain's rising defence costs. After four years of precarious peace France had invaded the Low Countries again in 1672. In the subsequent war Spain and her allies – the United Provinces and the Empire – suffered one crippling defeat after another. Spanish armies were hard pressed in the Low Countries, Catalonia and Sicily, where local insurrection gave France an opportunity to intervene. At the Peace of Nymegen (August–September 1678) Spain had no credit, and was forced to cede Franche-Comté (hardly worth fighting for) and further strategic territory in the Netherlands. Loss of distant provinces was less important than the strain on the Spanish economy. Now more than ever the government needed to economize. From 1677 Castile began to endure its most profound economic crisis of the seventeenth century, perhaps in its entire history.[38] In this area of government Don John could provide no leadership. As the economic crisis worsened and the government looked on helplessly, there was growing disillusionment. A satirical paper circulating in Madrid asked: 'Are there less taxes? Less *donativos*? Has the price of food come down? Have the fleets been repaired? Have we lost less in war? Are the prospects better that the people will be relieved, the kingdom saved and our condition improved?' Amidst mounting discontent Don John began to lose two specific bases of support, the army and the church. After a disastrous war and an ignominious peace, the military were now unoccupied and demoralized, and Don John had no panacea for their complaints. Meanwhile the hierarchy were having second thoughts about the messianic mission they had attributed to the new leader; their

[38] See below, pp. 392–402.

doubts were reinforced when they discovered that the clergy had less tax immunity than the aristocracy and were made to pay a higher *subsidio* as well as a *donativo*.

Don John reacted to criticism in two ways. He reshuffled his ministers, placing hard-core supporters, most of them second-rate, in presidencies, councils and viceroyalties. And he silenced opposition by the classical methods of the *caudillo*, driving his enemies into prison or exile. The crown itself was his prisoner. He had the king's every movement watched, every public appearance and audience supervised, every letter opened. But this was no substitute for policy. With his rule disintegrating, his government empty of ideas and resentment growing, Don John was only saved from political disaster by his death on 17 September 1679.

Return to Government

While the fall of Valenzuela brought to an end the seventeenth-century series of *validos*, the death of Don John terminated Spain's brief experiment with *caudillismo*. Between 1680 and 1691 Spanish government was rebuilt on sounder foundations and, in spite of the last leaderless years of Habsburg rule, left a legacy of improved administration. Charles II himself contributed nothing to this development. He occasionally awoke to political affairs during interludes of better health, but in general his physical and mental abnormality forced him to abandon government to other men. These were prime ministers, not *validos*, for paradoxically to abdicate responsibility to a *valido* a king needed a modicum of determination in order to sustain his favourite against opposition. The new prime ministers reached power not as the personal choice of the king but through intense political intrigue. The successful candidates were a compromise between the needs of government and the demands of the aristocracy. They therefore combined some qualities of statesmanship, the minimum requirement of a country in prostration, and social qualifications, the test of their acceptability to the nobles. They were not slaves of their class, but they had to work within the existing social structure and they inevitably found this an obstacle to reform. Moreover a new dimension had been added to politics. In 1679 Charles II married Marie Louise of Orléans, niece of Louis XIV. The marriage had political implications. Having defeated Spain in war, the French now hoped to dominate her in peace and diplomacy; while Spanish opinion preferred a French to an Austrian marriage on the ground that one Austrian in the royal family – the queen mother – was enough. But this, and Charles's subsequent marriage to Mariana of Neuburg, brought strong-willed queens and their diplomatic backers into Spanish politics and intensified the struggle for control of the crown.

After the death of Don John it took some time to reconcile the various interests and to find a prime minister acceptable to the aristocracy, the administration and the two queens (Charles's mother and wife). Eventually, on 21 February 1680, the king appointed the Duke of Medinaceli, explaining 'I now recognize that the form of government appropriate to my monarchy and the exigencies of the moment both call for a prime minister.'[39] Medinaceli, one of the wealthiest of the grandees, was an unassuming and uninspiring man with administrative experience as president of the Council of the Indies.[40] He was not exclusively tied to noble interests – he had not signed the manifesto of the grandees in 1676 – and he did not claim to be a saviour of the nation. He saw his duty more simply – to relieve the king of all responsibility of government, to use the existing administration to provide law, order and a sense of direction, and in particular to see the country through the great economic crisis of the years after 1677. He maintained the hard deflationary policy already devised by the financial administration.[41] But he also thought beyond economic restraint, necessary though it was. In an attempt to get the economy moving again he brought in a new president of the Council of Finance, Carlos de Herrera, former councillor of the Indies and of Castile, governor of Seville, and a man familiar with economic problems and merchant interests.[42] Medinaceli showed an interest in commercial-colonial reform untypical of the higher aristocracy and of his predecessors. He further strengthened his administration by recruiting José de Veitia Linaje, former treasurer of the *Casa de la Contratación*, secretary of the

[39] On the Medinaceli administration see Maura, *Vida y reinado de Carlos II*, i, pp. 352–424.
[40] E. Shäfer, *El Consejo real y supremo de las Indias*, i, p. 277.
[41] See below, pp. 396–8.
[42] Shäfer, *El Consejo real y supremo de las Indias*, i, p. 363.

Council of the Indies, and author of a celebrated treatise on American trade. Appointed *Secretario del Despacho Universal* in April 1682, Veitia Linaje worked as a kind of special consultant to the prime minister on plans to revive colonial trade and its yield. There was a vigorous attack on the more flagrant abuses of foreign commercial penetration at Seville–Cadiz, and greater attention was paid to imperial defence.[43] For the first time in decades the government itself, as distinct from the bureaucracy, showed an awareness of the problems and an anxiety to tackle them. It would not be easy to reverse the trend towards foreign domination of Seville and Cadiz, but in spite of wars, piracy and ceaseless contraband, the Indies trade survived and in the last decades of the century yielded among the highest returns in the whole of the colonial period, many of them to foreigners but some also to Spain.[44]

The fabric of Spanish life was too exhausted to be capable of sudden rejuvenation. The most that the Medinaceli administration could do was to provide political stability, recruit new talent, and improve the standard of government. It also had the courage to stand by its severe deflationary policy, and it refused to take the easy way out by manipulating the monetary system as previous administrations had done. This meant that life continued to be hard for the mass of the people, and even the aristocracy felt the pinch. On the basis of reports of acute distress in the peninsula, Louis XIV struck once again, invading the Low Countries and Catalonia. This was a small war, it is true, but it imposed painful defence costs and yet another punishing peace treaty (Ratisbon, August 1684), which deprived Spain of Luxemburg.

By 1684 Medinaceli was living on promise rather than performance and he had exhausted his credit with his sponsors. He agreed therefore to share the burden with someone else. In June 1684 the Count of Oropesa, a member of the Council of State since 1680, was appointed president of the Council of Castile. Oropesa was of sufficient stature to turn his appointment into virtual co-government, and with the capricious support of the two queens and of disappointed aristocrats he gradually eased out Medinaceli. The latter resigned in April 1685. Charles II neither chose his

---

[43] Girard, *Le commerce français à Séville et Cadix*, pp. 159–70.
[44] See above, pp. 278–86.

prime ministers nor dismissed them: he had them imposed upon him by a kind of aristocratic agreement; and he accepted the arranged succession of Oropesa without demur.

The author of a paper written some years later to discredit Oropesa described him as follows:

> He possesses considerable talent, sound judgement and wide knowledge of affairs acquired from study. He applies himself to business, has good understanding and a clear exposition. He is easy in his relationships and moderate in his conduct. All this may be enough for a good minister; but it is not enough for a good prime minister.[45]

Yet Oropesa was better qualified for the office than any other candidate. Between the needs of government and the demands of faction his appointment seemed to tip the balance towards the former. He was a man of ideas, capable and energetic, whose only apparent disadvantage was the possession of a notoriously pushing wife. Oropesa was also favoured with a first-rate colleague in the executive. Veitia Linaje had resigned along with Medinaceli and he was succeeded in the *Secretaría del Despacho* by Manuel Francisco de Lira, former diplomat, secretary for Italian affairs in the Council of State, an able if intolerant man.

Oropesa stood for a policy of fiscal, administrative and ecclesiastical reform, and was ready to boost the economy by a moderate dose of reflation.[46] Impressed by the French style of government, and suspecting the efficiency of the Council of Finance, he assigned fiscal affairs to a new office, the *Superintendencia de Hacienda*. There were few outstanding candidates for the appointment, and imitation of French methods could not in itself revive Spain's finances and economy. But the experiment is chiefly interesting as an early attempt to construct a ministry outside the conciliar system; as such it anticipated the Bourbon reforms of the eighteenth century. The Spanish Colbert was the Marquis of los Vélez, a benevolent and conscientious man though

[45] Maura, *Vida y reinado de Carlos II*, i, p. 419.
[46] For a fuller account of this policy see below, pp. 400–2. On the events of 1685–8 see the contemporary comments in 'Cartas del duque de Montalto a D. Pedro Ronquillo, embajador en Inglaterra (1685–1688)', *Colección de documentos inéditos para la historia de España*, lxxxix, pp. 299–475.

not greatly endowed with intelligence. According to current scur-
rility he was dissatisfied with his previous appointment as master
of the queen's horse because excessive obesity prevented him
from actually mounting a horse. As superintendent of finance he
was energetic enough and soon produced an extensive memorandum as a working paper for the preparation of a new tax
structure.[47] Oropesa and los Vélez thus gave a new stimulus to
fiscal reform, and this was designed not only to reduce the chronic budget deficit but also to introduce an element of social
justice into taxation. If their plans did not meet the success they
deserved this was due to the opposition of vested interests, the
aristocracy, the church and office-holders. But a number of minor
measures were implemented, and monetary readjustment brought
some relief to the economy. Like many rulers who shelve issues,
Oropesa was forced to divert his fiscal ideas into safer channels
by the appointment of royal commissions. He created a *junta de
medios* with membership drawn from the various councils and
presided over by los Vélez to consider reform proposals; and to
give greater weight to these proposals he appointed a *junta de
estado*.

Frustrated on the financial front, Oropesa turned his attention
to reform of the bureaucracy and the church.[48] Both institutions
suffered from excessive recruitment. Oropesa campaigned against
the number of false vocations in the church; he circulated the
bishops requesting a temporary suspension of ordinations, and he
sought to restrict the foundation of new religious houses. Under
his initiative a special junta investigated the power of the Inquisition. The committee criticized the inflated jurisdiction, privilege
and immunity of the tribunal; it recommended that there should
be no excommunication for temporal reasons, that there should
be right of appeal before secular courts against unjust sentences,
that the tribunal's *fueros* should be more closely defined and that
its fiscal frauds should be investigated. It was easier to make these
proposals than to implement them, but Oropesa kept up
the pressure and achieved something, if only in ventilating the
problem.

To threaten the aristocracy with taxation, the church with

---

[47] Maura, *Vida y reinado de Carlos II*, i, pp. 446–7.
[48] On administrative reform see below, pp. 402–11, 413–16.

reform and the bureaucracy with reduction, was to alienate the most powerful sectors of Spanish society. The Oropesa administration was not a failure; it made a contribution to Spain's slow recovery from prolonged depression, as will be seen. But many of its proposals were precocious and out of joint with the time and the place. They earned for Oropesa great unpopularity, which meant accusations of bad government by the interested parties opposed to his reforms. His opponents secured an ally in the new queen. After the death of Maria Luisa in February 1689 Charles II married Mariana of Neuburg, daughter of the Elector Palatine and sister of the Emperor Leopold. She was a calculating woman who easily dominated her husband and became the centre of much political intrigue. She also disliked prime ministers. But the Austrian marriage had further repercussions for Oropesa. It provoked Louis XIV to declare war on Spain yet again. As usual there were heavy defence costs with nothing to show for them, only predictable defeats in the Low Countries and Italy and the inevitable invasion of Catalonia. The prime minister was now vulnerable on domestic and foreign policy alike. Under pressure from the queen and a number of discontented grandees, Charles was persuaded, much against his will, to demand Oropesa's resignation; this he did on 25 June 1691.[49]

After the fall of Oropesa the government drifted without a prime minister. Queen Mariana, appropriating the sovereignty belonging to her husband, filled the Council of State with her own clients. Into the *Secretaría del Despacho* she put a particularly servile and uncultivated creature, Juan de Angulo, nicknamed *el Mulo*; and he was succeeded by another client of the queen, though a more presentable one, Alonso Carnero. In addition, a number of greedy German advisers were provided for in one way or another. But the Castilian aristocracy also had to be placated. There were so many aspirants to high office and the premiership that power was artificially divided among a number of competing candidates. On the advice of the Duke of Montalto Charles was constrained to issue a decree in 1693, the so-called *planta de gobierno*, constituting a kind of senior junta of ministers and dividing the spoils among them. The successful candidates re-

---

[49] Lira had already resigned from the Secretaría del Despacho; see Maura, *Vida y reinado de Carlos II*, i, pp. 542–5.

ceived the titles of lieutenant general and governor and were assigned different regions in which to deploy their talents. The Constable was appointed lieutenant general and governor of Old Castile; Andalucía and the Canaries went to the admiral, the Count of Melgar; Aragon and Catalonia to the Count of Monterrey; and New Castile to Montalto himself.[50] This arrangement was followed by further manoeuvrings which reduced the four supremos to a triumvirate. Montalvo took the government of the Aragonese kingdoms and Navarre, with the presidency of the Council of the Indies; Galicia, Asturias and the two Castiles went to the Constable, a singularly stupid and over-bearing man; and Andalucía and the Canaries to the admiral. And the triumvirate was finally reduced to two, Montalto and the admiral. These proceeded to squabble over the plunder, seconded by their respective factions, and the ridiculous territorial divisions gradually disappeared. In 1696 the queen demoted Montalto and dismissed Carnero. By now Spain was virtually without government, for the sole survivor from the *planta de gobierno*, the admiral, dared not make a move without the queen's approval. And she was interested in other things than the internal government of Spain.

One of the great obstacles to Spain's recovery in the second half of the seventeenth century was French imperialism. Any neighbour of France could expect to suffer from aggression, but Spain was particularly vulnerable because of the various fronts she presented. Territorially she lost to Louis XIV little of real importance, though he kept whittling away her possessions in the Rhineland and the Netherlands, and repeatedly struck her in northern Italy and Catalonia. The real cost to Spain was in men and money. Although she was still capable of sending subsidies to her overseas armies, these had to be paid in silver, which was in short supply in Spain where the currency was almost exclusively vellon. As for the peninsula itself, Spain's only defences were the patriotism of her subjects and their notorious aversion to foreign invasion or domination. The aristocracy no longer fulfilled a military role and material defences were almost non-existent. When a decree for general conscription was issued in July 1691 it was stated that the country had 'insufficient ships and troops for its defence . . . and in most towns one can hardly find a musket,

[50] Ibid., ii, pp. 45–6; Cánovas, *Casa de Austria*, pp. 383–4.

arquebus or pike'.[51] So Spain was in no position to resist Louis XIV's ultimate aggression, the War of the League of Augsburg, which brought further defeats in Milan, the Netherlands and Catalonia. Yet she emerged relatively unscathed: by the Peace of Ryswick (September 1697) Louis XIV returned all the gains he had made since the Peace of Nymegen. Spain's escape owed little to her own efforts. It was a consequence of two other factors. The combined pressure of the two great maritime powers, England and Holland, was at last turning the balance against France. And Louis XIV now had his eye on a greater prize, to be secured by diplomacy rather than war, namely the whole of the Spanish monarchy, or at very least a substantial part of it.[52]

By 1696–7 it was clear that Charles II had only a few years to live and would remain childless. An heir had to be found for Spain and her empire. The succession problem now obsessed the political life of the country and held government in complete suspense. For the real test of monarchy is the succession, and over this there was profound uncertainty. The two serious claimants were France and Austria, the former through Louis XIV's marriage to the Spanish Infanta, María Teresa, the latter through the emperor's marriage to Margarita Teresa. French and Austrian diplomatic pressure in Madrid, and the factions engendered in support of the rival causes, reduced the administration to impotence. Charles II suffered mental anguish in these years and in his desperate search for enlightenment had recourse even to exorcism. After intense lobbying, conflicting advice and constant vacillation, he finally made his will (2 October 1700) and left the Spanish dominions undivided to the French candidate, Philip, Duke of Anjou, grandson of Louis XIV. This decisions, the one moment of grandeur in his whole life, was influenced chiefly by the universal desire among Spaniards to keep their monarchy and empire intact under a strong ruler who would reside in Spain.

Charles II, browbeaten for so long by the women of his family, was most influenced in his last days by Cardinal Portocarrero, Archbishop of Toledo. On 29 October 1700 he signed a decree,

---

[51] Quoted by Domínguez Ortiz, *La sociedad española en el siglo XVIII*, p. 368 n. 4.

[52] See M. A. Thomson, 'Louis XIV and the Origins of the War of the Spanish Succession', *Transactions of the Royal Historical Society*, fifth series, iv (1954), pp. 111–34.

doubtless prepared by his mentor, ordering that in the event of his utter incapacity, the cardinal should govern with complete power in his name.[53] But Portocarrero only enjoyed his power for three days. On 1 November Charles died, and on the following day, in expectation of the arrival of the new king, a Junta de Gobierno was established.

[53] Valiente, *Los validos*, pp. 35, 191–2.

10

The End of Habsburg Spain

Promise and Prejudice in Eastern Spain

In the last decades of Habsburg rule Spain resembled a corpse, picked at by noble parasites and foreign marauders. This, it would seem, was the horrifying nemesis of a society which turned its face agains the world and the times in which it lived. Retribution was harsh and perhaps inevitable. Yet the conventional picture of Spain's final prostration has been overdrawn, or at least has lacked a sense of contrast and of movement. From the 1680s, amidst the ruins of government and economy, the country began to stir from its inertia and renew its life. Reform was in the air. Its authors were few in number, uncertain of themselves and frustrated by their fellows. But they cleared away some of the debris of the past and set up signposts for the future. This movement of recovery could be observed obscurely in Castile, more clearly perhaps in the periphery.

Eastern Spain moved independently of Castile. The second half of the seventeenth century was an Indian summer of provincial autonomy. After the costly failure to impose constitutional and fiscal uniformity, the central government left the regions severely alone. Don John appealed to Aragon and Catalonia – the first Spanish politician to do so – not to procure the vindication of their rights but to seek the support of rights already vindicated. To leave the regions alone was to leave them in the hands of their governing classes. In Aragon this perpetuated stagnation, and the province became an economic colony of France. In Catalonia it led to the first stage of economic advance. And in Valencia it led to peasant revolt.

In the last decades of the seventeenth century Catalonia began to emerge from its prolonged stupor.[1] It was assisted by two institutional conditions. Monetary autonomy saved it from the succession of state-imposed inflation and deflation experienced by Castile. In Catalonia monetary policy was determined by commercial not fiscal considerations. After 1659 the province enjoyed relative monetary stability; and it escaped the worst effects of the brutal deflation imposed on Castile in 1680. In the period 1688–99, however, Catalonia had enough inflation, without a corresponding wage rise, to ensure rapid accumulation of profits and conditions for further investment.[2] Another stimulus was provided by the freedom of commerce imposed in the Treaty of the Pyrenees (1659). While the neighbouring kingdom of Aragon was smothered by protection, which simply favoured low-quality goods and contraband, the Catalans enjoyed few tariff advantages and were forced to improve their own performance. Under the challenge of freer trade their textile industry underwent some renewal and expansion, shedding archaic privileges and equipping itself to compete more vigorously with French, English and Dutch goods.[3]

After a period of stagnation in 1664–74, maritime trade became more active from the late 1670s. On the evidence of *periatge* (guild merchant duty), it moved strongly ahead about 1680, and by the end of the century had expanded well beyond its level at the beginning.[4] In the late 1690s traffic in the port of Barcelona was almost double that in 1600. Barcelona now housed large-scale business firms, and these were turning from the narrow, preempted Mediterranean market towards the outer world, towards Cadiz and Lisbon, buying colonial goods – sugar, cacao and tobacco – and seeking to export Catalan products to the colonial markets.[5] The Catalan merchant marine was reconstructed and

---

[1] J. Vicens Vives, *Manual de Historia económica de España*, con la colaboración de J. Nadal Oller (Barcelona, 1959), pp. 422–3.

[2] Vilar, *La Catalogne dans l'Espagne Moderne*, i, pp. 639–41, 646.

[3] José Fontana Lázaro, 'Sobre el comercio exterior de Barcelona en la segunda mitad del siglo XVII. Notas para una interpretación de la coyuntura catalana', *Estudios de Historia Moderna*, v (1955 [1957]), pp. 197–219.

[4] This duty rose from 4,000 pounds a year in 1664–5, to 5,997 in 1680–1, to 9,785 in 1698–9; Smith, *The Spanish Guild Merchant*, p. 140.

[5] Vilar, *La Catalogne dans l'Espagne Moderne*, i, pp. 648–9.

armed to deal with corsairs. While Barcelona was the centre of commercial activity, actual production developed elsewhere. Artisan conditions in the capital itself were still depressed in the second half of the seventeenth century, particularly in the silk and textile industries. The provinces on the other hand were forging ahead. Wine and brandy production experienced a minor boom, being exported to all parts of Spain, particularly Andalucía, where it was beginning to break into the Indies trade. Brandy was also sold to the English and the Dutch, and this further outlet was sufficient to cause expansion of vineyards, while some of the returns went into other local industries. Textile production in the provinces was doing much better than in Barcelona, and showing signs of assimilating technical improvement from France. And the minor ports of the principality were active in small-scale shipbuilding. This economic decentralization was due not only to lower taxes in the provinces but also to rural population growth, which made the interior a good source of supply for labour. Whatever the reason, the inflation of agricultural prices was a sign of accumulation of rural profits.[6] In this period the bandits disappeared and the farmers got to work.

The atmosphere was heady enough to produce a number of ambitious projects for promoting foreign trade. These were a common enough phenomenon in the seventeenth century, but the Catalan proposals, unlike those of earlier Castilian *arbitristas*, were a sign of optimism and incipient revival rather than a reaction to depression. The ideas came, about 1680, from individuals and consortiums who were candidates for the lease of the Barcelona municipal taxes and were capable of guaranteeing on their own security capital amounting to between 140,000 and 170,000 Catalan pounds. The type of organization canvassed was the chartered company, as can be seen in the proposals of Narciso Feliu de la Peña, lawyer, historian, economist and businessman.[7] Feliu sought the progress of Catalan manufactures, if necessary by protection, 'so that the trade of Catalonia may rise again, like a phoenix from its ashes'.[8] He sought to beat the foreigners by

[6] Ibid., i, pp. 650–3.
[7] Ibid., i, pp. 653–67; Roland Dennis Hussey, *The Caracas Company* 1728–1784. *A Study in the History of Spanish Monopolistic Trade* (Cambridge, Mass., 1934), pp. 23–4.
[8] Quoted by Kamen, *Spain in the Later Seventeenth Century*, p. 82.

copying them, importing their workers, machinery, techniques. In 1681 Feliu outlined a plan for a trading company on the model of those existing in Holland, France and England. It would be formed in Barcelona with capital subscribed by fifty shareholders; it would make loans to captains of ships, merchants and manufacturers, and would finance the construction of shipping; and it would send two ships a year to America, exporting fruits, clothing, and manufactures of iron, copper and glass. Feliu de la Peña's call for a reorientation of Catalan trade away from the traditional Mediterranean market towards America reflected Catalonia's growing involvement in colonial trade. But this did not signify urban industrial growth. Barcelona was important: there an identifiable elite of ex-rural nobles joined the civic oligarchy in a unified ruling class.[9] But the recovery of the Catalan economy rested less upon Barcelona, whose manufacturing capacity was still rigidly controlled by the guild regime, than on the initiatives of the more flexible societies and economies of the countryside and the smaller coastal towns. Catalonia's economic expansion from the late seventeenth century was essentially a product of the rural environment, not the capital.

The economic recovery of Catalonia in this period can be exaggerated. Projects like those of Feliu probably overestimated the prospects of the principality. Yet almost immediately after the change of regime in Madrid in 1700 the Catalans again tried to secure official admission to the Indies trade; and when they failed they soon began to force their way in regardless of the law. Their ability to engage in overseas trade did not develop overnight. It was the result of lengthy, if confused, preparation in the previous decades when Catalonia disengaged itself from the general depression lying over the peninsula. And as Catalonia began to emerge from its former myopia so it became less inhibited in its attitude towards the rest of Spain. Between 1653 and 1697 Barcelona contributed the considerable sum of 6,377,591 pounds to the crown, financial co-operation of a kind which Olivares had not managed to secure. In 1674 the Catalans formally objected to being classified as foreigners in Cadiz – and to their goods being taxed as such on landing. While not forgoing any of their regional

[9] James S. Amelang, *Honoured Citizens of Barcelona: Patrician Culture and Class Relations 1490–1714* (Princeton, NJ, 1986), pp. 85–101.

prerogatives, they argued that Catalans were subjects of the crown and were 'Spaniards, Catalonia being indubitably of Spain.'[10] The crown acknowledged the justice of the complaint and by decree of 30 November 1674 removed the Catalans from the jurisdiction of the consul for foreigners.

Valencia, like Catalonia, enjoyed undisturbed possession of its *fueros* in the reign of Charles II. The crown exercised a limited power through its viceroy and its jurisdiction over a number of towns in the province. But the viceroy had to operate within the framework of the *fueros*. The city of Valencia was administered by the Council of Hundred, its membership drawn from the various social groups, the majority representation, though not the greatest influence, being held by members of the guilds. And the *Diputación*, or standing committee of the cortes consisting of two nobles, two clerics and two commoners, supervised observance of the *fueros* and the administration of taxes. Even in towns under royal jurisdiction the king's power was confined virtually to taxation, the yield of which was consumed locally. Most towns, and their inhabitants, were in noble or ecclesiastical jurisdiction, and here the king's writ hardly ran. Some of these nobles held titles of Castile, such as the Duke of Medinaceli and the Duke of Infantado; others, like the Duke of Gandia, were great territorial magnates, virtual sovereigns on their own estates.

The most significant event in Valencia's modern history was the expulsion of the moriscos, an event which damaged an already stagnant agriculture, and aggravated the problems of the province for many decades after 1609.[11] The consequences were felt outside the rural economy. For the numerous *censos* (mortgage loans) on property farmed by moriscos were supplied from capital owned by urban groups and ecclesiastical institutions. These investments were now at great risk. The crown sought to compensate landowners for loss of their labour force by, among other things, reducing the interest rate on *censos*; but in any case the

---

[10] Carrera Pujal, *Historia política y económica de Cataluña*, i, pp. 442–3; ii, p. 312.

[11] Juan Reglá, 'La expulsión de los moriscos y sus consecuencias en la economía valenciana', *Hispania*, xxiii (1963), pp. 200–18; Eduardo Asensio Salvadó, 'El arbitrista Jerónimo Ibáñez de Salt y su programa de recuperación de la economía valenciana en 1638', *Estudios de Historia Moderna*, iv (1954), pp. 225–72; Casey, *The Kingdom of Valencia*, pp. 5, 38–44.

difficulties of repopulating morisco farmlands meant that payments on *censos* were often in arrears or in default. Thus the expulsion of the moriscos first damaged agricultural production, then hurt the feudal aristocracy, and finally penalized the latter's creditors; many of these were from urban middle groups, and were forced to consume their savings, which precipitated the failure of the municipal bank of Valencia in 1613.[12] While the landed aristocracy were compensated to some degree for loss of their morisco vassals, they were also in a powerful position to dictate the terms of resettlement. Valencia lost over 25 per cent of its 450,000 inhabitants, and most of those expelled were tenants or vassals of the aristocracy. There was no great rush of immigrants to fill the vacuum: by the middle of the eighteenth century Valencia's population still had not reached the level of 1609.[13] The bargaining power of the aristocracy, therefore, did not derive from surplus of labour but from sheer territorial sovereignty. A few colonists entered from outside the province, and there was some internal migration as artisans from the towns and peasants from more depressed areas moved into morisco farms in search of a living. What they found was hardly a colonist's dream.

In the southern part of the province the newcomers were settled on the great estates of the Dukes of Gandia and Maqueda, the Marquises of Guadalest, Denia and Albaida, and the Counts of Cocentaina and Real. The terms of vassalage were harsh and extortionate. A typical example is provided by the settlement of Muro in the jurisdiction of the count of Cocentaina. The new tenants owed their lord tithes and first fruits; they forfeited all common land to the lord, could not move without his permission, and were bound to stay for at least five years; they had no property rights except by grace and favour of the lord, who also reserved to himself all civil and criminal cases in first instance; the establishment of bakeries, shops and taverns was monopolized by the lord; tenants had to grind their corn only in the lord's mill, and they were forbidden to buy flour from outside; anyone manufacturing anything had to pay the lord 10 per cent of production; on wines they had to pay a quarter of the product, and

[12] Reglá, 'La expulsion de los moriscos y sus consecuencias en la economía valenciana', pp. 206, 216–17.
[13] See above, pp. 65–9, 201–2.

on sugar half of the canes collected.[14] These were only a number
of major items of the pact; and similar terms were imposed by the
Duke of Gandia and the Marquis of Albaida. There was no escape
from an exclusively seigneurial relationship. The nobles – and the
church – held all the cards: they dominated the apparatus of
government, they owned the land, and they possessed jurisdiction. There was nothing to prevent them interpreting the pacts to
their own advantage. The agrarian economy of Valencia, therefore, was rebuilt not by a free peasantry but on the backs of
semi-servile vassals. This was one of the more glaring of the many
opportunities missed by Habsburg government, an example of its
crass neglect of responsibility and of its tendency to strengthen
rather than loosen the existing social structure.

On top of the burdens of their vassalage the peasants of Valencia suffered a long series of calamities in the course of the seventeenth century – conscription, taxes, bandits, locusts, bubonic
plague, earthquakes, the whole range of nation-wide afflictions in
miniature. Even so, many of these peasants had managed to pull
themselves up and to improve their economic position. Yet their
very success was cruelly turned against them. Grain harvests in
Valencia were very good in most years of Charles II's reign, but
while this lowered prices for the consumer it could spell disaster
for the producer. The combination of rich harvest and a reduced
population caused a continual decrease in the price of grain and
damaged the prospects of commercial farmers, men of previous
substance who had been accumulating property since the expulsion of the moriscos and who often owed seigneurial rents to
lords. 'Their dissatisfaction was probably a key factor in the
great peasant upheaval of 1693 . . . which attempted to get seigneurial rents lowered during this troubled period.'[15]

Valencia was a bastion of noble privilege. At least three-
quarters of the surface area was under secular seigneurial jurisdiction. At the top was a group of eight magnates – Infantado,
Lerma and Maqueda were notorious examples – who drew high
rents from the Valencian fiefs but usually lived and spent outside
the kingdom. If to these are added the middle nobility and lesser

[14] Francisco de P. Momblanch y Gonzalbez, *La segunda Germanía del reino
de Valencia* (Alicante, 1957), pp. 19–27, 43–9.
[15] Casey, *The Kingdom of Valencia*, p. 76.

gentry, total seigneurial rents in the seventeenth century came to 974,565 *lluires*, out of a total agrarian product of 4,676,000 *lluires*. The Valencian aristocracy therefore took about one-fifth of the output of the rural economy in feudal dues.[16] Many of these dues were taken in kind, and share-cropping, as distinct from morisco-type labour services, became common after the expulsion among incoming settlers, the going rate varying from one-third to one-fifth of the harvest. On top of tithes, taxes and seigneurial mono-polies, these were harsh rates. By the last decade of the century the situation of the Valencian peasants was hopeless, and in des-peration they had recourse to lawsuits against injustice and abuse. The territorial magnates, lay and ecclesiastical, were a closely-knit group, with common interests and a united front. There was no rift in their defences, and they cursorily dismissed requests for the lowering of seigneurial dues or change of any kind. The peasants had no representation in regional institutions: the lay and ecclesiastical nobility controlled two of the three estates of the cortes of Valencia, and they also dominated the *Diputación*. As far as the peasants were concerned the *fueros* of Valencia were a savage mockery of constitutionalism, and they were forced to seek their own remedies. A clandestine movement began to take shape, centred round the Játiva region of southern Valencia and under the leadership of Francisco García Menor, a farmer from Ráfol de Almunia in the jurisdiction of the Marquis of Almunia. By the early 1690s something like a peasant league existed, and its leaders initiated litigation before the viceroy, seeking a reduction of seigneurial dues and services on the ground that ancient privileges granted by the kings of Valencia exempted them from these exactions. But *fueros* were not for peasants. The Marquis of Castel-Rodrigo issued a series of viceregal edicts de-nying their claims and declaring that in the post-morisco settle-ment the lords had acquired property and fiscal rights over tenants, that these had been confirmed by royal grant, and that the settlers had known the terms and accepted them. The peasants then took their case to Madrid and petitioned the king, with no better result. From the church they could expect no support. The archbishop of Valencia, Fray Juan Tomás de Rocabertí, a lord of

[16] Ibid., pp. 102–3.

numerous vassals, issued a pastoral letter (8 July 1693) admonishing the clergy under pain of major excommunication to explain in pulpit and confessional the grave sin committed by those who without just cause withheld the services and dues owed to their lords.

The tension broke in the summer of 1693 when peasants refused to share harvest products with their lords in the customary proportions. On 9 July 1693 the Duke of Gandia's bailiffs imprisoned four peasants of the village of Villalonga for not paying their dues. Peasants in the rest of the *señorío* came out in revolt and released the prisoners, and the movement swept through the estates of the Marquis of Albaida, the Count of Cocentaina and other lords. Soon the insurgents numbered about 1,000 and were recruiting more. Francisco García was appointed *síndico* and assumed political direction, sending out emissaries throughout the province. And military command was conferred on José Navarro, a surgeon of Muro, who took the title *General del Eixercit dels Agermanats*, thus recalling the other *Germanía*, or brotherhood, of the 1520s. The rebel forces were organized into companies, eight in all, and captains were appointed; and as their numbers grew to about 2,000, villages came to their assistance with supplies. The plan was to assemble as large a force as possible and then march on the viceregal capital to place their cause before the crown and seek redress.

But the viceroy denounced the rebels as traitors and sent an army against them. On 15 July near the village of Cela de Núñez the peasant forces were scattered; a number of prisoners were taken and the rest fled in disorder to the mountains. The viceroy then offered an amnesty and a hearing to the rank and file; but to the leaders he offered nothing, and he placed a large price on the heads of the two principals, dead or alive. The villagers took the bait and again tried legal action, with no more success than before. So the movement was split, and three weeks after its beginning the rebellion was virtually over. García was never captured; but Navarro was taken and executed. Lesser rebles were sent to the galleys or heavily fined. In spite of the harsh repression the spirit of revolt was not extinguished. After 1700, during the War of Succession, the peasants of Valencia made another attempt to throw off their seigneurial yoke. But the Habsburg cause which they espoused was doomed, and the victory of Philip V was a victory for the landed aristocracy.

Castile's Tragic Decade

While Catalonia rebuilt its economy and Valencia erupted in social conflict, Castile passively endured its fate, trapped in a vicious circle of depression. A faulty agrarian structure and periodic pestilence precipitated demographic recession, which further diminished the consumer market for agricultural and industrial products.

Castile was the victim of two economic trends, one in the Atlantic sector, one internal. The Castilian interior lost its economic dominance and faced a future of separation from a more dynamic periphery increasingly integrated into international commerce. The dividing line was the mid-seventeenth century. The interior became depopulated, de-urbanized, de-industrialized; its rural economy became disengaged from the urban market, economically isolated and condemned to a cycle of production not far above subsistence level. In this process the role of Madrid was decisive. By drawing off income from the interior to spend in the exterior, without creating an alternative market for domestic manufactures, the relentless growth of the capital between 1560 and 1630 undermined the regional urban networks of Castile and contributed to the depression of the Castilian economy.[17] Falling output affected exports, which meant that Castile was unable to compete for European markets and even lost a major part of its American market. Shortage of foreign and colonial earnings perpetuated stagnation at home. This was almost a classical example of depression feeding upon itself. And in the background was a further factor, imperfectly understood by Spaniards who still believed that they possessed an El Dorado across the Atlantic if only it could be made to yield its wealth to them instead of to foreigners. They refused to accept that a fundamental shift of power had taken place within the Hispanic world, that the economic balance had now moved towards America, and that Amer-

[17] Ringrose, *Madrid and the Spanish Economy*, pp. 105–6, 251–2, 314–16.

icans now produced their wealth for themselves and their chosen markets, not for Spain.

Castile was hardly in a position to endure more. Yet its worst crisis, incredibly, was still to come. Between 1677 and 1687 the country was struck by every conceivable adversity, reducing an already enfeebled frame to its last gasp. In this decade Castilians were visited by scourges of biblical proportions. The most relentless enemy was their own climate.[18] This was not a new experience. The countryside had suffered from the very beginning of the reign. There had been harvest failures in 1665-8, causing a sharp rise in the price of agricultural products, with wheat more than doubling its price between 1663 and 1668.[19] In 1670 crops in the province of Granada were destroyed by locusts. But these were only preliminary warnings.

In the spring of 1677 torrential rainfall caused heavy loss of crops in southern Spain and led to famine conditions in Andalucía. This was followed by two years of drought in the same region, and then an earthquake in October 1680. After a brief respite Andalucía had two more years of drought in 1682-3, followed in the winter of 1683-4 by a great deluge. Rain fell incessantly in the whole of Andalucía; rivers overflowed their banks, crops were inundated, and the few cattle that remained after recent droughts were swept away in floods. In the province of Granada the first four months of 1684 were like a monsoon; crops, roads, bridges and mills were destroyed or impaired, and in the city of Granada alone 6,000 houses were damaged. After this catastrophe Andalucía could expect no harvest in 1684, and three years later the region suffered yet another drought. Meanwhile northern and central Spain had not escaped. There was heavy flooding in 1679-81 and crops were further destroyed by hail. The great rainstorms of 1684 reached as far as La Mancha, and in 1685 there was severe drought in Galicia.

These meteorological conditions were bound to affect food

[18] See the striking studies by Antonio Domínguez Ortiz, 'La crisis de Castilla en 1677-1687', *Revista Portuguesa de Historia*, x (1962), pp. 436-51; Kamen, 'The Decline of Castile: the last crisis', pp. 63-76; and José Calvo Poyato, 'La última crisis de Andalucía en el siglo XVII: 1680-85', *Hispania*, 46, 164 (1986), pp. 519-42.

[19] Earl J. Hamilton, *War and Prices in Spain* 1651-1800 (Cambridge, Mass., 1947), pp. 238-9.

supplies. Rural Spain was the basis of the economy and the harvest was its keystone. Crop failure meant calamity for the peasant and starvation for the rural poor. Drought destroyed communities, provoking fights for food and for irrigation rights. Andalucía in particular became a major disaster area and in 1683–4 the scene of a severe subsistence crisis; with food in scarce supply and prices soaring, oil, bread and other basic necessities disappeared from the market. Seville, normally one of the granaries of the south and a rich source of oil and livestock, reached the depths of depression. In 1684 the city authorities reported to the government on the plight of their people after eight years of drought or near-drought:

> The culmination of these afflictions came in the calamitous year of 1683, when drought left the fields barren and devoid of crops; food shortage became extremely critical, and people in their misery scratched the earth for grass and roots to keep alive.[20]

The chronicler Francisco Godoy recorded:

> During the whole of 1683, until the end of November, there was not a drop of rain. Almost the whole of Andalucía was in absolute drought. The crops were parched with heat, the trees burnt up, cereals destroyed.... Bread became so scarce and expensive that many people perished of hunger. No one in Andalucía escaped privation. There was a stock farmer whose 1,600 head of cattle was reduced to 200 because of drought and lack of fodder.... And I know another person who in addition to losing his cattle got only two bales of straw out of the 1,300 fanegas of grain he had sown.[21]

And when the rains came they brought no relief, only further disaster. All over Andalucía hungry peasants flocked to the towns in these years. The relief services provided by civil and ecclesiastical bodies broke down under the strain, powerless to prevent heavy mortality. Famine was a killer in itself. But its secondary effects were equally monstrous. Widespread malnutrition made the population easy prey to epidemic disease. And in a cruel coincidence pestilence now penetrated these debilitated regions.

---

[20] Quoted by Domínguez Ortiz, 'La crisis de Castilla en 1677–1687', p. 439.
[21] Quoted ibid., p. 440 n. 14.

The second half of the seventeenth century seems to have seen a reversal of the downward demographic trend, but there was a short-term recession in Castile in the 1680s, caused by the epidemics of 1676–85 which, while not as vicious as their two predecessors, were more prolonged. The plague began in Cartagena in June 1676, imported perhaps from the eastern Mediterranean.[22] Quarantine measures were ineffective and the infection swept through Murcia, then eastwards along the coast to Andalucía. Málaga was badly hit. Antequera reported the loss of 12,000 inhabitants. Many villages lost half their inhabitants, and municipal resources suffered as local revenues were expended on preventive measures and quarantine regulations. The disease fed particularly on eastern Andalucía. From 1679 to 1681 Granada suffered grievously, and almost simultaneously Jáen, Córdoba and Seville were infected. In the area of southern Córdoba 74.8 per cent of those infected died, and deaths amounted to 5.5–6.5 per cent of the population.[23] In Seville a preacher promised immunity if the theatres were closed; the advice was sound enough on quarantine grounds and it was observed, but by then the infection had taken root. The poor harvests of 1682–3 enabled the epidemic to flare up again in a second wave which lasted from 1683 to 1686. While it revived in Andalucía, it now also penetrated parts of La Mancha and Extremadura. Terror struck the court when it reached Castile and approached Madrid itself; there were heavy losses in the provinces of Burgos, Toledo, Madrid and Valladolid. The demographic impact was less than imagined but serious enough. Total losses in the decade of death from 1676 amounted perhaps to 250,000.[24] The fatal setbacks occurred during the prolongation of crisis in the years 1680–4 when climate, crops and contagion all worked against the people of Castile and reduced their ranks once more. The economy also suffered. Trade was damaged by quarantine measures, which disrupted communications without preventing contagion; the revenue from taxes diminished; and labour shortage affected agriculture and other sectors of the economy.

On top of these natural calamities Castile experienced its worst

[22] Domínguez Ortiz, *La sociedad española en el siglo XVII*, pp. 75–81.
[23] Calvo Poyato, 'La última crisis de Andalucía', p. 531.
[24] Domíguez Ortiz, *La sociedad española en el siglo XVII*, pp. 75–81.

monetary crisis of the century. Monetary disorder was more than a symptom of an ailing economy: it exacerbated as well as reflected depression. The basic object of monetary inflation was to bridge the gap between falling revenue and rising expenditure and to make good the failure of the economy to yield more wealth. Ironically the best industrial machinery in Spain was the mint at Segovia, installed by German technicians. Here and at other minting centres Philip IV had practised coinage debasement with reckless abandon. Inevitably gold and silver were driven out of circulation, and from the 1660s to the 1680s vellon may have constituted at least 95 per cent of money spent in Castile. Government inertia in the first fifteen years of Charles II's reign allowed the problem to drift without solution. The premium on silver, the measure of public distrust of vellon, having fallen to 50 per cent following Philip IV's violent deflation of 1664, rose to 115.5 per cent in New Castile by mid-1665, to 175 per cent by 1670, and to 275 per cent by 1680.[25] Commodity prices in New Castile rose from an index of 69 in 1662 to 98 in 1670.[26] The following decade saw inflation at its peak, with the index moving from 96 in 1671 to 113 in 1679. In New Castile the price of wheat almost doubled between 1676 and 1678. This great price rise was conditioned to some degree by mutations in the coinage, the price curve almost coinciding with monetary inflation. In the case of agricultural prices, which reached their highest point in 1678, it was also aggravated by climatic conditions and crop failures from 1677, especially in Andalucía. According to the French ambassador, the Marquis of Villars, on the basis of his experience in 1679–81 prices in Madrid were twice as high as the most expensive city in Europe.[27]

The cycle of inflation-deflation-inflation, the monetary and economic chaos, made life intolerable for Spaniards, destroying their savings and disrupting their trade. The ratio of wages to prices appears to have been favourable to wage-earners, and nominally they may have had sufficient for the necessities of life;[28] but the monetary disorder prevents serious estimate of the

[25] Hamilton, *War and Prices in Spain* 1651–1800, pp. 9–35.
[26] Base 1671–80; see Hamilton, *War and Prices in Spain* 1651–1800, pp. 119, 121, 240.
[27] Marquis de Villars, *Mémoires de la cour d'Espagne*, 1678–1682 (London, 1861), p. 3.
[28] Hamilton, *War and Prices in Spain* 1651–1800, p. 219.

real value of wages; and in any case the continual depreciation of vellon, the only currency available to the poorer classes, eroded their earnings, while heavy taxation further reduced their actual income. Commerce was dislocated and Spanish merchants had real difficulty in conducting overseas transactions; and inflation was too rampant to be a stimulus to the economy.

Eventually the government of Charles II shed its lethargy. In response to public clamour for deflation, a decree of 10 February 1680 reduced the tariff of the 'rich vellon' struck under the ordinance of October 1660 by 50 per cent; that of imitation vellon was reduced by three-fourths; and coins counterfeited abroad were cut by seven-eighths of their denominational value.[29] The law of 1641 limiting the premium to 50 per cent, which had been inoperative for 40 years, was reaffirmed. The premium now actually fell from 275 to 50 per cent when the deflation took place and remained there for more than six years. By decree of 22 May 1680 the 'rich vellon' was demonetized, and the owners were paid its value in 'current money'. Pure copper vellon with extrinsic value slightly above its intrinsic worth was authorized. There were no further changes in the vellon coinage during the Habsburg period; the output of vellon was rigidly limited, if only through inability to secure copper; and no more sudden doses of inflation and deflation perturbed economic life.

The massive devaluation of the currency in 1680, which in effect reduced the value of a mark of vellon by 75 per cent, from 12 to 3 reales, necessary as it may have been in the long term, was excruciating in its immediate effects. The object was to entice gold and silver into circulation. It was also sought to bring down prices, which had become intolerably high for all those with fixed incomes. They were therefore accompanied by further decrees, notably that of 27 November 1680, fixing prices at an artificially low level. The combination of deflation and price-control produced a price collapse unparalleled in Spanish history: commodity prices fell by almost 50 per cent in two years. Everyone suffered, from the beggar to the king. Shortage of money paralysed almost every sector of the economy. The government tried in vain to augment the amount of money in circulation by coining American silver when it arrived, by purchasing silver objects for minting and by prohibiting the manufacture of articles from

[29] Ibid., pp. 20–1.

copper needed for vellon. But money disappeared from circulation, labourers were unpaid, people lost their savings and local trade was paralysed. Artisans, peasants and landowners continued to complain bitterly of the absolute lack of money and the minimal prices obtained for their products. Towns and villages could not pay their taxes, and the government was forced to condone arrears, especially in central Castile. In October 1681 the Council of Finance discussed the possibility of suspending all taxes created since 1656, lowering the municipal *sisa*, and making a new assessment of *alcabala* quotas, because communities simply could not pay the present level.[30]

The poor prices of agricultural products affected the whole Castilian economy, and the repercussions were felt in trade and industry. The calling in of old coin under the decrees of 1680 led in many parts of the country to a virtual stoppage of local trade, and some parts of Castile fell back on barter for lack of good currency. Merchants were unable to meet their liabilities or collect money owed to them. Administrators and lessees of public money, who had only old coinage in their possession, were left insolvent. The credit of financiers collapsed, and bankers lost half their capital through devaluation. Overseas trade was also affected. According to the French ambassador, 'The wool trade of Segovia, almost the only trade from which Spaniards still make a profit, slumped heavily as a result of devaluation, which caused the price of wool to double. Foreigners would no longer buy it unless the Spaniards would reduce its price proportionately.'[31] Altogether the years 1680–2 were tragic ones for Spain, among the most demoralizing ever experienced by its people. And the agony continued.

Committees of inquiry sat in continuous session, but solutions were difficult to find. In November 1683 the government admitted that shortage of money was damaging trade and revenue as well as the income of the church and private landowners, and the Council of Castile was asked to propose a remedy. The Council could not agree on policy and gave an assortment of advice, none of it very convincing. The news reaching Madrid from the south of Spain in 1684 could hardly have been worse. In reply to a

[30] Domínguez Ortiz, 'La crisis de Castilla en 1677–1687', p. 449.
[31] Villars, *Memoires*, p. 276.

demand for greater tax efforts came a series of reports containing only lamentations. Córdoba, for example, insisted on its utter ruin:

> Great privation is suffered in this city and province. The flight of people from the countryside has filled the town with so many beggars that they have to be fed out of common stocks. But food is in short supply. The diminution of the harvests, the dearth of cattle, the destitution of labourers, the great bankruptcy of ecclesiastical and secular incomes, has left the greater part of the countryside uncultivated, and this is the only wealth of the province. So labourers are without work, owners without income; commerce is halted by lack of currency and by the export of money to buy grain from abroad.... And to crown all the plague continues for its seventh year.[32]

Although Andalucía headed the list of distressed areas, New Castile was not far behind. In the course of 1684 the Council of Finance received numerous petitions from communities requesting a reduction of their tax quota on the grounds of depopulation, shortage of money and poor prices. Many villages complained that their population had fallen steeply since 1680, one from 1,286 to 792, another from 500 to 158, others from 400 to 200, and from 200 to 80. And invariably the reason given was the low price of agricultural products since the savage deflation of 1680. A report of a minister of the Council of Castile in 1685 summed up the situation:

> The state of the whole kingdom of Castile is utterly wretched, especially Andalucía, where the aristocracy are without funds, the middle elements poverty-stricken, artisans reduced to vagrancy or beggary, and many dying of hunger, buried by the Brothers of Charity who used to give them relief but now have nothing to give. The women are also suffering. Necessity forces them to beg from door to door, for work does not yield a sustenance; others never leave the house, even to go to Mass, so destitute are they; and others – the worse pity – have prostituted themselves at all ages, simply to eat.[33]

[32] Quoted by Domínguez Ortiz, 'La crisis de Castilla en 1677–1687', p. 449.
[33] Quoted by Maura, *Vida y reinado de Carlos II*, i, p. 396.

One of the objects of the great deflation of 1680 was to bring gold and silver into circulation. In 1686 the government effected a partial revaluing of silver, a measure which had been demanded for some time as an economic stimulus and a means of preventing the flight of specie abroad.[34] By decree of 14 October the silver coinage was devalued by approximately 20 per cent. The premium on the new issue in terms of vellon was fixed at 50 per cent, and on the old at 87.5 per cent. And they remained fairly constant at this rate for the rest of the century. This devaluation of silver, the first in two centuries, was in effect an inflationary measure, but a sound and justified one. It put an end to a long period of monetary instability; silver came out of its hiding places and began to enter the market again; prices ceased to fall and underwent modest recovery; and the government helped things along by giving some tax relief. Even the weather improved, so that for a number of years harvests were more abundant. And the country was spared major epidemics for the rest of the century. The patient did not undergo a miraculous recovery. Periodic hunger and privation continued to visit the Castilian masses, and the Council of Finance was obliged to give further tax relief to numerous towns and villages unable to meet their quotas. But after 1685 the worst features of depression began to lift and Castile turned its back on the tragic decade.

Was optimism justified? Was the recovery of Castile merely the attenuation of the adversities of 1676–85, or was it a true revival, the starting point of eighteenth-century growth?[35] The first signs of demographic recovery can be observed in the 1660s; the plague of 1676–85 was a set back but it passed. In towns of Old Castile such as Valladolid, Medina del Campo and Peñaranda, and in regions of Valencia and Catalonia, population growth was already making headway. Segovia's recovery after mid-century, like that of other places, was slow and halting, but there were indications that rural as well as urban populations were emerging from depression.[36] In Galicia contemporaries were aware that numbers were increasing from about 1670, and evidence from baptisms

[34] Hamilton, *War and Prices in Spain* 1651–1800, pp. 22–3, 31.
[35] For varying interpretation see the three studies cited in n. 18 and Kamen, *Spain the Later Seventeenth Century*, pp. 67–112.
[36] Kamen, *Spain in the Later Seventeenth Century*, pp. 42–5, 61–2; García Sanz, *Desarrollo y crisis del Antiguo Régimen en Castilla la Vieja*, pp. 74–6.

shows that the worst of the crisis was now over.[37] Spain continued to suffer disease and famine, and to lose people through
emigration, but the transition from regression to recovery had
been made, and the turning point was the 1660s. Economic
growth came slightly later. The establishment of the *Junta de
Comercio*, or Committee of Trade in 1679 was important less for
immediate results or specific projects than for evidence of state
interest in the economy and the possibility of new investment in
manufactures.[38] In spite of the agrarian crisis of 1680–4, agriculture remained responsive to population growth and capable
still of extending land under cultivation. Castile achieved a rise in
agricultural production, and the evidence from tithes indicates
that grain output in Andalucía and Segovia was returning to the
level of more prosperous times.[39] Meanwhile Basques and Catalans embarked on a course of commercial and industrial expansion. From about 1680 rural production in Catalonia was moving
upwards and seeking markets abroad, while new manufacturers
and exporters were also at work. In Catalonia stable agricultural
prices, a rise in rural production and an increase in population
created a firm basis for a long period of prosperity which can be
dated from the 1670s.[40]

After 1686 the country enjoyed fourteen years of monetary
stability, and Habsburg government bequeathed to its successor
at least a sound currency. There was also a slow and modest rise
in prices. The severe deflation of 1680 had brought commodity
prices in New Castile down from an index of 113.4 in 1679 to
57.7 in 1686. In the subsequent period prices remained weak but
showed a tendency to improve. In New Castile they rose from an
index of 57.9 in 1687 to 67.1 in 1699; in Old Castile from 57.4 to
75.2; in Andalucía from 60 to 63.7.[41] This stabilization of prices
lasted from the mid-1680s to the 1730s to be followed by a
stronger rise, especially in the second half of the eighteenth century. In prices as in currency therefore, there was no abrupt break
in 1700. The trough of Spain's great depression may be limited to

---

[37] Saavedra, *Economía, política y sociedad en Galicia*, pp. 70–3.
[38] Kamen, *Spain in the Later Seventeenth Century*, pp. 75–81.
[39] Ibid., pp. 89–90; García Sanz, *Desarrollo y crisis del Antiguo Régimen en
Castilla la Vieja*, p. 105.
[40] Vilar, *La Catalogne dans l'Espagne Moderne*, i, pp. 640–53.
[41] Hamilton, *War and Prices in Spain 1651–1800*, pp. 119, 136.

the period 1640–85, and its greatest depth to the years 1676–85. The savage devaluation of 1680, the child and father of crisis, eventually restored confidence in Spanish currency, which in turn gave encouragement to financiers and manufacturers. And the slow and dependable price rise after 1686, if not a generator of growth, was at least a sign that the great depression had now spent itself; and the economy began to respond to moderate inflation. Perhaps the last decade of Habsburg rule was a time of hope rather than tribulation.

Bureaucracy and its Reform

While the later government of Charles II was restoring confidence to Spain's monetary system, it was also taking the first steps in administrative reform, anticipating in some degree the more successful efforts of Bourbon reformers in the following century. The problem was clear enough. National revival was impeded by defective institutions. The bureaucracy, which had once been the strength of Spanish government, was now failing the country. In view of the vested interests involved, however, it was an achievement to get the matter on to a government agenda.

Spain had too many officials. Pursuit of office had become a mania, fed by the universities, current social values, the patronage system and the government's own improvidence. The universities of Salamanca, Valladolid and Alcalá, among others, produced each year hordes of law graduates. Many of these had procured a virtually free education through entry in the *colegios mayores*, now a monopoly of the aristocracy; and many of them were sons and relatives of existing officials. With a university degree a man was almost guaranteed appointment in the law courts, the *audiencias* and the chancelleries, and from these he could expect promotion in due course to one of the councils. The normal career track of a *colegial* was from a chair of law, to a post in a provincial *audiencia*, and then through the conciliar hierarchy in Madrid (Finance, Orders, the Indies) to the Council of Castile. This was not a career open to talent. The *colegios mayores* were socially exclusive institutions which kept membership in the family and then assisted their members for life. The strong association between university entrance and bureaucratic appointments tended to create a closed circle of administrators who monopolized public careers. Under Philip IV and Charles II *colegiales* were appointed to 70 per cent of all vacancies in the Council of Castile.[42] The system nurtured a legal profession which behaved not as an administrative caste but as part of the nobility; the *letrado* elite had overcome the triple tests of nobility, purity of blood and graduation from a *colegio mayor*, and they spent the rest of their lives not only seeking office but also accumulating land, entails and annuities, while less privileged types including many *conversos* swarmed among the foothills of the law. But times were changing. In the years around 1680 a devaluation of university degrees and a fall in university enrolments began to affect the composition of the councils. By the reign of Philip V the sons of councillors of Castile were less likely to go to university or to enter an administrative career and much more likely to enter the Church or the army than they had been under Philip IV, an indication perhaps that the *letrado* was losing prestige and status. This did not affect the power of the councils, which reached its peak in the reign of Charles II. As the French adviser Jean Orry observed in 1703, 'It is the councils which rule the state and allocate all the offices, all the favours and all the revenues of the kingdom.'[43]

For those who did not have a degree but possessed compensatory qualifications – aristocratic status or family relationship with officials – there was another means of entry into the bureaucracy, by way of offices known as *de capa y espada*. These appointments depended solely on royal favour and patronage; there was no limitation as to their number; no standards or formal qualifications were required; and the salaries of these additional officials were an excessive charge on government revenue. Appointments of this kind so greatly exceeded the needs of the councils that periodic attempts had been made to control them; in 1661, for example, Philip IV decreed that *capa y espada* councillors appointed to the *Junta de Guerra* should wait for a vacancy before joining it, though they could receive salaries from the date of nomination.

---

[42] Janine Fayard, *Les membres du Conseil de Castille à l'époque moderne (1621–1746)* (Geneva/Paris, 1979), pp. 35–58, 205–10.
[43] Quoted ibid., p. 171.

Bureaucratic growth was both superfluous and harmful. In the Council of the Indies no less than seventy-two councillors were appointed in the thirty-five years of Charles II's reign. Of these, twenty-four were appointments *de capa y espada*. A total of forty-eight were *consejeros togados* (legally qualified councillors); of these twenty-three died in office, thirteen of them after serving only a short term, while nineteen were quickly promoted to the Council of Castile. This lack of continuity in service was a serious obstacle to efficient administration: in the course of thirty-five years only ten councillors served for more than ten years on the Council of the Indies.[44] But there were further anomalies. One of these, of recent growth, was the habit of appointing super-numerary councillors, both *togados* and *de capa y espada*, who already held appointments elsewhere, frequently abroad. The sole object of this exercise was to augment salaries. Don Pedro Ronquillo, for example, while holding appointment in the Netherlands and then as ambassador in London, was appointed councillor of the Indies (and also of Castile), without ever setting foot inside the council chamber.[45] And former secretaries of the Council of State were sometimes appointed to the Council of the Indies simply as a form of pension on retirement.

Finally, there was a further entry to office, through purchase. This was regarded as patriotism, not corruption, and the office so bought became a piece of property, usually with right of renun-ciation, which meant that the owner could sell it, bequeath it or give it away. Sale of office extended not only to notarial and municipal office, both very large groups, but to salaried offices in the central administration, including legal offices which were strictly speaking unsaleable. By the end of Philip IV's reign senior administrative posts of a judicial and financial kind, whose sale was generally regarded as inappropriate, were being put up to purchasers almost as a matter of routine.[46] The system embodied two abuses: it placed people in posts of responsibility for which they were morally or intellectually unfitted; and it encouraged peculation, as successful candidates had to pay off the interest on

[44] Schäfer, *El Consejo real y supremo de las Indias*, i, p. 269.
[45] Ibid., i, pp. 269–70.
[46] Parry, *The Sale of Public Office in the Spanish Indies under the Habsburgs*, pp. 5, 48.

PLATE 8 *Caballero de Golilla*, by Murillo (reproduced by kind permission of the Museo del Prado, Madrid)

capital borrowed to purchase the office. In the reign of Charles II abuses multiplied. Now even conciliar appointments were sold. At least two *capa y espada* councillors of the Indies, both high-ranking aristocrats, the Duke of Guastala and the Marquis of Iscar, obtained their appointments through payment of a substantial *servicio*. And although all purchase of legal office was forbidden in law, Martín de Solis was appointed fiscal of the Council of the Indies on payment of 14,500 ducats. Towards the end of the reign a child of nine years, the Marquis of La Laguna, Count of Paredes, inherited his father's office in the Council of the Indies along with other items of property.

Subordinate officials multiplied even more rapidly. In 1690 the Council of the Indies alone had seventy-five officials. Its total strength of one hundred included fifty supernumerary officials on salary in all grades from councillor to porter. This expansion occurred not in response to increase of business but to demands of patronage. Surplus staff were a great financial liability, and wages were usually in arrears, by August 1668 164,453 ducats in arrears. This may not have been serious for aristocratic supernumeraries, but it meant that lower officials lived constantly on credit or corruption. Apart from salaries – and pensions for widows – council officials also received a number of bonuses and fringe benefits, all of which were an additional burden for the councils financial allocation, at a time when its quota of remittances from Peru was becoming more and more irregular. So the financial position of the Council of the Indies was worse in the reign of Charles II than in any previous period. And this was one council alone. The others had similar problems of personnel and finance.

As the bureaucracy became a form of social security for its own members, so it deteriorated as an instrument of government. Its methods called for drastic overhaul. The *consulta*, originally a useful means of summarizing subjects and opinions, degenerated into a long-winded and pointless exercise. The practice of recording the opinion and arguments of each individual councillor was rigidly followed even when these were unanimous or in substantial agreement. There was, moreover, a certain chicanery in the construction of *consultas*. By the mid-seventeenth century councillors had adopted the practice of leaving the council table after debate, recording their opinions in private, and then either incorporating them in a completed *consulta* or sending them direct to the king outside conciliar channels. Repeated prohibition of this practice in the 1650s and 1660s suggests that it was difficult to eradicate.[47] Further attempts to reform *consulta* procedure were made in the reign of Charles II, though without much success.[48]

At a certain level conciliar government could function with some efficiency; the receipt of reports by individual councils and the transmission of outgoing replies and instructions, these tasks were performed well enough. But between these two stages, when the sovereign or his minister had to receive, consider and resolve material from a large number of councils, lay the weak link in the whole system and the point where it frequently broke down. Apart from the accumulation of business, the government did not possess an efficient registry; this meant that neither the councils nor the executive could lay their hands quickly on papers relevant to the file under discussion. The state archives at Simancas, outside Valladolid, were remote from the central organs of government; great delay could ensue if it were necessary to call for previous papers, especially as the filing system at Simancas was somewhat primitive.[49] Philip IV had attempted to remedy this situation. He ordered the creation within the royal palace of a current registry modelled on the permanent archives at Simancas. Here all conciliar papers would be filed for orderly consultation; material four years old would be removed and deposited in Simancas, but a classified inventory of their contents would be kept in the registry.

This large family of councils and their numerous offspring, the juntas, squabbled incessantly over jurisdiction. Overlapping areas of competence were a fertile source of dissension and kept the councils in permanent agitation, so that many of their *consultas* were concerned not with policy but with their own authority and alleged encroachment by other councils. Material which had come to a council, been processed into a *consulta* and remitted to the sovereign for decision, frequently had to be sent for execution to other interested councils, including the Council of State with its universal brief. These councils would then wish to see the original

[47] Valiente, *Los validos*, pp. 201–2.
[48] See 'Orden de la Reina Gobernadora', 26 July 1672, ibid., pp. 209–10.
[49] See the complaints of Philip IV, ibid., pp. 199–200.

consulta from the first council, and if they disagreed with its contents they would start all over again, with new deliberations and new *consultas*. Philip IV on more than one occasion ordered this nonsense to stop. But relations among councils and cross-reference between their *consultas* continued to cripple conciliar government, causing endless paper work and retarding executive action.[50]

The only hope of success under this system lay in the quality of the executive. A strong minister could override or by-pass the councils in order to speed decisions and action. This was the crucial argument in favour of a prime minister, whether or not he was a *valido*. But the single executive which emerged in the seventeenth century, culminating in straightforward prime ministers under Charles II, depended on two further innovations to operate effectively. Prime ministers needed to consult frequently with other ministers without going through the cumbersome machinery of the councils; and the executive needed an efficient secretariat of its own independent of the conciliar secretaries. In the eighteenth century the Bourbons worked their way towards a kind of cabinet council, consisting of the king or first minister and a few ministerial colleagues. The idea at least had been anticipated. There were signs, obscure at the end of Philip IV's reign, more clear during the reign of Charles II, that government was moving towards this kind of extraconciliar consultation. Prime ministers and their colleagues, the presidents of councils, assembled together with some regularity and acquired a secretariat of their own. This was the *Secretaria del Despacho Universal*, which emerged from the secretariat of the Council of State but seems to have detached itself from it. The *Secretario del Despacho* was not confined to a specific area of foreign affairs, as were the two secretaries of the Council of State, but had a universal brief and combined the functions of consultant and secretary to the head of government, whether this was a Junta de Gobierno or later a prime minister. The holders of the office were men of some status and distinction, Blasco de Loyola, Pedro Fernández del Campo, Jerónimo de Eguía, José de Veitia Linaje, Manuel de Lira. The stature of the office made it an object of great competition, and accounts for the surprise evinced by the appointment of unworthy incumbents in the 1690s.

[50] Ibid., pp. 162, 196–8, 205–6.

In the reign of Charles II these developments were limited by the mediocrity of the crown and the power of the grandees. Until the political power of the nobles had been broken by a powerful crown, absolute in practice as well as in theory and capable of choosing its prime minister irrespective of whether he were a grandee, then the executive could never completely bypass the aristocratic councils or fully control the administration. One attempt was made to provide an alternative to conciliar administration. In 1687 the count of Oropesa created a new office, the *Superintendencia de Hacienda*, designed as a single executive over financial affairs. This was inspired by French practice and was a curious precursor of eighteenth-century developments. But the functions of the office and its relation with the Council of Finance were never closely defined.[51]

The government of Charles II, therefore, had to accept the existence of councils and try to improve them. It made three attempts at reform. The first came in 1677 and its object, as defined by the royal decree of 6 July, was 'to obviate the great delay in the efficient dispatch of business caused by the increased number of ministers, as well as the rising cost of salaries'. The details are known only for the Council of the Indies, but similar provisions seem to have been made for the other councils. The personnel of the Council and of the Cámara de Indias was limited to a president, eight councillors, a fiscal, two secretaries and eight minor officials; and it was insisted that the councillors should have had experience of service in the colonies.[52] Yet this admirable reform was virtually annulled by its final provision: it was conceded that no present incumbent would be retired, and that the Council would be reduced to its new size simply by not filling vacancies when they occurred. In view of the great numbers involved this would take a long time. As long as government was conceived in terms of grace, favour and patronage, there was little chance of basic reform. This decree had little effect, and the old abuses continued.

Under the inspiration of Oropesa the government returned to the problem in 1687. A decree of 31 January ordered the total suppression of purchased offices in the councils, leaving to the proprietors only the title and status and 5 per cent interest on

[51] See above, pp. 377–8.
[52] Shäfer, *El Consejo real y supremo de las Indias*, i, pp. 275–6.

the sum paid for the office. The decree also suppressed super-
numerary places acquired by grace and favour when they became
vacant, and stated that on no account were there to be super-
numerary offices in the future.[53] This was a limited measure, but
it seems to have been more effective in practice than that of 1677.

The major reform was that of 1691. This too was prepared by
Oropesa, though his dismissal prevented him from implementing
it personally. By decree of 17 July membership of the councils
was reduced in the interests of efficiency and economy. In the
case of the Council of the Indies this meant a strength of one
president, eight councillors *togados*, two *de capa y espada*, two
secretaries and a fiscal, and nine minor officials. These were to
continue to receive the customary salaries, but the numerous
bonuses were reduced. All councillors over and above this number were to be retired, though they would remain on half salary
with an option on vacancies when they occurred.[54] As a general
measure the decree annulled all *mercedes* and grants made by the
administration itself without royal cognizance. Similar decrees
were issued for the other councils, and the whole can be regarded
as an important announcement of administrative reform. But statements of good intentions were not enough, and the test came in
the execution. These measures did not solve the financial problems of the councils or make good the arrears of salary. In 1694,
it is true, the Council of Finance became the sole administrator
of taxes in Castile, another anticipation of eighteenth-century
rationalization, but it was not given financial control over the
bureaucracy. So each supreme council continued to have its own
financial apparatus and its own income, and they were not controlled and paid by the treasury. Moreover, to accommodate
clients, exceptions were immediately made – in two cases were
written into the decree itself – allowing additional councillors *de
capa y espada*. Finally, the execution of the decree was seriously
handicapped by the collapse of government after the departure of
Oropesa, though it might be added that early Bourbon government found it just as difficult to implement bureaucratic reform.
For all these reasons the situation drifted back to normal. When
in 1700 the Habsburg regime came to an end, the councillors of

[53] Ibid., i, p. 278.
[54] Ibid., i, pp. 279–85.

the Indies, whose number had been fixed at ten by the decree of 1691, had grown to nineteen, seven of them *de capa y espada*; and substantial portions of salaries were five years in arrears.[55]

The Precursors

The years around 1680 were critical ones for Spain. It was then that the great depression of the seventeenth century, at its most acute from 1640, reached the most severe intensity. Yet the blackest period yielded the first glimmers of enlightenment. After the corruption and improvisation of the last *validos* and the first *caudillo*, the country was given political sanity and stability under the premierships of Medinaceli and Oropesa, an advance which was only halted by the intervention of the succession problem. Catalonia began to emerge from its provincialism, to renew its economy and to raise its sights towards the outer world. On the basis of monetary soundness and moderate inflation, Castile laid the foundations for future economic recovery. With more mouths to feed agriculture expanded its land use and output. And a programme of administrative reform was initiated, which promised more than it fulfilled, it is true, but which was subsequently imitated by the first Bourbon. The evidence, fragmentary though it is, justifies perhaps the projection of a new framework for modern Spanish history. For if this hypothesis is correct the chronology of depression must be revised. Spain did not pass suddenly from obscurantism to enlightenment in 1700 with the death of the last decrepit Habsburg and the advent of the first reforming Bourbon. If the performance of later Habsburg government was superior to its actual resources, that of the early Bourbons fell short of expectations. An alternative chronology, therefore, would postulate a period from 1685 to about 1760, in which successive governments arrested, if they did not reverse, the downward trend; this was followed, from 1760 to about 1790,

[55] Nevertheless the Council of the Indies managed to produce in 1681, seventy-eight years after the project was initiated, the *Recopilación de Leyes de las Indias*, a compilation of 6,400 laws in four folio volumes, 'a notable monument of colonial legislation'; see C. H. Haring, *The Spanish Empire in America* (New York, 1952) p. 102.

by a programme of more vigorous reform which modernized Spain's government and strengthened its economy.[56]

In Castile ministers attempted to build upon the monetary reform of the early 1680s by putting the government's own finances in order. During the first half of the reign these continued in their pristine chaos. There were too many taxes, too many officials and tax farmers, and too little actual yield; income was further eroded by exemption and fraud, by the cost of collection and by inflation.[57] The government survived by assigning taxes and other forms of revenue years in advance to bankers and creditors in return for immediate cash, and by borrowing from financiers and individuals on the security of *juros*. The latter became a dead weight of permanent obligation. Heavy liability had been inherited from the previous reign, for on 15 November 1663 Philip IV had declared his final bankruptcy and converted his debts into *juros*. A *juro* was a contract whereby a person or institution in return for an advance of capital to the crown, either voluntary or forced, was given an annual pension charged on a specific revenue.[58] This then became a piece of property which could be inherited or traded. The owners were hospitals, monasteries, widows, minors, *caballeros*, townspeople, all those people unable or unwilling to engage in work or business. But under Philip IV many merchants and businessmen were forced to buy *juros*, or received them in payment for sequestered capital.[59] Influential people such as bankers and *asentistas* speculated in these instruments, buying up depreciated *juros* and then persuading the treasury to pay the full income on them. Already by the reign of Philip III *juros* represented the massive sum of 4.5 million ducats, almost half the total revenue of the crown, and they were charged on the most lucrative and secure revenues. By 1667 they amounted to 9 million ducats and had become the treasury's biggest liability. The superintendent of finance, the Marquis of los Vélez, reported on 10 May 1687:

[56] There are, of course, further refinements of chronology in the eighteenth century; see Lynch, *Bourbon Spain 1700–1808*, pp. 9–10.

[57] See above, pp. 374–8.

[58] Domínguez Ortiz, *Política y hacienda de Felipe IV*, pp. 315–29.

[59] Although it is convenient to call *juros* government bonds, they were not bonds in the modern sense, for they were backed only by specific items of public revenue, not the whole.

For all the great machine of this monarchy there remains to your Majesty no more than the revenue contributed by the provinces of Castile, whose value comes to 84,197,790 *vellon reales*: what is alienated and destined for *juros* comes to 122,971,550 reales, leaving a deficit of 41,578,230 reales.[60]

A substantial part of the revenue raised from *juros* was assigned to defence expenditure. This continued to be the biggest drain on government resources. In 1680 projected expenditure amounted to 19.5 million escudos, available revenue to 8.7 million; deficit for the year, 10.8 million.[61] As silver was the only Spanish currency acceptable abroad, the crown had to use its bullion on foreign payments while trying to live on vellon at home, the currency in which its taxes were also collected. The premium on silver rose to 190 per cent in 1675, and 275 per cent in 1680. To send 1 million ducats to the Low Countries cost 2,750,000 ducats.[62]

From 1683 to 1685 the government initiated discussion of reform of the tax structure. In 1686 the *junta de medios* of the Council of Castile lent its support to the view that the incidence of taxation should be shifted from the lower to the upper income groups. It proposed that the *millones*, a tax on vital articles of food, should be reduced, while the *alcabala* and other taxes which fell more heavily on the affluent should be increased. The point was taken up in 1687 by the Marquis of los Vélez, the newly appointed superintendent of finance, who produced an extensive memorandum on financial reform.[63] According to this, revenue was falling to 7–9 million ducats, while expenditure was rising to 10–11 million. The drop corresponded to the *millones*, which had originally been introduced as a tax on basic articles of consumption as an alternative to direct taxation of the privileged classes, the nobles and the clergy. The yield of the *millones* was gradually eroded by the excessive bureaucracy it attracted, by the charging of *juro* payments upon it, and by the frauds committed by nobles and clergy, who sold tax-charged articles from their own estates direct to the consumer and kept the tax for themselves. Vélez

[60] Quoted by Kamen, 'The Decline of Castile: the last crisis', p. 65.
[61] Ibid., p. 66.
[62] Domínguez Ortiz, 'La crisis de Castilla en 1677–1687', p. 443.
[63] Maura, *Vida y reinado de Carlos II*, i, pp. 446–7.

concluded that 'the *millones* is the most unjust and burdensome tax in the kingdom', as it fell primarily on the poor, benefited the rich not the treasury, and now yielded no more than 1.5 million ducats.

Although the majority of ministers agreed that the *millones* should be abolished and replaced perhaps by a direct tax, they feared the sudden loss of 1.5 million ducats without a secure replacement. So the crown appointed another committee of the Council of Castile, headed by the superintendent of finance, to examine the financial situation in general and the proposal to reduce the *millones* in particular. And meanwhile an attempt was made to purge the tax of its administrative abuses and to charge it on the clergy. Strictly speaking the clergy were not exempt from the *millones*, but they resented it and took refuge in the periodic papal sanction which was required. On this occasion, with the excuse that papal permission had not yet arrived, the Archbishop of Toledo, Cardinal Portocarrero, refused to allow the tax in his diocese and threatened the tax-collectors with excommunication. He remained adamant in spite of the pleas of Oropesa, the royal confessor, and Charles II himself. Then, in February 1688, the Vélez committee reported; it concluded that while it was vital to alleviate the tax burden, the *millones* must be maintained, as it was needed for defence expenditure. It might have added that it was also a substitute for direct taxation of the privileged classes.

Frustrated in major reform by the rigid social structure of Castile, the Oropesa administration did what it could to adjust the fiscal system. The Council of Finance began to look more closely at contracts for tax collecting, usually farmed out to businessmen and financiers, most of them natives of Vizcaya or Portugal, and some of them *conversos*. In the years from 1650 to 1680 the council had accepted a number of impractical offers, which usually drove the farmers into bankruptcy through failure to perceive the economic changes adversely affecting revenue. From the early 1680s the Council of Finance began to make more realistic contracts with tax farmers, insisting that applicants provide adequate capital backing and financial guarantees.[64] The

[64] Carmen Sanz Ayán, 'La figura de los arrendadores de rentas en la segunda mitad del siglo XVII. La renta de las lanas y sus arrendadores', *Hispania*, 47, 165 (1987), pp. 203–24.

council also attempted to cut expenditure, and in fact reduced the budget for the royal household to 1.5 million ducats, a level little higher than that of seventy years previously. Offices were pruned, including those purchased, and those that survived were subject to a forced loan equal to a *media anata*.[65] There was a determined attack on pensions and *mercedes*: some were stopped, others were cut and all were taxed, the only exceptions being those of service veterans and their widows, and the widows of ministers, though even these were taxed. While none of this added up to a complete programme, it was evidence of reform within the existing structure. And reform went beyond mere fiscal pressure. Not only did Oropesa and los Vélez try to tap the rich, they also sought to alleviate the poor. This can be seen in the removal of abuses attached to the *millones*, in the abolition or reduction of the *sisa* on a number of consumer goods, and in the lowering of the tax quota for communities who were particularly hard pressed. And they extended the hand of reform to the church, negotiating with Rome for increased revenue from the clergy, and initiating a campaign against the excessive number of clerics and false vocations.

Meanwhile, in response to mounting criticism from reformers and taxpayers, the government had launched a major campaign against *juros*. The crown had already added to the heavy *juro* liability inherited from its predecessor, particularly from 1672 when this device was used to finance defence expenditure against France. *Juros* of course had not been allowed to escape completely: in classical seventeenth-century manner, what weak governments had been unable to prevent they had taxed, by means of a *media anata*, equivalent to the first half-year's income from each *juro*. But from 1677 the government began a basic reform of *juro* finance, and attempted to divide its revenue fairly between past and present claimants.[66] In this year a distinction was made between (1) *juros antiguos* acquired before 1635, and (2) *juros modernos* acquired since then. The state annulled half the value of the first type, and charged a *media anata* and a tax of 5 per cent on

[65] Maura, *Vida y reinado de Carlos II*, i, p. 508.
[66] Alvaro Castillo Pintado, 'Los juros de Castilla. Apogeo y fin de un instrumento de crédito', *Hispania*, xxiii (1963), pp. 43–70, especially pp. 64–6; Maura, *Vida y reinado de Carlos II*, i, p. 508; Domínguez Ortiz, *Política y hacienda de Felipe IV*, pp. 328–9.

what remained. The second type, which had attracted greater speculation, were also annulled to half their value, and the remainder were charged a *media anata* and taxed at 15 per cent. Subsequent decrees of 1685 and 1687 reduced the exemptions allowed under the 1677 enactment, and further annulled *juros* by 50–75 per cent, restricting interest payments to 4 per cent. From the 1685 operation alone the state saved 4 million ducats. By a further decree of 1688 the government drew up a list of priorities on revenue, reserving an annual portion for state expenditure, and applying the balance in specific proportions to servicing debts and paying *juros*, salaries and pensions. The attack on *juros* between 1677 and 1687 was part of the government's reaction to the great crisis which engulfed Castile in those years. Like the draconian monetary policy of 1680, the liquidation of *juros* caused great suffering in the short term, as individuals and institutions suddenly found their annuities annulled or devalued, and commercial houses involved in *juro* business lost some of their assets. But the new policy ended speculation in these instruments, penalized non-productive activities and anticipated the final liquidation of the *juro* debt in 1727. As such it was a measure of long-term recovery.

The reforming aspirations of Charles II's ministers did not stop at public finance. They also tried to penetrate more deeply into Spain's industrial and commercial problems. In these sectors their efforts were piecemeal and confused, and they were overwhelmed by the magnitude of the task. They are evidence of promise rather than performance, of partiality to the idea that the state should play a more positive role in economic planning; and they foreshadowed more successful action by later governments. A law of 1679 sought to improve the status and conditions of factory owners by granting them, among other things, the right to import raw materials duty-free and reducing their liabilities for *alcabala*. Laws of 1682 and 1692 made it clear that industrial and entrepreneurial activities were legally compatible with nobility.[67] And by decree of 29 January the government set up a *Junta General de Comercio*, consisting of four ministers from the Councils of Castile, War, Finance and the Indies, with a varying number of

---

[67] *Novísima Recopilación de las Leyes de España* (6 vols, Madrid, 1805–7), V, xii, 2; VIII, xxiv, 1.

experts, and designed to deal with problems of depopulation and industrial depression; and it was instructed to found *montes de piedad*, or credit banks, to facilitate movement of capital. The Junta did not live up to expectations, but on the other hand it kept returning to the major problems. Plans were prepared to improve transport on internal waterways, measures taken to restore Spain's decaying merchant marine, and subsidies granted to industrial initiatives. Thus a number of flaws in the Spanish economy were identified – the transport bottleneck, escape of profits to foreign merchant shipping and shipyards and lack of incentives for industry – and appropriate action was attempted. The policies also lured out a number of capitalists in Castile who were willing to commit themselves to manufacturing if they could obtain government support. State intervention of this kind – tax exemption, attraction of foreign craftsmen – led to some success, and Palencia and Córdoba developed new textile manufactures, though entrepreneurs found it difficult to break into a market long controlled by distributors of foreign textiles.[68] Most of the attempts at industrial revival in this period were made by foreigners, tempted into Spain by the absence of competition and acting essentially on their own initiative, though with Spanish government backing. In 1679 Flemish workers founded a paper mill at Arco in Segovia; a number of foreigners started new silk factories in Madrid and woollen factories in Cuenca; and in 1687 Frenchmen established a cloth factory in Sigüenza.[69] In the last decades of the century four stocking factories were established in Madrid and three in Valencia, with some export to England. Cloth was manufactured at Toledo and Segovia as well as at Cuenca and Sigüenza, but the product was coarse and had no market beyond the poorest classes. The silk factories of Valencia, Granada and Andalucía were still productive, though again the product was not of high quality.[70] Those at Valencia seem to have been profitable as well as productive, and before the War of

[68] William J. Callahan, 'A note on the Real y General Junta de Comercio, 1679–1814', *Economic History Review*, 21, 3 (1968), pp. 519–28; Kamen, *Spain in the Later Seventeenth Century*, pp. 75–81.

[69] Kamen, 'The Decline of Castile: the last crisis', pp. 68–9.

[70] N. Barozzi and G. Berchet, *Relazioni degli stati europei*. Ser. 1, *Spagna* (Venice, 1660), ii, pp. 642–5; this is, however, an overrated source, containing inaccuracies and false impressions.

Succession employed some 800 workers.[71] But none of this activity was sufficient to overcome the deep depression in the Spanish textile industry. Spain still remained unattractive to the best foreign experts. In 1677 the government tried to secure Dutch and English textile experts to revive the industry; but apparently they imposed conditions which the Spanish authorities found unacceptable.[72]

Commerce was almost as intractable as industry. In the eighteenth century, more particularly under Charles III, the government undertook a vast programme of commercial and colonial reform designed to appropriate the fruits of empire for its owner. In the late seventeenth century projects of this kind never left the council table, though at least they were extensively debated and the ideas canvassed are not without significance. Interested parties advanced a number of projects for chartered companies on the model of the English and Dutch East India Companies, some of them providing for the retention of the fleet system but with the administration of colonial trade and navigation focused in a single private corporation.[73] In 1683 the *Junta de Comercio* was reconstituted and initiated discussion of various reforms. One of the subjects under debate was a company for American trade, first proposed by Narciso Feliu, This envisaged a chartered 'armed company for the trade with the Indies', as a means of reviving Spanish manufactures and destroying foreign contraband in America; it would be modelled on English and Dutch companies, and foreigners might be admitted.[74] The Junta accepted the proposal and advised the government to give its sanction, which it apparently did, though the company was never actually created. For about a decade after 1687 the Council of the Indies considered a proposal for a company in the Netherlands, to be granted the sole right to trade to Hispaniola and Puerto Rico; it would be open to all Spanish subjects and even to capitalists of other

[71] Santiago Rodríguez García, *El arte de las sedas valencianas en el siglo XVIII* (Valencia, 1959), p. 26.

[72] Lonchay, Cuvelier and Lefèvre, *Correspondance de la Cour d'Espagne sur les affaires des Pays-Bas au XVIIᵉ siècle*, v, pp. 257, 282.

[73] Hussey, *The Caracas Company*, pp. 8–34; José Muñoz Pérez, 'El comercio de las Indias bajo los Austrias y los tratadistas españoles del siglo XVII', *Revista de Indias*, xvii (1957), pp. 209–21.

[74] See above, p. 386.

friendly nations. Again, although the Council of the Indies seemed to favour the proposal, there was no outcome.

The most striking ideas came from the pen of Manuel de Lira, a cultivated and much travelled man who had spent some time in Holland. Lira was an official of independent views; as has been seen, he was Secretario del Despacho Universal from 1685 to 1691 when he left the administration in disgust at court intrigue and factionalism.[75] In 1690 the government appointed a junta to advise on the promotion of American trade, and subsequently asked Lira to comment on its report, which simply recommended rigid prohibition of trade with foreigners. Lira reacted sharply against the growing xenophobia, and he denounced prohibitive and unrealistic regulations and taxes. He argued that it was pre-cisely the ban on trade with foreigners that induced the English, the Dutch and the French to establish settlements in the Indies. 'Excessive rigour has many disadvantages. I am convinced that it is better to govern with less absolutism.' It was one thing, he maintained, to prevent trade with enemies, another to prohibit trade with friendly foreigners. As an exponent of open trade and a critic of the Castilian monopoly, Lira advocated the formation of a commercial company at Seville or Cadiz; this would be open to all subjects of the crown and to the traders of England, the Low Countries, the Baltic ports and other nations friendly or allied to Spain; to accommodate them they should be granted freedom of religion in Spanish ports. In addition to reviving and expanding American trade, which in turn would stimulate Span-ish manufactures and merchant marine, Lira believed that his proposals would convert England and the United Provinces into firm allies, for they would have a stake in a vital sector of the Spanish economy and an interest in combating illicit trade.[76] Lira himself appreciated that his ideas had little chance of being accepted; and in fact they were not. Many of them would have simply legalized existing practice, and the government could not bring itself to do this. The proposal to admit foreigners to the

[75] See above, p. 379.
[76] Manuel Francisco de Lira y Castillo, 'Representación dirigida a Don Carlos II', in Juan Sempere y Guarinos, *Biblioteca Española Económico-Política* (4 vols, Madrid, 1801–21), iv, pp. 1–44; Antúñez y Acevedo, *Memorias históricas sobre la legislación y gobierno del comercio de los españoles con sus colonies en las Indias Occidentales*, p. 276.

American trade went far beyond the ideas of the time, including those of other nations. Even in 1765, when the government of Charles III began to reorganize colonial trade on the principles of *comercio libre*, it stopped short of admitting foreigners to the trade.

All of these schemes rose or fell in favour according to Spain's ability to defend her empire from foreign penetration. And they all failed. Shortage of capital, lack of confidence by foreign investors in Spanish officialdom and the relentless opposition of the Seville *consulado* to any formal attack on its monopoly made failure inevitable. In any case the new promoters were attempting to copy the form of foreign trading systems without the substance; Spain did not possess the capital and industrial resources of her rivals. More than this, they missed the whole point of the crisis in colonial trade. They believed that it was sufficient to retrieve the trade from foreigners, whereas it was now the Americans themselves who appropriated the fruits of empire. Nevertheless it was only two decades later that the device of the chartered company was actually implemented and the Caracas Company was launched with Basque capital. The discussion had begun and the ground had been prepared in the reign of Charles II.

In the twilight of the Habsburg regime the balance sheet of progress was still unfavourable, in spite of the efforts of the precursors; and the mass of the Spanish people had little to show for the sacrifices demanded of them. After the fall of Oropesa in 1691 the reform movement begun in the 1670s lost its impetus; the political energies of the nation were now concentrated on the succession problem, and government virtually ceased to govern. The English ambassador reported in 1694, 'This country is in a most miserable condition; no head to govern, and every man in office does what he pleases, without fear of being called to account.'[77] For the common people the century ended as it had begun, with living conditions hard and foodstuffs in short supply. In April 1699 there were bread riots in Madrid. A mob of 5,000 stormed through the town, frightened the grandees into hiding and rampaged outside the royal palace. The prostrate king was

[77] Stanhope to Godolphin, 8 October 1694, in *Spain under Charles II; or Extracts from the Correspondence of the Hon. Alexander Stanhope, 1690–1699* (London, 1844), p. 53.

forced to concede a change of corregidor, and to struggle from his sick-bed to appear in person before the mob with promise of redress. In May there were violent riots in Valladolid. Meanwhile peasants swarmed into the capital in search of food: 'We have an addition of above 20,000 beggars flocked from the country round, to share in that little there here is, who were starving at home, and look like ghosts.'[78] Scarcity of food reached famine proportions, and people fought like beasts over bread. It was a long haul out of the depression of the seventeenth century.

[78] Stanhope, 21 May 1699, ibid., p. 138.

Appendix I

Currency, Weights and Measures

Maravedí. The basic unit of account.

Real. Standard silver coin; equalled 34 *maravedís*; the *real de a ocho* equalled 272 *maravedís*.

Ducado. Ducat. Originally a gold coin but by the seventeenth century a unit of account; equalled 375 *maravedís*.

Escudo. Standard gold coin; from 1609 equalled 440 *maravedís*.

Peso. American treasure was expressed in pesos. The *peso de mina* equalled 450 *maravedís*. But this usage ceased in the course of the seventeenth century and the normal unit became the *peso fuerte*, or the *peso de a ocho reales*, which equalled 272 *maravedís*. For purposes of conversion it equalled 20 *reales de vellón*.

Vellón. A fractional coin, originally a mixture of silver and copper; by seventeenth-century pure copper.

Lliura. A Catalan pound; equalled 10 *reales*, or just under a ducat.

Libra. A weight, roughly a pound.

Arroba. Equalled 25 *libras*.

Quintal. Equalled 100 *libras*.

Fanega. A measure of bulk; equalled about 1.6 bushels. A *fanega* of cacao, however, was a weight; equalled about 116 *libras*.

Tonelada. Had different meanings at different dates. Chaunu has devised a conversion factor for reducing original data into a standard draft tonnage of 2.83 cubic metres.

Appendix II

Table A
Index Numbers of Commodity Prices, 1651–1700
Base = 1671–1680[1]

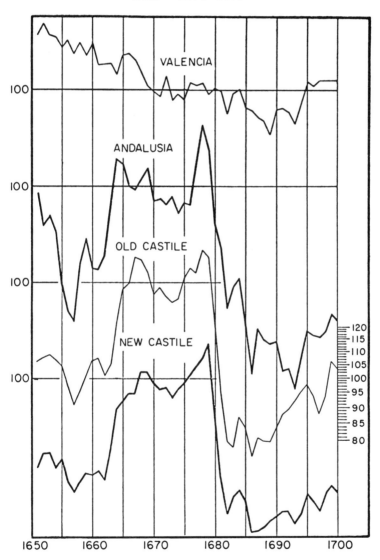

[1] Reprinted from E. J. Hamilton, *War and Prices in Spain 1651–1800* (Harvard University Press, 1947), p. 120.

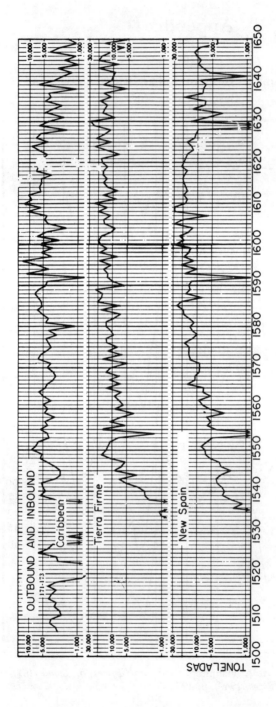

Table B

The Indies Trade, 1500–1650, as shown by the Tonnage of Shipping between Spain and the Principal Regions of America[1]

[1] From P. Chaunu, *Séville et l'Atlantique* (S.E.V.P.E.N., 1957), vii, p. 68.

Bibliographical Essay

General

The works of Antonio Domínguez Ortiz have notably advanced the study of early modern Spain in recent decades and have found expression too in a number of more general works, starting with *The Golden Age of Spain 1516–1659* (London, 1971), of which there is a Spanish version, *Desde Carlos V a la Paz de los Pirineos 1517–1660* (Barcelona, 1974), continuing in *El Antiguo Régimen: los Reyes Católicos y los Austrias* (2nd edn, Madrid, 1974), *Crisis y decadencia de la España de los Austrias* (Barcelona, 1984), and culminating in *Instituciones y sociedad en la España de los Austrias* (Barcelona, 1985), which contains original research as well as general interpretation. The great themes of Catalan history are treated in detail and in general by Ricardo García Carcel, *Historia de Cataluña, siglos XVI–XVII. 1. Los caracteres originales de la historia de Cataluña. 2. La trayectoria histórica* (2 vols, Barcelona, 1985). Henry Kamen, *Spain 1469–1714: A Society of Conflict* (London, 1983), combines research and revisionism in an interesting synthesis. Bartolomé Bennassar, *The Spanish Character. Attitudes and Mentalities from the Sixteenth to the Nineteenth Century* (Berkeley and Los Angeles, 1979), reflects on the life and work of Spaniards in historical perspective. J. H. Elliott, *Spain and its World 1500–1700* (London, 1989), reappraises the American, European and peninsular world of early modern Spain in a series of memorable essays.

The seventeenth century is studied in a number of general histories of Spain. *Historia de España Ramón Menéndez Pidal* (vols 23–5, Madrid, 1979–90) gives a comprehensive, though uneven, coverage of the period. *Historia de España*, Manuel Tuñón de Lara, ed. (Edn Labor, Barcelona, 1980–), and *Historia general de España y América* (vol. 8, Edn Rialp,

Madrid, 1986) are the leading modern works of reference and interpretation. Among the numerous regional histories, *Historia de Andalucía*, Antonio Domínguez Ortiz, ed. (Barcelona, 1980–1), is outstanding.

Spain's great depression has continued to exercise historians, who have sought to clarify the data and refine their analysis. Students and experts alike will profit from the following: J. H. Elliott, 'Self-Perception and Decline in Early Seventeenth-Century Spain', *Past and Present*, 74 (1977), pp. 41–61; R. A. Stradling, 'Seventeenth-Century Spain: Decline or Survival', *European Studies Review*, 9, 2 (1979), pp. 157–94, and the same author's 'Domination and Dependence: Castile, Spain and the Spanish Monarchy', *European History Quarterly*, 14 (1984), pp. 77–91. A. W. Lovett, 'The Golden Age of Spain: New Work on an Old Theme', *The Historical Journal*, 24, 3 (1981), pp. 739–49, and 'From Prosperity to Decadence: The Experience of Early Modern Spain', *The Historical Journal*, 32, 1 (1989), pp. 201–9, provides a framework and a guide to the new economic and social history produced in Spain and France. James Amelong, 'Society and Culture in Early Modern Spain', *The Journal of Modern History*, 65, 2 (1993), 357–74, reviews current trends among an 'emerging generation of Hispanists'.

The Later Habsburgs

Philip III and his government have been rescued from neglect by Patrick L. Williams in a series of carefully researched articles: 'Philip III and the Restoration of Spanish Government, 1598–1603', *The English Historical Review*, 88 (1973), pp. 751–69; 'El reinado de Felipe III', in *Historia General de España y América* (Vol. 8, Madrid, 1986), pp. 419–44, 514–15; 'Lerma, 1618: Dismissal or Retirement?', *European History Quarterly*, 19 (1989), pp. 307–32; and 'Lerma, Old Castile and the Travels of Philip III of Spain', *History*, 73, 239 (1989), pp. 379–97.

The government of Olivares, set amidst Spain's great crisis, is the subject of the outstanding work by J. H. Elliott, *The Count–Duke of Olivares. The Statesman in an Age of Decline* (London, 1986). Jonathan Brown and J. H. Elliott, *A Palace for a King* (New Haven, Conn. and London, 1980), describe the Buen Retiro and its collections, monuments to king and favourite alike. The king himself, long relegated to second place by the sheer dominance of his minister, is expertly studied in new and unaccustomed detail by R. A. Stradling, *Philip IV and the Government of Spain 1621–1665* (Cambridge, 1988).

Charles II and the end of Habsburg Spain are less researched than the reigns of his predecessors. Henry Kamen, *Spain in the Later Seventeenth Century 1665–1700* (London, 1980), is the first and still the only modern history of the reign of Charles II, a basic study whose research extends into society and economy as well as institutions. The chronology, nature and extent of the last great crisis of the century is also discussed by José Calvo Poyato, 'La última crisis de Andalucía en el siglo XVII: 1680–1685', *Hispania*, 46, 164 (1986), pp. 519–42.

The institutional history of the period has made significant advances on various fronts. José Antonio Escudero, *Los secretarios de estado y del despacho, 1474–1724* (2nd edn, 4 vols, Madrid, 1976), can be consulted for developments in the royal secretariat. Francisco Tomás Valiente, *Los validos en la monarquía española del siglo XVII* (2nd edn, Madrid, 1983), skilfully interprets the evidence on the emergence and status of the *validos*. Central government is also the area of Feliciano Barrios, *El Consejo de Estado de la monarquía española, 1526–1812* (Madrid, 1984). The tendency of recent historiography is to qualify absolutism by underlining the trend towards political devolution. I. A. A. Thompson, *War and Government in Habsburg Spain* (London, 1976), detects between 1560 and 1620 a steady retreat from the attempts of Philip II to nationalize military industries and their administration; under pressure of defence costs, his successors conceded their private ownership. The same author draws attention to other areas of decentralization in 'The Rule of Law in Early Modern Castile', *European History Quarterly*, 14 (1984), pp. 221–34. The retreat of centralized justice in favour of local courts is the theme of Richard L. Kagan, *Lawsuits and Litigants in Castile 1500–1700* (Chapel Hill, NC, 1981). The *letrados*, their status and their careers can be studied in the same author's *Students and Society in Early Modern Spain* (Baltimore, 1974), and in Jean–Marc Pelorson, *Les letrados: juristes castillans sous Philippe III* (Poitiers, 1980); their place in the conciliar hierarchy is expertly investigated by Janine Fayard, *Les membres du Conseil de Castille à l'époque moderne (1621–1746)* (Geneva, 1979). Sale of office, another example of weakening government control, can be studied in Francisco Tomás Valiente, 'Venta de oficios públicos en Castilla durante los siglos XVI y XVII', in *Gobierno e instituciones en la España del Antiguo Régimen* (Madrid, 1982), pp. 151–77, and Rafael de Lera García, 'Venta de oficios en la Inquisición de Granada (1629–1644)', *Hispania*, 48, 170 (1988), pp. 909–62. The cortes of Castile is also part of the story of absolutism, and one can begin with Charles Jago, 'Habsburg Absolutism and the Cortes of Castile', *The American Historical Review*, 86, 2 (1981), pp. 307–26, continuing with I. A. A. Thompson, 'Crown and Cortes in Castile, 1590–1665', *Parliaments, Estates and Representation*, 2 (1982), pp. 29–45, and 'The End of the Cortes of Castile', *Parliaments, Estates and Representation*, 4 (1984), pp. 125–33. The financial history of the period is also a history of the *conversos*, well told by James C. Boyajian,

Portuguese Bankers at the Court of Spain, 1626–1650 (New Brunswick, NJ, 1983). Political and social ideas have a perceptive historian in José Antonio Maravall, *Poder, honor y élites en el siglo XVII* (Madrid, 1979), and *Estudios de historia del pensamiento español* (3 vols, Madrid, 1984).

A study of international history can begin with R. A. Stradling, *Europe and the Decline of Spain: A Study of the Spanish System 1580–1720* (London, 1981), which places Spanish power and its limits in a national and a wider context; in a smaller frame see the same author's 'Olivares and the Origins of the Franco–Spanish War, 1627–35', *English Historical Review* 101 (1986), pp. 68–94. Spain's policy in northern Europe and determination to establish her sea power between the peninsula and the Netherlands and to extend it into the Baltic are made more credible by José Alcalá-Zamora y Queipo de Llano, *España, Flandes y el Mar del Norte (1618–1639)* (Barcelona, 1975); see the same author's *Razón y crisis de la política exterior de España en el reinado de Felipe IV* (Madrid, 1977). Peter Brightwell takes an expert look at the options open to Spain in the Netherlands in 'The Spanish System and the Twelve Years' Truce', *English Historical Review*, 89, 350 (1974), pp. 270–92, and concludes that the decision to renew the war in 1621 was neither rash nor unreasoned. On Spain's approach to the Thirty Years War see the same author's 'The Spanish Origins of the Thirty Years' War', *European Studies Review*, 9 (1979), pp. 409–31, 'Spain and Bohemia: The Decision to Intervene, 1619', *European Studies Review*, 12 (1982), pp. 117–41, and 'Spain, Bohemia and Europe, 1619–21', ibid., pp. 371–99. Geoffrey Parker, *Spain and the Netherlands, 1559–1659* (London, 1979), concludes that there was no discernible reduction in the provisions sent to the Low Countries before 1642–3, when it was the revolt of the Catalans rather than the exhaustion of Castile and its American treasure that caused resources to be diverted from the north. J. I. Israel, *The Dutch Republic and the Hispanic World, 1606–1661* (Oxford, 1982), places Spanish policy towards the Netherlands in a wider imperial context.

Economy and Society

A comprehensive economic history of the seventeenth century will be found in V. Vázquez de Prada, *Historia económica y social de España*, Vol. III, *Los siglos XVI y XVII* (5 vols, Madrid, 1978). Recent contributions to demographic history include Alberto Marcos Martín, *Auge y declive de un núcleo mercantil y financiero de Castilla la Vieja. Evolución demográfica de Medina del Campo durante los siglos XVI y XVII*

(Valladolid, 1978), a study which shows a town struck by plague, whose numbers at last began to recover in the later 1660s and continued to increase until the end of the Habsburg period. María F. Carbajo Isla, *La población de la Villa de Madrid. Desde finales del siglo XVI hasta mediados del siglo XIX* (Madrid, 1987), charts the growth and levelling out of the capital's population. On the impact of plague, drought and dearth important research is embodied in Vicente Pérez Moreda, *Las crisis de mortalidad en la España del interior, siglos XVI–XIX* (Madrid, 1980), and Jesús Maiso González, *La peste aragonesa de 1648 a 1654* (Zaragoza, 1982). Agrarian history can be approached through David E. Vassberg, *Land and Society in Golden Age Castile* (Cambridge, 1984), mainly based on the sixteenth century; Gonzalo Anes Alvarez, *Las crisis agrarias en la España moderna* (Madrid, 1970), is basic for the subject and contains data on the seventeenth century. The world of shipbuilding and navigation is newly explored by Carla Rahn Phillips, *Six Galleons for the King of Spain* (Baltimore, MD, 1988).

The trend towards regional studies has brought new areas of knowledge and revised chronology into the framework of the seventeenth century, permitting a reassessment of the limits of depression and the onset of recovery. Galicia is now endowed with precise demographic data, production statistics and estimates of social and fiscal burdens, thanks to Pegerto Saavedra, *Economía, política y sociedad en Galicia: la Provincia de Mondoñedo, 1480–1830* (Madrid, 1985). Angel García Sanz, *Desarrollo y crisis del Antiguo Régimen en Castilla la Vieja. Economía y sociedad en tierras de Segovia, 1500–1814* (Madrid, 1977), studies the transition from industrial growth to agricultural survival in a key area of Old Castile. Bartolomé Yun Casalilla, *Sobre la transición al capitalismo en Castilla. Economía y sociedad en Tierra de Campos (1500–1830)* (Madrid, 1987), can be consulted for further evidence of progress and regression in the Tierra de Campos region, province of Palencia. Laureano M. Rubio Pérez, *El Señorío Leonés de los Bazán: aproximación a su realidad socio-económica (1450–1650)* (La Bañeza, 1984), presents another case of falling population and grain prices, with signs of recovery about 1655. New Castile has also been brought into focus. Carla Rahn Phillips, *Ciudad Real, 1500–1750: Growth, Crisis, and Readjustment in the Spanish Economy* (Cambridge, Mass., 1979), provides a further example of blighted growth and regional readjustment. Jerónimo López-Salazar Pérez, *Estructuras agrarias y sociedad rural en la Mancha (siglos XVI–XVII)* (Ciudad Real, 1986), shows that La Mancha suffered less demographic adversity than the rest of Castile but that grain production still became depressed through rising costs and falling demand, and peasants were still victims of mortgage and rent payments. The Spanish interior was strongly influenced by Madrid, whose spending classes wanted the agricultural but not the industrial products of Castile, a theme developed by David Ringrose, *Madrid and the Spanish Economy, 1560–1850* (Berkeley and Los Angeles, 1983). The port of Cadiz exerted another kind of influence, as a entrepôt and a market for its agricultural hinterland, as shown by Francisco M. Traverso Ruiz, *Riqueza y producción agraria en Cádiz durante los siglos XVI y XVII* (Cadiz, 1987). Modern historiography has also reappraised eastern Spain. James Casey, *The Kingdom of Valencia in the Seventeenth Century* (Cambridge, 1979), shows in masterly fashion that the revival of Valencia after the expulsion of the moriscos and other adversities was slow and incomplete.

The social history of the period is widely interpreted by Manuel Fernández Alvarez, *La sociedad española en el siglo de oro* (2nd edn, 2 vols, Madrid, 1989), and at a more popular level by J. Alcalá Zamora y Queipo de Llano, ed., *La vida cotidiana en la España de Velázquez* (Madrid, 1989). The social history of the aristocracy undertaken by Domínguez Ortiz has been extended by particular studies: Charles Jago, 'The "Crisis of the Aristocracy" in Seventeenth-Century Castile', *Past and Present*, 84 (1979), pp. 60–90; I. A. A. Thompson, 'The Purchase of Nobility in Castile, 1552–1700', *Journal of European Economic History*, 8 (1979), pp. 313–60. One of the few attempts to identify a regional elite is made by James S. Amelong, *Honoured Citizens of Barcelona: Patrician Culture and Class Relations 1490–1714* (Princeton, NJ, 1986). The popular sectors continue to be elusive, though on social agitation see Claude Larquié, 'Popular Uprisings in Spain in the Mid-Seventeenth Century', *Renaissance and Modern Studies*, 26 (1982), pp. 32–54. As Linda Martz, *Poverty and Welfare in Habsburg Spain: The Example of Toledo* (Cambridge, 1983) shows, the relief of poverty was still pursued during the years of depression, though in ever worsening conditions. On the margin of society the moriscos continue to receive attention. Antonio Domínguez Ortiz and Bernard Vincent, *Historia de los moriscos* (Madrid, 1978) sums up the results of research since the work of Halperín Donghi, Caro Baroja and Lapeyre in the 1950s and adds new data of its own. Tulio Halperín Donghi, *Un conflicto nacional: moriscos y cristianos viejos en Valencia* (Valencia, 1980), republishes his previous researches in a convenient form. Juan Aranda Doncel, *Los moriscos en tierras de Córdoba* (Córdoba, 1984), writes the total history of the morisco community in a specific region, with a good account of the expulsion and its consequences. For a study of the expulsion in an even smaller locality see Encarnación Gil Saura, 'La expulsión de los moriscos. Análisis de las cuentas de la bailía de Alzira: administración y adjudicación de bienes', *Hispania*, 46, 162 (1986), pp. 99–114.

Religion

Diccionario de historia eclesiástica de España, Quintín Aldea Vaquero, *et al*, eds (4 vols, Madrid, 1972–5) is a useful work of reference. For a general account of the seventeenth-century church see Ricardo García Villoslada, ed., *Historia de la iglesia en España, vol. IV, La iglesia en la España de los siglos XVII y XVIII* (Madrid, 1979). Christian Hermann, *L'Eglise d'Espagne sous le Patronage Royal (1476–1834)* (Madrid, 1988), is a researched study of church-state relations under the royal patronage. The Spanish Inquisition has been subject to intense investigation in recent years. Henry Kamen, *Inquisition and Society in Spain in the Sixteenth and Seventeenth Centuries* (London, 1985), adds new archival sources and conclusions to his 1965 work. An outstanding Spanish contribution, which also includes a guide to archival sources, is Joaquín Pérez Villanueva and Bartolomé Escandell Bonet eds, *Historia de la Inquisición en España y América. Tomo I* (2nd edn, Madrid, 1984). Bartolomé Bennassar, ed., *L'Inquisition espagnole (xvᵉ–xixᵉ siècle)* (Paris, 1979), is a comprehensive collection of particular studies. Other collections include Stephen Haliczer, ed., *Inquisition and Society in Early Modern Europe* (London, 1986); Gustav Henningsen and John Tedeschi, eds, *The Inquisition in Early Modern Europe: Studies on Sources and Method* (DeKalb, Illinois, 1986); Angel Alcalá, ed., *The Spanish Inquisition and the Inquisitorial Mind* (New York, 1987). Jean-Pierre Dedieu, *L'Administration de la foi: L'Inquisition de Tolède XVIᵉ–XVIIIᵉ siècle* (Madrid, 1989), stands out for its detailed research and long time-span, as does Stephen Haliczer, *Inquisition and Society in the Kingdom of Valencia 1478–1812* (Berkeley and Los Angeles, 1990). Gustav Henningsen, *The Witches Advocate: Basque Witchcraft and the Spanish Inquisition* (Reno, Nevada, 1980), studies the struggle for a more enlightened policy towards witches.

Spanish America

The following select bibliography can be regularly expanded by reference to the *Suplemento de Anuario de Estudios Americanos. Sección Historiografía y Bibliografía*, published by the Escuela de Estudios Hispano-Americanos, Seville; Sylvia L. Hilton, *El Americanismo en España*, Centro de Estudios Históricos, Departamento de Historia de América, CSIC, Madrid; and *Handbook of Latin American Studies*, University of Florida Press, Gainesville. Older general works by Haring, Parry and Gibson have not been entirely superseded, though subsequent scholarship has produced a number of notable syntheses. These are led by Lyle McAlister, *Spain and Portugal in the New World 1492–1700* (Oxford, 1984), which can be supplemented by James Lockhart and Stuart B. Schwartz, *Early Latin America. A History of Colonial Spanish America and Brazil* (Cambridge, 1983), and by Leslie Bethell, ed., *The Cambridge History of Latin America*, vols I and II (Cambridge, 1984), also valuable for its bibliographies. For a good Spanish synthesis, with documents, consult Guillermo Céspedes del Castillo, *América Hispánica (1492–1898)* (*Historia de España*, Manuel Tuñón de Lara, ed., vols 6 and 13, Barcelona, 1983–6); see also the appropriate volumes of the other general histories of Spain cited above, including *Historia de España*, Antonio Domínguez Ortiz, ed., vol. 8, *Descubrimiento, colonizacion y emancipación de América* (Madrid, 1989). The search for American identity through study of the chronicles in their imperial and creole traditions is admirably conducted by D. A. Brading, *The First America. The Spanish Monarchy, Creole Patriots, and the Liberal State 1492–1867* (Cambridge, 1991).

The colonial economy has been studied in various contexts. Ruggiero Romano, *Conjonctures opposées: La "crise" du XVIIe siècle en Europe et en Amérique ibérique* (Geneva, 1992), considers the opportunity for autonomous growth in colonial America opened by the European 'crisis' of the seventeenth century. The internal market has been opened up by Carlos Sempat Assadourian, *El sistema de la economía colonial. Mercado interno, regiones y espacio económico* (Lima, 1982); and by Juan Carlos Garavaglia, *Mercado interno y economía colonial* (Mexico, 1983). The results of Pierre Chaunu's monumental account of the Indies trade to 1650 can be studied in the author's own synthesis, *Sevilla y América. Siglos XVI y XVII* (Seville, 1983). The transatlantic trade from 1650 is the subject of basic new research: Lutgardo García Fuentes, *El comercio español con América, 1650–1700* (Seville, 1980), and 'En torno a la reactivación del comercio indiano en tiempos de Carlos II', *Anuario de Estudios Americanos*, 36 (1979), pp. 251–86; Antonio García-Baquero, *Cádiz y el Atlántico (1717–1778)* (2 vols, Seville, 1976), with a backward glance to 1680. To these can be added Nicolás del Castillo Mathieu, 'Las 18 flotas de galeones a Tierra Firme (1650–1700)', *Suplemento de Anuario de Estudios Americanos. Sección Historiografía y Bibliografía*, 47, 2 (1990), pp. 83–129. Catalan trade with America has been authoritatively studied by Carlos Martínez Shaw, *Cataluña en la carrera de Indias 1680–1756* (Barcelona, 1981). On public and private income from America pride of place now goes to Michel Morineau, *Incroyables gazettes et fabuleux métaux. Les retours des trésors américains d'après les gazettes hollondaises (XVIe–XVIIIe siècles)* (Cambridge, 1985), who has rewritten the history of treasure returns. For a study of the Seville monopoly in the light of the new research see John Lynch, 'El comerç sota el monopoli Sevillà', *2nes Jornades d'Estudis Catalano-Americans. Maig 1986* (Barcelona, 1987), pp. 9–30. An authoritative synthesis of the Indies trade, its organization, personnel, and quantities, is provided by Antonio García-Baquero González, *La Carrera de Indias: Suma de la contratación y Océano de negocios* (Seville, 1992).

The defence of trade and empire is now better known thanks to a number of archive-based monographs. The leading examples of these are Bibiano Torres Ramírez, *La Armada de Barlovento* (Sevilla, 1981); Fernando Serrano Mangas, *Los galeones de la carrera de Indias 1650–1700* (Seville, 1985); Pablo Emilio Pérez-Mallaína Bueno and Bibiano Torres Ramírez, *La Armada del Mar del Sur* (Seville, 1987). In spite of the defence system fraud, contraband, direct trade and other evasions of the Seville monopoly still prevailed. Notable examples have been studied by Enriqueta Vila Vilar, 'Las ferias de Portobelo: apariencia y realidad del comercio con Indias', *Anuario de Estudios Americanos*, 39 (1982), pp. 275–340. Foreign penetration of the Río de la Plata has been identified by Zacarías Moutoukias, *Contrabando y control colonial en el siglo XVII* (Buenos Aires, 1988). The role of the *peruleros* has been clarified by Margarita María Suárez Espinosa, *Las estrategias de un mercader: Juan de la Cueva, 1608–1635* (Memoria para obtener el grado de bachiller, Pontificia Universidad Católica del Perú, Lima, 1985). Attack and counter-attack in the Pacific is comprehensively studied by Peter T. Bradley, *The Lure of Peru. Maritime Intrusion into the South Sea, 1598–1701* (London, 1989). The naval infrastructure is now better understood, thanks to Lawrence A. Clayton, *Caulkers and Carpenters in a New World: The Shipyards of Colonial Guayaquil* (Athens, Ohio, 1980).

Mexico in the seventeenth century was long studied through the eyes of Chevalier and Borah, whose works are still of value but now subject to modification by later research and revision. For a good analysis of the present state of research see José Morilla Critz, 'Crisis y transformación de la economía de Nueva España en el siglo XVII. Un ensayo crítico', *Anuario de Estudios Americanos*, 45 (1988), pp. 241–72. Demographic history still owes most to established masters. Sherburne F. Cook and Woodrow Borah, *Essays in Population History* (3 vols, Berkeley and Los Angeles, 1974–9) return to the problem of Indian population figures, on the basis of previous totals established for Central Mexico: 1518, 25.2 million; 1532, 16.8; 1568, 2.65; 1605, 1.075. When did attrition end? From a revenue list of 1646 they compute a total of 702,929, and place the low point in 1620–5, when the Indian population of Central Mexico was approximately 3 per cent of its size at the time the Europeans first landed. See *Essays*, iii, pp. 1–102. Mexican mining was really placed

BIBLIOGRAPHICAL ESSAY

upon the map of history in the early 1970s, when Peter J. Bakewell, *Silver Mining and Society in Colonial Mexico: Zacatecas 1546–1700* (Cambridge, 1971), established new knowledge of organization, production and development, and when D. A. Brading and Harry E. Cross, 'Colonial Silver Mining: Mexico and Peru', *Hispanic American Historical Review*, 52, 4 (1972), pp. 545–79, suggested a new chronology of mining cycles. Since then publication of royal treasury records has yielded new data suggesting further growth of silver production, and although such treasury data has been subject to criticism and revision in recent years (see *Hispanic American Historical Review*, 64, 2 (1984)), it remains an important guide to relative trends and continues to yield fruitful results, as seen in the works of John J. TePaske, *La Real Hacienda de Nueva España: La Real Caja de México (1576–1816)* (Mexico, 1976); and John J. TePaske and Herbert S. Klein, 'The Seventeenth-Century Crisis in New Spain: Myth or Reality?', *Past and Present*, 90 (1981), pp. 116–35. Further confirmation of mining recovery is found in new strikes and a return to smelting in the later seventeenth century: see Peter Bakewell, 'Mining in Colonial Spanish America', in Bethell, ed., *The Cambridge History of Latin America*, ii, pp. 105–51. For a useful survey of the state of mining research see Rosario Sevilla Soler, 'La minería americana y la crisis del siglo XVII. Estado del problema', *Suplemento de Anuario de Estudios Americanos. Sección historiografía y bibliografía*, 47, 2 (1990), pp. 61–81.

Rural history since Chevalier can be approached through the valuable essay by Eric Van Young, 'Mexican Rural History since Chevalier: The Historiography of the Colonial Hacienda', *Latin American Research Review*, 18, 3 (1983), pp. 5–61, and Enrique Florescano, 'The formation and economic structure of the hacienda in New Spain', in Bethell, ed., *The Cambridge History of Latin America*, ii, pp. 153–88. In this field regional studies have been the principal agency of advance: see William B. Taylor, *Landlord and Peasant in Colonial Oaxaca* (Stanford, Calif., 1972), and the same author's *Drinking, Homicide, and Rebellion in Colonial Mexican Villages* (Stanford, Calif., 1979). John C. Super, *La vida en Querétaro durante la colonia 1531–1810* (Mexico, 1983), studies a region which had a manufacturing as well as an agrarian sector. In general the hacienda is now seen as a commercial enterprise rather than a subsistence institution; this is also confirmed by Jan Bazant, *Cinco haciendas mexicanas: tres siglos de vida rural en San Luis Potosí, 1600–1910* (Mexico, 1975). New research on the social structure of seventeenth-century Mexico and its significance for the imperial bureaucracy is contributed by J. I. Israel, *Race, Class and Politics in Colonial Mexico* (Oxford, 1975). Research up to 1980 is represented in

the interesting synthesis by Colin M. MacLachlan and Jaime E. Rodríguez O., *The Forging of the Cosmic Race. A Reinterpretation of Colonial Mexico* (Berkeley and Los Angeles, 1980).

Peru experienced progress and regression in the seventeenth century.
There is evidence of both in the notable study by Kenneth J. Andrien,
Crisis and Decline: the Viceroyalty of Peru in the Seventeenth Century
(Albuquerque, 1985), where economic and fiscal prospects are shown to
have been damaged by inferior government and short-term objectives.
The works of Andrien and Bradley (cited above) show among other
things the rising amounts of revenue retained for expenditure in Peru,
whose administrative and defence costs consumed a large part of the
viceregal budget; this is also confirmed by John J. TePaske and Herbert
S. Klein, *The Royal Treasuries of the Spanish Empire in America* (3 vols,
Durham, NC, 1982), and John J. TePaske, 'The Fiscal Structure of
Upper Peru and the Financing of Empire', in Karen Spalding, ed., *Essays
in the Political, Economic and Social History of Colonial Latin America*
(Newark, Delaware, 1982), pp. 69–94. Agricultural production was increasingly commercialized and sought the regional markets of Peru and
its neighbours. Knowledge of the agrarian history of coastal Peru is
extended by Robert G. Keith, *Conquest and Agrarian Change: the
Emergence of the Hacienda System on the Peruvian Coast* (Cambridge,
Mass., 1976), and Nicholas P. Cushner, *Lords of the Land. Sugar, Wine
and Jesuit Estates of Coastal Peru, 1600–1767* (Albany, NY, 1980). The
formation of haciendas in the Andes and their implication for rural
production and the internal market is well studied by Luis Miguel Glave
and María Isabel Remy, *Estructura agraria y vida rural en una región
andina: Ollantaytambo entre los siglos XVI y XIX* (Cuzco, 1983). The
mining industry underwent slow rather than catastrophic recession.
Peter J. Bakewell has again accomplished important work of measure-
ment: 'Registered Silver Production in the Potosí District, 1550–1735',
*Jahrbuch für Geschichte von Staat, Wirtschaft und Gesellschaft
Lateinamerikas*, 12 (1975), pp. 67–103, while the infrastructure of mining (and other issues) are studied in his *Silver and Entrepreneurship in
Seventeenth-Century Potosí. The Life and Times of Antonio López de
Quiroga* (Albuquerque, NM, 1988). The economic, social and fiscal
implications of obligatory labour in the mines are fully explored in Peter
Bakewell, *Miners of the Red Mountain. Indian Labor in Potosí, 1545–
1650* (Albuquerque, NM, 1984), and Jeffrey A. Cole, *The Potosí Mita
1570–1700. Compulsory Indian Labor in the Andes* (Stanford, Calif.,
1985). Forced labour was one, though by no means the only, cause of
Indian population losses, which were also the consequence of disease,
drought and war; the subject has been expertly treated by Noble David

Cook, *Demographic Collapse. Indian Peru, 1520–1620* (Cambridge, 1982). Another Indian resource subject to Spanish pressure was the indigenous transport system, a subject rediscovered in the archives by Luis Miguel Glave, *Trajinantes: caminos indígenas en la sociedad colonial, siglos XVI/XVII* (Lima, 1989).

Index

mining: in America, 271; Mexico, 241,
273, 285–6, 287–8, 303–10; Peru,
285–6, 316, 327–34
Miranda, count of, 30, 31
mita: in Peru, 318, 321, 323, 325,
331–4
Mixteca, 302
Moluccas, 261
Moncada, Sancho de, *arbitrista*, 5,
11–12, 214, 219, 350
Mondoñedo, Galicia, 174
Montalto, duke of, 379–80
Monteleón, duke of, viceroy of
Catalonia, 72
Monterrey, count of, 369, 380
Montesclaros, marquis of, 138
Monzón, 135, 146–7
Monzón, treaty of, 102
Morgan, Henry, 257, 264
moriscos, expulsion of, 8, 56–64; its
consequences, 65–9, 173–4, 175,
176–7, 202
Mosquito Shore, 264
Moura, Cristóbal de, 30, 31, 37
municipal government, 358;
aristocracy in, 358–9; and taxation,
128–30
Münster, treaty of (1648), 166, 258
Murcia, 122, 174, 395

Naples, 42, 43; revolution in, 164, 167
Narborough, John, 263
Navarra, Melchor de, 367
Navarre, 132, 174, 211
Navarro, José, 391
navy *see* Armada
negroes: slave trade, 253–4, 289; in
Mexico, 306; in Peru, 316, 321
Nestares Marín, Francisco de, 335
Netherlands, Spanish: expenditure in,
50, 116, 170; and Germany, 97,
108–9; Peace of Pyrenees, 170;
revenue from, 43, 132; truce of
1609, 55–6; under Charles II, 363,
373, 376, 379, 380; under Philip III,
46, 54–5
Netherlands United Provinces of: in

Andalucía, 195; and Brazil, 81–2,
98, 103, 107, 141, 151–3, 259,
274–5; in Caribbean, 252, 253–5,
258; in Pacific, 165, 261–3, 296;
and Portuguese empire, 78–80; and
revolt of Portugal, 155, 156; and
Spanish American trade, 103, 229,
281, 284–5, 289; trade with Spain,
208, 220; treaty of Münster, 166,
258; Triple Alliance, 364; truce of
1609, 55–6; and vessels in American
trade, 218–19, 247–8, 274; war of
League of Augsburg, 381
Nevis, 255
New Christians *see* conversos
New Granada, 278, 321
Nicaragua, 264, 265, 295, 296, 342
Nithard, John Everard, *valido*, 361–5
Nozca, Peru, 321
Núñez Saravia, Juan, 194

Oaxaca, 302
obrajes: in Mexico, 301; in Peru,
325–6
office, sale of, 112, 404–6; in America,
227, 335–7; aristocracy and, 31,
187–8, 402–3; commoners and, 190
Olinda, 151
Olivares, Gaspar de Guzmán, count
duke of: and aristocracy, 159–60,
184, 187, 188, 355; and Catalonia,
136–40, 141–3, 145–6; and
conversos, 194–5; and cortes of
Castile, 126, 127; fall of, 157,
160–1; financial policy, 112–14,
119–20, 337; and institutions of
government, 349; and Portugal,
149–52, 154, 155, 157; rise to
power, 84, 86, 87–9; theory of
empire, 132–3; and Thirty Years
War, 94–110; Union of Arms,
133–5, 236; *valido*, 19, 89–91
Ollantaytambo, 323
Oñate, count of, 108, 109, 139
Oquendo, Antonio de, 141
Orpesa, Manuel Joaquin Alvarez de
Toledo, count of: and revolt of

Portocarrero, Pedro, inquisitor
general, 19, 29
Porto Viejo, Peru, 296
Portugal: and American trade, 229,
245, 259, 276, 289; and Brazil, 79,
81–2, 150–3; fiscal independence,
43, 78, 132; independence of, 156–7,
171, 178; New Christians, 78, 81,
111, 194–5; and Olivares, 133, 141;
revolt of, 149, 156; in Spanish
America, 79–80, 83, 153–5, 244–5;
under Philip III, 75–83
Potosí, 258–9, 307, 346, 347; foreign
penetration, 243–4; mining and
output, 318, 320, 327–34;
Portuguese in, 79, 153–4; supply of,
325–6
Prada, Andrés de, 31–2
prices: and American trade, 233,
270–1; in Castile, 8–9, 118, 119;
and grain, 9–10
Priego, marquis, of, 187
Puebla, 299, 302
Puerto Rico, 101, 255, 418
Pyrenees, treaty of, 148, 156, 170, 226,
384

Querétaro, 314
Quevedo y Villegas, Francisco de, 85,
86–7
quinto, 236, 240, 307

Ráfol de Almunia, Valencia, 390
Ramírez de Guzmán, Juan, procurator
of Seville, 125–6
Realejo, Nicaragua, 295, 342
Recife, 151, 156
repartimiento (labour), in Mexico, 305,
306–7, 311–12; in Peru see mita
Ribera, Juan de, archbishop of
Valencia, 58–9, 61
Rimac, Peru, 325
Rio de Janeiro, 152
Río de la Hacha, 289
Río de la Plata: foreign penetration,
243–4; Portuguese in, 79–80,
153–4; trade to Potosí, 258–9, 328

Rocroi, battle of, 165
Rojas, Antonio de, 292
Ronquillo, Pedro, 404
Rosellón, 146, 148, 170, 174
Ruidiaz de Pineda, Francisco,
procurator of Seville, 125–6

Sá, Salvador de, 153
Saavedra Fajardo, Diego: in Germany,
108; on valido, 37
St Kitts, 255
St Martin, 255
Salamanca: in cortes, 122;
depopulation, 203; señorío, 357;
university, 402
Salces, 143
Salinas, count of, 77
San Lucar de Barrameda, 232, 249,
252, 253
San Luis de Potosí, 303, 304–5
San Sebastian, 175, 208, 216
Santa, Peru, 325
Santa Barbara, Mexico, 303
Santa Catalina (Old Providence),
254–5
Santa Coloma, count of, viceroy of
Catalonia, 143–4
Santa Cruz, marquis of, 102
Santa Cruz de la Sierra, 328
Santander, 7, 175, 176, 221, 277, 282
Santo Domingo, 253, 255
Sarmiento de Valladares, Diego, 367
Schapenham, Hugo, 262
secretario del despacho universal, 376,
377, 379, 408
secretary of state, office of, 32–3
Segovia: agriculture, 401; in cortes,
122; industry, 191, 212–13, 219,
417; population, 175, 400; señorío,
357
señorío: secular, 3, 66–7, 119, 183,
185–6, 187, 205–6, 357–8, 387,
388–91; ecclesiastical, 351, 357
Sessa, duke of, 160
Seville: American trade, 229–33, 238,
239–40, 278, 282, 285; aristocracy,
358; businessmen, 185, 190–1; in